Rebelocracy

Conventional wisdom portrays war zones as chaotic and anarchic. In reality, however, they are often orderly. This work introduces a new phenomenon in the study of civil war: wartime social order. It investigates theoretically and empirically how new forms of order emerge and function in conflict zones. By theorizing the interaction between combatants and civilians and how they impact wartime institutions, the study delves into rebel behavior, civilian agency, and their impact on the conduct of war. Based on years of fieldwork in Colombia, the theory is tested with qualitative and quantitative evidence on communities, armed groups, and individuals in conflict zones. The study shows how armed groups strive to rule civilians, and how the latter influence the terms of that rule. The theory and empirical results illuminate our understanding of civil war, institutions, local governance, nonviolent resistance, and the emergence of political order.

Ana Arjona is Assistant Professor of political science at Northwestern University. She is the coeditor of *Rebel Governance in Civil War* (Cambridge University Press, 2015). Her work has been funded by the Harry Frank Guggenheim Foundation, Social Science Research Council (SSRC), the United States Institute of Peace, Columbia University, Northwestern University, and Yale University in the United States; the International Development Research Centre in Canada; the Folke Bernadotte Academy in Sweden; and the Department for International Development and the Economic and Social Research Council in the UK.

Cambridge Studies in Comparative Politics

General Editor
Margaret Levi   *University of Washington, Seattle*

Assistant General Editors
Kathleen Thelen   *Massachusetts Institute of Technology*
Erik Wibbels   *Duke University*

Associate Editors
Robert H. Bates   *Harvard University*
Stephen Hanson   *University of Washington, Seattle*
Torben Iversen   *Harvard University*
Stathis Kalyvas   *Yale University*
Peter Lange   *Duke University*
Helen Milner   *Princeton University*
Frances Rosenbluth   *Yale University*
Susan Stokes   *Yale University*
Sidney Tarrow   *Cornell University*

Other Books in the Series
Christopher Adolph, *Bankers, Bureaucrats, and Central Bank Politics: The Myth of Neutrality*

Michael Albertus, *Autocracy and Redistribution: The Politics of Land Reform*

Ben W. Ansell, *From the Ballot to the Blackboard: The Redistributive Political Economy of Education*

Ben W. Ansell, David J. Samuels, *Inequality and Democratization: An Elite-Competition Approach*

Leonardo R. Arriola, *Multi-Ethnic Coalitions in Africa: Business Financing of Opposition Election Campaigns*

David Austen-Smith, Jeffry A. Frieden, Miriam A. Golden, Karl Ove Moene, and Adam Przeworski, eds., *Selected Works of Michael Wallerstein: The Political Economy of Inequality, Unions, and Social Democracy*

Andy Baker, *The Market and the Masses in Latin America: Policy Reform and Consumption in Liberalizing Economies*

Continued after the index

Rebelocracy

Social Order in the Colombian Civil War

ANA ARJONA
Northwestern University

CAMBRIDGE
UNIVERSITY PRESS

One Liberty Plaza, New York NY 10006, USA

Cambridge University Press is part of the University of Cambridge.

It furthers the University's mission by disseminating knowledge in the pursuit of education, learning and research at the highest international levels of excellence.

www.cambridge.org
Information on this title: www.cambridge.org/9781107126039

© Ana Arjona 2016

This publication is in copyright. Subject to statutory exception and to the provisions of relevant collective licensing agreements, no reproduction of any part may take place without the written permission of Cambridge University Press.

First published 2016

Printed in the United States of America by Sheridan Books, Inc.

A catalog record for this publication is available from the British Library

ISBN 978-1-107-12603-9 Hardback

Cambridge University Press has no responsibility for the persistence or accuracy of URLs for external or third-party internet websites referred to in this publication, and does not guarantee that any content on such websites is, or will remain, accurate or appropriate.

To Eudald Lerga

Contents

List of Figures and Tables		*page* xii
Acknowledgments		xv
Abbreviations and Glossary of Terms		xxi
1	Introduction	1
	Civilian–Combatant Interactions, Wartime Institutions, and the Study of Civil War	4
	A Theory of Social Order in Civil War	9
	Research Design	14
	Looking Ahead	19
2	Wartime Social Order: What Is It and How Does It Vary?	21
	Defining Wartime Social Order	21
	A Typology of Wartime Social Order	26
	Assessing the Quality of the Typology	29
	Current Understanding of Rebel Governance and Collective Civilian Resistance	35
3	A Theory of Social Order in Civil War	41
	The Argument	41
	Assumptions	43
	Long-Term Horizons and the Emergence of Order	48
	Short-Term Horizons and the Emergence of Disorder	50
	Rebelocracy and Civilian Cooperation	55
	Rebelocracy and the Byproducts of Control	58
	The Costs of Running a Rebelocracy	60
	Aliocracy and Civilian Resistance	62
	A Theory of Collective Civilian Resistance to Rebelocracy	65
	Relaxing Assumptions	74

	Caveats	78
	Conclusion	82
4	Research Design: Studying War Zones in Colombia	84
	A Study of Colombia: Advantages and Limitations	85
	The Colombian Armed Conflict: An Overview	88
	The FARC, the ELN, and the Paramilitaries	94
	Empirical Strategy	100
	Advantages and Limitations of the Research Design	107
	Conclusion	109
5	The Determinants of Social Order	111
	Reconstructing the History of Local Communities in War Zones	111
	Sample and Data-Gathering Methods	112
	The Determinants of Order	124
	The Determinants of Rebelocracy and Aliocracy	138
	Conclusion	157
6	Creating Rebelocracy, Aliocracy, and Disorder	159
	The Process of Creating Social Order in War Zones	160
	Community Structure and Armed Groups' Strategies	162
	Measuring and Describing Order and Disorder, Rebelocracy and Aliocracy	170
	The Creation of Rebelocracy in War Zones	173
	Life under Rebelocracy	180
	Collective Resistance, Bargaining, and the Paths to Aliocracy	193
	The Paths to Disorder	201
	Collective Civilian Resistance	209
	Conclusion	210
7	How Local Institutions Matter: A Process-Driven Natural Experiment	212
	Life in the Coffee Haciendas	215
	An Agrarian Movement Is Born	219
	Institutional Innovations in the Struggle for Land	221
	Self-Governance: Institutions to Preserve Public Order and Adjudicate Disputes	224
	Zama, Tellus, and Librea: Divergence in Local Institutions	229
	Comparing Processes Across Villages	234
	The FARC in Tellus and Librea	235
	The FARC in Zama	246
	Civilian Resistance	248

	A New Wave of Violence: The Paramilitaries Attack in Viotá	252
	Causal Inference: The Effect of Institutional Quality	255
	Conclusion	260
8	Testing the Microfoundations: Social Order and Recruitment	262
	Who Joins Rebel Movements?	264
	Wartime Social Order and Recruitment	267
	Evidence on Communities in War Zones	269
	Evidence on Joiners and Nonjoiners	282
	Conclusion	295
9	Conclusion	297
	Caveats	300
	Scope Conditions and External Validity	302
	Implications	305

Appendix 1: Fieldwork and Sources of Empirical Evidence   313
Appendix 2: Supplemental Materials for Chapter 5   330
Appendix 3: Supplementary Materials for Chapter 6   355
Appendix 4: Supplemental Materials for Chapter 8   357
References   361
Index   387

Figures and Tables

Figures

2.1	Types of presence of non-state armed groups at the local level	page 24
2.2	Typology of wartime social orders	26
3.1	Causal paths	42
5.1	Descriptive statistics of sampled municipalities (histograms)	115
5.2	Timeline in *memory workshops*	120
5.3a	Order by warring side (histograms)	125
5.3b	Order by locality	126
5.4	Bivariate relationship between order and explanatory variables	128
5.5	Effect of indiscipline and competition on order	133
5.6	Effect of indiscipline on order (adjusted predictions)	134
5.7	Effect of competition on order (adjusted predictions)	135
5.8	Effect of high-quality institutions and strategic territory on order	135
5.9	Effect of valuable resources on order	136
5.10	Effect of indiscipline and competition on order (additional model specifications)	137
5.11	Economic influence	139
5.12	Political influence	140
5.13	Public goods provision or regulation	140
5.14	Social regulation	141
5.15	Social interaction	141
5.16a	Rebelocracy by warring side (histograms)	142
5.16b	Rebelocracy by locality	143
5.16c	Cluster analysis of armed groups' influence on localities	144

5.17	Rebelocracy and explanatory variables	145
5.18	Effect of institutional quality on rebelocracy	147
5.19a	Effect of high-quality institutions on rebelocracy (adjusted predictions)	148
5.19b	Effect of high-quality institutions on rebelocracy in communities ruled by the state (adjusted predictions)	149
5.20	Effect of high-quality institutions and strategic territory on rebelocracy	149
5.21	Quality of preexisting institutions by source	150
5.22	Institutional quality and potential indigenous influence	153
5.23	Effect of high-quality institutions on rebelocracy (instrumented)	155
5.24	Effect of past resistance on rebelocracy (instrumented)	157
6.1	Stages in the process of creation of social order	161
6.2	Example of concatenation of social orders in a community throughout the war	162
6.3	Types of social order in sampled localities	172
8.1	Recruitment by municipality	271
8.2	Recruitment and rebelocracy measures	272
8.3	Recruitment and rebelocracy by warring side	273
8.4	Recruitment and attributes of localities	275
8.5	Multilevel models for recruitment	276
8.6	Effect of rebelocracy on recruitment	277
8.7	Multilevel models for recruitment (deviation from cluster means)	278
8.8	Recruitment and high-quality institutions by warring side	279
8.9a	Effect of high-quality institutions on recruitment	280
8.9b	Effect of high-quality institutions on recruitment (adjusted predictions)	280
8.10	Population and sample of ex-combatants	283
8.11	Bivariate relationship between individual-level attributes and recruitment	289
8.12	Bivariate relationship between community-level attributes and recruitment	290
8.13	Social order, joiners, and nonjoiners	291
8.14a	Guerrilla rebelocracy and recruitment	293
8.14b	Paramilitary rebelocracy and recruitment	294
A1.1	Mind mapping exercise on memory	319

Maps

5.1	Random sample of municipalities	113
5.2	Random sample of localities	118

7.1	Viotá in Colombia	216
8.1	Municipalities where former combatants lived at the time of joining an armed group	285
8.2	Sample of municipalities for survey with civilians	286

Tables

3.1	A theory of social order in civil war	42
3.2	Social order in territories with different strategic value	75
4.1	Guerrilla groups included in the empirical evidence	95
4.2	Paramilitary groups included in the empirical evidence	95
4.3	Research design components	102
4.4	The empirical basis of theoretical propositions	107
5.1	Institutional biography in a locality	120
6.1	Community structure and armed groups' strategies to build order	163
6.2	Entry strategies to build rebelocracy	175
A1.1	List of interviews and focus groups (conducted by the author 2007–2015)	324
A1.2	List of cases	329
A2.1	Coding of variables used in Chapter 5	331
A2.2	Linear multilevel models for order	341
A2.3	Bayesian multilevel models for order	344
A2.4	Multilevel linear models for rebelocracy	347
A2.5	Bayesian multilevel models for rebelocracy	349
A2.6	Multilevel linear models for rebelocracy using an instrumental variable	350
A3.1	Sources on civilian resistance	355
A4.1	Multilevel linear models for recruitment	358
A4.2	Linear multilevel models for recruitment (aggregate data at the dyad level)	360

Acknowledgments

I decided to embark on the study of the dynamics of civil war in the early 2000s. Colombia was still enduring some of the worst years of the armed conflict between the state, insurgents, and paramilitary groups. I was initially determined to investigate how countries can recover from the wounds that war leaves behind. But I quickly realized that I would not be able to understand the challenges that societies endure in a postwar period without an understanding of what happens *during* war. Even though I was concerned about the intense violence that often characterizes civil wars, I realized that much more changes in war and we did not know much about it. In particular, war seemed to entail not only the destruction of a preexisting reality but also the emergence of multiple new local realities. There was a sense of normality during lulls in the fighting in conflict zones – but such normality was quite different from place to place, and it seemed to shape civilians' lives in profound ways. I set out to understand which new forms of order emerge in conflict zones, what roles do civilians and combatants play in that process, and what are the consequences for the conduct of war.

This book comes from my doctoral dissertation. I was fortunate to start a PhD in political science at Yale University in the same year that the Program on Order, Conflict and Violence was born. It was a tremendously stimulating place, with professors and students asking new questions, crafting innovative theories, and conducting dedicated fieldwork across the globe. I benefited from the insights and mentoring of an outstanding dissertation committee. The scholarship and teaching of my advisor, Stathis Kalyvas, influenced my approach to social science research in ways that transcend this book. I thank him for continuously challenging me to think deeper, for supporting this project at its different stages, and for being a caring friend. I learned much from the teaching and research of Elisabeth Wood, and her constant effort to work following the most demanding ethical principles. I thank her for giving me invaluable feedback every time I needed it, and for being tender and demanding at the same time. Ian Shapiro believed in the relevance and viability of this project since its inception. He graciously agreed to guide me in the study of how political philosophers have approached the problem of order. I am grateful for his support over the years, and for caring about me and my family.

In developing this project, many others at Yale gave comments, feedback, and support. Although I cannot list them all here, I am especially grateful to Cameron Ballard-Rosa, Laia Balcells, Gina Bateson, Robert Blair, Mario Chacón, Kush Choudhury, Francesca Grandi, Don Green, Adi Greif, Sandy Henderson, Amelia Hoover, Corinna Jentzsch, Stephen Kaplan, Matt Kocher, Dominika Koter, Pierre Landry, Meghan Lynch, Jason Lyall, Haris Mylonas, Shivaji Mukherjee, Tatiana Neumann, Ana de la O, Leonid Peisakhin, Gemma Sala, Kenneth Scheve, Luis Schiumerini, Jonah Schulhofer-Wohl, Livia Schubiger, Abbey Steele, Sue Stokes, and Steve Wilkinson.

As a postdoctoral fellow at Columbia University, I learned much from Macartan Humphreys, whose support I deeply appreciate. I also thank Guy Grossman for being so welcoming. In New York, Zachariah Mampilly was a great interlocutor. I deeply appreciate his support and generosity.

At Northwestern University, I have enjoyed insightful discussions with Lina Britto, Edward Gibson, Jim Mahoney, Wendy Pearlman, Will Reno, Rachel Riedl, and outstanding graduate and undergraduate students who have read and criticized parts of this book. The support and positive atmosphere of my department made this book better.

I am also indebted to the scholars who participated in a book conference held at Yale University in 2013, with the support of the Program on Order, Conflict and Violence: Kate Baldwin, Francesca Grandi, Kosuke Imai, Michael Kalin, Stathis Kalyvas, Matt Kocher, Roger Petersen, Michael Reed, Scott Straus, Andrés Vargas, and Elisabeth Wood.

Over the years, I received insightful comments on different parts of this book from many friends and colleagues. I mention some of them here: Yuen Yuen Ang, Desmond Arias, Deborah Boucoyannis, Luis de la Calle,

Andres Casas, Sarah Daly, Todd Eisenstadt, Jon Elster, Andreas Feldman, Yvan Guichaoua, Michael Gilligan, Patricia Justino, Pablo Kalmanovitz, Morgan Kaplan, Ken Kelly, Nelson Kasfir, Ed Malesky, Mike McGovern, Anna Gryzmala-Busse, Jorge Domínguez, Ben Lessing, Monika Nalepa, Marc Opper, Sam Plapinger, Didier Precard, Lincoln Quillian, María Paula Saffond, Alberto Simpser, Dan Slater, Richard Snyder, Guillermo Trejo, Ben Valentino, Philip Verwimp, Lucan Way, Erik Wibbles, and Timothy Wickham-Crowley. I also thank participants at conferences and workshops at the University of Michigan at Ann Arbor, Brown University, El Centro de Investigación y Educación Popular (CINEP) (Bogotá, Colombia), CIDE (Mexico), Columbia University, EAFIT University (Medellín, Colombia), Sussex University (Brighton, UK), Duke University, MIT, Harvard University, Los Andes University (Bogotá, Colombia), Ohio State University, Oxford University (Oxford, UK), the University of Chicago, the University of Pennsylvania, and the University of Virginia. The authors of the volume *Rebel Governance in Civil War* that I coedited with Nelson Kasfir and Zachariah Mampilly also offered valuable feedback.

In Colombia, many persons provided comments and supported my fieldwork in various ways, especially Gerson Arias, Alvaro Agudelo, Camilo Echandía, Fernando Enciso, Rodolfo Escobedo, Alexander Herrera, Ana María Ibañez, María Victoria Llorente, Claudia López, Marcela Melendez, Claudia Medina, Juliana Monsalve, Dario Restrepo, Mauricio Romero, Francisco Sandoval, Fabio Sánchez, Mauricio Solano, Fany Uribe, Teófilo Vásquez, María Alejandra Vélez, and María Emma Wills. I also thank CINEP, the School of Economics at Los Andes University, CITPax, and the *Agencia Colombiana para la Reintegración* for their support in my fieldwork. Fernán González and Francisco Gutierrez provided invaluable feedback and encouragement.

I am deeply grateful to all the people who trusted me and my research team in Colombia, sharing their memories and views with us. Their hospitality and generosity were demonstrative of the kindness that persists even in the wake of violence. In particular, I am indebted to Alvaro, Douglas, Lucia, Omar, and Roger for helping me so much in Cordoba and Cundinamarca. I do not use their last names to protect their identities.

The work of several researchers and research assistants was essential to the completion of this project. Many thanks to Eduardo Alvarez, Andres Felipe Aponte, Kaitlyn Chriswell, Andres Clavijo, Camilo Corredor, Victor Herrera, Adelina Pak, Natalia Perez, Camila Reyes, Javier

Revelo, Brian Yost, and Sara Zamora. Ana María Zuluaga was particularly helpful when conducting fieldwork in Viotá, and I thank her and her family for their hospitality. I also thank Laura Otalora for her help with data processing and Laura García, Salma Al-Shami, and Jacob Schauer for their help with specific components of the statistical analysis. Silvia Otero was an outstanding research assistant, and an excellent interlocutor. Rana Khoury and Sasha Klyachkina edited the book and offered insightful comments.

I am also grateful to the institutions that provided financial support for this project: The Social Science Research Council's International Dissertation Research Fellowship, the Harry Frank Guggenheim Foundation's Dissertation Writing Grant, Yale University's John Enders Grant, MacMillan International Dissertation Grant, and Robert Leylan Prize, as well as research grants from the United States Institute of Peace, the Folke Bernadotte Academy (Sweden), Canada's International Development Research Centre, and the Department for International Development (DFID) and the Economic and Social Research Council (ESRC) Grant for Development Research (UK).

While turning a manuscript into a book, I benefited from the insightful advice of anonymous reviewers and the guidance of my editor, Lew Bateman. I also thank Kathy Thelen and Erik Wibbles for the inclusion of this book in the *Comparative Politics Series*.

Conducting the research that I present in this book took a long journey. Every single stage along the way was made possible in many ways by the dedicated support of my partner, Eudald Lerga. When he moved from Barcelona to New Haven so that I could join the PhD program at Yale University, I thought that was the ultimate demonstration of love. But three years later, when the time for fieldwork came – and we had six-month-old twins – he showed me that that had been just the beginning. Not only did he and my sons come with me to Colombia but they also traveled with me around the country – always staying in safe places – so that I could do fieldwork. Since then, he has supported my work in every possible way. I cannot thank him enough for his generosity over the years. His genuine interest in my research also made him a wonderful interlocutor. I dedicate this book to him.

I owe much to our families in Colombia and Catalonia. They have made every effort to help us in every imaginable way. My parents have always supported me – in every project I have pursued – unconditionally. I thank them for everything they have done.

Finally, our sons, Esteve and Miquel, now nine years old, have been extremely patient and supportive. Growing up with the book that was born right at the same time as they were, their interest on the work I do has been persistent. Their love, energy, and creativity have infused my life in every possible way. Thank you.

As Colombia gets close to a peace agreement between the insurgent group FARC and the government, my hope is that this book contributes to our understanding of how war transformed communities and individuals – and how such transformations should be taken into account as the country transitions into peace.

Abbreviations and Glossary of Terms

ACC	Peasant Self-Defense Forces of Casanare (Colombia)
ACCU	Peasant Self-Defense Forces of Córdoba and Urabá (Colombia)
AMV	Self-Defense Forces of Meta and Vichada (Colombia)
AUC	United Self-Defense Forces of Colombia
BACRIM	Emerging Criminal Bands (Colombia)
C.	Case number
CAJAR	Colectivo de Abogados José Alvear Restrepo (Colombia)
CNAI	Fundación Nuevo Arco Iris (Colombia)
CP	Communist Party of Colombia
DDR	Disarmament, Demobilization, and Reinsertion
DRC	The Democratic Republic of Congo
ELN	National Liberation Army (Colombia)
EPL	Popular Liberation Army (Colombia)
FARC	Revolutionary Armed Forces of Colombia
FATA	Federally Administered Tribal Areas (Pakistan)
FMLN	Farabundo Marti National Liberation Front (El Salvador)
HRW	Human Rights Watch
IDEs	Individually demobilized combatants
IELN	Individually demobilized former ELN members
IFARC	Individually demobilized former FARC members
Int.	Interview number
IPARAS	Individually demobilized former paramilitary members
JAC	Juntas de Acción Comunal (Communal Action Association)
M19	April 19 Movement (Colombia)
MOE	Misión de Observación Electoral (Electoral Observation Mission)
NPLF	National Patriotic Front of Liberia

NRA	The National Resistance Army (Uganda)
NYT	*New York Times*
PKP	Communist Party of the Philippines
PLA	The People's Liberation Army (China)
RCD	Congolese Rally for Democracy
RUF	Revolutionary United Front (Sierra Leone)
SPLA	Sudan's People Liberation Army
SPLM	Sudan's People Liberation Movement
TPLF	The Tigray's People's Liberation Front (Ethiopia)
UNITA	The National Union for the Total Independence of Angola

I

Introduction

The FARC were everything in this village. They had the last word on every single dispute among neighbors. They decided what could be sold at the stores, the time when we should all go home, and who should leave the area never to come back .... They also managed divorces, inheritances, and conflicts over land borders. They were the ones who ruled here, not the state.

Local leader, village of Librea, municipality of Viotá[1]

We did interact with the FARC all those years. A little more than a decade. [At first] they came here, walked by, told us things, asked that we did certain things like not talking to the army .... Then they started to set rules and tell us how things needed to be done. They wanted to take power over these people and this land. But they couldn't. We had to obey them in certain ways, of course, because they have the weapons. But we [the peasant leaders] are the authority here. People recognize us as such. They could not take that away from us. They didn't rule us.

Local leader, village of Zama, municipality of Viotá[2]

These are the testimonies of two individuals who lived in neighboring villages, less than 2 km apart, in the Colombian Andes. The Revolutionary Armed Forces of Colombia (*Fuerzas Revolucionarias de Colombia*, FARC), one of the world's oldest guerrilla groups, controlled the area for about twelve years, but did so in drastically different ways in the two

---

[1] Personal interview, village of Librea, Viotá, Cundinamarca, Colombia, 2007. Given that the Colombian conflict is ongoing, I do not use the real names of my interviewees or their communities, only their municipalities.
[2] Personal interview, village of Zama, Viotá, Cundinamarca, Colombia, 2007.

places. In the village of Librea, the FARC ruled over the political, economic, and social life of the population. Most people cooperated with the rebels and obeyed rules governing everything from mobility, public speech, and domestic violence to economic activities and conflict resolution. Things were quite different in the village of Zama, where civilian leaders remained the ultimate authority. The FARC regulated some aspects of civilian conduct, but locals remained in charge of arbitrating disputes, deciding the rules that guided social interaction, and holding meetings to discuss community problems and decide important issues. Whenever the FARC tried to intervene in their affairs, the community successfully limited their influence.

The situation of these villages illustrates a puzzling aspect of civil war: far from being chaotic and anarchic, war zones are often orderly. Although fear and violence exist, chaos is seldom the norm. In many places there is a sense of normality – even if different from that of peacetime – and people have expectations about what might happen. There is a new order in place, which civilians recognize, that marks many aspects of daily life. Furthermore, different forms of order frequently coexist in areas controlled by the same non-state armed group. Adjacent villages, or even neighborhoods, end up living under very different institutions – understood broadly as the formal and informal rules, norms, and practices that structure human interaction (North 1990) – which give way to different patterns of being and relating. In some cases, rebels establish institutions to regulate a myriad of conducts, while in others their intervention is minimal. What explains the emergence of order in war zones? Why, when order emerges, does it take different forms?

Media coverage of war and commonplace understandings of war zones are far from what these villages experienced. Most of what we hear about war entails destruction, death, and disruption. This is certainly part of the story, and we are prone to focus on it for obvious reasons – war is indeed a deeply devastating event. But much more than violence happens during war. Armed actors do not only kill, but also create institutions, endorse ideologies, form alliances with local actors, provide public goods, recruit, and, in so doing, transform the societies in which they operate. Civilians, on the other hand, do not only suffer from war – they also cope with it, adapt to it, and shape it. They bargain with armed actors, influencing how their communities are governed, and how they live. In sum, life goes on in war zones and we need to understand how.

This book investigates social order in civil war conceptually, theoretically, and empirically. Conceptually, I propose a typology to distinguish, first, between conflict zones in which civilians live with great uncertainty, which I call *disorder*, and those where a formal or informal social contract between civilians and combatants allows them to form clear expectations, which I call *order*. Second, the typology distinguishes between situations of order where rebels (or counter-rebels) intervene broadly in civilian affairs, which I call *rebelocracy*, and those where rebels rule in a minimalist way, leaving most local affairs in the hands of others – be it state officials, traditional leaders or some other local actor – which I call *aliocracy*.[3] Hence, the book introduces and conceptualizes a novel phenomenon in the study of civil war.

Theoretically, I propose a model to explain variation in wartime social order across time and space by examining the interaction between the warring sides, on the one hand, and between civilians and combatants, on the other. There are two factors that determine what kind of social order will emerge in conflict zones: armed groups' time horizon – that is, whether or not they care about future outcomes more than they do about present ones – and the quality of preexisting local institutions, particularly those for adjudicating disputes. First, I argue that rebels with short-term goals will produce disorder in the territory. Most groups operate under long-time horizons most of the time, but when they face internal indiscipline or competition with other warring sides, their preferences shift and they care more about present outcomes than future ones. This may also happen under certain peace negotiations. It is in these situations that disorder emerges, forcing civilians to live under great uncertainty. Second, rebels with long-term horizons will seek a rebelocracy. In areas where local institutions are effective and legitimate, civilians have bargaining power because they can threaten rebels with collective resistance. In such cases, the rebel group has incentives to settle for aliocracy as its form of rule. On the other hand, where preexisting civilian institutions are either ineffective or illegitimate, civilians are unlikely to resist collectively, and therefore lack bargaining power. In these cases, rebels are able to establish rebelocracy.

Empirically, the book undertakes two tasks. First, it describes in great depth how distinct forms of social order function in Colombian conflict

---

[3] The neologisms *rebelocracy* and *aliocracy* come, respectively, from the Latin words *rebello*, which means "rebel," and *alios*, which means "other." The Latin root *cracy* forms nouns meaning "rule by" or "government by." I provide a formal definition of these terms in Chapter 2. This typology, together with some of the material in Chapters 1 and Chapter 2, was introduced in a journal article in Arjona (2014).

zones. Using surveys, interviews, and memory workshops, I reconstructed the history of interaction between non-state armed groups and seventy-four local populations throughout the country, creating a large dataset as well as local histories that provide a nuanced account of social order in conflict zones. Based on these sources, I present evidence on the institutions that armed actors have established, as well as on the local dynamics that those institutions engender. I also recount how different aspects of daily life change with the new order, and how civilians and combatants perceive those changes.

The second empirical task is to test the theory. I rely on a multi-method approach to test the central hypotheses that emerge from the model, as well as their underlying microfoundations – that is, the assumptions on individual behavior on which the argument is built – and mechanisms. I take advantage of the strengths of various methods to achieve distinct goals, and rely on different kinds of evidence that I collected on civilians, combatants, communities, and armed groups in multiple waves of fieldwork conducted between 2004 and 2012 in Colombia.

CIVILIAN–COMBATANT INTERACTIONS, WARTIME INSTITUTIONS, AND THE STUDY OF CIVIL WAR

The existing literature on irregular civil wars – those fought by at least one nonconventional force – has widely recognized that this type of conflict entails a close interaction between civilians and combatants. Moreover, the quality of this interaction is often seen as a key determinant of war outcomes: the idea that popular support is essential for victory has been stressed by rebel theorists, military historians, and scholars alike (Galula 1964; Trinquier 1964:8; Taber 1965; Mao 1978; Guevara et al. 1997). Debates about counterinsurgency also revolve around the importance of civilian collaboration with the warring sides in conflicts ranging from Vietnam, to El Salvador, to Iraq and Afghanistan.

Civilian–combatant interactions are crucial also because they shape the context in which both civilians and combatants make a wide range of choices. Understanding the terms of those interactions is therefore central when we ask why people join rebels and militias, why families decide to flee, why combatants kill, why locals support or boycott counterinsurgency operations, and why former fighters successfully reintegrate into their communities or fail to do so. Even when we ask questions about macro-level outcomes such as the duration of war, the stability of peace agreements, or the effects of peacekeeping operations, our theories and interpretations of empirical results rely on assumptions about how actors make decisions on the ground – and such decisions are deeply influenced by the nature of civilian-combatant relations.

Despite the centrality of the interaction between civilians and combatants, its variation has seldom been described systematically, let alone theorized. To be sure, there are excellent studies of civilian–combatant relations and of the fate of populations in conflict zones. However, scholars have mostly focused on rebel behavior, or on how civilians experience war and cope with it, instead of theorizing and documenting the interaction between the two.

For a long time, what happens in areas where rebels or paramilitaries are present was essentially a black box that the literature depicted with two contrasting views. The first relies on the "hearts and minds" metaphor, portraying rebels as freedom fighters who try to gain popular support on the basis of good behavior and ideological propaganda. The second view emphasizes the criminal behavior of non-state armed organizations: combatants are assumed to rely only on coercion to induce cooperation from local populations. This dichotomy leads to the simplistic assumption that civilians are either politically supportive of the rebels or cowed and victimized by them. Accounts that explain war dynamics on the basis of rebels' criminal or idealistic nature have further advanced this view. For example, according to Weinstein (2007), idealistic groups recruit ideologically motivated individuals, limit their use of violence against civilians and provide them public goods, and garner popular support; predatory groups, on the other hand, attract greedy persons to their ranks, exploit local populations, and fail to obtain civilian support.

Evidence of life in war zones, however, confounds this view. A given guerrilla or militia group often opts for different strategies towards neighboring local populations. The Chinese People's Liberation Army, for example, followed strict rules governing its treatment of some communities, while, in others, combatants showed little restraint (Hinton 1966; Girling 1969; Hartford 1995). What is more, while an armed group may rule in one place as an occupying army that controls only security and taxation, in other communities it can become a proto-state by functioning as the police, court, and public-goods provider.

Civilians, for their part, exercise agency despite the hardship of war and can respond to the presence and behavior of armed groups in different ways: some cooperate enthusiastically, others passively obey, and others resist fiercely. For example, even under the surveillance of one of the world's most powerful armies, civilians in Afghanistan have often helped the Taliban in a myriad of ways – from hiding rebels in their homes, to flying kites to signal the arrival of American troops (*NYT* 2010b). At the same time, others have taken risks to aid American forces in areas where the Taliban has a strong presence (*NYT* 2010a). Civilians can also choose to flee when living in a war zone becomes too risky or strenuous. Furthermore – and despite common beliefs – civilians can resist armed groups' ruling attempts. Instances of armed resistance have been documented in many cases like Mozambique (e.g., Weinstein 2007), Kenya (e.g., Anderson 2005), and Peru (e.g., Isbell 1992). An emerging literature shows that peaceful resistance to armed actors has also emerged in many armed conflicts – from Peru to Colombia to Sudan to Indonesia (e.g., Hancock & Mitchell 2007; Kaplan 2013b). Ethnographic evidence on several rebellions has also shown that civilians find ways to make demands on the rebels, bargain with them, and strike deals (Weber 1981; Vlassenroot & Raeymaekers 2004b; Lubkemann 2008; Arjona 2015; Barter 2015; Förster 2015).

Clearly, civilian–combatant relations can take many forms, leading to substantial variation in the nature of daily life in war zones. Even though this variation is staggering in its range across and within civil wars, our understanding of its causes and effects is still quite limited. A new literature on rebel governance has made excellent contributions but, for the most part, has focused on variation *across* armed groups, rather than *within* them. In addition, the few existing accounts focus on explaining why combatants govern civilians or not, rather than on why they govern them *differently*. Furthermore, the focus of these studies tends to be rebel provision of public goods rather than the creation of new institutions.[4]

The neglect of wartime institutions is actually quite widespread in the literature on civil war more generally. Despite the general agreement that institutions shape behavior, the study of how civilians and combatants make choices in war zones tends to overlook the role of wartime institutions. Disregarding the effect of institutions in the analysis of individual and collective behavior would be astounding in many social sciences; however, it has endured in civil war studies perhaps because war is assumed to be chaotic and anarchic, as the widespread use of concepts

---

[4] I discuss this and other literature in Chapter 2.

such as failed states, collapsed governance, and ungoverned spaces suggests (Justino 2013).

Yet, the emergence of local institutions – and, with them, order – in the midst of war makes sense. To start with, war often weakens, and sometimes destroys, state institutions. Different literature has shown that in contexts where access to effective institutions is lacking, new informal institutions are likely to emerge. For example, rural communities that depend on limited, public natural resources often develop norms that facilitate collective action (Ostrom 1990). Illegal markets where property rights and contracts cannot be enforced by law also tend to develop their own parallel institutions (e.g., Gambetta 1996; Volkov 2000; Varese 2001; Skarbek 2011). Some theorists have argued that every tight social group develops norms that encourage cooperative behavior (Ellickson 2009:167). The emergence of the state itself has been explained as a process whereby one actor offers institutions and protection in exchange for taxation, thereby transforming a situation of anarchy into one where clear rules allow for higher predictability, productive activities, and capital accumulation (e.g., Tilly 1985; Olson 1993). Even within contexts where institutions do exist, actors often attempt to provide private orderings to "realign incentives and embed transactions in more protective governance structures" (Williamson 2002; see also Dixit 2007:438). These insights suggest that when prewar institutions are weakened in war zones, some sort of new institutions that establish order are likely to emerge.

The existence of wartime institutions should not be surprising for another simple reason: armed groups have incentives to create them. First, as Tilly (1978) suggests, in order to overcome their competitors, warring sides try to monopolize the means of violence, extract resources from local inhabitants, and, at the same time, promote capital accumulation. Even though Tilly was referring to a long historical process, armed actors fighting civil wars are likely to learn that in order to advance their cause, they need to create a sustainable system of resource extraction to fund their operations. Such a system, in turn, requires some security and limited taxation for civilians to engage in productive activities (Olson 1993) – in other words, it requires institutions. In addition, as I will argue in this book, armed groups interested in controlling territory have incentives to establish institutions because doing so helps them to both gain territorial control and strengthen their organizational capacity.

Overlooking wartime institutions and the emergence of new forms of order has important implications. Theoretically, by ignoring the different ways in which armed groups approach civilians, we fail to understand how the former seek obedience and support, how they are able to grow and survive, and how their behaviors affect local populations. At the same time, overlooking the roles that a given armed group comes to play within a given community leads us to investigate civilian behavior without paying attention to the institutional contexts in which civilians live. Hence, our understanding of civilians' decision to cooperate with armed actors, flee, or join or oppose combatants, ignores a crucial aspect of the context in which they make their decisions.

Neglecting the different forms that war takes on at the local level also has important consequences for our understanding of post-conflict outcomes. Civil war triggers many processes that transform economic activities, infrastructure, demographic patterns, social fabric, and political identities, among others (Wood 2008; Arjona 2009; Justino 2013). Yet, assuming that these processes are homogeneous across regions or within an armed group is inconsistent with available empirical evidence. Precisely because the way in which armed groups occupy territories varies across time and space, we cannot assume that these processes affect all local populations – even those in the same region – in the same way. Ethnographic evidence shows that there is great variation in how neighboring communities within a province experience war (e.g., Vlassenroot & Raeymaekers 2004a). As I show in this book, systematic data supports these findings. The effects of war cannot, therefore, be assumed to be constant within a country or its regions. Accounting for that variation is essential to understanding both wartime dynamics and their effects in the post-conflict period.

Concerning policy, understanding the behavior of armed groups and civilians is essential to identifying the challenges and opportunities for different sorts of intervention. Efforts to limit civilian casualties, prevent displacement, or promote development in war-affected areas have to be grounded in a realistic assessment of the local dynamics of war. Civilian-combatant relations are also at the core of counterinsurgency studies. The idea that gaining popular support is essential for victory has been invoked to plan, or criticize, counterinsurgency strategies across the globe. Yet, such strategies cannot be evaluated without assessing how armed groups gain territories, settle in them, and secure civilian obedience and support, as well as how civilians respond in different contexts.

Finally, if institutions are, as many disciplines believe, an essential building block of economic, social, and political phenomena, we need to understand how they are transformed by war, and how this differs across localities. The challenges and opportunities for reintegration, reconciliation, poverty alleviation, and institution-building may well vary depending on the type of social order that emerged during the war. Yet, as Blattman and Miguel (2010) note, the institutional legacies of armed conflict have been largely neglected.

Challenging the assumption that civil wars are characterized by chaos and "collapsed governance" (Justino 2013; Risse 2013; Reno 2011), I argue that our understanding of the conduct of war as well as its legacies demands a theory of the creation of social order during wartime. By offering such a theory, this book aims to open the black box of civilian–combatant relations and institutional arrangements that characterize war zones. In the remainder of this introduction, I lay out the central components of the theory (which is presented in Chapter 3), the research design, and the organization of the book.

A THEORY OF SOCIAL ORDER IN CIVIL WAR

I propose a theory of the creation of social order in irregular civil wars by analyzing the interaction of state and non-state armed actors as well as between them and civilian populations. My central argument is that, in any given war zone, the length of an armed group's time horizon determines whether or not it establishes a social contract with the local population, giving place to local order. In situations where a social contract is established, I argue that the quality of the preexisting local institutions – defined as their legitimacy and efficacy – determines whether rebelocracy or aliocracy emerges.

The logic of the argument is as follows: I assume that rebels aim to control territories as a means of pressuring the incumbent and increasing their strength. I also assume that a secondary goal is to maximize the byproducts of that control – such as obtaining material resources, attracting recruits, and expanding their networks – which help rebels build their organizational capacity. Given these two goals, I argue that rebels prefer order to disorder and, among the possible types of order, they prefer rebelocracy to aliocracy.

Order is instrumental to maintaining territorial control, which is hardly possible in the absence of clear rules that regulate both civilian and combatant behavior. Such rules facilitate rebel monitoring of civilian conduct (such as helping the enemy), and also make civilians more likely to voluntarily obey and offer support. Rebels, therefore, have incentives to establish a social contract with the local population, where both sides are subject to certain rules. However, as Olson (1993) argued, establishing a social contract pays off in the long run: actors incur the costs of limiting their behavior in the present for the sake of future benefits. When rebels have short time horizons, they have incentives to reject any commitments that limit their present behavior.

I identify two conditions under which a given armed group, or one of its units, operates under short time horizons. The first is when a group faces armed competition with other warring sides in a given territory, which forces it to focus on defense. When fighting to preserve territorial control, rebels have fewer incentives to restrain their behavior and abstain from conduct that they expect will increase the odds of winning that territory. A social contract with the local population becomes a burden, as it does not help the group to achieve its short-term goals and can, on the contrary, hamper its success. Furthermore, preserving order becomes too costly, as the group prefers to devote resources and manpower to fighting its enemy. Disorder, or the absence of a social contract, is therefore likely to emerge when two or more warring sides actively compete for territorial control. This argument is consistent with theories of rebel and criminal violence and predation (e.g., Kalyvas 2006; Metelits 2010; Skaperdas 2001), in which armed competition pushes armed actors to use more violence and neglect social contracts.

The second condition under which armed groups operate on a short time horizon is when they lack internal discipline. Different factors can affect the internal organization of armed groups, such as their social networks, ideology, and the type of recruits they attract (e.g., Weinstein 2007; Staniland 2014), making them more or less disciplined. In the absence of an internal structure that makes combatants follow rules and orders from their commanders, fighters are likely to engage in behaviors to satisfy their individual preferences. Rules that limit combatant behavior are often disobeyed, and civilians face great uncertainty about how combatants will act. Disorder is, therefore, more likely to emerge when combatants can disregard the orders of their commanders. This argument is consistent with theories that stress the role of organizational structures in rebel violence and governance (Weinstein 2007).

In the absence of armed competition and indiscipline, armed actors are more likely to operate under long time horizons, establishing a social contract with the local population. The ensuing social order may take one of two forms. The first form of social order is *rebelocracy*, or the rule of rebels, where armed groups intervene broadly in civilian affairs, regulating behavior beyond the spheres of taxation and security. For example, combatants may regulate public and private conduct, establish a justice system to adjudicate disputes and enforce contracts, and provide public goods. The second form of social order is *aliocracy*, or the rule of others, where armed groups only intervene in civilian affairs by collecting taxes and regulating conducts related to security, while others – such as civilian authorities, state institutions, or traditional leaders – regulate the remaining aspects of local life. To use the language of the state, under rebelocracy the armed actor adopts the functions of an interventionist state, while in aliocracy it resembles a minimalist one.

I argue that armed groups with long time horizons prefer *rebelocracy* to *aliocracy* for three reasons. First, *rebelocracy* facilitates territorial control, as the group can directly regulate and monitor many activities. Second, it allows the group to create and transform institutions in the social, political, and economic spheres both to build its organizational capacity and further its interests. And finally, by influencing local life in profound ways, the group also manages to elicit civilian cooperation. Such cooperation, in turn, reinforces territorial control. In this way, the group reshapes local life in accordance to its interests, needs, and principles. In addition, thanks to what we could call an economy of smallness, rebelocracy is not hard to implement. A few local informants who are willing to report on instances of disobedience of rules, together with exemplary punishments, often suffice for civilians to follow the new rules that combatants establish. It follows that once they target a territory to settle in, rebels prefer *rebelocracy* to *aliocracy*.

But civilians do not always give in. While one of the tenets of decades of research on guerrilla warfare is the centrality of civilian support for rebel survival and success, the bargaining power that such a position proffers civilians has been widely ignored. Yet, if civilians resist collectively, they can endanger armed groups' territorial control and its byproducts. To avoid such a costly outcome, the armed group prefers to settle for a social order in which its influence on locals' lives is limited, yet still allows it to preserve control of the territory. Armed groups are, therefore, better off by tailoring their strategy to each community based on their expectation of collective resistance.

The question that follows, then, is under what conditions do civilians resist collectively? I argue that the likelihood of collective resistance to rebelocracy in a given local community is a function of the quality of the local institutions in place prior to the arrival of the group, in particular, dispute institutions – those that adjudicate disputes, enforce contracts, and protect property rights. By quality of institutions, I mean their legitimacy – that is, that they are recognized as valid by most community members – and their efficacy, meaning the extent to which they tend to be observed. Two mechanisms are at work: first, the quality of institutions influences individuals' preferences for preserving the current form of governance and therefore their desire to resist an insurgent's ruling attempts; and second, it shapes the community's capacity to launch and sustain resistance, which I conceptualize as a collective action problem.

When armed groups approach local communities with high-quality institutions, they anticipate resistance and prefer to establish a social contract that respects the existing governance scheme. In exchange, combatants demand obedience to rules regarding their security and the fulfillment of material contributions. This agreement is often the result of prodding and negotiations. The ensuing social order, *aliocracy*, is substantially different from a social order of *rebelocracy* in two ways: first, civilian affairs remain mostly in civilian hands in *aliocracy*, whereas combatants are highly influential in *rebelocracy*; and second, under *rebelocracy* the armed group is more able to shape the economic, political, and social life of the community in ways that benefit its interests. Still, both arrangements help the group to preserve territorial control more than *disorder* would.

Finally, some territories are so important for the group that tolerating civilian autonomy is too costly. Areas where high-level commanders live, or where new recruits are trained, are good examples. Other territories are highly valuable because of their geographic location, such as corridors that would allow the group to bring in weapons, export illegal resources, or connect factions deployed across the country. In these strategic territories, armed groups need tight population control and broad cooperation, and therefore do not tolerate civilian autonomy, even if they expect resistance. Communities that demand civilian autonomy are therefore likely to be targeted, often with the aim of displacing all their members from the area. *Disorder* is the likely outcome.

In addition to rebel and civilian behavior, the theory explains the role of the state in wartime. I distinguish between the state's armed forces and its other agencies, which can create and change local institutions. If the state's forces compete with other warring sides, I expect disorder to emerge. If other state agencies established high-quality institutions – in particular dispute institutions – prior to the arrival of the armed actor,

I expect the latter to establish aliocracy instead of rebelocracy for fear of organized resistance.

Although the theory focuses on social order as an outcome, describing and explaining the process by which new social orders are consolidated is essential to this book. How do armed groups actually penetrate communities and rule them? How do civilians manage to limit rebels' ruling aspirations? What are the modes of resistance? How is civilian cooperation sought? How do guerrilla and paramilitary commanders earn deference or disdain? By investigating when and why distinct types of social order are likely to emerge, I delve into these questions and address the process by which armed groups make their way into communities and rule them – or fail to do so. I also assess how ideology, community structure, state agents, and alliances between armed groups, on the one hand, and elites and other sectors of the population, on the other, shape these processes.

The theory is meant to explain variation in non-state armed groups' strategies towards local populations, the latter's responses, and the ensuing forms of social order in areas where armed groups have an *ongoing* presence. Interactions between civilians and combatants in areas where the former are only sporadically present are not part of the universe of cases that the theory aims to explain. Put differently, I aim to investigate prolonged interactions of civilians and combatants, as opposed to their contact in isolated events like sporadic attacks.

The theory should apply to all *irregular* civil wars – the most common type of civil war since the 1950s (Kalyvas & Balcells 2010) regardless of the main division fueling them: secessionist, center-seeking, and ethnic-based groups are expected to follow a similar logic. However, several factors that shape the explanatory variables identified by the theory may co-vary with these types of conflicts, making a particular form of social order more or less likely. An important scope condition, however, is that armed groups should seek to control territory. The theory does not seek to explain social order in areas where armed organizations do not want to control territory. For example, secessionist rebel groups may only want to control territory in the area they want to "liberate," but not in other regions of the country in which they operate. Other civil wars are characterized by armed actors that engage in genocide, rather than territorial expansion. This book does not explain their interaction with civilians. Finally, conventional civil wars, where clear battle lines exist, are also not within the scope of this project.

RESEARCH DESIGN

I test several implications of the theory, as well as its microfoundations and mechanisms, with data on individuals, communities, and armed groups in the Colombian armed conflict. Colombia exhibits great variation in the factors that, according to the theory, shape wartime social order: several rebel and paramilitary groups have participated in the conflict, which allows for testing the argument on organizations with different internal structures and goals; the quality of local institutions also varies greatly across the territory, as they may come from the state, ethnic authorities, and *sui generis* forms of peasant self-governance; and finally, the value of local territories and competition for territorial control change across time and space. In addition, there is great variation in ethnicity, geography, and state presence, which allows for testing the theory in a wide variety of contexts.

Even though the conflict has lasted for more than four decades, there is great disparity in the duration of war at the sub-national level as armed groups expand to new areas of the country and abandon previous strongholds. For this reason, while some communities interacted with armed actors for only two years, others have coexisted with them for decades. This variation allows for testing the argument in communities that have experienced the war for substantially different lengths of time.

It is important to note that all armed groups in Colombia have been impacted, directly or indirectly, by the market of illicit drugs. This raises the question of whether the dynamics in Colombia can be found in civil wars where rebels lack valuable natural resources to fund their operations. It could be possible, for example, that armed groups that lack such resources are unable to establish institutions to rule populations. However, in later chapters I offer evidence of armed groups' creation of rebelocracies in many countries around the world – some of which have natural resources and some of which do not. This evidence suggests that rebelocracy is appealing and can be established by rebels even in the absence of profitable goods. To be sure, it is still possible that the factors that lead armed actors to create disorder, rebelocracy, and aliocracy vary depending on whether natural resources are available or not. This is an open question that can only be resolved with new data.

The research design consists of different tests of observable implications of the theory regarding the determinants of social order, as well as the underlying mechanisms and microfoundations. I rely on original data that I collected between 2004 and 2012 with different methods, including three original surveys, structured and open interviews, in-depth case studies, and memory workshops to produce timelines and what I have called *institutional biographies*. The analysis relies on a mix of methodologies, including statistical analysis, process tracing, and natural experiments.

The Determinants of Social Order

The first component of the research design tests hypotheses on the determinants of variation in social order across time and space. I selected a random sample of local communities in different regions of Colombia that had lived under guerrilla or paramilitary presence. With a survey that used vignettes to elicit responses, I gathered data on the interaction between armed groups and communities. While they do not necessarily offer an in-depth view of local histories, these vignettes were an effective way to get snapshots of the forms of social order that emerged in the sampled communities. Based on this initial coding, I randomly selected a sub-sample to focus on. Relying on interviews, memory workshops, and primary and secondary sources, I reconstructed the history of interaction between seventy-four communities and all the armed groups that had been present in their territory (more than thirteen armed groups in total, including several guerilla and paramilitary groups). Using multilevel models, the statistical analysis confirms strong correlation between social order on the one hand, and preexisting local institutions, armed competition, and armed groups' indiscipline, on the other. By design, I compare communities that are similar in many ways – they belong to the same municipality, have the same local government, and often the same local economy. However, to better identify the causal nature of these relationships, I rely on instrumental variables – a widely used method that helps to isolate causal effects.

I also test the central mechanism underlying the relation between the quality of local institutions and social order, to wit, the threat of civilian resistance. I find that rebelocracy is less likely to emerge in communities that had previously engaged in collective resistance against an armed actor, suggesting that those communities are more likely to bargain with groups that want to rule them, and that the latter are more likely to give in.

It is worth explaining why this is a theory-testing exercise rather than a theory development one. Although my theory had been informed by the dynamics I had observed in my fieldwork in two municipalities in Colombia (and qualitative evidence on many cases beyond Colombia), the main test of the hypotheses uses data on a random sample of communities throughout the country that were not available when the theory was developed. The survey questions were designed to test specific hypotheses, and the in-depth interviews were conducted to gather detailed data on previously theorized mechanisms.

Processes and Mechanisms: The Creation of Social Order

While the statistical analysis identifies the effect of the explanatory variables on social order, it fails to shed light on the processes by which new orders come to be. Put differently, the statistical analysis can only expound on social order as a static outcome; however, it is essential to understand it as a dynamic process. In order to illustrate how armed groups approach local communities at different stages, and how the latter react, I rely on both qualitative and quantitative information. The evidence comes from the in-depth studies of the sample of communities previously alluded to, as well as from in-depth interviews with civilians and ex-combatants of guerrilla and paramilitary groups. I use this evidence to illustrate how civilians and combatants interact in a dynamic fashion, facilitating the consolidation of new social orders.

The data also serves to test specific claims about mechanisms and microfoundations. For example, by relying on interviews and local histories, I show that civilian cooperation is more common under rebelocracy than under other forms of social order.

Given the central role civilian resistance plays in the argument, I rely on primary and secondary data to assess whether resistance in Colombia has been observed under the conditions specified by my theory. I built a dataset based on the existing literature on civilian resistance in Colombia to see whether patterns coincide with the expectations of the theory. In particular, the argument implies that resistance is not triggered by armed groups with long time horizons, unless the territory has a high strategic value. Although this is not a random sample and may not be representative of all Colombian war zones, it is a good plausibility test of the mechanism. I find that the large majority of cases of resistance do take place under the conditions specified by the theory.

A Process-Driven Natural Experiment

The third empirical component of the project entails an in-depth study of three local communities in the municipality of Viotá that interacted with the FARC for about twelve years each. Located in the Colombian Andes, Viotá was home to one of the most successful agrarian movements in the country between the 1930s and the 1950s. Successful collective action by this peasant community not only led to a radical transformation of land tenure, but also to the emergence of effective self-governing schemes, which were responsible for arbitrating disputes as well as defending the population from violent attacks, state repression, and a bloody civil war during the 1950s. Yet, around 1960 a fortuitous event – a gift of land to one of the key agrarian leaders – triggered the migration of most leaders to a specific village. Over time, the movement became concentrated in that village, while the local institutions that had marked collective action and self-governance faded away elsewhere.

This exogenous shock on local institutions created a unique natural (or quasi-natural) experiment. All the villages had been formed due to the successful agrarian reform led by communist cadres throughout the municipality. Furthermore, popular participation in the different forms of collective action between 1930 and 1960 was massive all over the municipality. By 1960, most peasants in all of the villages had acquired land. It was only when most agrarian leaders moved to a single village that differences in community organization and local institutions started to emerge across villages. I exploit these differences to assess whether the quality of local institutions had a significant impact a few decades later when the FARC settled in the municipality: did variation in local institutions affect the FARC's strategies towards the different villages? Were locals' reactions where institutions were still legitimate and effective different from reactions where they were not? Did a different form of social order emerge in these communities?

Combining the logic of causal inference of natural experiments and process tracing,[5] I provide detailed evidence on the trajectories of three of the villages to argue that the quality of local institutions shaped the collective action capacity of their communities; their bargaining power vis-à-vis the FARC; and the ways in which the latter ruled. This approach allows me not only to test a complex mechanism but also to offer

---

[5] See Arjona (2016b) for a discussion of this approach.

a detailed account of civilian–combatant relations, civilians' experience of war, and the creation of new forms of order during wartime.

I find that the FARC established aliocracy in the village where legitimate, well-functioning institutions were in place. Despite the FARC's full military control over the entire municipality, this community managed to remain relatively autonomous for years. Meanwhile, rebels became the de facto rulers elsewhere in the municipality – including the main urban center where the police, court, local government, and other state agencies operated. Rebels ruled over every facet of life in those communities – from solving private disputes, to regulating economic activities and social behavior, and to deciding the results of local elections. However, they were unable to take over the tiny village where they encountered strong self-governing schemes. Furthermore, years later when the FARC started to abuse the general population, this village resisted – and succeeded.

This comparison suggests that armed groups' strategies, civilians' responses, and the resulting social order can be radically different, even within a municipality, if there is variation in the quality of local institutions. Furthermore, it shows that when armed groups fully disregard civilian agency, communities with high-quality institutions are able to organize successful resistance, often without relying on violence.

Finally, this study provides detailed evidence on the processes that lead to different forms of social order, with a focus on the choices of both civilians and combatants. By delving into the history of three small communities, interviewing leaders, common peasants, and combatants who operated in the area, I was able to record the protagonists' perceptions, learn about the small events that triggered great changes, and capture the nuances in the interactions between the FARC and these local communities under varying circumstances. This study demonstrates directly the operation of institutions – and rebels reacting to them. It also shows the complex roles that the state plays in conflict zones. Not least, it provides an intimate sense of how life in war zones goes on under different forms of social order.

Testing the Microfoundations: Social Order and Recruitment

In order to rigorously evaluate the microfoundations of the theory, I test the observable implications on recruitment. The argument is built on the assumption that civilian cooperation is higher under rebelocracy: I argue that one of the reasons why armed groups prefer rebelocracy is that it leads to higher levels of civilian cooperation, which in turn is crucial to maintain territorial control. Being a particular form of civilian cooperation, recruitment should be higher in local communities where rebelocracy emerged – where armed groups became de facto rulers and intervened broadly in community life. I use the data on local communities mentioned before, as well as on a large-scale survey with about 800 former combatants and 600 civilians that I conducted in collaboration with Stathis Kalyvas in Colombia. The data include detailed information on the profiles, families, and communities of ex-combatants prior to joining an armed group, as well as of civilians who did not join, but lived in municipalities where at least one person joined a group.

The analysis overcomes a problem shared by most studies with survey data on former combatants. These studies usually rely on data on ex-combatants' and civilians' characteristics either before the war started or after demobilization. In contrast, I rely on ex-combatants' responses about their life one year prior to enlisting, and on civilians' responses about their situation at different time periods. This allows me to build a dataset where the control group is made of civilians who were living at the same time and place where surveyed former combatants made the choice of enlisting in an armed group. This is important because war may transform many aspects of a person's life; the real comparison group for recruits should be their peers who did not choose to join a group despite living in the same place, at the same time.

The substantial contribution of this analysis goes beyond testing the microfoundations of a theory of social order. It suggests that recruitment is not only highly endogenous to the presence of armed groups (Kalyvas 2006; Arjona & Kalyvas 2011), but also – and more so – to the form of social order that emerges in war zones. Understanding recruitment thus requires opening the black box of civilian–combatant relations and theorizing how wartime institutional arrangements – and the beliefs and preferences that often result from them – shape communities and individuals. Neglecting the importance of civilian–combatant relations would amount to studying people's choices without considering the very context in which such decisions are made.

LOOKING AHEAD

The book is organized as follows. Chapters 2 and 3 present the theory. Chapter 2 introduces a new phenomenon in the study of civil war, wartime social order, and presents a typology. It also discusses current accounts of rebel behavior and civilian choice in civil war, and identifies how this project builds on, and differs from, them. Chapter 3 presents the theory of social order, focusing on the determinants of variation at the level of the locality.

Chapter 4 presents the research design, and introduces the Colombian armed conflict, as well as the main non-state armed groups involved. Chapter 5 presents the results of the statistical tests on the determinants of social order. Chapter 6 focuses on social order as a process by examining its development, and theorizing and illustrating mechanisms and microfoundations. It offers rich, detailed evidence on civilian–combatant interaction and daily life in war zones throughout Colombia. I start with a stylized view of the process, beginning with the moment an armed group enters a community and ending with the consolidation of a new social order. I then focus on each stage, discussing the underlying mechanisms shaping civilian and combatant behavior.

Chapter 7 presents the process-driven natural experiment. It offers a detailed history of the municipality of Viotá based on primary and secondary data as well as interviews. It then reconstructs the history of the interaction between the FARC and three local communities where institutions took different paths. The chapter concludes with a discussion of plausible alternative explanations. Chapter 8 evaluates the microfoundations of the theory by testing its implications on recruitment.

Chapter 9 concludes by summarizing the argument and findings, addressing their limitations, and exploring implications beyond the Colombian case, as well as beyond civil wars.

2

Wartime Social Order

What Is It and How Does It Vary?

This book investigates a new phenomenon in the study of civil war: social order in war zones. How do we define "wartime social order" – a seemingly paradoxical term given the common portrayal of war zones as chaotic and disorderly? How does social order vary? Which dimensions should we focus on? In this chapter, I define the concept of wartime social order. I also propose a typology and assess its quality by discussing the relevance of the variation that it captures, whether it identifies real types, and its parsimony. I then consider the insights that the current literature provides for understanding the emergence of different forms of social order in war zones as well as of collective civilian resistance. Assessing both their contributions and shortcomings, I address the ways in which I build on and depart from these theories.

DEFINING WARTIME SOCIAL ORDER

We often think of civilians living in war zones as victims trapped in a state of uncertainty, where "normal life" does not exist. Yet, a closer look at civil wars shows a different picture: despite fear and violence, new rules of behavior often operate, and civilians plan their daily lives around them. A new routine becomes ingrained, and people have expectations about what might happen. I refer to the existence of this predictability as *order*.

Every form of order is built on a set of institutions – that is, formal or informal rules, norms, and practices that structure interaction (North

1990:3),[1] allowing for such predictability to exist. In war zones, such institutions can vary greatly as they prescribe different conducts for civilians, combatants, or both. With a variety of rules comes a variety of expectations. Civilians' and combatants' expectations about others' behavior create specific patterns of social, economic, and political interaction. I define "wartime social order" as the particular set of institutions that underlie order in a war zone, giving place to distinct patterns of being and relating.[2] By war zone, I am referring to a territory where at least one non-state armed actor has a continuous presence.[3]

Even though the notion of social order in wartime may seem puzzling – war is, after all, a situation in which the preexisting order is being challenged – empirical evidence suggests that many areas where armed groups are present are quite orderly. Clear rules exist and people perceive the likely consequences of their conduct. It is actually common to find detailed studies of life in war zones describing the emergence of a new order – for example, Weber's (1981) study of Nicaragua; Nordstrom's (1997) and Lubkemann's (2008) on Mozambique; Vlassenroot and Raeymaekers' (2004a; 2004b) on the Democratic Republic of Congo; and Strachota's recent reports of The Islamic State of Iraq and the Levant (ISIS) governance in Syria (2015).

Available evidence suggests that order is not only common in war zones but also manifests in a variety of forms across time and space. As I will mention later in the chapter, studies of armed groups across the globe show that these organizations do not adopt the same strategy in every territory where they are present. On the contrary, they intervene in

---

[1] Throughout the book I use this definition of *institutions*. Formal institutions are "rules and procedures that are created, communicated, and enforced through channels widely accepted as official"; informal institutions are "socially shared rules, usually unwritten, that are created, communicated, and enforced outside of officially sanctioned channels" (Helmke & Levitsky 2004:727).

[2] *Order* has been defined in terms of regularity by many scholars, including legal anthropologists (Roberts 2013) and sociologists (Simmel 1964). Under this approach, the term *social order* refers to the building blocks of such predictability – be it formal institutions, customs, norms, values, or social structures. However, the foundational problem of social order has often been defined in terms of what holds society together, preventing individuals and groups from breaking away, and avoiding universal conflict (Lockwood & Wrong 1994). My definition of wartime social order builds on both approaches.

[3] To be sure, defining a threshold for what counts as *continuous* is difficult. Conceptually, I am referring to situations where there is a frequent interaction between civilians and combatants, beyond sporadic strikes or visits. In the empirical chapters, I focus on conflict zones where armed actors have operated for at least six months. But a rebel group can certainly engage in an ongoing interaction with civilians for a shorter period of time.

different spheres of local life depending on the time and place, bringing about different forms of social order. While the emerging literature on rebel governance has focused on whether or not rebels rule civilians, it has largely overlooked the great variation that exists in the specific ways non-state armed groups transform local institutions, and with them, the patterns of behaving and relating in war zones.

This book aims to explain both the emergence of order in war zones and the particular form order takes. In particular, it investigates how the interaction between combatants and local actors – including regular civilians, state officials, and non-state organizations – influences the institutions that regulate civilian affairs, thereby creating a new form of local order. By "civilian affairs," I am referring to any realm of private and public life, including politics, economics, social relations, religious practices, and sexual behavior.

When a civil war erupts, it is likely to affect people even if they do not live in war zones. However, this book is a study of the ways in which social order changes when civilians and combatants interact frequently. Areas of the country in which these groups engage only in sporadic actions (which can take the form of violent attacks, economic extraction, or mobilization) are not within the scope of the study. By focusing on war zones, I aim to explore why ongoing interactions between civilians and combatants vary over time and space – a question that is essential to understand the conduct of war as well as its legacies.

War zones include contested and "liberated" areas – that is, those under full rebel control – as well as anything in between. The only condition of a war zone is that at least one non-state armed group has an ongoing presence in the area. Such presence may entail a constant dispute with another warring side, sporadic confrontations, or full control over the area. Figure 2.1 shows a classification of local territories depending on the type of presence of armed groups.

The conceptual unit of analysis is the community–armed group pairing or dyad at a given time. By "community," I am referring to the people who inhabit a given local territory and "interact directly, frequently, and in multi-faceted ways" (Bowles & Gintis 2002:420). Hence, the community is a fairly small unit: in rural areas, it is the village or town; in cities, it is the neighborhood. I selected this small unit of analysis on the basis of both theoretical reasons and empirical observation. From theory, one should expect armed groups to choose their strategies at this disaggregated level because neighboring communities can react quite differently to their strategies. From empirics, variation in such choices, as well as in the

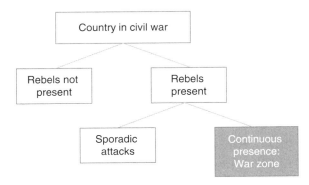

FIGURE 2.1 Types of presence of non-state armed groups at the local level

ensuing social orders, is observed within relatively small regions, cities, and towns in a number of conflicts. Focusing on larger geographical units would therefore cloud the different forms of social order that emerge within their population. For example, Evans' (2009) study of the Federally Administered Tribal Areas (FATA) in Pakistan shows spatial variation in social order within areas of Taliban presence. If I were to treat the greater region as my unit of analysis, I would overlook the different ways in which the Taliban transforms social order in villages and neighborhoods.

Communities may interact with more than one armed group or experience different cycles in their interaction with the same actor throughout the war. Hence, in any given community, multiple forms of social order may emerge during the war. For analytical purposes, it is convenient to separate each cycle, and analyze its origins, evolution, and termination, as we tend to do with regimes. This is why I focus on the community–armed group dyad as the central unit. However, in Chapter 6, I come back to the idea of cycles where a preexisting social order is transformed, a new one is consolidated, and transformed again. I discuss the stages involved in these processes and provide detailed evidence of each stage.

Before presenting a typology of social order, other concepts must be clarified. I use the term *armed group* to refer to all non-state armed organizations that are fighting the war. These include rebels who challenge the government and paramilitaries who aim to defend the status quo. I explicitly refer to state armed forces by the terms "national army," "state forces," or "governmental forces." Therefore, whenever

I mention "armed groups," I am referring only to *non-state* armed groups. Although the theory does not seek to explain the behavior of the state, it certainly takes state forces into account as a factor that can influence armed groups' and civilians' behavior, which will be discussed in Chapter 3.

I use the words "rebels," "combatants," and "non-state armed groups" interchangeably. I aim to theorize the behavior of both insurgents and irregular counterinsurgents (e.g., irregular paramilitaries and militias), but I do not make this explicit throughout the text. Instead, I use these different terms to remind the reader that I am referring to all kinds of irregular, non-state armed groups fighting within a civil war. Likewise, I talk about civilians, noncombatants, and locals interchangeably to refer to all persons who live in a given local territory, do not participate in hostilities, and are not full-time members of any state or non-state armed organization. Noncombatants include, therefore, both regular civilians and public officials who work at government or state agencies in the local territory.[4]

Lastly, scholars have used the terms "support," "participation," and "collaboration" to refer to civilians' involvement with armed groups. The terms "support" and "participation" can be misleading because they signal a positive motivation for such involvement, like political agreement. "Collaboration" can be misleading as well as pejorative because it has been widely used to denote civilian involvement with the Nazis and the Axis powers during World War II. To avoid these limitations, I use the term "civilian cooperation" to denote the behaviors of civilians that directly benefit the armed group, independent of the motivations that underlie them. Therefore, cooperation includes both voluntary acts to help the group and obedience of its commands.[5] The opposite of civilian cooperation is resistance, meaning either disobedience (failing to follow rebel commands) or opposition (engaging in behaviors that may negatively affect the group, such as aiding the enemy).[6]

---

[4] To be sure, telling combatants and civilians apart can be quite challenging. For a lengthy discussion, see Kinsella (2011).
[5] In this book I approach civilian cooperation without disaggregating it for the sake of parsimony. However, cooperation may entail very different conducts (Petersen 2001; Wood 2003; Barter 2012; Parkinson 2013). I discuss the conceptualization of civilian choice elsewhere (Arjona 2016a).
[6] In this book I focus on unarmed resistance. I discuss further my definition of resistance in Chapter 3.

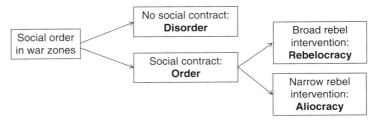

FIGURE 2.2 Typology of wartime social orders

A TYPOLOGY OF WARTIME SOCIAL ORDER

Social order in a war zone can vary across multiple dimensions. Just as in peacetime, the institutions that sustain social order during war can be more or less legitimate, participatory, effective, or stable. I propose a typology on the basis of two dimensions (Figure 2.2). First, whether a social contract has been established between the armed group and local residents. By social contract, I mean that both parties – civilians and combatants – have shared expectations about their behavior.[7] While this contract is seldom spelled out, every social order relies on an implicit notion of the duties or commitments of both the ruler and the ruled. I refer to the existence of such social contract as a situation of *order*. This dimension can be operationalized as the existence and enforcement of rules of conduct, which allow for predictability.[8]

When combatants, the local population, or both fail to abide by a set of defined rules, there is no social contract between the two and unpredictability is high. I refer to this situation as *disorder*. When combatants do not abide by clear rules, local residents have few solid beliefs about the likely outcomes of alternative choices. Even if an armed group is in full control of civilian behavior, the absence of limits for those in power leads to high levels of unpredictability. A parallel with an impulsive dictator or the state of exception in a democracy serves to illustrate this situation: the government in

---

[7] Hence, I do not use the term "social contract" to suggest that there is a moral or political obligation of the subjects to the ruler.
[8] Other scholars have conceptualized the interaction between civilians and combatants on the basis of the existence of a social contract – or its lack thereof (Wickham-Crowley 1987; Metelits 2010; Keister 2011). However, these approaches only differentiate between coercive and noncoercive relations. The typology that I develop here builds on this insight but I am especially interested in studying the different forms that a social contract may take.

power can have tight control over the population, but at the same time display unpredictable behavior. To be sure, this does not imply that combatants behave randomly or that internal rules constraining their behavior toward civilians fully disappear. Instead, there is great variation across cases of disorder in armed groups' tactics. Yet, what unites these cases is that civilians do not expect rebels to follow a set of rules and, therefore, the level of predictability is low.

Disorder may also emerge when local actors – regular civilians, authorities, or other agents present in the locality – fail to abide by known rules, even if combatants themselves do honor the social contract. Consider a village where local residents pick and choose which rules to follow or decide to disobey entirely. There would be no social contract and unpredictability would be high.

It is important to note that these social contracts do not necessarily rely on the consent of civilians – indeed, they seldom do. Civilians may dislike some of the ways in which rebels rule and even the very existence of a rebel government. But the mere existence of clear rules that both sides – the ruler and the ruled – follow indicates that there are shared expectations regarding behavior. There is a stark difference between this situation and one in which a social contract is absent and uncertainty reigns.[9]

To be sure, order varies along a continuum. As Lockwood and Wrong (1994:9) note,

Like virtually all conceptualizations of social relations, social order is a matter of degree. Order is never so fully present in concrete social reality as to exclude all deviations, unpredictabilities, mistaken perceptions and accidents. Nor is it ever so utterly absent that complete random behavior, unremitting total conflict, or social interaction confined to the minimum required by biological necessity prevails.

Although the reality of a particular conflict zone falls somewhere between these two extremes of nil and total uncertainty, the concepts of order and

---

[9] To be sure, a situation of disorder can vary along different dimensions, the most important being violence. Consider two villages living under disorder: the population may suffer in both due to chaos, but those living in the most violent village would obviously suffer more. I do not differentiate between these realities because this book is not about the causes of violence against civilians – there is a large literature on this topic. However, in Chapters 3 and 6 I do discuss how victimization and order interact. Although this simple distinction between order and disorder captures two very different realities, further disaggregating disorder might be necessary when studying certain research questions.

disorder do capture two distinct realities: under the first one, people can form expectations regarding most domains of their life, most of the time; under the second one, people cannot.

When a social contract between the local population and the armed group does exist, the form of order varies depending on the scope of the group's intervention in local affairs. I call a social order in which the armed actor intervenes broadly *rebelocracy*, or the rule of rebels; I call the social order in which the armed actor intervenes minimally *aliocracy*, or the rule of others, because most civilian affairs are in the hands of others – be it state officials, traditional leaders, religious figures, or other authorities.[10]

As with order and disorder, the scope of rebel intervention is likely to vary along a continuum from narrow to broad. I define aliocracy as a social order in which armed groups do not intervene beyond the two most basic realms of rule: security, which is the minimal condition for governance (Weber 1968; Hobbes 2010); and taxation, which is often necessary for the ruler to be able to rule (Levi 1989), although not all armed groups need to tax civilians because some have other sources of funding.

Rebelocracy is defined as a social order in which armed groups intervene beyond security and taxation. The specific domains in which armed groups rule under rebelocracy vary. Most of the time, they include the provision of mechanisms to adjudicate disputes, ranging from informal procedures to formal courts. Often, armed groups regulate different economic activities beyond taxation, and establish rules on conduct that belongs to the private sphere – such as how people can dress, their sexual behavior, and their use of alcohol or other mind-altering substances. Many armed actors also intervene to provide or regulate the provision of basic services like education and health. A few groups also establish political institutions to structure some form of representation. I provide several examples of armed groups' influence in these different realms of local life later in the chapter.

The channels through which a group rules under rebelocracy can vary as well. In some places, it relies on combatants, who are permanently deployed in the locality and rule directly. In others, it relies on militias, who are part-time members of the organization, live within the community (and are often members of it), and report directly to

---

[10] As mentioned in Chapter 1, *rebelocracy* and *aliocracy* come, respectively, from the Latin words *rebello*, which means "rebel," and *alios*, which means "other." The Latin root *cracy* forms nouns meaning "rule by" or "government by."

a commander. In other cases, the group rules in a more indirect way through a sector of the population that it has allied with, co-opted, or coerced. For example, some armed groups make alliances with a political party, some co-opt a social movement, and some even create boards or cooperatives to serve as governing bodies. In some cases, armed actors manage to coerce, infiltrate, or co-opt the formal local government.[11]

It is important to note that rebelocracy does not imply that sources of authority other than armed groups are absent. As later chapters show, war zones can exhibit a complicated structure of authority where state officials, religious figures, ethnic leaders, and other actors play important roles even when combatants are the de facto rulers. While this typology focuses on the influence of non-state armed groups, it does not rule out the presence and sway of other actors. Furthermore, in many contexts rebelocracy preserves a clandestine character, even though rebels do rule in the sense of being the ones making the decisions. For example, the slums of large cities in countries undergoing civil war are often governed by insurgents or militias to a great extent, even though state agencies do continue to work there. What is more, many localities under rebel control are surrounded by localities under state control; even though the rebels are the de facto rulers, the façade of state control is maintained and secrecy still surrounds rebel activity.

ASSESSING THE QUALITY OF THE TYPOLOGY

How robust is this typology? Although there is no consensus on the criteria to evaluate concepts and typologies (Doty & Glick 1994; Gerring 1999), a good typology should meet at least three conditions, beyond internal consistency: (1) It should identify variation that matters either because it is a relevant phenomenon in and of itself, or because we can expect it to shape relevant phenomena; (2) it should identify types where within-group variation is minimized and between-group variation is maximized; and (3) it should be parsimonious: it should identify as few types as possible while having the greatest descriptive and explanatory potential. In what follows, I assess the quality of this typology along these three conditions.

---

[11] In Chapter 6, I revisit these differences and explain why armed groups opt for one strategy over another when attempting to build rebelocracy.

Relevance

In the introductory chapter of this book, I argued that it is important to understand whether civilians and combatants interact in a context of order or disorder as well as the type of institutions that sustain order when it does emerge. In this section I elaborate on some of those arguments to assert that explaining social order in war zones is important to advance our understanding of relevant questions about civil war, assess the potential implications of wartime policies and interventions, and address challenges in the post-conflict period.

First, I suggested that opening the black box of civilian–combatant relations would shed light onto many questions on the conduct of war. Insofar far as institutions shape behavior – as many social scientists believe they do – taking into account the institutions that operate in war zones is essential to understand how civilians and combatants behave on the ground.

Consider armed groups' use of violence. Every social contract includes provisions to enforce rules. In a war zone, combatants are usually the enforcers. As they rely on violence to enforce their rules, they are likely to use it in different ways depending on the type of social order in place. For example, while combatants may use violence to ensure the observance of a myriad of rules on economic and political behavior in rebelocracy, they are likely to use violence only to enforce minimal rules about security and taxation in aliocracy. Furthermore, who is targeted and why may well vary depending on the form of social order. For example, armed groups may be suspicious of civilians trying to mobilize others for autonomy under rebelocracy, but not under aliocracy.

Let us now turn to civilians' experience of war, their reactions to it, and the impact it has on them. Whether a person lives in order or disorder is likely to have important implications on many spheres of her life because living under great uncertainty is nearly incapacitating – how do you make a living, how do you educate your kids, how do you maintain social relations? Even if she lives in a situation of order, whether her daily life is meticulously ruled by an armed group or not is likely to have different repercussions. People's options, trade-offs, beliefs, and motivations are all impacted by the context in which they live. If we take into account that in some cases – like the Colombian one – entire generations in certain communities grow being ruled by armed actors, the effects of living under rebelocracy or aliocracy can be drastically different. Furthermore, in our quest to understand why civilians join armed groups, why they flee, why they take risks to aid combatants or state forces, it is essential that we take a closer look at the local realities in which they live.

Improving our understanding of social order in war zones could also inform our contentions about the macro-level dynamics of civil war. For example, when we inquire about changes in the endowments of armed groups, failed state policies, or natural disasters that might impact the duration of war, our arguments always rely on assumptions about how combatants, civilians, or both react. The better we understand the context in which they make their choices, the more suited we are to infer how they will respond to changes in the course of the war.

Turning to the post-conflict stage, as we strive to understand how communities cope with the legacies of war and which policies might be more helpful, the study of war zones becomes crucial. We need to acknowledge the great variation that exists in the ways of relating and behaving across conflict zones within a single country because they are likely to shape the patterns of reintegration and reconciliation.

Furthermore, the mammoth task of understanding the evolution of states could gain insights from a better understanding of war zones. While we have investigated the macro-level effects of external war on state capacity (Tilly 1985), we have yet to learn how the dynamics of civil war transform the trajectory of state building – both at the national and sub-national levels. Insofar as new forms of order emerge and endure in conflict zones, it is possible that new identities, interest groups, elites, conflicts, and alliances arise. We should expect these changes to leave legacies in the aftermath of the war.

Ideal Types and Parsimony

How well does this typology reflect the variety of ways in which civilians and combatants interact in conflict zones? To be sure, these are ideal types. I do not expect reality to fit neatly into these categories because order is a matter of degree. Likewise, the level of intervention of the armed actor in civilian affairs is likely to vary along a continuum from narrow – aliocracy – to broad – rebelocracy. Despite the obvious limitations of ideal categories to account for the subtle nuances that we observe on the ground, the available evidence suggests that this typology does capture distinct local realities in conflict zones.

The first way to assess whether the typology captures types that exist on the ground is by looking at actual cases (i.e., war zones or conflict areas) in very different contexts and seeing whether we can identify disorder, aliocracy, and rebelocracy. Although systematic data on wartime local institutions are rarely available, there is an ample supply of detailed, qualitative evidence on armed groups and conflict zones around the world. A survey of this literature suggests that the typology indeed captures three ideal types that are often found on the ground.

There are numerous accounts of armed groups bringing about disorder when occupying territories. The groups fighting in Sierra Leone and Liberia are perhaps the most salient examples due to their predatory strategies and limited engagement in the establishment of clear rules (Ellis 1998; Johnston 2004; Weinstein 2007). The Lord's Resistance Army is also a well-known example. This rebel group created widespread uncertainty with its hectic and abusive behavior. It raided villages, especially at night, "looting, burning, and abducting" (Weber and Rone 2003:17). Thousands of children were abducted and forced to become soldiers. Communities living in fear of these raids experienced a situation of disorder.

Armed groups that are well-known for ruling civilians, like the Tamils in Sri Lanka, often display this type of unconstrained behavior as well (Korf 2004). In fact, detailed studies of daily life in war zones usually show that populations often endure periods of both order and disorder when armed actors are present in their territory. In Iraq, for example, while both insurgents and counterinsurgents created order in some areas under their control, at times they brought about chaos, resulting in great uncertainty in everyday life (e.g., Robben 2010).

What are the attributes of the new orders that emerge in war zones? Case studies from different civil wars provide evidence of both aliocracy and rebelocracy. Several cases fit the definition of "aliocracy." Renamo established this form of presence in most occupied territories in Mozambique. Traditional chiefs, known as regulos, ruled civilian affairs, but they had to ensure food provision to Renamo as well as civilians' abidance by a set of rules (Young 1997a; Weinstein 2007). Similarly, accounts of the interaction between the Sudan People's Liberation Movement (SPLM) in Sudan and local communities in Tei Town portray the relation between the SPLM and civilians as a tense agreement, in which local chiefs assured some minimal compliance in exchange for greater safety of the community (e.g., Johnson 1998).

Until recently, the existence of rebelocracies in war zones had been largely overlooked – often, even experts on civil wars doubted they existed at all. The emerging literature on rebel governance – which I discuss later in this chapter – has helped to counter this omission, especially by showing that armed groups often provide public goods. Recent coverage of governance by rebel forces in Syria and Iraq has also drawn attention to this phenomenon in the Middle East. Yet, case studies have shown for a long time that rebelocracy has been a common phenomenon across the globe, and during multiple time periods.

In Africa, descriptions of rebels providing public goods and creating new institutions are bountiful. The Eritrean People's Liberation Front, for example, provided health care, education, and dispute resolution schemes. It also implemented land reform and created a formal system of taxation and political councils (Cliffe 1984; Barnabas & Zwi 1997; Connell 2001; Pool 2001). The Tigray People's Liberation Front (TPLF) in Ethiopia is also known for its provision of services and implementation of land reform (Young 1997b). In the late 1980s, the National Union for the Total Independence of Angola (UNITA) "succeeded in establishing a sophisticated socio-economic infrastructure that effectively amounted to a state within," building, among others, 6 hospitals and 189 clinics, as well as 22 secondary schools and around 700 primary schools (Potgieter 2000:262).[12]

The National Resistance Army (NRA) and the Rwenzururu Kingdom Government in Uganda have also been described as insurgencies engaged with ruling civilians comprehensively. Kasfir (2004, 2005) and Weinstein (2007) found that the NRA set up a system of civilian administration in the Luwero Triangle (especially at times when armed competition with the state forces was low). Both authors stress the democratic character of the ruling system that the NRA tried to set up as well as its provision of health services. The group was also in charge of the maintenance of order in the localities, and the provision of food for the central committee (Ngoga 1998:97). The Rwenzururu Kingdom Government, on the other hand, developed a broader system of service provision for civilians than the NRA did (Kasfir 2004). Evidence of rebel intervention in civilian affairs beyond security and taxation can also be found in many other conflicts in the continent.[13]

Insurgencies in Latin America have also established rebelocracies. Wickham-Crowley (1987, 1991, 2015) provides a comprehensive list of

---

[12] On UNITA see also Heywood (1989), Radu and Arnold (1990), and Malaquias (2001).
[13] Several papers developed within the University of Ghent's comparative project on governance in protracted conditions of crisis in Sub-Saharan Africa provide insightful evidence on cases in this region. See *Afrika Focus* Vol. 21, 2 (2008).

insurgent groups from the 1950s to the 1970s that acted as rulers in areas where they operated – including well-known cases, like Cuba and Nicaragua, and more obscure ones, like Venezuela. In Cuba, several authors have described how rebels created administrative councils to deal with public health, the collection of taxes, and the enactment of new laws (e.g., McColl 1969; Guevara et al. 1997). Studies of the Shining Path in Peru provide evidence of the group's intervention by policing, adjudicating private disputes, and even organizing recreation (e.g., Manrique 1998; La Serna 2012). A rich literature on rebel courts in Colombia shows how common this practice is among guerilla groups throughout the country (e.g., Aguilera 2001, 2013; Molano 2001; Espinosa 2003; García-Villegas and Espinosa 2015).

Asia and Europe are not exceptions. The Liberation Tamil Tigers of Tamil Eelam (LTTE) in Sri Lanka ruled civilian affairs in a comprehensive fashion. Mampilly (2011) and Stokke (2006) offer a detailed account of their effective civil administration, which included education and health systems, a legal code with its corresponding judiciary, a police force, and even a bank. The Maoist Rebels of Nepal also created institutions to distribute land and food and set up courts to solve disputes (Kattel 2003). The resistance groups that fought against Soviet occupation in Afghanistan developed a bureaucracy that, while not sophisticated, was in charge of several regulatory tasks in local territories (Rubin 2002; Sinno 2008:126–127). The Taliban also engaged early on in state-like activities in areas where they were present in Afghanistan, and have developed a complex judicial system with mobile courts (e.g., Giustozzi et al. 2013; Sinno 2008). Rebel forces engaged in rebel governance in Greece too, setting up institutions and providing public goods (McColl 1969; Kalyvas 2015). Across Southeast Asia, rebelocracies were manifest as well.[14]

Evidence on the ways in which paramilitaries and counterinsurgent irregular groups interact with civilians is more difficult to find, as these groups are understudied (Jentzsch et al. 2015). However, some case studies suggest that they also often establish rebelocracies. For example, in the different armed conflicts that Afghanistan has endured over the last decades, several non-state armed groups became the de facto guarantors of local order, provided public goods, and co-opted or eliminated other sources of authority in their areas of influence. Warlords' organizations like Massoud's and Wahdat – two of the many that were competing for

---

[14] For example, McColl (1969) presents an overview of multiple sources on rebel governance in insurrections in Vietnam, the Philippines, Malaya, and Thailand.

power after the Najibullah regime collapsed in 1992 – created and developed civilian institutions in some of the territories under their influence (Sinno 2008:193, 217).

It is important to stress that even though these rebel and counterinsurgent groups have provided public goods, institutions, or a system of dispute resolution, their interactions with civilians are not exclusive to rebelocracy; these groups often also interacted with civilians under disorder and aliocracy. In other words, there is variation across time and space in the form of social order that a given armed group brings about.

Taken together, this evidence suggests that the typology I propose does capture variation that we see in war zones. Yet, it classifies rebels' influence on institutions – when institutions do exist – into two discrete categories. Are "rebelocracy" and "aliocracy" capturing two distinct realities?

This typology was developed in 2009, prior to collecting detailed data on social order in a random sample of Colombian conflict zones. The typology was, therefore, not inductively informed by the evidence, which I collected at a later time. A good test of the depth and parsimony (Gerring 1999:380) of the typology is therefore to inspect the data in order to assess whether the typology captures "natural" groups. In Chapter 5, I use cluster analysis to show that the data gathered suggest that aliocracy and rebelocracy are indeed quite distinct and internally homogeneous groups – that is, each contains elements that are very close to the other elements in that group while being clearly different from the elements in the other type. In other words, "aliocracy" and "rebelocracy" do capture distinct types of social order in war zones. Throughout the book, and especially in the conclusion (Chapter 9), I will show why this simple classification not only captures distinct realities but also has great explanatory power as several local dynamics of war are likely to be affected by whether aliocracy or rebelocracy emerges.

CURRENT UNDERSTANDING OF REBEL GOVERNANCE AND COLLECTIVE CIVILIAN RESISTANCE

What explains the emergence of order and disorder? When order is created, when does it take the form of rebelocracy? When does it become an aliocracy? The literature on civil war dynamics offers some insights about the emergence of order; however, it falls short in explaining variation in the ways rebels rule when such order does emerge. In the next section, I discuss the current understanding of these outcomes and why they are insufficient. In Chapter 3, I present my theoretical account.

While violent rebel behavior has received substantial attention in recent years (e.g., Humphreys & Weinstein 2006; Kalyvas 2006; Weinstein 2007; Downs 2008; Wood 2009; Cohen 2013; Balcells 2017), other behaviors of these organizations, and their consequences for civilians, have received little attention. Although several anthropologists and political scientists have written extensively about specific non-state armed organizations that display state-like functions (e.g., Appleby et al. 2001), theorizing rebel governance – its sources, its variation, and its implications – has seldom been the goal of the literature. The generalized use of concepts like "failed states" and "ungoverned spaces" has only aggravated the dismissal of institutions that operate in wartime (Justino 2013), and the role that armed groups play as rulers.

Rebels and military historians, however, have long been aware of the strategic importance of rebel governance. Successful rebel leaders (Cabral 1970; Mao 1978; Guevara et al. 1997), as well as those studying their actions (e.g., Galula 1964; Trinquier 1964; Thompson 1983; Thompson 1989), realized that rebel groups cannot succeed without gaining popular support – the well-known "hearts and minds" approach. They argued that regulating civilian life in controlled territories, guaranteeing public order, and providing public goods were valuable means to gain such support.[15] Yet, these authors failed to account for the variation that we observe on the ground. If civilian support is so important to wage irregular war, and governing civilians helps to achieve that end, why don't all armed groups engage in governance? And why do those who do govern civilians opt for radically different approaches?

A rich literature on the economics of organized crime and an emerging field on rebel governance have provided some answers to these questions. Although these two literatures have evolved separately, both have aimed to explain the conditions under which non-state armed actors (rebels or criminals) provide public goods (Gambetta 1993; Skarpedas & Syropoulos 1995; Volkov 2000; Arias 2006; Weinstein 2007; Berman & Laitin 2008; Berman 2009; Keister 2009; Metelits 2010; Skarbek 2011; Wolff 2015); become a recognized authority

---

[15] See for example Beckett (2001) on Mao; Guevara et al. (1997), especially chapter III; McColl (1969); and (Galula 1964).

(Wickham-Crowley 1987); allow civilians to participate and share power with them (Kasfir 2004; Weinstein 2007); set up systems of civil administration (Mampilly 2011); provide security and taxation (Sánchez de la Sierra 2015); or develop specific economic relations with local populations (Zahar 2001).

In order to explain variation along these different dimensions of rebel governance, most authors turn to the extensive literature on state-building (e.g., Tilly 1985; North and Weingast 1989; Olson 1993). Some have concluded that the conditions in which the European nation-state emerged – on which most of this literature focuses – differ greatly from those in which armed groups behave in a state-like fashion (e.g., Kasfir 2002; Mampilly 2007); others, however, rely heavily on this literature (Wickham-Crowley 1987; Weinstein 2007; Sánchez de la Sierra 2015). Taken together, these studies point to three determinants of rebel governance: national-level conditions, the attributes of armed groups, and sub-national war dynamics.[16]

National conditions include state penetration both before the onset of war (Skarpedas & Syropoulos 1995; Mampilly 2011) and during wartime (Berman and Laitin 2008; Berman 2009); the existence of a legitimate authority (Wickham-Crowley 1987); war duration (Wickham-Crowley 1987; Mampilly 2011); and truces and ceasefires (Mampilly 2011). Yet, national-level factors cannot explain why two armed groups would exhibit different behaviors within the same civil war, like the NRA and the LRA in Uganda. Both operated within the same national conditions, yet the NRA provided public goods to civilians (Kasfir 2004) while the LRA raided and looted without ever setting up a system of civilian administration (Van Acker 2004). Such variation across armed groups is quite common in most civil wars. For this reason, scholars tend to focus on the armed group, rather than the country or the war, as the unit of analysis.

Other hypotheses point to the attributes of rebel groups as determinants of rebel governance: their internal organization (Skarpedas & Syropoulos 1995; Mampilly 2011); their endowments – both domestic (Weinstein 2007) and foreign (Keister 2009; Mampilly 2011); their attempts to mobilize support before launching their armed struggle (Kasfir 2004); and their ideology and ties with civil society actors (Mampilly 2011). While these arguments can explain variation across armed groups within civil wars, they cannot account for variation *within*

---

[16] This section is based on Arjona (2008).

a given organization – and most armed groups do exhibit variation in the strategies they adopt towards civilians. This variation becomes evident both in detailed accounts of war zones and by comparing the evidence gathered by scholars on different regions and time periods within the same civil war. I give a few examples below.

In Africa, UNITA engaged in public goods provision in many areas where it operated within Angola, but not in others. In the area of Jamba it created schools, hospitals, and even radio stations, which led several journalists to claim that UNITA had created a new government in the area; however, in other areas of the country, it neglected governance and was much more coercive and predatory (Heywood 1989; Radu & Arnold 1990; Malaquias 2001). Likewise, in the Democratic Republic of Congo (DRC), rebel groups have exhibited distinct behaviors in terms of ruling local populations. According to Raeymaekers et al.(2008), predation in some areas was pervasive while in others the rebels negotiated and cooperated with different types of local actors, including traditional chiefs and entrepreneurs. In some cases, alliances were made on the basis of shared economic interests, while in others they were based on the need for security and protection.

Observers have also documented variation in rebel governance within armed groups in Latin America. To illustrate, the Farabundo Marti National Liberation Front (FMNL) in El Salvador has been described as an organization committed to allowing democratic civilian participation (McClintock 1998). However, Wood (2003) provides detailed evidence of variation in the organization's strategies and describes the FMNL performing the role of authority in some areas, while behaving as a purely coercive force in others. Likewise, the author shows that the group's stand towards peasant organization, especially cooperatives, varied across time and space. As this book will show, there is also great variation in how both left-wing guerrillas and right-wing paramilitaries approach civilians in Colombia over time and space.

Studies of insurgencies in Asia also reveal variation in patterns of rebel governance within organizations. The People's Liberation Army in China (PLA), for example, seems to have combined different methods to interact with civilians during the war. In some places, it created councils that performed administrative and juridical functions, which included regulating health care, education, taxes, and the maintenance of public order (McColl 1969). Yet, these services and institutions were neglected in other areas. Several authors also show that the group's relation with landless versus middle-class peasants varied greatly across regions (Hinton 1966; Girling 1969; Hartford 1995). Rubin (2002) and Sinno (2008) provide detailed evidence that shows how the Taliban have adopted different strategies across and within regions in Afghanistan.

In sum, armed groups often display different strategies towards local communities. Even the NPLF and RUF in Liberia and Sierra Leone respectively – both known for being predatory and highly violent (e.g., Ellis 1998; Johnston 2004; Humphreys & Weinstein 2006) – were involved in some form of governance of populations in certain areas under their influence (Bangura 2000; Reno 2015). Given this variation, a theory of wartime governance should not only account for patterns across armed groups, but also for variation within them.

A few scholars have argued that armed competition over territory or over valuable resources precludes rebel governance (Skarpedas & Syropoulos 1995; Kasfir 2005; Metelits 2010; Sánchez de la Sierra 2015). Focusing on criminal groups, others have contended that local political structures (Arias 2006; Blake 2013), and state presence and abuse (Wolff 2015) explain whether these organizations provide security and public goods to local populations in urban contexts. These are the only hypotheses that can potentially explain why a single armed group rules only at certain times and places. However, these accounts do not explain variation in the way in which rebels rule when they do so.

It is useful to think of the local realities that emerge in war zones as "regimes." If there is something like local regimes in war zones, we need to conceptualize these structures and identify distinct types in order to theorize why they emerge, how they function, how they shape rebel and civilian behavior, and what their legacies are during and after the war. This book proposes a novel typology and an approach to wartime order that moves our discussion in that direction.

In developing that perspective, this book also offers a theory of collective civilian resistance against rebel groups. The empirical literature on civilian resistance has demonstrated that this is not a rare phenomenon. In recent years, scholars and activists have written about "peace communities" or "zones of peace" – instances of organized, peaceful resistance during wartime. Most of this work is primarily empirical, describing how local communities have confronted rebels and militias, especially in Colombia and the Philippines (e.g., Hancock & Mitchell 2007; Hernández 2004), while a few also theorize the consequences on civilians' safety (Kaplan 2013a, 2013b). Other forms of less structured resistance come up in studies that stress the importance of negotiations between civilians and combatants in war zones, as well as daily forms of hidden resistance (Vlassenroot & Raeymaekers 2004a; Uribe de Hincapié 2006; Lubkemann 2008; Raeymaekers et al. 2008; CNRR 2011; Mampilly 2011; Förster 2015). These studies highlight the importance of civilian resistance and, just like the studies on rebel governance, they too call for an explanation: why does it take place at certain times and places, but not others?

Theories of resistance to oppressive states and occupation forces (e.g., Petersen 2001; Darden 2016), and recent accounts of resistance to insurgents (Kaplan 2013b; Mouly et al. 2015; Schubiger 2015), have argued that social networks, identities, and victimization lead civilians to organize and defend themselves. What needs to be incorporated is how the nonviolent strategies of armed actors, and the interaction between civilians and combatants, shape the emergence of resistance.

Lastly, although several case studies offer valuable insights,[17] little effort has been made to gather systematic evidence on the ways in which civilians and combatants interact on an ongoing basis, let alone to theorize them. Wood's (2008) discussion of the social processes that are transformed by war suggests how complex this interaction is and how deep the consequences are for local communities. Theories that account for such nuances and variations in civilian–combatant relations are essential to advancing our understanding of the changes that war brings about, both during the war and in its aftermath (Wood 2008; Arjona 2009). Building such a theory is the task of Chapter 3.

---

[17] For example Theidon (2004) on Peru; Ngoga (1998) on Uganda; Paul and Demarest (1998) on Guatemala; and multiple studies of municipalities in Colombia (e.g., Torres 2004; Gutiérrez Sanín et al. 2006).

3

A Theory of Social Order in Civil War

According to the typology of wartime social order I presented in the previous chapter, there are three possible outcomes when a community and an armed group interact: *disorder, aliocracy,* and *rebelocracy*. In this chapter I develop a theory to explain when, and why, each of these forms of social order is most likely to emerge. While the preferences of armed groups are integral to shaping social order in war zones, my theory contends that civilians, too, wield a significant amount of agency in determining whether aliocracy or rebelocracy are consolidated. This chapter thus aims to theorize how civilians and combatants interact, shaping each other's behavior as well as the form of social order in which they live.

In reality, social order is the outcome of a complex process. There are initial approaches, subtle signaling, and bargaining. For analytical purposes, I start by providing a general theory about the outcome – that is, specifying the conditions under which each form of social order emerges in a given time and location – abstracting the process that leads to it. In Chapters 6 and 7, I theorize the process by which social orders are created, and discuss further the microfoundations of the theory.[1]

THE ARGUMENT

I start by assuming that armed groups are equally interested in establishing their dominance over all the territories where they have an ongoing presence – an assumption that I relax later in the chapter. There are two factors that determine what kind of social order will emerge in the areas

---

[1] Some of the material presented in the section on collective civilian resistance appeared in Arjona (2015).

TABLE 3.1 *A theory of social order in civil war*

		Quality of preexisting local institutions	
		High	Low
Armed group's time horizon	Long	Aliocracy	Rebelocracy
	Short	Disorder	

where they operate: their time horizon and the quality of preexisting local institutions, particularly those for adjudicating disputes. First, I argue that rebels with short term horizons will give rise to disorder in the territory. This is most likely when armed groups are undisciplined and in situations in which they face competition with state or non-state armed forces. Second, rebels with long term horizons will prefer a rebelocracy. However, in areas where preexisting local institutions are efficient and legitimate, civilians are likely to resist collectively because they value their form of governance and have a high capacity for collective action. In such cases, civilians have bargaining power and rebels are likely to settle for aliocracy, rather than rebelocracy, as a form of rule.

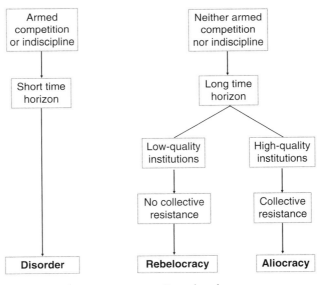

FIGURE 3.1 Causal paths

Table 3.1 summarizes the argument and Figure 3.1 shows the causal paths. To explain the argument, I proceed as follows through the chapter. First, I identify the assumptions on which the theory is built. Second, I theorize the behavior of armed groups by identifying the conditions under which they bring order or disorder about; I then turn to their choice between rebelocracy and aliocracy when they do opt for order. Third, I propose a theory of collective civilian resistance. Fourth, I extend the model by relaxing some of its assumptions and discussing the implications. In particular, I allow the strategic value of local territories to vary, armed groups' information of civilian resistance to be imperfect, and communities' capacity for collective action to be endogenous to wartime order. Finally, I discuss caveats related to the role of the state, armed groups' ideology, and community structure.

ASSUMPTIONS

Armed Groups' Preferences

In conventional civil wars, regular armies confront each other in the battlefield. The army that defeats the rival wins the war. But most civil wars are fought by asymmetric sides that engage in what is known as irregular warfare (Kalyvas & Balcells 2010). This theory aims to explain social order in *irregular civil wars*. In such wars frontlines are absent because the weak actor avoids confronting the strong side directly. Think of the Vietcong or the Taliban fighting against the US Army: they are better off avoiding battles against powerful American troops. Instead, they disperse their combatants and try to engage in hit-and-run operations, which force the powerful army to keep reacting wherever it is attacked. Over time, guerrillas are able to control small territories, which the state cannot recover unless it concentrates its forces in a few locations and thereby leaves many others unprotected. The more territories rebels control, the more they can expand and grow their operations, while making it increasingly difficult for the government to regain territories under rebel control.

Under this logic, rebels try to disperse as much as possible so that the state cannot respond to the multipronged challenge it faces (Galula 1964; McColl 1969; Guevara et al. 1997; Kalyvas 2006). This expansion leads to the fragmentation of space, whereby some areas are under rebel control, some are under state control, and others are contested (Kalyvas 2006:88). In some cases, rebels manage to create an "insurgent state" or "liberated zone" – an entire region fully under their control; however, it is very common to find small territories controlled by the rebels surrounded by areas controlled by the government and vice versa. This is why maps depicting the distribution of control in irregular wars "show up as messy patchworks" (ibid.).

Several scholars and military theorists have stressed the centrality of territorial control as a determinant of rebel behavior.[2] Kalyvas (2006) explains armed groups' use of violence against civilians as a strategy in their quest to control territory. US Army general Petraeus largely based his counterinsurgency manual on his understanding of the ways in which rebels attempt to gain and defend local territories (Petraeus et al. 2008). Even Che Guevara's (1997) and Mao Zedong's (1978) influential guides on guerrilla warfare consist, to a great extent, of instructions for gaining and defending territory. Based on this insight, the theory of social order that I propose assumes that, when deciding whether to bring order about and which form to pursue, rebels are principally driven by their goal of securing territorial control. An important scope condition of this theory is, therefore, that the non-state armed group does want to control territory.[3]

It is important to note that this condition is not as restrictive as it may seem. First, controlling territory is the way in which most insurgents actually fight their wars: this is a way to pressure the government, grow their ranks, and enlarge their organization.[4] Second, armed groups that

---

[2] Control can be defined as sovereignty – that is, the exclusion of enemy presence in the territory. Kalyvas (2006:88), for example, defines insurgent control as a situation in which rebels can prevent operations by government forces day and night, as well as the government's performance of basic functions like collecting taxes.

[3] I am agnostic about the leading divisions that drive the warring sides. The theory should apply equally to secessionist, center-seeking, class-based, and ethnic-based groups insofar as they fight an irregular civil war and have incentives to control territory.

[4] Evidence of armed groups controlling local territories or entire regions abound. In 1969, McColl (1969) provided detailed evidence on rebel-controlled areas in the insurrectionary wars of China, Vietnam, the Philippines, Malaya, Thailand, Cuba, and Greece. For Latin America, evidence goes from the well-known wars of Cuba, Colombia, Peru, and El Salvador, to guerrillas that failed quickly, like those in Venezuela (e.g., Wickham-Crowley 1987; Stoll et al. 1993; Moroni Bracamonte & Spencer 1995). In Africa, detailed evidence of rebels taking over cities, towns, and regions is available for a number of groups, such as the EPLF (Pool 2001) and the SPLM/A (Mampilly 2011). Even in countries where the state is not weak, rebels are often able to take over full areas. The Naga insurgencies in India (Suykens 2015) and the LTTE in Sri Lanka (Stokke 2006; Mampilly 2011) are two examples. The existing literature also shows that rebels often gain control of specific communities within large areas controlled by the state – especially shanty towns in big cities, including country capitals (e.g., Taw & Hoffman 1995). Kalyvas (2006) offers secondary evidence of many non-state armed groups that controlled territories in countries across the globe.

profit from valuable natural resources often need to control territory to undertake their activities. For example, "the asset-specific nature of the diamond regions in southern and eastern Sierra Leone required the RUF to occupy much of the territory it controlled" (Johnston 2008:129). This is the case of other organizations that needed to develop infrastructure or rely on extensive labor to extract natural resources, such as diamonds, like UNITA in Angola (Malaquias 2001), or narcotics, like the Taliban in Afghanistan or the FARC in Colombia (Sanín & Giustozzi 2010). The argument does not apply, however, to non-state armed groups that do not seek to control territory, for example, because they aim to commit genocide in order to cleanse a country or region. Cases like the 1994 civil war in Rwanda – which consisted of a genocide (Straus 2008) – are therefore beyond the scope of this theory.[5]

While the quest for territorial control is widely recognized as a key factor shaping armed groups' behavior, a second, related goal, tends to be overlooked: maximizing the byproducts of that control. This omission obscures the fact that while preserving territorial control will remain rebels' core goal, they will try to use that control to maximize a wide range of benefits. Indeed, control can translate into acquiring economic resources, accessing key networks, recruiting new members, and gaining popular support. In order to understand rebel behavior and civilian–combatant interactions, we need to take these potential benefits into account. I assume, therefore, that (1) armed groups seek, above all, to gain and preserve territorial control; and that (2) once control is secured, they will try to maximize the benefits it can render.

To be sure, armed groups are not monolithic entities. In some cases combatants' preferences differ from those of the leadership, or leaders are, themselves, not interested in winning the war, but rather in obtaining economic rewards (Keen 1998; Reno 1998). I refer to these situations later in the chapter.

The Fundamental Role of Civilians

One of the central contentions of the literature on irregular warfare is that an armed group's success in controlling territories largely depends on

---

[5] Even though the scope of the theory is limited to irregular civil wars fought by armed actors that do seek to control territories, it has implications for other contexts in which an armed actor seeks to expand its control over territories and populations, as I argue in Chapter 9.

civilians. It is civilians who provide information on the enemy and its supporters, allow combatants to take refuge among the population, and help combatants to wage attacks (e.g., Guevara et al. 1997:56, 99; Wood 2003:122–159; Kalyvas 2006:ch.5). Mao (1978:93) captured the crucial role that civilian cooperation plays in his famous dictum that the population is like a sea in which the guerrilla swims like a fish. When the sea dries up, the rebels are often defeated.

Building on this insight, several studies have argued that rebels choose their strategies largely based on their need to garner civilian cooperation (e.g., Wood 2003; Kalyvas 2006; Steele 2016). The theory and practice of counterinsurgency have been deeply shaped by this assumption as well: the most influential theorists of counterinsurgency have argued that winning the "hearts and minds" of the civilian population is a necessary condition for success (e.g., Galula 1964; Trinquier 1964; McChrystal & Hall 2009).

I assume, therefore, that armed groups need help from civilians in order to achieve their primary goal, to wit, control territory. However, I refine this assumption by differentiating *obedience* – complying with combatants' commands – from *spontaneous support* – voluntarily offering them help. I argue that armed groups need *massive* obedience and *some* spontaneous support and, what is more, that both are necessary conditions for preserving territorial control.

Let us start with obedience. Unless civilians follow certain rules, the security of the armed group can be easily compromised. For example, one peasant providing information on the whereabouts of a rebel camp can be enough for the army to attack and destroy it. Because civilians can hinder rebel control of territory, ensuring universal obedience is of paramount importance.

Yet, obedience is rarely sufficient for a rebel group to prevail. To start with, the group needs at least some civilians to voluntarily offer information. No armed group can fully protect itself without help from civilians because combatants cannot monitor every inch of the territory they control – they need locals to tell them what they hear and see. Consider, for example, the civilians who flew kites in Afghanistan to alert the Taliban about the arrival of American troops, facilitating their escape (*NYT* 2010b). This kind of spontaneous support is crucial to armed groups. Likewise, if a local is secretly helping the troops of the enemy, the ones most likely to find out are his neighbors, not combatants. The armed group needs informants who are willing to offer such information.

While it is true that rebels can mandate that people speak up when they see any signs of defection, or the arrival of enemy troops, obtaining high-quality intelligence through coercion is quite hard, as Wood (2003:156) argues. Studies of civil wars in contexts as diverse as Lithuania, Greece, El Salvador, Colombia, and Sudan have found that pure coercion is not sufficient for armed groups to bring about the type of civilian cooperation they need to preserve territorial control (Wickham-Crowley 1987; Petersen 2001; Gutiérrez Sanín 2003; Wood 2003; Gutiérrez & Barón 2006; Kalyvas 2006; Uribe de Hincapié 2006; Weinstein 2007; Keister 2009; Mampilly 2011; Förster 2015).

Furthermore, different literatures suggest that political rule in general requires at least some voluntary support. Several political theorists, for example, have argued that political order cannot rely on coercion alone; rather, positive beliefs about the ruler and even emotions like love, loyalty, or honor are needed for political rule to be long-lasting (Machiavelli 1984; Olson 2000; Hobbes 2010). Even Hobbes – whose *Leviathan* is often described as having unlimited power – recognized that "the sovereign who violates natural law should anticipate instability, disorder, and eventually the loss of power. It follows that order cannot, and should not, be preserved on the sole basis of terror" (Shapiro 2010:xiv). The empirical literature on dictatorship has also found that, to stay in power, authoritarian rulers need at least some support – be it from allies or from a sector of the population that endorses the regime (Wintrobe 1990; Slater 2010). In sum, like any ruler, rebels too need at least some voluntary cooperation to prevail.

The theory that I propose assumes, therefore, that armed groups need civilian cooperation to control territories, and that such cooperation must include both massive obedience of certain rules, and at least some spontaneous, voluntary support.

I also make two simple assumptions about civilians' preferences: first, they want to be safe – that is, they want to avoid death and any form of physical harm. And second, they care about how they are governed, but there is variation across and within communities regarding civilians' preferences for governance. The first assumption is based on the basic understanding of humans' instinct for survival. The second simply states that people care about the institutions they have to follow, and the decisions that those in power make and affect the population – a basic contention that often underlies the study of politics.

LONG-TERM HORIZONS AND THE EMERGENCE OF ORDER

Given armed groups' preferences – controlling territory and maximizing its byproducts – why do they opt to bring order in a war zone? I argue that rebels have incentives to establish a social contract with a local population and bring order when they have long time horizons; that is, when they care about future outcomes more than they do about present ones. On the contrary, when they have short time horizons – that is, when they focus on more immediate goals – a social contract is not appealing.

When an armed group is operating under a long time horizon, it is concerned about its capacity to preserve control over the locality in the long run, while maximizing the benefits it can obtain. A social contract with the local population entails both sides committing to abide by a set of rules. I argue that the armed actor has incentives to establish such a contract because it leads to greater civilian cooperation – both in the form of obedience and spontaneous support – as well as to larger benefits.

To start with, combatants have incentives to establish rules on civilian conduct because they need civilians to behave in certain ways, for example avoiding providing information to the enemy, to maintain control. By making those rules explicit, rebels can communicate to civilians what is expected of them, increase predictability, and more easily monitor compliance and punish disobedience.

Rebels also have incentives to establish clear rules on *their own* behavior. If they do not, the incentives for civilians to obey would diminish. Consider a person living in a locality where rebels are present. Under a social contract where the rebels have clearly established rules on both civilian and combatant behavior, civilians know that providing information to the army carries a punishment, while obeying the rules ensures their safety. They can alter their behavior to increase their own security. In a situation where combatants have not established a social contract to constrain themselves, civilians know they may be killed whether or not they talk to the army. Under these unpredictable circumstances, aiding the army may even be a way out. All else equal, the likelihood that civilians decide to cooperate with the rebels is higher when a social contract is in place.

It follows that both combatants and civilians are better off under a social contract – for the former because they obtain greater civilian obedience, and for the latter because they can adapt their behavior to avoid being harmed. This logic is similar to that of social contract theories where the social contract is a solution to a prisoner's dilemma. In these theories, the parties to the contract are better off if everyone cooperates, but they have incentives not to cooperate because they expect that others will not do so. Adopting an enforced social contract solves this dilemma by making disobedience costly to both parties, in this case civilians and combatants.

In addition to creating incentives for civilians to obey due to fear of punishment, a social contract can also promote voluntary obedience, that is, civilians complying with rules willingly. Having at least some civilians obey because they want to, rather than because they have to, is quite important. As Levi (1989: 49) argues, "Enforcement is nearly always imperfect. Even with considerable coercive power and effective techniques of measurement and monitoring, a ruler cannot achieve total compliance unless there is a policeman on every corner." As with any other ruler, an armed actor is more able to control the behavior of its subjects if at least some of them willingly comply.[6] This allows rebels to allocate precious resources to pursuing their goals instead of spending them on monitoring civilians.

In order to foster civilians' willingness to obey, the group can set up rules that locals approve of, even if those rules do not directly increase combatants' ability to control the territory. Consider a village where rape is widespread. By forbidding rape (and punishing offenders), the armed group can gain recognition and at least partial support for its rule, which can lead some civilians to voluntarily comply with rebel regulations more generally. Several studies show that rebels often intervene to address key problems related to public order, and that civilians welcome it. For example, civilians applauded the efforts of the Shining Path in Peru (Starn 1995:551) and The Greek People's Liberation Army (ELAS) in Greece (Kalyvas 2015:127) to curb robberies. In Chapter 6, I provide detailed evidence of people's positive response to so-called "social cleansing campaigns" by guerrillas and paramilitaries in Colombian conflict zones, which sought to eliminate rape, robbery, and drug use.

Yet, a social contract is better for the armed group not only because it renders more civilian obedience but also because it makes spontaneous

---

[6] Several theorists have stressed the importance of voluntary obedience for any system of law to function. To Kauffman (1999), for example, a system of law that is based on mere fear of punishment not only faces important normative challenges, but also promises to be more insecure and unstable. Levi (1989:52–54) specifies the benefits that rulers obtain from fostering what she calls quasi-voluntary compliance.

support more likely. All else equal, civilians are more prone to endorse rebel rule under order than under disorder. People dislike living with high uncertainty; they value order over disorder, even when it is imposed on them (Silver 1965; Förster 2015). This preference is illustrated by the situation in an Afghan district of Baghlan province, where local militias who were supposedly fighting for local defense lost civilian support to the Taliban when failing to honor a social contract with the local population: "'To be honest, the people prefer the Taliban,' said Mr. Khan, the tribal elder. 'These [local] Arbeki men are cruel, violent, taking everything by force from the shopkeepers. They are walking in the bazaar with their rifles, extorting the drivers and traders.'" (*NYT* 2010b). Civilians are unlikely to offer spontaneous support to an armed group that engenders disorder. Mao was well aware of how important it is for guerrillas to follow strict rules in their treatment of civilians. After listing the specific guidelines that troops should follow – which include not stealing from the people and avoiding searching the pocketbooks of those arrested without authority to do so – he proclaimed: "It is only undisciplined troops who make the people their enemies and who, like fish out of its native element, cannot live." (Mao 1978:93).

Finally, a rebel group that aims to maximize the byproducts of territorial control is better off establishing order because such byproducts often depend on civilian behavior. As both civilian obedience and spontaneous support tend to be higher under order, so are the benefits that armed groups obtain from them. For example, armed actors are more likely to obtain material contributions, political support, and recruits under order than under disorder.

In sum, bringing about a situation of *disorder* is a poor strategy for armed groups with long time horizons because it creates fewer incentives for civilians to cooperate, therefore making it more difficult to preserve territorial control. Establishing a social contract, on the other hand, facilitates monitoring and makes both obedience and spontaneous support more probable, which in turn favor territorial control as well as its byproducts.

SHORT-TERM HORIZONS AND THE EMERGENCE OF DISORDER

Combatants do not always care about future outcomes more than they do about present ones: sometimes they only value short-term benefits or heavily discount future ones. When operating under short time

Short-Term Horizons and the Emergence of Disorder

horizons, incentives for self-restraint decrease; social contracts are not established (or honored) and, in the absence of clear rules that most people follow, disorder emerges. Olson's (1993) famous metaphor of roving versus stationary bandits helps explain the reasons why social contracts are not appealing for rebels with short time horizons: while stationary bandits limit their abuse in order to increase long-term benefits, roving bandits prefer to do as they please to maximize immediate gains.

To be sure, time horizons cannot be directly observed; they are an actor's relative preference for events happening in the near or distant future. I identify three conditions under which an armed group, or one of its units, focuses on present rather than future outcomes: group indiscipline, armed competition, and certain changes in the macro-politics of the war. Under these conditions, present outcomes are more valued than future ones, affecting armed groups' incentives to establish a social contract that imposes limits on their own conduct.

When an armed group has problems of internal discipline – that is, of enforcing its rules and orders within its organization – the rank and file can act upon their own short-term interests rather than those of their organization. Under this situation, disorder emerges *not* because the commander has ordered combatants to operate outside of the social contract, but because combatants disobey their commander.

As Weinstein (2007) argues, this is the case when combatants are motivated by immediate spoils because they are not willing to make long-term sacrifices. However, I argue that group discipline is a requisite for the establishment of social contracts even if combatants are motivated by ideology and do care about their organization's capacity to control territories in the long term, gain civilian cooperation and, ultimately, win the war.

Consider an armed group whose combatants are ideologically committed to their group. In their daily life, however, they may be hungry and crave for food. They have incentives to steal food from peasants, in spite of also desiring to advance the goals of their organization. Even if they have been well trained and know that stealing from peasants will harm the group's ability to obtain civilian cooperation in the future, they are tempted to break the rule, knowing that a single incident is unlikely to ruin the cause. We can think of the situation as a free-riding problem: all the ideologically motivated combatants prefer that everyone else in the group treats civilians well at all times; but each of them has incentives to indulge once in a while to satisfy short-term preferences. By breaking rules on the treatment of civilians, these acts jeopardize the social contract.

This logic also applies to profit-driven combatants whose ability to achieve economic goals depends on a long-term relationship with the local population. As Weinstein (2007) argues, some profit-seeking rebels pursue activities that require territorial control and civilian labor, for example, the cultivation of coca crops. Civilians may also be needed for a market to function. Raeymaekers and Menkhaus (2008:44) found such dependency of profit-seeking rebels on civilians in their study of The Rally for Congolese Democracy (RCD) in the Democratic Republic of Congo; according to them, "[t]o secure their dominance over the exploitation and trading of local resources ... the rebels depended on the willingness of individuals and groups to align with them, in return for protection of their economic interests." In these cases, a social contract is necessary to organize labor and maintain control over the territory. Yet, even if every combatant understands that a social contract is important to obtain long-term profits, they also have incentives to break the rules in order to obtain short-term benefits. Discipline ensures that the long-term goals of the organization drive combatant behavior, taking precedence over their short-term interests.

To be sure, different factors may affect combatants' preferences for abusing civilians (Wood 2016), such as their political training (Hoover 2011), their endowments (Weinstein 2007), and their patterns of recruitment (Weinstein 2007; Cohen 2013). I am agnostic about the causes of armed group discipline as well as of combatants' preferences for civilian abuse. My claim is that, all else equal, in the absence of group discipline combatants are less likely to observe a social contract that imposes restraints on what they can and cannot do in their interaction with civilians.

Armed actors learn that having combatants that overlook rules on the treatment of civilians can be quite costly. For this reason, many armed groups allow civilians to submit complaints when combatants have misbehaved. In Afghanistan, for example, "a system of checks and balances has developed in which civilians and Taliban members can appeal to higher authorities when insurgents abuse their power" (Bergen & Tiedemann 2012:35). In some cases, like the Communist Party of the Philippines (PKP), the leadership identifies "bad elements" in its ranks and tries to overcome the problem with better recruitment or intensive education within the organization (Kerkvliet 1977:229). However, dealing with opportunistic individuals proves to be a pervasive problem in other cases like the RUF in Sierra Leone (Gberie 2005), and Charles Taylor's National Patriotic Forces in Liberia (Ellis 1998; Johnston 2004). In these cases, predation of local populations becomes widespread and disorder is likely to reign.

In sum, order is attractive for groups that, regardless of their goal, need long-term cooperation from civilians, and have internal discipline to control the behavior of the rank and file.

The second condition under which armed groups operate on a short time horizon is when they face competition with other warring sides. Under competition, the main goal is to expel the rival and preserve territorial control, while other goals become secondary (Kasfir 2004). As with any other expanding armed actor, the first step is to win; only then does the question of how to occupy and rule the territory become salient. Hence, when competing with other warring sides, armed groups tend to highly discount the value of future outcomes. Metelits (2010) and Sánchez de la Sierra (2015) also argue that competition creates uncertainty about long-term economic benefits, which shifts the group's time horizon. This preeminent focus on preserving control in the present impacts the group's incentives to establish or honor a social contract for several reasons.

To start with, when territory is disputed, observing a social contract can hinder a group's capacity to preserve control. As Kalyvas (2006) argues, under competition civilians are unlikely to inform the armed actor about those who cooperate with the rival side because they do not believe that the group can protect them.[7] Deprived of good information and seeking to minimize the possibility that enemy forces obtain good intelligence, the group has incentives to use violence on the basis of simple suspicions. Furthermore, as Balcells (2017) and Steele (2016) argue, combatants may rely on collective identities like prewar partisanship or ethnicity to infer locals' likelihood of cooperating with the enemy and use violence against potential defectors. A social contract would prevent such acts of violence because they are based on individuals' attributes, rather than on their actual disobedience of a rule. In this way, even though a social contract would increase civilian cooperation – and, thus, territorial control – in the long term, in the short run it could prevent the group from stopping civilian cooperation with its rival, leading it to lose control over the territory.

---

[7] In his model, this happens to both armed groups in zone 3; to the incumbent in zones 4 and 5; and to the rebels in zones 1 and 2 (Kalyvas 2006).

In addition, under competition armed groups expect civilians to break the social contract as well. Suppose that a rebel group sticks to the social contract while its enemy, a paramilitary group, uses violence to induce civilian compliance. Some civilians may prefer to cooperate with the paramilitary group (the most violent of the two) as a survival strategy, therefore breaking the social contract with the rebels. Anticipating this outcome, the rebels have incentives to do what it takes in order to eliminate potential allies of the paramilitaries – that is, act in a manner unconstrained by a social contract – to avoid losing control.[8] Put differently, a social contract between the rebel group and civilians does not necessarily create the conditions for civilian cooperation because the paramilitaries are also affecting civilians' payoffs. As Kalyvas (2006:114) argues, rebels "would rather be disliked and feared than liked but not feared when their rival is feared."[9]

Armed actors also have incentives to break a social contract because the opportunity costs of using resources and manpower to maintain order are much higher under competition. Enforcing rules that are not immediately related to the group's capacity to control the territory is not worthwhile when those resources could be used to fight the enemy. Furthermore, the armed group may simply be incapable of maintaining order because, under competition, none of the groups possesses the monopoly over the use of violence. Civilians face disorder because none of the armed actors are able to fully enforce its rules and uncertainty is high.

In addition to indiscipline and armed competition, an armed group's time horizon may shift to the short-term in the advent of certain macro-level changes. The proximity of negotiations, for example, can shift the group's preferences for immediate territorial expansion, which would

---

[8] This is not to say, however, that all combatants have the same leeway when facing armed competition. As mentioned before, armed groups' internal institutions and control mechanisms may limit the behavior of their members (Hoover 2011), even in situations of disorder. Furthermore, the absence of a social contract does not mean that violence is not used strategically.

[9] A social contract would make sense only if *all* competing armed actors were to commit to observe certain rules in their treatment of civilians – otherwise, they would be honoring a social contract while leaving their enemy the opportunity to gain more cooperation and win through coercion. Achieving such agreement between two or more armed groups is extremely difficult, and therefore does not happen frequently. However, some communities – often called "peace communities" – have managed to do that. See Kaplan (2013b) for a detailed study of a case in which such an agreement was reached and sustained. In this case, a peasant community in Colombia managed to convince two armed actors to allow a civilian commission to investigate suspects of cooperating with either of the groups before killing them. The study finds that the groups honored this agreement and violence was substantially reduced.

increase its bargaining power at the negotiating table. In this situation, combatants may not care much about their ability to secure civilian cooperation in the long term but, rather, about their capacity to signal military power in more parts of the national territory. Creating social contracts in those new territories would not make sense given that the benefits of social contracts materialize in the long run. Likewise, if an end to the conflict seems imminent, combatants may no longer have incentives to make present sacrifices in territories under their control for benefits that would only be appropriable in the future. Finally, insofar as rebels' capacity to use violence increases their bargaining capacity, they have incentives to use coercion against civilians even if it violates the terms of a social contract. As Hultman (2007:206) suggests, killing civilians can be "a militarily cheap and easy strategy to raise the government's costs for standing firm and continuing fighting."

To be sure, depending on the terms of the agreement, the group may have incentives not to maximize its expansion, but rather to gain more support among the population. If, for example, the agreement involves the transition of the rebel group into a political party, the group may adopt strategies that maximize electoral support in anticipated elections. At the same time, the group may have an incentive to restrain its behavior because it anticipates having to reintegrate with the civilian population, and face charges for crimes committed. Macro-level changes can therefore both favor and decrease the likelihood of a social contract.

In sum, when armed groups operate with short time horizons due to internal indiscipline, armed competition or macro-changes in the war, they lack the incentives or the capacity to establish social contracts. A situation of *disorder* is thus likely to emerge, where armed groups fail to abide by established rules, and civilians are subjected to high levels of uncertainty. Since indiscipline and armed competition are common factors affecting many armed groups, the empirical chapters of this book focus on their effect on social order, leaving out the effect of macro-changes in the war. However, it is important to note that an implication of the theory is that any event that alters armed actors' discount rate of future outcomes is likely to impact the likelihood of order and disorder.

REBELOCRACY AND CIVILIAN COOPERATION

When an armed group has incentives to establish a social contract with a local population and create order, it prefers rebelocracy to aliocracy because the former helps it to advance the twin goals of securing territorial control and maximizing its byproducts. The quest for long-term territorial control is to a great extent a quest for civilian obedience and spontaneous support. Rebelocracy's greatest advantage is that it can trigger both forms of cooperation.

Several attributes of rebelocracy spur civilian cooperation. One of the most important is the administration of justice. By creating formal or informal courts or some other mechanism to adjudicate disputes, armed groups centralize power and build an aura of legitimacy.[10] To start with, establishing a court or its equivalent helps the armed actor to create order, which benefits both civilians and combatants. The centrality of courts as means for order was obvious to the legal chief of the Sri Lankan Tamil Tigers, who stated: "we have to maintain law and order in the areas controlled by us. For this purpose we need the court system" (Kamalendran 2004). By settling disputes among locals, the armed actor also obtains valuable information about the members of the community: their networks, divisions, and alliances – all of which helps combatants to exert social control. In addition, creating a mechanism to adjudicate disputes often entails providing a much needed public service that civilians quickly appreciate.

Furthermore, as Bilz's (2007) insightful discussion of why people delegate revenge to the state suggests, monopolizing punishment plays a key role in conferring power on the avenger while legitimizing its rule. Once an armed group becomes a recognized authority, beliefs about combatants change in ways that either directly or indirectly favor cooperation: some civilians obey and even offer spontaneous support to the group because they come to see it as the right thing to do; others do so to be on good terms with those who hold power; and others cooperate to follow social norms, either to avoid social sanctions or because they have internalized such norms. Elsewhere I discuss other mechanisms by which recognizing an armed actor as an authority leads to voluntary obedience and spontaneous acts of support (Arjona 2016a).

It is quite common to find rebels and militias playing the role of alternative courts – and people welcoming them. In Sri Lanka, the Tamil Tigers created a judicial system with both district courts and high courts.

---

[10] Although justice institutions can be conceived of as a public good, I treat them separately throughout the book given the central role that they play in my argument. Hence, when I talk about public goods, I am referring to the provision of services like health and education, and the construction of roads.

Many civilians often decided "to take their claims to the Tamil Eelam courts rather than the Sri Lankan courts" (Stokke 2006:1027–1028). The SPLA in Sudan also played this role in its strongholds, appointing judiciary officers who oversaw local chiefs' courts, and even creating a system of appeals overseen by higher-rank members of the organization (Johnson 1998:67–69). The Maoists in Nepal established courts to settle disputes related to various types of conflict, including damage by animals, stealing, and rape. They also banned polygamy. In 2004, a report estimated that these courts operated in twenty-five of Nepal's seventy-five districts (Dubey 2004). In Ethiopia, the Eritrean People's Liberation Front set up judiciary committees that treated legal problems by "criticism and self-criticism and through judiciary examination" (Pool 2001:122). In the town of Decamhare, the committees dealt with more than 1,400 cases within six months of their creation (ibid.).

Accounts of daily life in Taliban-dominated areas in Afghanistan illustrate how effective this practice is for gaining locals' cooperation. According to Giustozzi (2007:111), the Taliban's strategy in Afghanistan to develop a base of popular support included "setting up their own 'no-frills' administration," which was "centered on the judiciary, whose services were in high demand in the countryside because of the total failure of the central government to establish a reasonably reliable judicial system." In those areas where courts had not been established, field commanders were often in charge of "mediating local disputes and administering justice." Recent news reports and research point to the Taliban's offer of fast and accessible justice as a key means for gaining civilian cooperation and territorial control throughout the country.[11]

Perhaps the best indication of how beneficial it is for rebels to create their own courts is the great effort that they often put into becoming locals' preferred actor to solve disputes. In the Palestine rebellion in the 1930s, rebels invited civilians to resolve their problems at rebel courts, as opposed to British courts. Furthermore, as a British schoolteacher declared, they conducted "a continuous and largely successful propaganda to show that their courts [were] more just, and above all more speedy, than the King's courts" (Ghandour 2010:102). Several armed groups operating in Southern Syria, including al-Nusra and Ahrar al-Sham, came together to create a unified court as "part of a pragmatic effort by the Southern Front to win civilian hearts and minds" (Sosnowski 2015).

---

[11] See for example (Baczko 2013; Ahmed 2015; Kaplan 2015).

García Villegas (2008) offers detailed accounts of judges who were forced by members of guerrillas and paramilitaries in Colombia to abstain from adjudicating disputes because that was the armed organization's prerogative. The importance of courts for consolidating power and obtaining civilian cooperation is clearly captured by the fact that the Maoists in Nepal "regard[ed] their court system as the heart of their 'People's Government'" (Haviland 2006).

Rebelocracy also triggers cooperation by positively transforming beliefs about the rebels, the social contract, or both. By creating efficient institutions, improving the provision of public goods and services, or influencing the formal political discourse, combatants can build a positive reputation among locals, which, in turn, favors cooperation via reciprocity, emotional responses, or expectations about future benefits. A good reputation can create support elsewhere as well: as McColl (1969:622) argues, areas where guerrillas rule are "a strong propaganda weapon in the struggle for the support of the population."

Another important way in which rebelocracy facilitates civilian cooperation is by simply making non-cooperation costly. When rebels become an influential local actor, the costs of civilian apathy and resistance increase: in a context in which access to jobs, goods, and services is mediated by an armed group, opposing it entails material penalties. Even social status and power might well depend on a person's standing with the de facto ruler. For example, in Raqqa, Syria, after ISIS took control over the city in 2015, "it quickly became clear that every spot in the social order, and any chance for a family to survive, was utterly dependent on the group" (*NYT* 2015). Civilians may therefore cooperate in order to be on good terms with the rebels and avoid jeopardizing their own well-being, particularly if they are unable to exit the war zone.

Finally, rebelocracy can generate new social, political, and economic dynamics that can affect civilians' beliefs about the war and the warring sides; awaken powerful emotions; and give place to new social norms. Many of these changes can push civilians to offer cooperation. I explore these dynamics and their impact on civilians' choices elsewhere (Arjona 2016a).

REBELOCRACY AND THE BYPRODUCTS OF CONTROL

Rebelocracy also allows armed groups to maximize the byproducts of control – their second most important goal. In order to keep expanding, these groups need to build their organizational capacity and weaken that of the enemy. Rebelocracy offers the possibility of strengthening their economic, military, and political standing.

Economically, governing civilian affairs beyond public order and taxation is instrumental for rebels because their physical survival often relies on civilians, who provide food, shelter, and clothing. In addition, rebels can engage in profitable activities by organizing labor: for example, to extract diamonds, as several rebel groups in the Democratic Republic of Congo have done, or to grow coca, as the FARC in Colombia and the Shining Path in Peru have done. Structuring these economic activities under a social contract prevents excessive expropriation of civilians, which would risk the group's food security and funding sources in the long run (Olson 1993).

Militarily, rebelocracy gives armed groups access to networks and intelligence. Providing information to the armed actor in control is one of the ways in which civilians cooperate. By becoming a central actor in local life, the armed group can more easily penetrate networks and obtain information, which in turn helps it consolidate control. Rebelocracy also provides a more secure refuge than aliocracy given the higher level of civilian cooperation. Non-coerced recruitment – a key form of voluntary cooperation – is also likely to be substantially higher under rebelocracy, as I show in Chapter 8.

Politically, rebels gain from interfering in local politics and shaping political behavior. They can alter the results of elections when they are held, organize massive protests, have access to regional or national political networks, and even intervene in the allocation of governmental funds. Deals between armed groups and politicians have been documented in many conflicts, including cases as dissimilar as Liberia (Reno 2015), Côte d'Ivoire (Förster 2015), Aceh (Barter 2015), and Colombia (López 2010). In addition, some rebel organizations value putting in practice some of their political goals (Mampilly 2011), like land distribution. For example, although land reform is seen as a key instrumental move by the PLA in the Chinese civil war, some authors also suggest that the organization insisted on popular education and class consciousness as goals, rather than simply means, of the revolution (Hinton 1966).

Rebelocracy might even bolster rebels' image abroad. Mampilly (2011) provides several examples of armed groups that showed their high-quality government to international observers for this purpose. In Sudan, for example, the author finds that "ultimately, the SPLM/A was more concerned with constructing the façade of democratic institutions to impress international donors than actually gathering feedback on the provision of services to local communities" (p. 132). Similarly, Heywood (1989:62) describes how UNITA in Angola asked international observers and journalists to attend their meetings and tour their villages. This helped the organization to "support its claim of being a counter-government, especially since it has had the ability to implement a number of 'showcase' social-economic programmes"(Ibid., 62). The ability to persuade international organizations or observers that they were providing institutions and services to civilians resulted in economic benefits and increased international legitimacy.

In sum, by intervening in the social, economic, and political realms, rebels can obtain high levels of civilian cooperation, which, in turn, makes territorial control more likely to prevail; they also obtain economic, political, and military benefits, while having the opportunity to put into practice at least part of their ideology. Given these benefits, armed groups prefer rebelocracy to aliocracy. Yet, they must determine whether the benefits outweigh the costs of running a rebelocracy.

THE COSTS OF RUNNING A REBELOCRACY

Establishing a rebelocracy is not as costly as one might expect. The armed group is already employing the resources needed to control the territory, including establishing ties with civilians who inform the group about potentially dangerous activity. The added cost of rebelocracy is having those informants also report on the disobedience of other rules, as well as on problems affecting the community that need attention. Sometimes the group delegates its power to resolve certain matters to a local actor that follows the orders of the group. This could be a civilian who works with the armed actor, a committee created by it, or a preexisting organization that has allied with the group or is co-opted or coerced by it. In other words, rebels take advantage of the economies of smallness: creating rules and enforcing them is much easier in a small community than in a large society. I provide examples of the different ways in which armed groups can rule in both direct and indirect ways in Chapter 6.

For rebelocracy to work, combatants also need to create expectations of strict enforcement. This entails imposing punishment for disobedience early on, which sends a clear signal to civilians and decreases the likelihood of misconduct in the future. Often, combatants rely on locals – especially on those who become part-time members of the group – or governance boards (Sinno 2008, Ch. 1) to impose some of these punishments. Sometimes combatants are in charge of imposing the punishment themselves. Over time, however, disobedience becomes rare as civilians develop expectations about punishment. In Chapter 6, I provide detailed evidence of how those expectations are created as well as of the high levels of obedience of armed groups' rules within rebelocracies.

Running formal or informal courts requires human resources. In some cases, this is done by delegating to a person or local committee the role of judge, as the rebel group Free Aceh Movement (GAM) did with Ulamas (religious leaders) in Aceh, Indonesia (Barter 2015). Similarly, the coalition of rebel groups in Southern Syria appointed sixteen judges to serve in the House of Justice in Gharz (Maayeh & Sands 2014). Often, minor disputes are resolved by locally appointed committees or representatives, while serious cases are reported to the rebels directly. This was the case, for example, during the Palestinian rebellion of the 1930s (Ghandour 2010:100), and in some territories under FARC control in Colombia (Penhaul 2001).

While some armed groups do pay their appointed judges a salary, like the Taliban does in Afghanistan (Giustozzi et al. 2013:19), in many cases elders and local committees do not receive payments. Furthermore, the costs involved in the actual process of adjudicating disputes tend to be substantially lower for armed groups than for state bureaucracies. To start with, armed groups usually fail to incorporate most elements of a due process, such as the defendant's right to cross-examine witnesses or be represented by a lawyer, which makes the process shorter and simpler. In addition, in most cases the armed actor listens to the parties involved once and makes a decision immediately, as evidence on rebel courts from Nepal suggests (Haviland 2006).[12] In most cases, no records are kept, which also decreases the costs involved.[13] Despite these conditions, these courts solve a central problem for communities and people often welcome them.

Even in cases where running a parallel judiciary requires substantial resources, the benefits seem to outweigh the costs. As discussed earlier, by setting up a system to settle disputes armed actors gain power, access to information, legitimacy, and civilian cooperation, all of which facilitate

---

[12] While in many cases such decisions are not subject to appeal, some armed groups do offer this possibility, like the Sri Lankan Tamil Tigers (Kamalendran 2004), and the Taliban in Afghanistan (Giustozzi et al. 2013:14). However, given civilians' fear of retribution, appealing tends to be uncommon (ibid.:23).

[13] I have only been able to find evidence of one armed group keeping records of the disputes that it settles: the rebels during the rebellion in the late 1930s in Palestine (Ghandour 2010:102).

territorial control. As a Syrian rebel in Qobtan Jebel, near Aleppo, said: "We spend a lot of time dealing with petty issues while fighting a war at the same time.... But if you don't listen to everyone, we'll lose the people and then the revolution" (Levinson 2012). I come back to the central role of judicial institutions later in the chapter.

Finally, rebelocracy often goes beyond the creation of formal or informal institutions. Armed actors often decide to provide, or intervene in the provision of, services such as education, health, and the maintenance of infrastructure. Providing these services directly requires resources, while organizing locals or pressuring state agencies to do so is a matter of enforcing additional rules. Which types of services a given group provides, and to what extent, is likely to depend on its ideology and endowments. While obtaining 50 million dollars per month from selling oil (Hendawi & Abdul-Zahra 2015), ISIS could offer a wide range of services that would have been simply impossible to most rebels in the world, such as implementing infrastructure projects, providing food, and maintaining electricity lines and water mains (Caris & Reynolds 2014). However, even poor rebel groups have often found ways to provide, or intervene in the provision of, basic services. For example, Wickham-Crowley (1987) offers a detailed account of rebel provision of such services by poor, left-wing insurgencies in many Latin American countries.

In sum, creating institutions to regulate many realms of local life does not require investing substantial resources. Armed groups can rule without spending much beyond what is required to simply keep territorial control, as it usually requires a few locals who are willing to monitor compliance of a longer list of rules. While armed actors may devote a substantial amount of resources to create a formal judiciary or to provide public goods, rebelocracy does not require such investments.[14] Overall, most armed groups create rebelocracies with few resources and obtain in return large benefits – mostly in the form of social control, economic gains, and substantial civilian cooperation, all of which facilitate territorial control. In Chapter 6 I provide evidence of the relatively small costs involved in running a rebelocracy.

ALIOCRACY AND CIVILIAN RESISTANCE

Given the extent to which the benefits outweigh the costs, armed groups with long time horizons – whose goals are to control territories and

---

[14] How much a particular armed group spends is likely to vary depending on its revenue and the opportunity costs of the resources at its disposal.

maximize its byproducts – prefer rebelocracy to aliocracy. Yet, rebels sometimes do establish a social order of aliocracy. Why do they opt for what is essentially their second-best option?

Social orders are not created in a vacuum. Despite the harsh conditions of war, civilians have agency (Petersen 2001; Wood 2003; Kalyvas 2006; Lubkemann 2008; Mampilly 2011; Barter 2012; Parkinson 2013), and their reactions can alter rebels' payoffs. I argue that civilians have bargaining power vis-à-vis combatants when the former can make a credible threat of resisting rebelocracy collectively. By collective resistance, I mean instances of concerted opposition to the armed actor by disobeying its mandates, making demands on it, or both.[15] If most or all members of a community deny obedience and spontaneous support, rebelocracy becomes too costly and unlikely to endure, therefore endangering both territorial control and its byproducts.[16] Anticipating the possibility of compromising its two goals, rebels have incentives to establish aliocracy instead. Although studies of civil war have long recognized that rebels need civilian support, the bargaining power that such a position proffers civilians has been widely ignored.

Let us consider how the costs and benefits of establishing rebelocracy vary depending on civilian resistance. In communities where resistance is not organized, armed groups can easily control a number of activities by establishing new rules, relying on their reputation as rule enforcers, and using reliable sources of information about misconduct. In this way, the process of identifying disobedience and punishing it only requires that a few civilians agree to provide information on the behavior of community members, making it unnecessary for combatants to monitor locals directly. Hence, rebelocracy requires only a few strong supporters

---

[15] By civilian resistance I mean *local* resistance, not the creation of a new armed group. Creating a new armed organization that enters the war usually requires the involvement of external actors, like the state, tribal leaders, regional elites, or even foreign governments. I do not investigate this form of opposition to rebel rule in this book.

[16] It might seem odd to merge disobedience and opposition in one category. These are, indeed, two different options, and they may have different implications for civilians on the ground. For this reason, denying cooperation is often labeled neutrality rather than resistance. However, denying obedience is in many cases an act of resistance. It does not mean offering support to the other side or engaging in acts against the armed group, but it does entail abstaining from doing things the group has asked for. For the purpose of this theory, the more parsimonious definition that differentiates spontaneous support, obedience, and resistance suffices. Others have argued that neutrality is indeed closer to resistance than to "absolute" neutrality. See for example Galeano (2006:86).

and massive obedience, while the benefits, as explained before, can be quite large.

If collective resistance is organized, the consequences for the rebels depend on its success. In the first scenario, the community fails to expel the group from the area directly, but it denies information, relies on its own institutions rather than those established by the group, and rejects the intervention of combatants by disobeying their mandates. The costs of establishing rebelocracy become quite high, as punishing disobedience without some local support requires intense monitoring. In addition, the advantages of rebelocracy – civilian cooperation; political, economic, and military benefits – do not materialize as they all pass through the hands of civilians. Even more, rule that relies on coercion alone tends to be unstable as discussed before, and combatants may end up losing control over the territory. In sum, by imposing rebelocracy when civilians resist collectively, rebels face high costs and risk losing both territorial control and its byproducts in the long run.

In the second scenario, resistance is so successful that the community expels the armed group from the territory. In this case, the group loses both control and its byproducts immediately; it may also bear negative externalities elsewhere due to reputational losses.

Since attempting to establish rebelocracy when civilians resist is likely to bring high costs and low benefits in the long run, rebels have incentives to limit their ruling aspirations, and thus opt for a less intrusive social contract that does not trigger resistance. It might seem unrealistic that a group of powerful, armed combatants bends to the preferences of civilians. But micro-level evidence of war zones shows just that. In his criticism of common approaches to "warlordism," for example, Marchal (2007:1996) argues that in Somalia "[the] warlord had to accept a number of social patterns that were beyond his own will: often he was as dependent on his people as they were on him." Examples from other cases abound (Hancock & Mitchell 2007; Arjona 2015; Arjona et al. 2015; Barter 2015; Förster 2015).

Although the armed actor has incentives to compromise when civilians resist rebelocracy, it does not when establishing aliocracy due to the lack of an acceptable alternative. Consider a locality where civilians resist aliocracy, the most minimal form of intervention that the armed group could offer that still allows it to control the territory. Opposition to aliocracy amounts to hindering the armed group's control over the territory altogether. Control being its principal goal, the group lacks incentives to give in to such opposition. For this reason, civilians have bargaining power when they resist rebelocracy but not when they resist aliocracy.

Civilians do not have much influence over armed groups' decision to abandon disorder either. When disorder is caused by group indiscipline, there is not much civilians can do to change combatants' behavior. If the latter have not established a social contract, it is because they do not need civilian cooperation to obtain their short-term goals or because they have incentives to free ride. Under both circumstances, civilians lack bargaining power.

When disorder is caused by armed competition, the warring sides do care about civilian cooperation. In fact, as I have explained, the main reason why a social contract is not established is because combatants prefer to be able to use violence as they see fit in order to obtain as much civilian cooperation as possible, by any means. Civilians' promise not to cooperate with the rival in exchange for a social contract is not credible because none of the armed actors possesses a monopoly over the use of violence. If the rival uses coercion in order to obtain cooperation, civilians are likely to adapt their behavior in order to survive. Under these circumstances, civilians' commitment to honor a social contract is not credible and the community lacks bargaining power. This dynamic could be avoided if all armed groups are convinced about civilians' commitment to noncooperation – a difficult task that, although not common, has been documented (e.g. Kaplan 2013b), as previously mentioned.

In sum, I argue that armed groups will bring about order when they have a long time horizon and disorder when they do not, regardless of civilians' choices. When they do bring order about, their choice between aliocracy and rebelocracy is based on their expectations about whether or not they will face collective resistance from locals: they will establish rebelocracy whenever they do not anticipate collective resistance to it, and they will settle for aliocracy when they do expect concerted civilian opposition. The question that follows, then, is what explains expectations regarding collective resistance to rebelocracy?

A THEORY OF COLLECTIVE CIVILIAN RESISTANCE TO REBELOCRACY

Whether a community resists rebelocracy collectively or not might seem to be a matter of political preference: if locals support rebels' goals, they should welcome rebelocracy; if they oppose those goals, they should resist it. Yet, to the community the issue is not whether it supports the political goals of the armed actor. Rather, it is about how to respond to an actor aspiring to rule over it. Locals may endorse the political goals of the group but still desire to resist rebelocracy; in other words, they may want to cooperate with insurgents – but not be ruled by them. Thus, while rebels' political programs and ideologies matter, they are not the determining factor shaping civilian resistance to rebelocracy.

Several scholars have noticed this tension between the grand goals of an insurgency and the interests and expectations of common citizens. In the 1970s, some students of peasant rebellions advanced what we could call a localist view of civil war, according to which local realities often matter more than the grand narratives and macro cleavages that are at stake in the war. Scott (1979:111), for example, noted that for peasants the most relevant unit is their village – or perhaps their municipality or the nearby marketing town and its surroundings. He argued that this localism has enormous consequences for rebellion: "[I]t is clear that peasants will normally experience their interests as local interests, not as national or even provincial interests, and that a revolution will have to contend with this disparity of social horizons and solidarity." In other words, civilians' responses to a rebel group are largely driven by their local reality. More recently, scholars have identified specific ways in which local interests, norms, conflicts, and networks drive civilians' decision to denounce their neighbors to armed groups (Kalyvas 2006), join local opposition to foreign invasion (Petersen 2001), and support insurgents (Wood 2003; La Serna 2012; Parkinson 2013).

Similarly, while for insurgents bringing order and establishing rebelocracy in the territories they occupy are means to advance their cause, to civilians the difference between aliocracy and rebelocracy has dramatic consequences on the kind of lives that they can live during the war. They may strongly support the goals of the insurgency, but they might be better off without rebelocracy, and the converse could also be true. To understand resistance, we need therefore to inquire about civilians' preferences for new rule.

However, *desiring* to resist is insufficient: civilians must also be *able* to do so. And resisting an armed organization is not an easy task. Imagine living in a village where the rebel commander gets to decide who gets a job, how a dispute over property rights is resolved, or who gets a seat at the local school. Most people would have strong incentives to be on good terms with the rebels. Even if the majority of the community does not want to live in a particular social order established by the group, they still have incentives not to resist. Opposing the group is risky, and individuals who do not do so would still enjoy a "free ride" from the benefits of successful resistance.

While cooperating with an insurgency is often portrayed as an instance of collective action (Olson 1965; Silver 1974; Popkin 1979; Wood 2003), I argue that in many cases it is resisting against an armed group, rather than aiding it, that entails a risky enterprise, the benefits of which cannot be delivered to participants alone. When an armed group has high levels of control over a territory, cooperation is, in fact, the dominant strategy as it leads to pleasing the armed actor and potentially obtaining numerous benefits.[17] Resistance, on the other hand, is a quintessential collective action problem.

To explain collective resistance, we should, therefore, not only identify the conditions under which the members of a community would *want* to resist, but also the conditions under which they would be *able* to launch and sustain such risky mobilization. I contend that the quality of local institutions in place prior to the arrival of the armed group shapes civilians' preferences for their current form of governance – and therefore their *willingness* to resist rebelocracy; they also impact the community's capacity for collective action, which, in turn, determines its *ability* to launch and sustain collective resistance.

I define the quality of institutions on the basis of their legitimacy and efficacy. Legitimacy refers to whether most members of the community believe that those institutions are fair and should regulate their interactions. The members of a community may agree or disagree with the validity of institutions for a myriad of reasons, including their origin, their effects, the procedure by which they were designed, or the principles that they embody. Insofar as most community members see their institutions as just, they are legitimate under my definition.

Efficacy – as commonly used in legal theory (Kelsen 2009:29–44) – means most people obey the rules, that is, the rules are effective. Institutions are ineffective when many in the community disobey them, regardless the reason. As with legitimacy, there are many causes of efficacy, such as the level of internalization of the rules, how much they reflect people's preferences, the likelihood and severity of sanctions for

---

[17] The same may happen in territories under dispute, although for a different reason. As Kalyvas and Kocher (2007) argue, when two or more groups compete for territorial control, the insecurity for civilians can be so high that joining one of the warring sides may be safer than not doing so.

disobedience, and whether the rules are established by a recognized authority (Weldon 1953; Milgram 1963; Becker 1968; Kauffman 1999). Under this definition, institutions are effective whenever they are widely observed, regardless the cause.

The quality of institutions is high when institutions are both legitimate and effective, and low when they are either illegitimate or ineffective. I recognize that this classification fuses together communities that can have deeply different structures and power dynamics. However, I argue that this minimalist distinction is sufficient to capture how institutions impact the likelihood of collective civilian resistance. Communities with legitimate and effective institutions are likely to be both willing and able to resist rebelocracy; communities with either illegitimate or ineffective institutions are, on the contrary, unlikely to do so.

Although many institutions structure interaction in a community, I argue that dispute institutions play a predominant role in shaping collective resistance to rebelocracy and limiting armed groups' ability to consolidate their power. Dispute institutions are the formal and informal rules for adjudicating disputes, defending property rights, and enforcing contracts within a community (Abel 1974). I am referring not only to formal institutions but also informal, and I am agnostic about the source of such institutions – they may come from the state, from traditions, or from local processes of self-governance. My focus is on their quality. In what follows I explain why dispute institutions play a predominant role in driving civilians' preferences for new rule, and why they also impact their capacity for collective action. I then explain why high-quality dispute institutions deprive rebels from one of their most effective means to consolidate their power.

Civilians' Willingness to Resist

Civilians' preferences for rebelocracy are driven by the quality of their current structure of governance. In a community with high-quality institutions, people value their form of governance and have a strong preference for preserving it. Under low-quality institutions, on the other hand, it is less likely that the majority has a strong preference for preserving the current form of local governance. What is more, some community members may even desire change, given how illegitimate or ineffective they perceive institutions to be. Overall, only in communities with high-quality institutions do preferences against new rule tend to be strong and shared across individuals so that they are willing to resist collectively.

The quality of dispute institutions plays a predominant role in shaping civilians' preferences for their governing structure for two reasons. First, dispute institutions are essential for society to function – much more so than many other components of governance – and therefore impact civilians' daily lives tremendously. And second, the quality of dispute institutions embodies the quality of local governance more generally, as it often impacts central aspects of its social order.

Let me develop each of these points further. I start with the first, to wit, that dispute institutions are an essential building block of society. Conflict is inherent to human interaction. In any given community, economic, political, and social life is made up of numerous, small interactions that entail the possibility of a dispute – from lending money to neighbors to organizing childcare to doing business to hunting in groups. Dispute institutions are essential because they prevent conflict by decreasing uncertainty, reducing the number of available choices, and creating precedent; furthermore, when conflict erupts, dispute institutions are responsible for solving it (North 1990; Sweet 1999; Roberts 2013). When dispute institutions are of low quality, people struggle to form expectations about the actions of others, who may fail to honor agreements and follow the rules in the absence of a mechanism to enforce compliance. In such an environment, all kinds of interactions suffer, and conflict is likely to become widespread.[18]

Different literatures have recognized, both theoretically and empirically, the paramount importance of dispute institutions for society to function well. To start with, the existence of dispute adjudication institutions is ubiquitous in most societies, "stretch[ing] from song duels and witchcraft to moots and mediation to self-conscious therapy and hierarchical, professionalized courts" (Felstiner 1974:63), suggesting they are an essential component of societal life. Furthermore, dispute institutions are often considered one of the most important elements of governance because they help to preserve order (Benson 1989; Roberts 2013), and allow for coordination, which is, in turn, crucial for mutually beneficial economic, social, and political interaction (Levi 1989:41; Sweet 1999:149). Dispute institutions are also an important determinant of

---

[18] As Hart argues, perhaps only very small, cohesive communities can preserve order without dispute institutions, because they can rely on social control alone. For most societies, however, dispute institutions are an essential building block of social order. Hart, Herbert L. A., 1961. *The Concept of Law*. Oxford University Press. Cited by Benson (1989:4).

economic outcomes because they can decrease transaction costs[19] (North 1990; Coase 1998), and increase social capital (Knack & Keefer 1997; Adler & Kwon 2009; Dasgupta & Serageldin 2000; Ackerman 2002; Ostrom & Ahn 2003). In sum, dispute institutions are essential for people to live together peacefully and engage in mutually beneficial cooperation.

The second reason dispute institutions are a primary determinant of civilians' preferences for new rule is that they often impact the quality of local governance more generally. A system of dispute resolution that is impartial is likely to increase equality among community members in other domains of local life; in contrast, a community with dispute institutions that discriminate or are biased, for example, to favor elites or an ethnic majority, is likely to foster discrimination more broadly. Likewise, a community where dispute institutions are effective is a society that has managed to enforce rules pertaining to the protection of property rights, enforcement of contracts, and conflict resolution. It is likely that this community also has effective institutions in place to regulate other local matters. In fact, several studies of local governance in rural communities show that the persons, committees, or organizations responsible for adjudicating disputes are often also in charge of many other aspects of local governance and community organization, such as crime, disaster relief, and public goods provision, in contexts as varied as China (Huang 2008), India (AnanthPur 2004), Uganda (Wunsch & Ottemoeller 2004), Peru (Gittitz 2013), and Colombia (Sandoval Forero 2008).

Given that dispute institutions are a necessary enabler of peaceful and beneficial interaction among the members of a society, their quality is an important determinant of civilians' preferences for their governance structure. People living under dispute institutions that are illegitimate or ineffective are unlikely to have a strong desire to preserve – let alone defend – those institutions. On the other hand, members of a community with high-quality dispute institutions are unlikely to welcome the establishment of new rule.

Civilians' Ability to Resist Collectively

I have stressed that wanting to resist is not sufficient for collective resistance to materialize: civilians also have to be *able* to do so,

---

[19] Transaction costs are those costs associated with the definition, maintenance or transfer of property rights (Coase 1998).

which requires solving a collective action problem. The quality of dispute institutions plays a central role in fostering the community's capacity for collective action. Building on a broad literature, I argue that legitimate and effective dispute institutions foster communities' ability to launch and sustain collective action. Such institutions influence the extent to which community members rely on shared norms of behavior and conflict resolution schemes, as well as their capacity to coordinate, their interpersonal trust, reciprocity, and social cohesion. These factors have been repeatedly found to affect communities' capacity to initiate and sustain collective action (e.g., Ostrom 1990 1998; Putnam et al. 1993; Flora et al. 1997; Temple & Johnson 1998; Dasgupta & Serageldin 2000; Petersen 2001; Habyarimana et al. 2009). Communities that rely on legitimate and effective dispute institutions are therefore more likely to be not only willing to oppose rebelocracy, but also able to unite and do so.

Furthermore, communities that have legitimate and effective institutions to adjudicate disputes often rely on the same actors involved in adjudicating disputes to coordinate important collective action. As mentioned before, they often coordinate other important activities for the communities such as responses to disasters, communicating with state officials, organizing the provision of public goods, and coordinating assistance to community members in need. This provides an effective and legitimate preexisting leadership structure that can be repurposed for civilian resistance against armed actors.

Detailed evidence on a few cases supports these contentions. For example, high-quality local institutions seemingly allowed communities in Peru to resist the penetration of the rebel group Shining Path. In the region of Cajamarca, for instance, peasants had developed since the 1970s local committees called *rondas campesinas* to maintain order and adjudicate disputes. These committees gained massive recognition among peasants, were seen as legitimate, and were quite effective at controlling petty crime, transgressions to public order, and even corruption (Lair et al. 2000; Picolli 2009; Gittitz 2013). Several authors argue that the *rondas*, by allowing peasants to mobilize, impeded the rebel group's expansion in the region (Lair et al. 2000; Picolli 2009). Local institutions also seem to explain variation of Shining Path's success *within* other regions of Peru. In Ayacucho, Heilman (2010:195) found that Shining Path militants "fared best in those areas rife with sharp internal conflict, abusive authorities, and gamonalismo." Similarly, La Serna (2012) argued that in Ayacucho Shining Path met resistance in communities whose systems of justice were effective, and found acceptance where such systems were ineffective. Chapter 7 provides detailed evidence of the ways in which legitimate and effective institutions enabled collective action in Colombia.

Dispute Institutions as the Foundation of Rebelocracy

In addition to shaping civilians' desire and ability to resist rebelocracy, high-quality dispute institutions deprive armed actors of one of the most effective means to consolidate their power: creating new dispute institutions and becoming the de facto administrators of justice for local populations.

Despite being largely overlooked in social scientific research, work across disciplines has shown the importance of dispute institutions in how rulers come to power. Anthropological studies of law have found that "those in power seem invariably to have provided dispute institutions to their subjects" and, what is more, that "'courts' have historically played a central role in colonial expansion" (Roberts & Palmer 2005:222), whilst legal analysts have shown how "conquerors use courts as one of their many instruments for holding and controlling conquered territories" (Shapiro 1981).

The instrumental value of dispute institutions is threefold. First, they increase the ruler's social control over the population. According to Roberts and Palmer (2005:223), rulers seldom establish dispute institutions with the sole purpose of settling disputes: as "central was the ambition to remain in power; and certainly in much of the Medieval European world, for example, the principal means available to the monarchs for controlling their subjects was the judge." Second, they allow the ruler to enforce rules, which often entails not only applying existing regulations but also interpreting them and creating precedent, which contributes to the consolidation of the regulatory system that the ruler aims to establish. Finally, having the power to decide the proper resolution to a dispute – that is, arbitrating justice – can garner legitimacy. As Shapiro (1981:22) argues, "governing authorities seek to maintain or increase their legitimacy through the courts."[20]

Even though courts have been neglected in the study of state building, recent scholarship provides compelling evidence of the centrality of courts as a means to consolidate rule. In an analysis of legal norms,

---

[20] Quoted in Roberts and Palmer (2005:223).

Bilz (2007) argued it was crucial for European state building that citizens delegated to the state their right to seek revenge when harmed by others. In her impressive study of premodern state formation, Boucoyannis (2017) finds that the power of rulers to build integrated court structures shaped their extractive and hence their military capacity, rather than the reverse, as assumed by most of the literature.

Although studies of rebel behavior have overlooked the strategic value of rebel courts, case studies of insurgencies have highlighted their instrumental role for territorial expansion. In his study of the Taliban courts in Afghanistan, Baczko (2013:iv) argues that by creating a judicial system that goes "beyond individual conflicts and identity-based divisions" the group has been able to gain legitimacy in many areas of the country. Likewise, in his study of rebel courts by Colombian guerrillas, Aguilera (2013) argues that adjudicating disputes was highly effective for gaining popular legitimacy and consolidating territorial control.

Rebels quickly learn that gaps in dispute institutions offer a unique opportunity to penetrate a community, obtain information about its members and their networks, gain legitimacy, and control civilian behavior. Once the dispute institutions established by the armed group become the preferred mechanism for adjudicating disputes, the organization becomes a central figure in the community. Locals are likely to seek its help when involved in a conflict; to defer to its judgment in order to solve community problems; and to treat it as a ruler. The armed group can then easily expand its influence and power over other areas of community life. And if some civilians do not welcome such influence, it is usually too late – the group already has supporters, allies, and the means to identify and punish defectors. The possibility of coordination of collective action is largely reduced at that point, because coordinating opposition under the surveillance of informants is extremely hard. Thus there is an inverse relationship between rebel consolidation of social control and the likelihood of civilian resistance in war zones.

When the preexisting dispute institutions in the community are legitimate and effective, on the other hand, civilians are unlikely to turn to the armed actor to solve their disputes. By depriving combatants from the possibility of becoming the de facto judge, high-quality dispute institutions make it much more difficult for their organization to consolidate their power and, eventually, establish a full-fledged rebelocracy.

RELAXING ASSUMPTIONS

The previous sections relied on three non-trivial assumptions. First, armed groups require the same kind and level of civilian cooperation in all the territories they aim to control. Second, local capacity for collective action is static within each interaction between a community and an armed actor: living under the presence of combatants does not change it. Third, armed groups have perfect information about local institutions and, therefore, can accurately predict civilian resistance. In this section I discuss these assumptions and theorize the implications of relaxing them.

Armed Groups' Different Use of Local Territories

I have argued that armed actors strive for control over territory. Although I have so far assumed that all territories are equally valuable, this is certainly not the case. Armed groups use territories for different purposes, which are often deemed more or less valuable than others. Some places are targeted, for example, because they are easy to conquer, and simply add to the lot of territories under rebel control; others are deemed economically important; others function as safe havens, where leaders are well-protected, wounded combatants can be healed, and new recruits can be trained; and other places are used as corridors for smuggling weapons in, and illegal resources out.

These different uses of territory have important consequences on the type of civilian cooperation sought. Consider a region that is not located in a crucial area of the country. The group benefits from rebelocracy because it helps the group accumulate territorial control and provides valuable benefits. Yet, it can tolerate aliocracy too if the community is likely to resist; rebelocracy is not crucial in this territory because there are few, if any, secondary benefits to controlling the territory.

But this is not the case of highly strategic territories such as safe havens: an area in which high-level commanders hide requires extreme measures to be protected. Groups often secure such a haven by creating rings of security around the territory. Civilians closer to the core experience higher pressure to fully cooperate with the group. In this context, civilian autonomy cannot be tolerated. Hence, the armed actor does not adapt its behavior to avoid resistance: on the contrary, if resistance is expected, it may massively displace the population or even annihilate it so that it can then resettle strong supporters to the territory, or keep it solely for military

TABLE 3.2 *Social order in territories with different strategic value*

		Quality of preexisting local institutions	
		High	Low
Armed group's time horizon	Long	Low-value territory: Aliocracy High-value territory: Disorder	Rebelocracy
	Short	Disorder	

purposes. Communities with high-quality institutions are therefore likely to face disorder if their territory is highly valuable for the rebels, even if the group operates under a long time horizon.

An implication of this argument is that violence against communities with high-quality institutions should be higher in strategic territories, even when there is neither armed competition nor armed group indiscipline. Another implication is that resistance is more likely when the territory is highly strategic to the group, because this is when combatants are less likely to settle for aliocracy.

Table 3.2 shows how taking into account the value of territories changes the predictions of the theory.

Changes in Communities' Capacity for Collective Action

I have argued so far that civilian resistance is determined by the quality of preexisting dispute institutions in the community when an armed group enters it. I am therefore assuming that a community's capacity for collective action cannot change under the presence of an armed actor. Yet, it might be that the capacity for collective action is dynamic rather than static in conflict zones. If over time civilians resent rebelocracy and develop capacity for collective action, couldn't they resist?

One possibility could be that armed groups create legitimate and effective institutions that, over time, facilitate the community's capacity for collective action. Although this institutional change is possible, armed groups have little incentive to sponsor a fully civilian-led government that would allow for such change, precisely because autonomy reduces combatants' capacity to shape local dynamics in ways that favor their organization. Rebels may create community organizations and foster mobilization, but always under their wing – either formally or by operating as a shadow government. For this reason, the chances of increased collective action under rebelocracy are quite low.

Still, a community's capacity for collective action may increase during war for at least two reasons. First, recent studies have found that violence triggers pro-social behavior, trust, and social cohesion (Bellows & Miguel 2009; Blattman & Annan 2009; Bateson 2012; Gilligan et al. 2013). High levels of violence may therefore lead to a greater capacity for collective action. Yet, most of these studies focus on either peaceful settings or post-conflict contexts. We ignore whether violence leads to collective action within a context of war, and how lasting such effect might be if perpetrators are still around, and armed. Furthermore, other studies have found the opposite effect: violence destroys trust and collective action (Cassar et al. 2013; Rohner et al. 2013; Grosjean 2014). If violence can indeed increase a community's capacity for collective action, an observable implication would be that highly victimized communities are less likely to experience rebelocracy in the future, as they have a higher capacity to resist. To account for this possibility, we would need to theorize the conditions under which violence does foster collective action – an important question that I do not pursue in this book.

The second reason why collective action may increase during wartime is that policy interventions sometimes work. There are numerous projects implemented by national and international NGOs and donors that can impact the institutional capacity of local communities (Kaplan 2013b; Castañeda 2014). Although further research is needed to understand when and how this might happen, it is possible that both top-down and bottom-up processes foster collective action. I do not develop this hypothesis in this book.[21] However, insofar as NGOs or other organizations impact communities' capacity for collective action, the theory expects their effect on social order to be the same that high-quality local institutions would have.

Imperfect Information About Local Institutions

According to the theory, full-fledged collective resistance is an off-the-equilibrium path – that is, an outcome that we should not observe – unless the territory is highly valuable. Civilians *threaten* the

---

[21] See Kaplan (2013b) for a study of how collective action capacity to reduce violence may develop during wartime.

group with collective resistance, and combatants – anticipating the disastrous effects of resistance – give in. If armed groups have accurate expectations of collective resistance, they should avoid it and we should not observe it.

A central assumption in this logic is that armed groups have perfect information about the likelihood of civilian resistance. I argue that assuming perfect information makes sense because armed groups rely on different strategies to make correct inferences. However, sometimes they do form poor expectations and fail to properly tailor their ruling strategy, triggering resistance. In what follows I discuss some of the strategies that combatants rely on to gauge the likelihood of civilian resistance.

First, armed groups learn from their experience, that is, they engage in institutional learning. As with any organization, commanders sharpen their capacity to link their behaviors to outcomes; trial and error shows what works and what doesn't; and training allows lessons learned by different commanders to illuminate the work of others. Several accounts of how armed groups operate on the ground suggest that they make conscious changes in their war tactics as they learn.

Moroni et al. (1995), for example, argue that in the civil war in El Salvador "while in the early years there were differences in the [FMLN's] organization of areas of influence from faction to faction, by mid-war the shared experiences and increased cooperation among the factions was such that each organization distributed its force in a similar manner throughout each front." Fonseca (1982) also argues that the Sandinista National Liberation Front (FSLN) in Nicaragua underwent a profound transformation in the early 1970s, after evaluating its poor performance during the 1960s. Kerkvliet (1977:230) provides extensive evidence on the PKP's self-criticism in the Philippines for not taking into account the preferences of the masses as well as the know-how acquired by its rank and file members. Overall, armed groups learn how to wage their wars, and part of that learning entails deciding how to treat civilians in ways that would induce the kind of civilian behavior that they desire.

One of the ways in which this institutional learning plays out is the discovery of cues: certain attributes of a local community help rebels gauge the community's capability to resist. They may learn that tribes with deeply embedded traditions and no internal divisions are more likely to resist, as are communities living in areas where the state functions well and solves problems through accepted, institutionalized means. Likewise, they learn that divided communities are easier to penetrate.

To be sure, strong communities sometimes emerge in areas where poor institutions abound, like islands of good governance despite state failure and the winding down of tradition. These communities often surprise armed groups when they deny cooperation and oppose rebel (or paramilitary) rule. Armed groups are therefore incentivized to devote resources to accurately measuring the potential of local collective action prior to attempting to penetrate a community. One way to do this is to gather intelligence. Groups often infiltrate communities to get a sense of how organized they are and who is able to mobilize others. Chapters 6 and 7 describe this tactic.

Rebels also "test" communities' strength of collective action by using violence as a measurement tool: by threatening or harming the local leaders, the group assesses whether collective action will prevail without them. In some cases, targeting leaders effectively destroys the possibility of collective resistance and rebelocracy ends up being consolidated. Yet, sometimes such violence triggers fierce resistance: attacking the leaders does nothing more than fueling the desire, and the means, for opposition. In this case, combatants will hardly achieve more than minimal obedience under a tense social order of aliocracy; furthermore, they may end up losing territorial control altogether. For this reason, the group is better off finding out how capable the community is of resisting before targeting anyone.

CAVEATS

So far the theory has not explicitly dealt with three important factors that can be expected to impact social order: the state, the ideology of the armed group, and the structure of the community. In this section I discuss them.

The Role of the State

It might seem counterintuitive to sidestep the state in a theory that aims to explain the behavior of irregular forces that fight against, or in favor of, the state. Yet, I argue that once we disaggregate state presence it becomes evident that the role it plays is already captured by the theory.

First, state presence affects the likelihood that an armed group manages to establish permanent presence in a given territory. For guerrillas or paramilitaries to have an ongoing interaction with civilians, the state has to be unable or unwilling to limit their behavior. The places where the state maintains a monopoly over violence are not part of the universe of cases to which this theory applies. In this sense, the state works as a selection device of the cases that fall within the scope of this theory.

Let us now turn to the communities where non-state armed groups *are* permanently present. There are two mechanisms by which the state can shape social order. The first one is by creating armed competition. In communities where the military capacity of the state is relatively higher, the state's armed forces will be more likely to compete for control with the insurgents. According to the theory, armed competition leads rebels to operate under short time horizons, which makes them less willing (and less able) to fulfill any social contract with the population. Disorder is therefore more likely than either rebelocracy or aliocracy where the state's military capacity is high. The effect of the state's military presence is, therefore, captured by the theory as it takes armed competition into account.

The second mechanism by which the state can shape social order is through its effect on the community's preexisting institutions. Following the theory, if the state provides effective and legitimate institutions, specifically dispute institutions, civilians should have strong preferences for preserving state institutions and a high capacity to resist armed groups' ruling attempts. Aliocracy is therefore likely to emerge. On the contrary, where the state is perceived to be illegitimate or ineffective, it will be easier for combatants to establish rebelocracy.

In this way, what matters is not only whether the state is present in a given area, but also *how* it is present, and the ways in which the local community perceives and interacts with it. Hence, while Mampilly (2011) argues that rebel provision of services depends on previous state penetration, I argue that whether rebels govern, and how, is shaped by the type and quality of state presence: its military capacity influences whether order emerges; and its institutional quality shapes whether aliocracy or rebelocracy is consolidated.

In addition, the state shapes specific attributes of social order – rather than its type – by being one of the actors involved in its creation. In many civil wars, state agencies are present in areas where non-state armed groups are present; often, a formal local government functions in an area where rebelocracy has emerged. In these cases, public officials may be coerced or co-opted by the armed actor. Often, combatants allow certain provision of services by the state. By shaping the terms of civilian–combatant interactions, and the relations among civilians, the state is an important player. I provide evidence of the many ways in which the state operates across distinct forms of social order in Chapter 6. In Chapter 7, I provide evidence on its involvement with paramilitaries.

The Role of Ideology

The ideology of the armed actor – that is, its stated motivations for fighting – is not considered in the theory. I argue that whether armed groups create social order and of which type is essentially a strategic choice driven by the logic of irregular warfare. However, ideology does affect in many ways *how* social orders are built as well as some of their attributes. In particular, armed groups can anticipate more voluntary cooperation from civilians whose preferences are closer to the stated goals of the organization. This expectation can have implications on how both rebelocracy and aliocracy are built. For example, aliocracy in some cases entails a tense agreement between the community and the rebels, as locals would prefer the armed group not to be present at all and only submit to minimal governance out of necessity. However, when civilians' care much about rebels' goals, aliocracy may involve relatively high voluntary cooperation despite the group's limited involvement in regulating civilian affairs. I develop these implications in Chapter 6.

The ideology of the armed actor can also impact its use of violence even in the absence of a social contract. Hence, disorder might be more or less violent depending on ideology, among other factors.

I have also argued that civilians' acceptance of rebelocracy does not reflect ideological support for the armed group, and, as well, that resistance does not entail disagreement with their cause. In Chapter 6, I give several examples of communities that welcome rebelocracy by insurgents and, years later, do not oppose the rebelocracy of counter-insurgent paramilitaries either. Chapter 7 provides a detailed study of a community where the most committed communists led resistance to the intervention of (also communist) FARC insurgents.

Nevertheless, the ideology of the local population does impact the way in which rebelocracy and aliocracy are consolidated and how they function. I return to these issues in Chapter 6, where I address the specific ways in which civilians and combatants interact in the different paths that give rise to disorder, rebelocracy, and aliocracy.

Community Structure

For simplicity, the theory treats the community as an actor. I focus only on whether or not its local institutions are legitimate and effective, without considering the specific ways in which internal divisions and inequalities within the community might impact the interaction of its members with armed actors.

The low-quality institutions that facilitate rebelocracy can emerge as a result of very different processes. Consider a community ruled by a faction that has established highly effective (i.e., enforced) dispute institutions that, however, lack generalized legitimacy. This is often found in highly unequal communities. When rebels attempt to establish their dispute institutions, those oppressed will not chip in to oppose them; quite the contrary, they may even welcome rebel institutions. Now consider a community with no strong divisions, but where dispute institutions are incapable of successfully solving pressing issues; they are legitimate but ineffective, and therefore obsolete. People struggle with problems of contract enforcement and robberies. Support for the current governing institutions is weak, so they will not undertake risky resistance to new rebel institutions. Although the reasons that lead people to be dissatisfied with their current institutions are different in these two communities, in both cases their dissatisfaction will limit their desire and ability to resist new rule. Furthermore, some locals may even desire change, given how illegitimate or ineffective they perceive their institutions to be. It follows that low-quality dispute institutions are sufficient for rendering resistance unlikely, regardless of the specific form of institutional failure.

For this reason, even though most communities are made up of population groups that differ from each other in their interests, values, identities, power, and resources, insofar as these differences lead to strong divisions and conflict, the typology captures them: it is unlikely that communities with strong tensions between ethnic groups, elites and workers, or estate owners and peasants have high-quality dispute institutions. I contend, therefore, that this simple distinction is sufficient to explain the conditions under which aliocracy and rebelocracy emerge.

I do argue, however, that the specific internal divisions of a community shape the *process* by which social orders are built. In particular, armed actors are likely to select their strategies – in terms of whom to approach and how – by paying attention to the particular form of institutional failure in the community and the divisions that it leads to. I develop these ideas in Chapter 6, where I derive hypotheses on armed groups' strategies towards different sectors of local communities, in particular their use of violence and ideological mobilization.

CONCLUSION

This chapter presented a theory of social order in war zones. To this end, I theorized armed groups' preferences and choices, as well as civilians' responses to them. I argued that when operating under short time horizons, armed groups lack incentives to establish social contracts with local populations. Three factors tilt rebels' preferences in favor of the short run: armed competition with other organizations, internal indiscipline, and macro-changes in the war, like some peace negotiations. When any of these factors are present, rebels are likely to bring about disorder, rather than order.

When armed groups have long time horizons, on the other hand, they prefer order to disorder. Order makes the task of preserving territorial control – the primary goal of armed groups – easier, as it facilitates civilian obedience and voluntary cooperation.

I also argued that when bringing order about, rebels prefer rebelocracy to aliocracy because the former maximizes their odds of preserving territorial control as well as of seizing the byproducts of that control. Yet, rebels' preferences do not always prevail; civilians that can resist have bargaining power because they can undermine rebels' goals by threatening their territorial control. Armed groups are better off establishing a social order of aliocracy when they anticipate that civilians will be able to resist against rebelocracy.

Civilian resistance is, in turn, a function of the quality of preexisting local institutions, in particular institutions to settle disputes. When institutions are both legitimate and effective, people not only have a strong preference to oppose rebelocracy, but also the capacity for carrying out collective resistance. When local institutions are either illegitimate or ineffective, on the other hand, locals are less likely to both have strong preferences for their form of governance and a high capacity for collective action. Anticipating these outcomes, armed groups try to establish rebelocracy in communities with low-quality institutions, but limit their ruling aspirations to aliocracy in communities with high-quality institutions.

This chapter also relaxes the theories' assumption about the value of local territories, the sources of civilian collective action, and armed groups' expectations of civilian resistance. I concluded that armed groups are not likely to tolerate aliocracy in highly strategic territories, and are therefore likely to victimize communities capable of resisting. Additionally, civilian resistance may not be static; external factors such as the work of NGOs or even armed group rule could increase locals' capacity for resistance. Lastly, armed groups may not have perfect information on communities' capacity to resist; in these cases, violence against local leaders is often used as a "measurement" mechanism.

Finally, I briefly discussed how the presence of the state, community structure, and ideology can impact the emergence of social order in conflict zones. I argued that the theory captures the effect of two dimensions of state presence – institutional quality and armed competition. I also argued that ideology and community structure are likely to impact the process by which social orders are built, rather than their type.

To assess the explanatory power of this theory, we need empirical evidence on the emergence of disorder, aliocracy, and rebelocracy in war zones. We also need to explore the quality of local institutions in these areas; the internal organization of non-state armed groups; and the patterns of territorial disputes. Chapter 4 introduces the empirical approach of the book, and Chapters 5 through 8 test the different components of the theory.

4

Research Design

Studying War Zones in Colombia

What does order look like within a war zone? How do different forms of social order come about? Does social order vary across time and space following the logic outlined in Chapter 3? How do civilians influence the process by which new social orders are consolidated? Are their choices consistent with the argument advanced so far?

In the remaining chapters of the book, I test several implications of the theory of social order, its underlying mechanisms, and its microfoundations – that is, the assumptions regarding individual behavior on which the argument is built. I also analyze and illustrate empirically the process by which each social order is consolidated, and provide detailed evidence on how it functions. I employ an integrated research design that takes advantage of the specific strengths of different empirical methods and types of data. I rely on unique qualitative and quantitative evidence that I collected on communities, armed groups, and individuals in Colombian conflict zones in multiple waves of fieldwork conducted between 2004 and 2012.

In this chapter I explain the research design of the book, to wit, how I use different methods and types of evidence to assess the explanatory power of my theory. I start by discussing the virtues and limitations of focusing on Colombia. How much can we learn about the phenomenon of wartime social order by looking at Colombia? What are the limitations of focusing on one country alone? The second section provides an overview of the Colombian conflict. The third describes the non-state armed groups on which the empirical analysis focuses. The fourth section summarizes the empirical strategy that I use in the following chapters. The fifth section summarizes the empirical basis for the theory, specifying how the book substantiates its assumptions and hypotheses. The final section concludes.

A STUDY OF COLOMBIA: ADVANTAGES AND LIMITATIONS

The theory of social order developed in Chapter 3 applies to all armed groups fighting irregular civil wars that control at least some territory. Based on this condition, many civil wars would be adequate cases to test the theory. What can we learn by focusing on Colombia alone?

The Colombian conflict is well suited to the study of wartime social order for several reasons. First, different armed groups have operated throughout the country, including right-wing paramilitaries and left-wing guerrillas; this scenario allows for comparisons across different types of armed groups while controlling for national-level conditions. Furthermore, since these groups often operate in the same localities, the design allows for comparisons across groups while holding local-level conditions constant. Second, there is great variation across Colombian localities in their local institutions, state presence, geography, ethnicity, traditional political affiliations, economy, and history of prewar violence. This variation allows for studying the role of local characteristics in armed groups' strategies and civilian choice while controlling for national and regional factors, as well as the type of armed group involved.

Third, although the Colombian conflict has lasted for more than four decades, there is tremendous variation in its duration at the subnational level. While some communities have interacted with non-state armed groups for short periods of time (two years), others have done so for decades. Fourth, the demobilization program advanced by the Colombian government when this project started offered a unique opportunity to conduct extensive research with ex-combatants of both guerrilla and paramilitary groups who had given up their weapons within the last two years. This allowed for gathering micro-level data on a variety of aspects of armed groups and their behavior toward civilians – a possibility seldom available to researchers of civil wars.

Finally, the increased presence of state forces in many areas of the country since the mid-2000s made fieldwork possible in forty-five municipalities in twenty-two of the thirty-two Colombian departments (the equivalent of states in the United States). Although the war has not ended, security conditions have improved over the years, which made talking to civilians in remote areas feasible. People were often receptive to the goals of the project and shared their memories with great generosity, often with a decisive will – even a need – to reclaim their courage and agency in areas where armed groups had successfully dominated the territory for years.

To be sure, the Colombian civil war does have some particular attributes. To start with, it is a protracted conflict. While the average length of civil wars is four years (Acemoglu et al. 2010:664), the Colombian war has lasted more than forty. Yet, as I mentioned before, some armed groups emerged two or three decades after the initial onset, and the conflict expanded to many areas of the territory several years later. These patterns allow for variation in the amount of time that communities and armed groups have endured the war.

Another factor that is likely to have affected the Colombian civil war is the market of illicit drugs. Again, not all armed groups started participating in this trade at the same time nor to the same extent. Furthermore, the rebels operated for at least a decade without being involved in the drug trade. Yet, it is possible that the logic of social order that I observed in Colombia is in some way driven by the presence of valuable natural resources. Although this would limit the generalizability of the findings, many other wars have seen natural resources exploited by rebel groups, such as the wars in Afghanistan, Iraq, Syria, Sierra Leone, and Liberia.

Not all conflicts involve both insurgents and paramilitaries, nor are paramilitaries always as connected to state forces and politicians as they have been in Colombia. However, I do not believe that this feature of the Colombian conflict substantially impacts the dynamics in areas where paramilitaries have never been present – and I conducted fieldwork in many of them. Furthermore, the presence of pro-state militias or paramilitaries is much more common than is often assumed (Jentzsch et al. 2015). But insofar as the emergence and growth of paramilitary groups affected the ways in which different sectors of the state treated civilians and responded to rebel groups, and even the reactions of society to war-related phenomena, it is plausible that some of the dynamics that I study in Colombia are not comparable to cases where paramilitaries did not operate. This issue could only be addressed with new data on those cases.

Finally, the Colombian conflict is a class-based conflict, not an ethnic one. In addition, rebels have a center-seeking agenda, not a secessionist one. Although the logic of the argument should apply to cases of secessionist and ethnic wars – insofar as the armed actors fight as irregular forces and aim to control territory – it is possible that the findings do not travel to these types of conflicts. Only additional tests can show whether the theory explains the construction of social order in these situations.

Although including comparisons across countries would certainly increase the generalizability of the results, devoting all the time and energy that this project entailed to one country was worthwhile for many reasons. In terms of the quality of the empirical evidence, the project collected very detailed information on the ways in which armed groups arrive in local territories, approach local populations, and set up different forms of rule. It also generated unique data on how civilians influence the decisions of armed groups, including many more instances of civilians making demands of – and also resisting against – guerrillas and paramilitaries than most scholars would expect to find. To my knowledge, this is the first project to collect qualitative and quantitative evidence on wartime institutions from a representative, random sample of local communities. Such detailed evidence contributes to our understanding of the scope of variation of wartime social order on the ground. Given how difficult it is to collect data on a random sample of localities in conflict zones, a comparison across countries would have necessarily led to sacrificing the quality of the evidence. This is particularly true for this project because it aims to explain wartime dynamics at a very disaggregated unit of analysis: the local community. In the Colombian case, data at this level are almost non-existent; while data at the municipality level abound, data on local communities (i.e., the neighborhood, or village) are simply not available beyond the few pieces of data recently collected by the census. Most of the evidence for this project had to be collected from scratch. Gathering the different kinds of evidence envisioned in the research design, and implementing it in many areas of the country, required not only a deep understanding of the country's different regions but also very demanding fieldwork.

In addition, collecting very detailed evidence on how armed groups control territories and rule local populations – or fail to do so – was much more useful for testing my argument than having less detailed data on other conflicts at a more aggregate level. To start with, wartime social order does vary at the level of very small units, such as neighborhoods and villages. Had I focused on larger units to collect data on a higher number of countries, I would have run into the ecological fallacy problem – that is, inferring about localities based on aggregated data on districts or regions. Furthermore, by focusing on one country I was able to collect the necessary evidence to test several components of my theory, as opposed to only its central propositions, such as the underlying mechanisms and microfoundations. Finally, as I will explain later, I was able to collect the necessary empirical evidence to implement two different approaches to testing causal effects: first, that of establishing the effect of explanatory variables (or treatments) on a large sample of units while adopting a strategy to address potential confounders; and second, that of tracing processes to test mechanisms while limiting alternative explanations by focusing on a natural experiment.

Needless to say, replicating part or all of the components of this research design beyond Colombia would allow for testing the generalizability of the findings, and would teach us much more about the complex interactions between armed organizations and local actors.

Beyond methodological considerations, conducting this study on Colombia was worthwhile for its contribution to the construction of a memory of the Colombian war, the understanding of its dynamics, and debates about post-conflict policy. As the country prepares for the demobilization of the FARC and the implementation of the peace accords, we need more information about what happened during the war. This book joins the efforts made by many Colombian scholars, journalists, and organizations to document the ways in which the war unfolded, and how it impacted individuals, families, and communities. Furthermore, we need more tools to understand why the war evolved as it did, and what could be done in its aftermath to help the country recover. This study shows that communities experienced the armed conflict in very different ways, and that the legacies of war are not homogenous across space. Current debates about the challenges and opportunities for reconciliation, reconstruction, social justice, and peace need to take this variation into account (Arjona 2009). This is a time to reflect on how the war transformed the country not only through its direct effect on victims but also by transforming social order at the local level.

THE COLOMBIAN ARMED CONFLICT: AN OVERVIEW

Colombia is a country where rough terrain surrounds the main populated settlements in the Andes, the valleys, and the Caribbean coast. This topography, together with a history of fragmented state presence, has led to starkly unequal development in different regions of the country (González et al. 2001). Colombia has struggled with many forms of inequality since independence from Spanish rule in the early 1800s, as its citizens have had unequal access to political representation, land, income, and state services; in addition, they have not enjoyed equality before the law (González et al. 2001; Palacios 2003). While the population is ethnically diverse, with approximately 11 percent of the population being Afro-Colombian and 4 percent being indigenous, ethnicity has not been the main source of conflict, despite the disadvantages that ethnic minorities face.[1]

Violence has been intermittently present for most of the country's republican history, often led by the elite members of the traditional political parties – the Liberals and Conservatives. Partisan identities led thousands of Colombian peasants to fight against each other under the banner of their political parties in different civil wars. The ongoing conflict can be traced back to one of these wars, called *La Violencia* ("Violence"), which took place between 1948 and the early 1960s. During that period, fighting between members of the Liberal and Conservative parties caused the death of at least 134,00 people – with some estimating the death toll over 400,000 (Guzmán et al. 1986; Palacios & Safford 2002:632). Violence decreased following an agreement between the two parties to alternate power until 1974. In the postwar period, the government was unable to effectively address pressing problems of inequality, rural development, and access to land. Students, peasants, and workers of different sectors engaged in strikes, protests, and other forms of mobilization throughout the country (Archila 1997: 192–7). State repression was common, and rural unrest was often quelled with extreme violence (ibid.:205).

In this context, several guerrilla groups with a communist agenda emerged, including the FARC, the National Liberation Army (ELN), the Popular Liberation Army (EPL), and the April 19 Movement (M19). For decades these groups were active only in a few peripheral areas of the country, and their military capacity was low. In the mid-1970s, however, many of these groups – with the exception of the ELN (Aguilera 2006:255)[2] – began using illicit drugs as a way to finance their operations; this allowed them to develop their military capacity and expand to new territories. They also used kidnapping and extortion as a means to raise additional funds, and targeted territories with natural resources like oil in order to tax companies and extract resources to sell in the black market.[3] Several studies suggest that while the FARC expanded within marginal

---

[1] The data are based on the 2005 census.
[2] The ELN did profit from drug trafficking much later – in the first decade of the twenty-first century (Bonilla 2014).
[3] See for example Aguilera (2006); Gutiérrez Sanín (2006); Pizarro (2006).

areas in the 1970s and mid-1980s, it turned to more integrated and economically developed regions in the 1990s (Vélez 1999; Bottia 2003). The ELN, on the other hand, was almost extinguished in the 1980s, but its successful strategy of extorting multinational companies, and an internal reorganization, allowed it to recover and expand (Aguilera 2006).

The accelerated expansion of the guerrillas and their funding techniques had a direct impact on the everyday lives of the country's regional and local elites, who were mainly landowners, cattle farmers, and emerald traders. As a result, they began to form paramilitary groups. In addition to the support given by traditional elites, these groups were backed (and on occasion created) by drug lords who were emerging as local elites (Cubides 1999). Following Romero (2003:18), the peace negotiation attempted by President Betancourt (1982–1986) with different guerrilla groups was also an important catalyst for the formation of paramilitary groups, as it implied a potential redefining of the political order that would favor the guerrillas and their sympathizers; this new order, in turn, entailed a risk and a threat to the preeminence of the regional power equilibria.

While a few paramilitary organizations were genuinely self-defense groups formed by peasants to confront the guerrillas, most of them quickly became mobile, switched from defense to offense, and sought to expand into new territories (Safford & Palacios 2002). Their operations were financed by voluntary and forced contributions from landlords and firms, as well as income derived from drug trafficking. In their fight against the guerrillas, the Colombian armed forces tolerated and abetted paramilitary groups in different areas of the country (HRW 2000; Richani 2013).

The peace talks that President Betancourt launched with several guerrilla groups in the 1980s, including the FARC, EPL, M19, and a faction of the ELN, fell apart after a few years. As part of the process, in 1985 the political party Patriotic Union (Unión Patriótica, UP) was created as a political vehicle for the guerrillas to participate in democratic politics. With the support of the Colombian Communist Party (PCC), the UP achieved significant electoral success, winning seats in the national congress, state assemblies, and municipal councils. In the presidential elections of 1986, the UP candidate received the highest support that the Left had ever obtained in a presidential election. Threatened by this success, paramilitary groups, drug traffickers, and state forces participated in a massive campaign to exterminate the UP. More than 3,000 UP militants were killed, including 2 presidential candidates and 13 members of Parliament (Dudley 2004). The violent persecution of UP members led the FARC to grow skeptic about the possibility of transitioning into a political party.

In 1985, the M19 took over the Palace of Justice, which served as the Supreme Court's headquarters in Bogotá. The military responded with a raid, and the siege ended with twelve magistrates dead, as well as nearly 100 others, including hostages, soldiers, and guerrilla members. Eleven persons were declared disappeared, some of whom have been found in common graves in recent years (*El Tiempo* 2015a). This bloody attack also harmed the prospects for a negotiated peace.

In the late 1980s, the intensity of the armed conflict and the levels of violence began to increase at unprecedented rates, with clashes among guerrillas, paramilitaries, and the Colombian armed forces growing more frequent and deadly, while the total number of attacks by armed groups (including homicides, massacres, kidnappings, attacks to infrastructure, sabotage of political events, and hijacking) increased steadily. The FARC emerged as the most powerful guerrilla group, followed by the ELN. Smaller guerrilla groups, including the EPL and the M19, negotiated their demobilization with the government of President Barco in 1990.

The 1990s were characterized by an unprecedented territorial expansion of the strongest guerrilla groups as well as of the paramilitaries. While the FARC had eight fronts in 1975, they had sixty-five in 1995. In the same period, the ELN moved from six to sixty-five fronts. The paramilitaries grew from around 4,000 members in 1997 to approximately 12,200 in 2002 (Echandía 2013:30). In 1997, several paramilitary groups formed an umbrella organization called the United Self-Defense Forces of Colombia (AUC). Although it aimed to build a unified organization with a clear leadership, it remained a conglomerate of units that responded to their own commanders, and with distinct internal structures.

By 2002, about half of the municipalities of the country registered the presence of an illegal actor (Sánchez and Chacón 2006:352). This expansion translated into very high levels of violence, a loss of state control over large portions of the country, and a general feeling of insecurity among the population. Human rights abuses by all armed groups, including the state forces, became more frequent (Pécaut 1999).

Within this context, President Andres Pastrana (1998–2002) attempted a peace negotiation with the FARC for which a large zone in the south of the country – the size of Switzerland – was demilitarized.

The negotiation failed, and when in 2002 the process was closed, there were strong signs that the FARC had not really intended to negotiate peace (Aguilera 2013:210–212) and had in fact used the demilitarized zone to strengthen its organization, train recruits, and profit from the illegal-drugs industry.

Alvaro Uribe won the presidential elections in 2002 with a proposal to crush the guerrillas by military means. From 2002 on, the state saw a steady recovery of areas that had been under guerrilla control, and violence decreased by most counts (Echandía 2008). Certain regions of the country, however, continued to exhibit high levels of violence, especially in the west and near the border with Venezuela. At the same time, denunciations of human rights abuses by the state became more frequent (e.g., *Noche y Niebla* 2008a, 2008b, 2009). Harassment of legal opposition, including journalists, unionists, and human rights organizations became widespread, and even public servants – like judges of the high courts – were subjected to illegal surveillance (Romero 2009; El Espectador 2015). The army was also involved in systematic extrajudicial killings (HRW 2015); Colombia's Prosecutor's Office has identified more than 4,000 victims of what came to be known as "false positives" – the killing of innocent civilians by members of the army to report them as guerrilla members killed in combat (*El Tiempo* 2015b).

In 2006, the infamous "*parapolitics* scandal" revealed that politicians had colluded with paramilitary groups throughout the country to get elected (Romero & Valencia 2007; López 2010). Paramilitaries wanted to "institutionalize and extend their illegal project throughout the country and influence directly on the passing of laws"; politicians, on the other hand, wanted to rely on paramilitary violence and coercion against voters and candidates of the opposition "in order to clear the way to being elected as members of the Senate or the House of Representatives" (Verdad Abierta 2013). By 2012, 200 members of congress and 470 public servants nationwide had been implicated in this scandal (Verdad Abierta 2012). While the judicial branch continues to investigate the links between many politicians and paramilitary groups, relatives and political allies of those who have been indicted continue to run for office and get elected (*El Tiempo* 2010; Avila 2014).

A parallel scandal, known as "*Farc-politics*," revealed links between the FARC and politicians. As with the *parapolitics* scandal, the investigations have implicated both local politicians and members of congress, but on a much lower scale. While different guerrillas – not just the FARC – have indeed co-opted local politics in many municipalities, their influence in national or departmental elections has not been major (Avila 2012). Indeed, there have been only a few judicial investigations against politicians for their ties with the FARC.

Under Uribe's presidency, the government launched a voluntary demobilization program in 2002 that by October 2009 had attracted more than 20,000 former combatants of guerrilla and paramilitary groups.[4] The government also implemented a peace agreement with paramilitary leaders that resulted in the demobilization of around 30,000 individuals who claimed to be members of various groups under the AUC. This demobilization process has been intensely debated. Some believe it was a key determinant of the steady decrease in violence that the country has experienced since 2002 (Restrepo and Spagat 2005). Yet, others assert that the inner political structure of the paramilitaries remained intact, which allowed them to continue and expand their project of penetrating the state (HRW 2005; López 2010). In addition, new small armies – known as emerging criminal bands (BACRIM) or neo-paramilitaries – were formed, often recruiting demobilized paramilitary fighters. These groups do not necessarily have a counterinsurgent agenda; they seek to exploit illegal markets, especially those of illicit drugs (López 2010). In the last few years, the BACRIM have been among the principal perpetrators of violence in the country, surpassing both the guerrillas and paramilitaries (CNAI 2009; *Semana* 2013).

After Uribe's two terms in office, President Juan Manuel Santos was elected in 2010. Soon after, he initiated peace talks with the FARC. Despite several obstacles and the firm opposition of an important sector of the population and of the political elite – including former president Uribe and his followers – a peace agreement was scheduled to be signed in early 2016, though its outcome remained unknown at the time of writing. The government also appeared on the precipice of initiating peace talks with the ELN. The success of both efforts would mark the end of almost fifty years of insurgency in Colombia.

The signing of the peace agreement, however, will not be enough to bring peace to the country. According to the Institute for the Study of Development and Peace (INDEPAZ), the neo-paramilitaries (or BACRIM or narco-paramilitaries, as they are also called) are present in 338 municipalities – a third of the country. What is more, at least 298 of these municipalities have endured the continuous presence of these groups for at least six years

---

[4] Public data from Colombia's office for disarmament, demobilization, and reintegration are available at www.reintegracion.gov.co/Es/proceso_ddr/Paginas/balance.aspx.

(Verdad Abierta 2015). Although these numbers surpass the official estimates, the latter do not paint a reassuring picture either: between 2014 and 2015, the Ombudsman's Office identified 171 municipalities in which civilians were at risk due to the presence of these groups (ibid.). The growth of neo-paramilitary groups is worrisome not only because they are devoted to profiting from illicit activities like drug trafficking and illegal mining (McDermott 2014), but also because they have opposed the peace process, targeted human rights activists, and fought against land restitution (Human Rights Watch 2013). Their expansion poses a real threat to the consolidation of peace in the country.

Although estimating the societal costs of civil war is always difficult – even counting fatal victims is quite challenging (Krüger et al. 2013) – the Colombian civil war has been undoubtedly bloody and destructive. According to Colombia's Center for Memory (CNMH 2013), between 1985 and 2012 – the last twenty-seven years of an almost fifty-year long conflict – the war led to more than 150,000 victims of selective killings and 11,000 victims of massacres; almost six million forcedly displaced persons; more than 10,000 victims of landmines; almost 2,000 victims of sexual violence; 25,000 forced disappearances; and almost 30,000 victims of kidnapping. In a country of about forty-five million people, these numbers show that the conflict has shaken society and has left many wounds behind.

THE FARC, THE ELN, AND THE PARAMILITARIES

As the previous section shows, Colombia has seen the formation of many insurgent and counterinsurgent groups. Some have been militarily defeated, others have surrendered their arms, and some are still fighting. This book presents evidence on many of these groups – more than fifteen fronts of five different guerrilla groups, and fourteen paramilitary blocs (some of which belonged to the AUC umbrella organization, and some which did not). Tables 4.1 and 4.2 list the guerrilla and paramilitary groups that are discussed in the next chapters.

Instead of providing a detailed account of every group that features in the empirical evidence, I describe the two guerrilla groups that are most prevalent: the FARC and the ELN. I do not do the same for each paramilitary group, because the next chapters provide evidence on many of them; rather, I provide a general description of paramilitary groups, pointing out some of the most important differences between them.

TABLE 4.1 *Guerrilla groups included in the empirical evidence*

Guerrillas (English)	Guerrillas (Spanish)
ELN (National Liberation Army)	Ejército de Liberación Nacional
EPL (Popular Liberation Army)	Ejército Popular de Liberación
ERP (People's Revolutionary Army)	Ejército Revolucionario del Pueblo
FARC (Revolutionary Armed Forces of Colombia)	Fuerzas Armadas Revolucionarias de Colombia
M19 (April 19 Movement)	Movimiento 19 de Abril

TABLE 4.2 *Paramilitary groups included in the empirical evidence*

Paramilitaries	Paramilitaries (Spanish)	Umbrella Organization[1]
Peasant Self-defense Forces of Casanare	Autodefensas Campesinas de Casanare	
The Carranceros (AKA Macetos)	Los Carranceros (AKA Macetos)	Alianza Oriente
Self-defense Peasant Forces of Meta and Vichada[2]	ACMV Autodefensas Campesinas del Meta y Vichada	
Bananero Bloc	Bloque Bananero	
Calima Bloc	Bloque Calima	
Catatumbo Bloc	Bloque Catatumbo	AUC, Autodefensas Campesinas de Córdoba y Urabá (ACCU)
Cordoba Bloc	Bloque Cordoba	
Metro Bloc	Bloque Metro	
Mineros Bloc	Bloque Mineros	
Mojana Bloc	Bloque Mojana	
Centauros Bloc	Bloque Centauros	
Martyrs of Guatica Front	Frente Mártires de Guática	Autodefensas Campesinas del Magdalena Medio (ACMM)
Winners of Arauca	Vencedores de Arauca	Bloque Central Bolívar
The Buitrageños	Los Buitrageños	None

[1] Some of the groups that belonged to the AUC were part of a regional alliance as well.
[2] The ACMV emerged from Los Carranceros and at some point did belong to the AUC. However, at the time of its demobilization in 2005, it was not part of it. See "Autodefensas Campesinas de Meta y Vichada", Verdad Abierta, www.verdadabierta.com/justicia-y-paz/831-autodefensas-del-meta-y-vichada [accessed on September 15, 2015]. The Bloque Central Bolivar was also part of the AUC until 2002. See "Los Tentáculos del Bloque Central Bolívar", Verdad Abierta, http://www.verdadabierta.com/bloques-de-la-auc/2939-los-tentaculos-del-bloque-central-bolivar [accessed on September 15, 2015].

Origins and Goals

The origins of the FARC and the ELN are still subject to debate. Most authors trace them back to *La Violencia,* which, as mentioned before, took place between the late 1940s and the 1960s. The ELN was formed in 1963 by liberal guerrilla fighters who were involved in *La Violencia,* along with politically disenchanted university students and recent graduates. It was directly supported by the Castro regime in Cuba, where many of its leaders were trained. The stated goal of the group was to improve the conditions of rural peasants (Offstein 2003).

The FARC were officially founded in 1966, although the group began operations in 1964. Formed by peasants, FARC originated as self-defense guerrilla groups that fought during *La Violencia.* Their move from a defensive to an offensive guerrilla force was triggered by a large military operation against their agrarian movement – an operation known as the *Attack on Marquetalia* (Medina Gallego 2009:61).

From their early years, the FARC were closely linked to the Colombian Communist Party, through which they received organizational and financial support from the Soviet Union. Most of the early members of the FARC were rural peasants. The stated goal of the group was to seize power in order to transform the structures of the state, not only to defend the interests of the peasantry but also to establish a new system based on the principle of equality in income distribution (Ferro & Uribe 2002). The total number of FARC combatants was estimated to be between 17,000 and 22,000 prior to the government's offensive in the early 2000s, and about 15,000 since 2006 (Gutiérrez 2008:12). The ELN, on the other hand, had around 5,000 combatants at the start of the century, and probably around 2,500 by 2006 (ibid.).

As mentioned before, several paramilitary groups emerged in different areas of the country in the 1980s as a reaction to the violence perpetrated by the guerrillas and to oppose the potential changes that the peace process that was being negotiated (and which ultimately failed) would bring about (Romero 2003). The stated goal of the paramilitaries was to do what the state was incapable of: defending their properties and their lives. In other words, these organizations claimed to be self-defense groups that also defended the state and its institutions. But several scholars point to the defense of local power and privileges as equally important goals (Cubides 1999; Romero 2003). In addition, their ties to drug traffickers are undeniable (Richani 2013). It is also clear that their goals quickly changed from mere defense to expansion (Reyes 1991; Palacios & Safford 2002).

Estimates of the total number of paramilitary combatants vary, especially after many more ex-fighters than expected joined the collective demobilization of different paramilitary groups. While estimates of the number of members that these groups had prior to the demobilization program range from 13,000 (Sánchez & Chacón 2006) to 15,000 (Gutiérrez 2008), the total number of officially admitted fighters into the governmental demobilization program is above 30,000, which suggests that many unarmed persons were included in the list of "beneficiaries" of the program.

Organizational Structure

Both the FARC and the ELN are insurgent guerrilla armies. They have a formal structure with well-defined hierarchies and rules. Both are organized in different blocs and fronts in many areas of the country. The commander of each front is somewhat autonomous and is usually responsible for financing the operations of his or her own group, but has to follow the guidelines set by the national leaders. Both groups operate mostly in rural areas, but they also have urban militias that undertake political and military tasks in towns and cities. In general, the ELN was thought to be stronger than the FARC in urban areas – at least until the 1990s.

In all dimensions, the guerrillas seem to be more demanding and require greater sacrifices from their fighters than do the paramilitaries (Ferro & Uribe 2002; Gutiérrez 2004; Arjona & Kalyvas 2008). Neither the FARC nor the ELN pay salaries or any other material reward to their combatants; the FARC requires a life-time commitment and only in rare occasions allows combatants to leave the group, usually reacting to defection with severe punishments including death; they ensure contact with friends and family is kept to a minimum by screening mail and allowing combatants to make only a few visits to their hometowns. Also, guerrilla fighters usually move around frequently, which makes it difficult for individual combatants to establish personal ties with civilians (Gutierrez 2008).

The guerrilla groups also seem to interfere quite significantly in the private lives of their members (Ferro & Uribe 2002; Gutiérrez 2004; Arjona & Kalyvas 2008). The FARC and the ELN seem to plan many details of the daily lives of their fighters, including determining whether couples remain together. They also regularly have sessions of ideological training – in some cases daily (Arjona & Kalyvas 2008). The FARC even decides if women can have children, and force some pregnant women to have an abortion (ibid.).

Both the FARC and the ELN seem to regulate combatants' conduct towards civilians, often punishing the use of violence by their fighters when not ordered by their commanders, as well as abuses such as robberies and rape (Arjona & Kalyvas 2008). Rules on internal behavior are also strict. Minor misbehaviors are severely punished and serious offenses usually lead to a summary execution. For example, most ex-guerrillas report that raping female combatants was absolutely prohibited and punished with death (ibid.).

Internal discipline regarding finances in particular has been, in most FARC and ELN units, highly successful. Both groups have relied on kidnapping and extortion as a source of income, and the FARC derive large profits from the illegal-drugs market.[5] Despite the incentives for combatants to appropriate these resources, both organizations are highly effective at controlling their management. Several accounts suggest that the FARC try to preserve strict discipline, purging its own ranks when misbehaviors are common (e.g., Verdad Abierta 2009b). However, there is variation across units within the FARC and the ELN, as well as over time, in their levels of discipline. For example, sometimes the unruly character of a commander has substantial influence on the internal norms of the unit it commands.

Like the guerrillas, the paramilitaries were also structured in an irregular army-like fashion; however, their internal structure was not as formal and centralized throughout the country as that of the guerrillas. In fact, at the beginning of the conflict the different paramilitary organizations that operated around the country were not formally connected with one other, and each operated under its own rules. In 1997 Carlos Castaño, the leader of the Peasant Self-defense Forces of Córdoba and Urabá (ACCU), one of the most powerful paramilitary groups, organized several paramilitary factions throughout the country into the AUC (United Self-Defense Forces of Colombia). The AUC resembled a confederation more than a cohesive, unified organization. It lacked a set of well-defined rules that regulated the structure of the groups, their mechanisms of internal control, and their methods of operation.

---

[5] The ELN, on the other hand, did not give up its rule against financing its operations with drug money (Aguilera 2006:211–212) until recently (Bonilla 2014).

Several authors argue that, at the beginning, the paramilitaries victimized vast numbers of civilians indiscriminately. Over time, however, they learned that they needed civilian support and apparently turned to more selective violence (Romero 2003). Their expansion was nonetheless highly violent, with brutal massacres and days-long attacks on local communities, where they tortured, killed, and raped (e.g., CNRR 2009a, 2009b). They successfully gained control of several areas of the country that had been strongholds of the guerrillas for many years. In some areas, competition for control was intense for a long period of time.

Regarding internal discipline, the paramilitaries were less strict than the guerrilla groups. They usually offered monthly payments to their recruits (some estimate it around 200 dollars per month); they allowed combatants to take some time off; and they usually allowed their combatants to stay in their hometowns, which meant family and other networks could be preserved. Becoming a paramilitary fighter did not require the life-long pledge guerrilla groups demanded and, in principle, any combatant could ask for full dismissal (yet, in reality this request was sometimes refused). The paramilitaries intruded less into the private lives of their combatants than the guerillas, for instance keeping away from decisions regarding couples and children (Gutiérrez 2008).

Several authors have found that opportunities for individual enrichment existed within the paramilitaries (Romero 2003; Gutiérrez 2008). Combatants of these groups had a greater opportunity to appropriate resources derived from extortion or drug trafficking than guerrilla combatants did. This was not necessarily a problem of indiscipline, as individual enrichment seemed to be accepted by the leadership of these organizations (Gutierrez 2008). However, when combatants relied on unauthorized means for private gain, paramilitary commanders often used exemplary punishments – including collective purges, and even killing entire units (Verdad Abierta 2008, 2010a).

There were, nevertheless, some important differences among the various paramilitary groups. A few blocs were known for being more like a private army at the service of drug trafficking than a counterinsurgent force. For example, in the department of Casanare, "the paramilitary groups, supposedly created to combat the guerrilla, killed each other fighting for control over drug trafficking, oil royalties, and the thousands of hectares of land" of the department (Verdad Abierta 2009a). Likewise, some groups exhibited less disciplined behavior than others. This was particularly the case of units that operated far away from where they were recruited and consolidated, like the Catatumbo Bloc.[6]

EMPIRICAL STRATEGY

The research design of this book aims to test the theory's hypotheses about the causes of variation in social order and about causal mechanisms (*how* the main explanatory variables impact social order), as well as its microfoundations (the underlying assumptions about individual behavior). In addition, the book aims to offer detailed descriptive evidence on a phenomenon about which we know very little – wartime social order. How do disorder, aliocracy, and rebelocracy emerge? How do they function? What are the specific strategies that armed groups adopt towards civilians? How do local communities respond?

To achieve these different goals, I exploit the advantages of different methods and types of evidence that complement each other. To test hypotheses on the determinants of social order, I rely on statistical analysis (using multilevel models) of a dataset on more than one hundred community–armed group pairs or dyads, which interacted for at least six months. To address potential endogeneity due to the potentially omitted variables, I use instrumental variables.

To test hypotheses on the underlying mechanisms, I use statistical analysis of the data on community–armed group dyads, as well as process tracing on a quasi-natural experiment. I also illustrate some of the mechanisms with qualitative and quantitative evidence on communities, armed groups, and individuals.

To test the microfoundations, I use statistical analysis of data on communities, civilians and combatants. I also illustrate some of the microfoundations with qualitative evidence on civilian and combatant behavior coming from interviews, surveys, and focus groups.

In addition to drawing causal inferences on the development of wartime social order using the aforementioned methods, *describing* wartime social order is a distinctive goal of the research design. In this sense, the data-collection component of the project is important in and of itself for several reasons. First, to my knowledge, this is the

---

[6] This bloc was formed in Cordoba (on the Caribbean coast, in the west of the country) and operated in the east, near the Venezuelan border.

Empirical Strategy

first study to offer systematic data on the nonviolent behaviors of armed groups at the local level. What do guerrillas and combatants do beyond killing, massacring, and displacing? How do these behaviors vary across armed actors as well as within them? Accordingly, descriptions of how communities are transformed by the presence of these groups tend to focus on violence, overlooking other important dimensions: How do formal and informal institutions change? What forms do civilian–combatant relations take? How does local governance change in wartime?

The evidence collected for this project provides a detailed account of life in war zones across Colombia regarding guerrilla and paramilitary behavior, civilian choice, and local governance. The data show great variation across local communities as well as clear patterns in the behavior of both civilians and combatants. The evidence also suggests that the nonviolent behaviors of armed groups are an essential component of their strategy, and stresses the importance of theorizing and researching civilian–combatant relations in different contexts. Finally, the evidence also shows that civilians bargain with, make demands of, and resist armed actors more often than expected.

A second reason why the empirical component of this book is significant is that, in focusing on the history of specific communities from peacetime to their wartime experiences, the data speak to the more general question of how order is created. In this sense, this research provides a micro-level take on how aspiring rulers come to power, as well as on the role that communities and individuals play in that process. In order to provide a rich description of wartime social order, I offer a stylized view of the process by which each form of order emerges. I then discuss how armed actors arrive, whom they approach and how, the specific ways in which combatants intervene in local affairs, and how civilians respond.

Table 4.3 summarizes the components of the research design. In what follows, I explain how each of these components aims to achieve a specific goal or set of goals.

Chapter 5: Identifying the Causal Effect of the Explanatory Variables on Social Order

The goal of this component of the research design is to identify the causal effect of my explanatory variables on the type of social order that emerges in a given time and location. Do armed competition and indiscipline lead

TABLE 4.3 *Research design components*

Chapter	Goal	Empirical Strategy
5	Identify the causal effect of the explanatory variables on wartime social order	Statistical analysis of a longitudinal dataset on wartime social order at the local level, using instrumental variables
6	Describe and analyze the process by which distinct forms of social orders are built in war zones, and illustrate the mechanisms and microfoundations	Analysis of qualitative and quantitative evidence on the history of interaction between local communities and armed groups
7	Identify the causal process linking local institutions and social order at the local level	Process tracing of three local communities exploiting a random shock on local institutions (a process-driven natural experiment)
8	Test the microfoundations of the theory: do civilians cooperate more under rebelocracy than under other forms of social order?	Statistical analysis of data on community–armed group dyads and descriptive individual-level data on both joiners and non-joiners of guerrilla and paramilitary groups

to disorder? Are communities with high-quality local institutions more likely to live under aliocracy than rebelocracy? Is aliocracy less likely to emerge in highly strategic territories?

I rely on an original dataset on a random sample of local communities where guerrillas, paramilitaries, or both, have been present. I built this dataset using an innovative approach that combined (1) short surveys in order to select the sample, where I used vignettes to measure social order; (2) memory workshops to build timelines of the history of each community as well as to create institutional biographies (which describe variation in institutions over time); and (3) long structured interviews or surveys to collect detailed, quantitative and qualitative evidence on the interaction between armed actors and local communities. I also rely on primary and secondary sources. The dataset includes information on 124 community–armed group dyads, over time. These dyads are composed of seventy-four localities and thirty-eight fronts or blocs of guerrilla and paramilitary groups, which interacted for at least six continuous months between 1970 and 2012. I provide a detailed description of this fieldwork in Chapter 5 and in Appendix 1.

Empirical Strategy

Using multilevel models, I test the effect of the independent variables on the emergence of disorder, aliocracy, and rebelocracry in a given community–armed group dyad at a particular time. The design tries to isolate the effect of the explanatory variables on social order in three ways. First, by design I compare communities that shared many attributes, including climate, local government, economy (except when economic activities vary within the municipality), and previous patterns of violence and migration. Second, to test the effect of time-varying variables I exploit the clustered structure of the data and use the deviation from the cluster mean as an instrument. And third, to test the effect of the quality of preexisting institutions – a time invariant variable – I use the potential effect of indigenous migration to the communities as an instrumental variable. In Chapter 5, I also test the mechanism underlying the effect of the quality of preexisting dispute institutions on social order, to wit, its effect on collective resistance.

Chapter 6: The Process of Creating Social Order

This chapter explores theoretically and empirically several aspects of the process by which different forms of social order are consolidated. In so doing, it undertakes several tasks: (1) it theorizes the strategies that armed actors adopt toward civilians, their treatment of different population groups within the community, and civilians' influence on armed groups' strategies; (2) it provides evidence that illustrates the mechanisms by which the independent variables affect the form of social order that emerges in a given community; (3) it elucidates the microfoundations by offering evidence on civilians' and combatants' behavior as well as their own recollections of why they behaved as they did; and (4) it provides a rich description of the ways in which disorder, aliocracy, and rebelocracy operate, impacting the modes of being and relating in the locality.

The empirical evidence presented in this chapter comes from different sources. First, I rely on testimonies and detailed descriptions of many aspects of civilian–combatant relations and the ensuing social orders. These testimonies were collected in almost 125 communities located in 43 municipalities, in 22 of the 32 departments of the country. Some testimonies come from 170 in-depth interviews with civilians, former combatants, NGO staff, and public officials; some evidence comes from the memory workshops described above; others come from interviews conducted in a random sample of 15 municipalities in 2006.

Second, I rely on the quantitative data on community–armed group dyads mentioned before, which contains detailed information on armed groups' strategies towards civilians at different stages of their interaction with them, civilian resistance, and the ensuing institutions. And third, I rely on a survey with more than 800 former members of guerrilla and paramilitary groups, as well as about 500 civilians. I come back to this survey in the next section of this chapter. The sources and data-gathering methods are described in Chapters 5 and 6. Additional details are given in Appendix 1.

Chapter 7: A Process-driven Natural Experiment

Although Chapter 5 tests the central implications of the theory by trying to isolate the causal effect of the explanatory variables on the type of social order that emerges, it does not offer a powerful test of the underlying mechanisms. It only shows that both high-quality preexisting dispute institutions and instances of collective resistance tend to lead to aliocracy, but it cannot show *how*. Chapter 6 offers a partial corrective by providing different pieces of evidence to illustrate how different forms of social order are built, and how the different explanatory variables come into play. However, that chapter focuses on many cases, making it impossible to provide a rigorous test of the mechanisms by which the explanatory variables shape armed groups' and civilians' decision-making. A focus on mechanisms is particularly needed in the study of civil war, where, as Lyall (2014:188) notes, "both crossnational and microlevel studies have increasingly adopted research designs built to measure the direction and magnitude of the relationship between independent variables and outcomes rather than the mechanisms that underpin this relationship."

Chapter 7 aims to identify the most complex causal process – and the most novel one – in the theory, to wit, the effect of preexisting local institutions on wartime social order. In order to do so, I combine the advantages of two methodologies: natural experiments and process tracing. Natural (or quasi-natural) experiments are research designs where units are assigned to treatment randomly (or as-if-randomly). Given random assignment, differences in the average outcome of interest between treated and non-treated units are likely to be caused by the treatment (Dunning 2012).

Although the logic of causal inference in natural experiments relies on comparing a large number of treated and non-treated units, in this study I rely on the logic of causal inference of process tracing. In this approach, causality is established not on the basis of several observations on distinct units but, rather, on the basis of several *causal process observations* (CPOs) within units – that is, "observations about context, process, or mechanisms" (Brady et al. 2010:24). By tracing the sequencing of CPOs, it is possible to show that they are consistent with the theory and inconsistent with alternative explanations, making it highly plausible that the relation between the explanatory variable (in this case institutional quality) and the outcome (in this case, collective resistance and social order) is causal.[7] In this way, process tracing relies on a different logic that does not depend on the number of units but, rather, on consistency between CPOs and the proposed causal mechanism.

The natural experiment consists of three neighboring communities that shared the same history of exclusion and exploitation, and participated in the same agrarian mobilization and land taking between 1930 and 1960, but experienced an exogenous shock that transformed their dispute local institutions in the 1960s: a gift of land to an emblematic leader of the agrarian movement propelled other leaders to eventually sell their plots and move to the same community to be together. The movement became concentrated in one of the villages, which was able to preserve its institutions for decades. However, self-governance decayed elsewhere in the municipality and two decades later it was practically gone.

Exploiting this sudden change in the trajectory of local institutions, I trace its effects on wartime social order thirty years later when the FARC took control of the area. I find that the absence of strong traditional institutions led to *rebelocracy* in two communities, while effective and legitimate institutions in the third community allowed civilians to interact with combatants under a social order of *aliocracy*. I use process tracing to identify the causal mechanisms by which institutions impact collective resistance, as well as by which the latter influence the strategies of armed actors. I also address alternative explanations. I rely on in-depth interviews and focus groups as well as primary and secondary sources.

Chapter 8: Testing the Microfoundations – Rebelocracy and Recruitment

Although Chapter 6 illustrates some of the microfoundations by offering evidence on combatants' and civilians' behavior, Chapter 8 aims to

---

[7] See Arjona (2016b) for a detailed discussion of this approach.

provide a more rigorous test of a central assumption about civilian behavior that is crucial for the theory, to wit, that rebelocracy is desirable for armed groups because it leads to higher civilian cooperation. If this assumption does not hold true, my contention that armed actors prefer to establish rebelocracy would crumble.

In this chapter I rely on the data on community–armed group dyads described before to test whether recruitment – a clear form of cooperation – is indeed higher under rebelocracy than aliocracy. Using statistical analysis, I test whether or not recruitment was more likely in communities living under rebelocracy. To identify the causal effect, I employ the same approach of Chapter 5: I compare communities within municipalities, and exploit the clustered structure of the data to create an instrumental variable for rebelocracy.

I also rely on individual-level data on joiners and non-joiners of guerrilla and paramilitary groups to offer additional evidence. I use data from a survey that I conducted in collaboration with Stathis Kalyvas in 2005 and 2006 with about 800 former members of guerrilla and paramilitary groups, and approximately 500 civilians living in areas where many of the ex-combatants lived prior to joining a non-state armed group. These data allow for building a refined control group for civilians. By showing that recruitment is much higher under rebelocracy, I demonstrate that social order does impact civilian cooperation in the way the theory assumes.

Summary of the Empirical Basis of the Theory of Wartime Social Order

Every theory is made up of multiple propositions. The theory that I developed in Chapter 3 is based on several assumptions, some of which rely on fairly well established facts, and some that do not. For the foundations of the theory to be strong, all assumptions should be defended not only theoretically but also, when possible, empirically. The main hypotheses about the determinants of order and disorder on one hand, and aliocracy and rebelocracy on the other, rely on more or less complex mechanisms. In other words, some hypotheses entail one main causal link, while others entail a concatenation of causal relations. This research design aims to offer a test of every causal link that underlies the theory.

Although I cannot test systematically every assumption and causal statement, the book does test systematically the most important

TABLE 4.4 *The empirical basis of theoretical propositions*

	Theoretical statement	Empirical basis
Assumptions	(1) Armed groups want long-term territorial control	Well established by the literature (Chapter 3)
	(2) Armed groups want to maximize the byproducts of control	Illustrated (Beyond Colombia: Chapter 3; Colombia: Chapter 6)
	(3) Civilian cooperation is essential to achieve (1)	Well established by the literature (Chapter 3)
	(4) Civilian cooperation is essential to achieve (2)	Illustrated (Beyond Colombia: Chapter 3; Colombia: Chapter 6)
	(5) Rebelocracy leads to higher civilian cooperation than disorder and aliocracy	Test of implication on recruitment (Chapter 8)
Causal statements	(6) Competition leads to disorder	Test on random sample of communities (Chapter 5)
	(7) Indiscipline leads to disorder	Test on random sample of communities (Chapter 5)
	(8) The quality of preexisting institutions creates the conditions for civilian resistance to rebelocracy	Test with process tracing in a natural experiment (Chapter 7)
	(9) Expectation of civilian resistance leads armed groups to settle for aliocracy	Test on random sample (Chapter 5) and test with process tracing in a natural experiment (Chapter 7)
	(10) Based on (8) and (9), high-quality preexisting institutions lead to aliocracy	Test on random sample (Chapter 5). Process-driven natural experiment (Chapter 7)

assumption that is not already backed up by a substantial literature, as well as every hypothesis on the causal links between the explanatory variables and wartime social order. Table 4.4 indicates the empirical basis for each proposition.

ADVANTAGES AND LIMITATIONS OF THE RESEARCH DESIGN

While the research design of this book offers several advantages, it also faces limitations. First, I am aware of the difficulties involved in relying on data collected mostly by asking people to remember how their life was a few years earlier – especially in a war zone. Memory may play tricks on respondents, all sorts of psychological mechanisms can lead to biases, and people can also consciously omit, overstate, or fabricate facts in their responses. However, talking to people from various sectors and networks who have experienced the armed conflict in different situations helps to lessen the possibility of painting a false story of any given locality. In addition, collecting data in randomly selected samples of communities across the country also makes me more confident about the reliability of the results. What is more, even though there are no systematic studies of social order in war zones in Colombia, existing case studies on particular topics and journalistic accounts of Colombian war zones are consistent with many of the findings. For example, the existence of what I have called *rebelocracy* in areas where institutions were very weak has been identified by scholars working on very different regions of the country (e.g., LeGrand 1994; Molano 1994; González 1999; Uribe de Hincapié 2001; González 2003).

Second, there are limitations to the ability of this research design to identify causal effects. In an ideal world, social scientists would be able to isolate the causal effect *and* causal mechanisms of the variables that are expected to impact the outcome of interest. Furthermore, they would be able to do so without fabricating conditions that are so removed from reality that the results would be of little use to understand real phenomena. Yet, isolating main causal effects or causal mechanisms is extremely difficult. Doing both is even harder. When planning my fieldwork, I considered several potential exogenous causes of variation of local institutions – such as religious missions, state policies directed only to coffee growers, natural disasters, and inter-family marriage – but none of these were truly random, and they did not allow for a study of wartime order in different regional contexts. The research design relies instead on a combination of methods that have different strengths and, together, offer strong empirical support for the theory.

The component of the research design that uses data collected on a large number of cases relies on instrumental variables to improve the quality of causal inference. I am aware that the validity of instrumental variables can be defended but, ultimately, not proven. Yet, there are several reasons that make the instrumental variables that I use – some of them exploiting the nested structure of the data, and one relying on the potential for indigenous migration since the early twentieth century – good candidates, as I argue in Chapter 5.

Turning to the process-driven natural experiment, the comparison of processes across the villages offers a window to the nuances of the Colombian civil war and the ways in which it shapes local politics and civilian agency. The study finds strong evidence of the similarity across the villages until the emblematic leader moved to one of them, as well as of the variation in local institutions across villages after that. The evidence also shows variation in social order two decades later, when the FARC ruled the municipality. However, there is a potential confounder: leadership. Although several CPOs do suggest that what drove aliocracy was the potential for civilian resistance, it is possible that both leadership and local institutions played a significant role in the process. I discuss this possibility in Chapter 7 and argue that this finding propels new questions about collective action and civilian bargaining with armed actors.

Although each approach employed faces limitations, the strength of the research design lies on what they achieve as a whole. On one hand, different types of very detailed evidence are consistent with the main hypotheses on the determinants of variation in wartime social order; on the other hand, evidence on the mechanisms and microfoundations also support the most important propositions that make up the theory. The combined results of statistical analysis of data on a large sample of communities throughout a very diverse country, an in-depth study of a natural experiment, and qualitative evidence on dozens of communities provide strong support for the theory.

Finally, even though this chapter explained why testing this theory on Colombia has many advantages, the generalizability of the argument depends on future tests on other cases. This is an evident limitation of a research design that studies sub-national variation within a single country; although I built this theory based on my analysis of evidence on a large number of conflicts – some of which are mentioned in Chapter 3 – such evidence is not systematic and cannot be used to test my argument. Future tests are therefore needed to assess the explanatory power of the theory beyond Colombia.

CONCLUSION

This chapter discussed the advantages and limitations of focusing on Colombia, provided an overview of the Colombian conflict, and introduced the research design. The project combines different methodologies to test hypotheses on variation in social order in a systematic way, while allowing for an in-depth analysis of the processes that underlie it. It also brings to the forefront the microfoundations on which the argument is built.

The data come from different stages of fieldwork where surveys, in-depth interviews, and case studies were combined to gather data on communities, armed groups, and individuals in several regions of the country. Combined, these sources offer rich evidence that not only allows for testing several implications of the theory, but also makes an important contribution by describing aspects of civilian–combatant relations, armed group behavior, and civilian agency for which evidence is rarely available.

The following chapters present each component of the research design. Each chapter describes the methods I used to collect the data, discusses its advantages and shortcomings, and presents the results. I revisit the implications of these findings in Chapter 9.

5

The Determinants of Social Order

This chapter tests the main implications of the theory on wartime social order presented in Chapter 3. Do armed competition and armed group indiscipline lead to disorder? Are low-quality preexisting institutions likely to facilitate rebelocracy, while communities with legitimate and effective institutions live under aliocracy instead? If so, does their willingness and ability to resist collectively explain why?

Using original data on Colombian communities, I investigate the determinants of variation in social order across communities and armed groups with a series of multilevel models – that is, models that take into account the similarities that may exist between communities in a given municipality, between communities interacting with the same armed group, and between observations on a given community over time. I also rely on an instrumental variables approach to better isolate the effect of the explanatory variables on social order.

The chapter is divided into four sections. The first section describes how the data were collected. The second section summarizes the central hypotheses to be tested on the determinants of order and disorder, which come from the theory developed in Chapter 3, and presents the results. The third section does the same with the hypotheses on the conditions that favor rebelocracy. The final section concludes.

RECONSTRUCTING THE HISTORY OF LOCAL COMMUNITIES IN WAR ZONES

Testing the theory developed in Chapter 3 requires data on local communities in war zones. Finding systematic evidence on the interaction between civilians and combatants is very difficult for most civil wars. The task is even harder when it comes to local level data, as studies usually focus on regions, cities, ethnic groups, or armed groups, but not on villages or neighborhoods. Ethnographies do provide invaluable evidence on local communities, but they seldom adopt a comparative approach. In the Colombian context, there are excellent case studies and cross-case comparisons at the level of the municipality, as well as a few in-depth studies of neighborhoods and villages. However, systematic data that allow for comparisons and identification of patterns are not available at such a disaggregated level of analysis. Furthermore, testing the argument requires measuring the quality of informal institutions; even though the importance of such institutions has been largely acknowledged (Dasgupta & Serageldin 2000; Helmke & Levitsky 2006), methods to measure them are surprisingly scarce. Measuring informal institutions *during conflict* is even more challenging.

In addition to collecting data on the main outcome I aim to explain – that is, social order – and the explanatory factors that my theory identifies, I also wanted to collect data that would allow me to assess *how* these variables shape the decisions of armed groups and civilians. In other words, I wanted to document the *process* by which different forms of order come to be in war zones and how they function.

Given the trade-offs between collecting cursory data on a large number of cases and obtaining in-depth data on a smaller sample, I designed an innovative approach that allowed me to build a large-n dataset as well as several rich, detailed local histories on the interaction between communities and armed groups. In what follows I describe this approach. The different kinds of evidence that I gathered are used in this chapter as well as in Chapter 6. Additional details are given in Appendix 1.

SAMPLE AND DATA-GATHERING METHODS

After developing the theory presented in Chapter 3, I collected data to test it in a systematic manner in two waves of fieldwork, which took place in 2010 and 2012. Each time, I selected a set of municipalities (eight in 2010, twenty-one in 2012) stratified by region to ensure geographical variation; in 2012, I also stratified based on additional variables to ensure variation in ethnicity and state presence.[1] The four regions included twenty-seven of

---

[1] See Appendix 1 for more details.

Sample and Data-gathering Methods

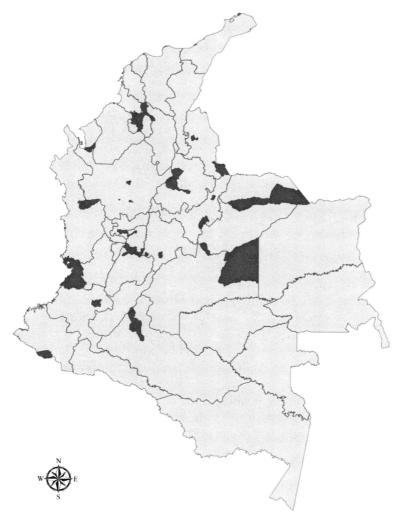

MAP 5.1 Random sample of municipalities

the thirty-three departments of the country (the equivalent to US states). I excluded five departments located in the Amazonian region, which are sparsely populated and have only recently seen the arrival of the armed conflict: Vichada, Guainía, Guaviare, Vaupés, and Amazonas. I also excluded San Andres and Providencia, the islands located in the Caribbean Sea, where armed groups had not been present until recently. Map 5.1 shows the sampled municipalities.

In total, the two samples include twenty-nine municipalities throughout Colombia where at least one non-state armed group had been present for a minimum of six continuous months since 1970.[2] The sample is quite diverse along several dimensions, including location (nineteen of the thirty-three departments), ethnicity, economic activities, abundance of legal and illegal natural resources, the structure of land tenure, and historical patron–client relations. By virtue of the geographical variation, the sample also includes very different conflict dynamics: some municipalities were strongholds of the FARC since the 1970s, while others have only experienced rebel presence since the 2000s. Likewise, some municipalities were bastions of paramilitary groups in the 1990s, while others encountered these organizations much later. Patterns of violence also vary greatly across municipalities, as do patterns of counterinsurgency and anti-narcotics policy.[3] Figure 5.1 shows descriptive statistics for several of these variables.

Once the municipalities had been selected, I developed a design that would satisfy several requisites. First, in order to build a sample of localities where I could control for various political, economic, and historical factors, I needed to select clusters of localities that exhibited variation in social order but belonged to the same politico-administrative unit. These localities also needed to be representative of other localities within such politico-administrative units. Second, my goal was to collect detailed data on the institutional history of these localities both before and during the war. I wanted to trace the processes by which particular forms of social order emerged in these places, and to have detailed descriptions of how they operate, and how civilians and combatants interact within them. Finally, I wanted measures of my main dependent and independent variables that could be comparable across cases. Survey research has convincingly shown that small changes in the ways questions are asked can substantially alter the answers we get. Even though I wanted to have in-depth testimonies and open conversations, I also wanted to have

---

[2] The scope of the analysis is limited to estimating the determinants of social order in a given locality, conditional on the fact that an armed group at some point chose to expand to that locality. Localities that have never experienced the presence of an armed group are beyond the scope of the theory advanced in this book.

[3] Additional details of how municipalities were selected in each wave are given in Appendix 1.

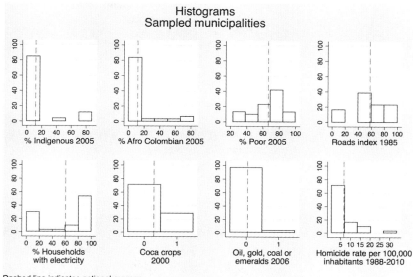

FIGURE 5.1 Descriptive statistics of sampled municipalities (histograms)

Sources

Demographic	Census, 2005
% Poor (multidimensional poverty index)	National Planning Department (DNP), Colombia, based on census data
Roads index	Social Foundation, 1985
% Households with electricity	Census, 2005
Coca crops (dummy)	Integrated Illicit Crops Monitoring System (SIMCI), United Nations Office on Drugs and Crime, 2000
Gold, oil, coal, or emeralds (dummy)	Agustin Codazzi Geographic Institute, 2006
Average homicide rate per 100,000 inhabitants	National Police, 1988–2010

data obtained in very similar ways for it to be comparable across cases.

To meet these goals, I collected data in three ways, leading to a dataset with systematic information on many aspects of civilian–combatant relations and social order, as well as a large set of local histories with detailed qualitative information.

Vignettes Survey: Rough Measures of Social Order

In Colombia, the municipality is the lowest politico-administrative unit. It has a county head called *cabecera*, where the local government operates. Each municipality has representation of the judiciary system, a mayor, and a local council. The mayor and council members have been elected by popular vote since 1988. Since 1991, local governments have become a central locus of power and governance because they are in charge, among others, of providing key public services like water, sewage, infrastructure, education, and health, as well as managing public funds.

In order to select a sample of communities within each municipality, I needed some measure of either social order or my independent variables to ensure variation. Given the absence of data on social order or the quality of local institutions, I designed an innovative approach that allowed me to obtain a rough measure of social order on a large number of cases. Using vignettes, I conducted a short survey that allowed me to identify which communities had mostly lived under rebelocracy, and which had mostly lived under aliocracy. This survey was conducted only on communities where at least one armed group had been present for at least six months at any point in the past. I excluded communities that had not experienced an ongoing interaction with combatants at all because they were not part of my universe of cases.

To code social order in each community, my research team interviewed around five persons in each municipality who were likely to be knowledgeable about the history of the area. I did not aim to interview a representative sample of locals, but rather a heterogeneous group of *experts*. In each municipality these experts usually included a civic leader, a politician, a priest, and NGO workers or public servants. They were asked about as many localities within the municipality as they knew well.

The interviewer read two vignettes that described community life in a hypothetical village under the presence of an armed group. The first vignette described in plain words a social order of *rebelocracy*, where the armed group intervened in several spheres of life. The second vignette described a social order of *aliocracy*, where the group was present and ruled over security and taxation but did not intervene in other aspects of local life. The interviewee was then asked to report which vignette resembled the situation in each locality more closely, and for which periods of time. The specific wording of these questions can be found in Appendix 1.

This survey facilitated the coding of social order – a variable that is complex and for which good proxies are difficult to find. Based on this measure, I was able to randomly select localities stratified by the scope of armed groups' involvement in local institutions. To be sure, for this method to work it has to provide a high-quality measure of social order. Can people classify localities they know well on the basis of these short descriptions of ideal types? Are these good measures of social order in war zones? How different would the picture be, had I collected more in-depth data on all these localities? The additional, detailed data that I collected allowed me to test the reliability of this measure. I will come back to this issue later in the chapter.

A Random Sample of Localities

Based on the rough measures of social order obtained with the vignettes survey, I randomly selected between two and four localities within each municipality to conduct a more in-depth study. I classified each locality as a case of aliocracy or rebelocracy based on the number of years it had lived under each form of social order; I then calculated the proportion of cases of aliocracy and rebelocracy in each municipality and selected cases respecting this proportion. Disorder was not taken into account to select the cases, because it is usually a transitory situation and most communities that live under disorder also experience another form of social order before or after it. Map 5.2 shows the sample of localities in which the memory workshops and surveys were conducted.[4]

In each selected locality, I combined several tools to obtain comparable and rich evidence on the history of interaction between the community and every armed group that operated in the area. My research team started with activities that were conducted collectively as part of a memory workshop, and then conducted individual surveys with each participant.

Memory Workshops

With the help of outstanding research assistants, in each selected community we conducted a memory workshop[5] with a group of locals that

---

[4] The descriptive statistics presented in this chapter take into account the sampling strategy by including sampling weights. The statistical models do not use sampling weights, although including them does not change the results in any substantial way. See Appendix 1 for more details.

[5] I use the term "memory workshop" to capture the twin goals of the activities that we conducted, to wit, to spur reflection about memory and to reconstruct collectively the history of specific wartime experiences. This term has been used by researchers in different fields and places to denote workshops seeking to elicit memory in some way. I build

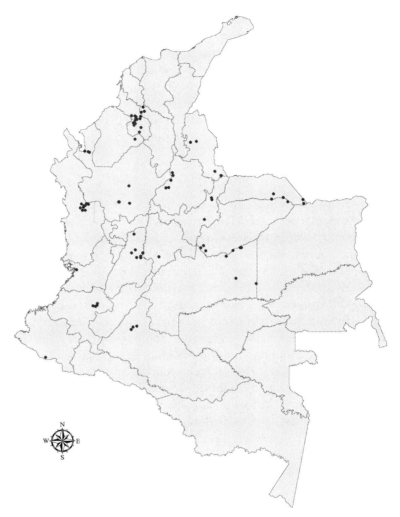

MAP 5.2 Random sample of localities

included a teacher, an elder, a local leader and, when possible, a merchant. These profiles were selected because they represent different

> particularly on the work of Pilar Riaño, who has proposed the use of memory workshops as part of a fascinating toolkit to create historic memory (CNMH 2009). Since the focus of this book is not violence, I designed a type of memory workshop geared towards capturing the wartime transformation of institutions – which, as I defined them in Chapter 2, include the rules, norms, and practices that structure human interaction in conflict zones. Memory workshops were conducted in the 2012 field wave.

sectors of the population and are, at the same time, persons who tend to know the dynamics of their communities well. In most cases, participants included at least one woman. It is important to stress that the goal was not to create a representative sample, but rather a sample of *local experts*.

The memory workshop included three activities, each of which served a different purpose. After the workshop, we conducted a survey with each participant.

The first activity of the memory workshop consisted of a reflection on the role of memory. Using mind-mapping techniques, we invited participants to reflect on whether memory matters and why, and on how their communities could build memory about the conflict in their territory. I describe this activity in greater detail in Appendix 1. The main goal was to invite participants to think about what remembering the conflict could entail in order to make a modest contribution to the construction of memory about the war in the community while making it easier for both interviewers and interviewees to talk about the past.

The second activity consisted of building a timeline of the history of the community where important events were identified. Participants first identified and dated events that took place before the first armed actor arrived at their territory. They then worked on a detailed timeline of events that took place during the times when at least one non-state armed group was present in their community, at any point in time since 1970. The goal of these timelines was to identify the most important events in the recent history of the community, and the time when they happened. The timelines proved to be extremely useful: not only did they provide valuable information about the community, but they were also used by interviewees to situate events in time in the next activities, and I used them to complement other information while reconstructing the local histories and building the dataset. Figure 5.2 shows an example of a timeline built by workshop participants.

The third activity consisted of creating what I call an *institutional biography* – the history of the informal institutions that regulated a single conduct before and during the war. This activity consisted of reconstructing the rules – either formal or informal – that regulated a particular conduct in the community. Participants were asked to write down one conduct that they deemed important in their community, such as fishing or solving problems with neighbors. One activity was then randomly selected, and participants were asked to describe the rules that regulated that conduct over time, noting when such rules changed. For

TABLE 5.1 *Institutional biography in a locality*

	Conduct: fishing		
Time period	1960–1970 (Before FARC arrived)	1971–1985 (Under FARC presence)	1986–1990 (Under FARC presence)
What rules regulated the conduct?	None	No fishing during closed season	No fishing during closed season and no fishing with large nets
Who established them?	Nobody	FARC	FARC
Did people perceive rules as just?	No	Yes	Yes
Did people obey the rules?	No	Yes	Yes
What was the punishment for disobedience?	None	Social work	Social work

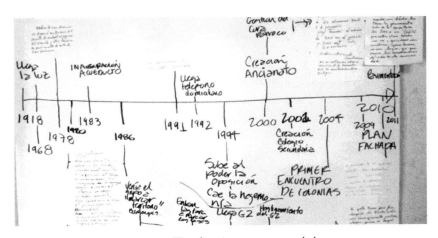

FIGURE 5.2 Timeline in *memory workshops*

each period in which a particular rule or set of rules regulated the conduct, participants were asked (1) who established those rules; (2) who was supposed to follow the rules; (3) whether most locals obeyed the rule; (4) whether the majority of locals deemed those rules legitimate; and (5) what was the punishment for disobedience. Participants discussed each question and the researcher filled in a similar table to the one depicted in Table 5.1, which depicts the biography of institutions regulating fishing in a locality where the FARC were present.

Sample and Data-gathering Methods

The goal of including this component in the workshop was to obtain a different measure of wartime social order. On the one hand, I wanted to have one single coding that came from the group of participants as a whole, rather than a set of individual responses to survey questions. Giving people the opportunity to share what they remembered about rules regulating a specific conduct made it easier to incorporate more information and improve the coding. On the other hand, I wanted to have a simple proxy that was comparable across cases. By reconstructing in the exact same way the history of regulation of a single conduct in each locality, it was easy to create a single, clear proxy of institutional change during wartime across localities. The quality of preexisting institutions is directly measured by asking whether rules regulating the conduct were seen as legitimate by most members, and whether they were followed. The form of social order is measured by identifying whether armed actors regulated the activity when they were present in the territory.

Creating institutional biographies collectively was a fascinating exercise. The evidence is quite effective in the sense that it tells us a lot about these communities with just a few data. It shows, for example, which communities had problems organizing themselves and solving basic problems in the prewar period. For example, some institutional biographies show that robberies were forbidden but the rule was largely overlooked. It also shows which communities had clear rules that were widely supported, and which did not. In some cases, local cleavages also became quite obvious – such as when a certain conduct was regulated by rules established by landowners, despite widespread disapproval.

The data gathered with the institutional biographies also allowed me to check the quality of the vignettes survey as a means to measure social order and, therefore, as an indicator for selecting localities. We can think of survey respondents and the group that participated in the workshop as two raters of the same phenomenon – that is, social order. In the former, individuals rate social order in a particular way; in the latter, they participate in a workshop and, with other individuals, indirectly rate social order by constructing institutional biographies. An inter-rater reliability check can tell us how close these two proxies are: in 80 percent of the cases, the vignettes survey and the institutional biographies coincided in their coding of social order, while only in 20 percent of the cases they did not.[6] Overall, these proxies

---

[6] These percentages were calculated as follows: for every observation (i.e., community-year under a given armed group), I calculated the percentage of respondents who selected the vignette that coincided with the coding based on the institutional biographies. I then

seem to be measuring a similar phenomenon – there is, to be sure, some measurement error, but it is not substantial.

Most participants appreciated these workshops. They enjoyed learning more about their communities and many participants left with ideas to foster conversations about their history, to rescue instances in which they came together as a community, and to commemorate difficult times. Some talked about incorporating certain content in classes at schools so that children would learn about what their communities had been through. Others imagined building monuments or expressing in some way their hopes for the future. In some localities participants did not want to receive any payment, which we offered to compensate them for their time (the workshop and survey took a whole day). They wondered why they should be receiving a payment when they had gained so much by participating. This reassured us that the workshop offered a space that was, in most cases, valued.

Survey with Local Experts

Each workshop participant responded to a long survey that contained both open- and close-ended questions. The survey asked specific questions about the quality of local institutions prior to the arrival of any armed actor to the locality, as well as about every stage of interaction between the community and the armed actor. Close-ended questions gathered specific data about the institutions that regulated conduct during war, as well as about specific characteristics of the armed groups that operated in the area. Open-ended questions elicited much more detailed accounts of daily life and the ways in which different sectors of the population interacted with combatants. Interviews lasted between one-and-a-half and three hours, and included around ninety questions on each armed group that was ever present in the locality.

Outcomes: Dataset of Community–Armed Group Interaction and Local Histories

Using the data from the survey, memory workshops, and primary and secondary evidence, I created a dataset with a rich, detailed description of

> calculated the average of these percentages for the entire sample. In other words, this number measures the proportion of community-years for which the coding based on vignettes and the coding based on the institutional biographies coincided. These calculations do not include cases in five municipalities where, due to time constraints, institutional biographies could not be completed.

how armed groups penetrated local communities, how civilians responded, and what kind of institutions operated over time.[7]

Given that in some localities several armed groups were present at the same time – sometimes establishing different institutions – the unit of analysis is not the locality–year, but the locality–armed group–year. Structuring the data in this way allows for assessing what different armed groups did when operating at the same time in a given locality.

The sample includes 1,248 observations on 124 locality–armed group dyads made up of 74 localities and 38 units of 10 different guerrilla and paramilitary groups, which interacted for at least 6 continuous months between 1970 and 2012.[8] About 8 percent of all dyads interacted for 5 years or less; 36 percent between 6 and 10; and 55 percent more than 10 years. There are more observations on dyads of guerrillas (62 percent) than paramilitaries (38 percent).[9] Of all the communities where the paramilitaries were present at least in one year, 56 percent had had guerrilla presence before.[10]

As in other civil wars, the Colombian conflict affected regions and localities at different times throughout the conflict. Of all the localities included in the sample, 45 percent interacted with only one non-state armed group; 31 percent interacted with two; 20 percent with three groups; and one locality interacted with four groups. However, 92 percent of all

---

[7] There are issues with memory, to be sure, but given the lack of archives or any other source where changes in local institutions have been registered for a few communities – let alone for a representative sample – we have to rely on oral testimonies. The combination of workshops, surveys, and secondary sources allows for triangulating sources and decreasing measurement problems.

[8] There are many ways to classify these armed groups. The ten organizations mentioned here include five major guerrilla groups – FARC, ELN, EPL, ERP, M19 – and five paramilitary structures: the Autodefensas Campesinas de Córdoba y Urabá, Bloque Central Bolívar and Autodefensas Campesinas del Magdalena Medio, all of which belonged to the AUC federation; the Buitragueños, which did not belong to any federation or regional structure; the Alianza Oriente, which was formed by a few groups operating in the oriental plains (*llanos orientales*); and a general category for paramilitaries that are not identified as belonging to a particular structure.

[9] This asymmetry is likely to be explained by the fact that, as mentioned in Chapter 4, while the guerrillas were formed in the 1960s, most paramilitaries emerged in the 1980s or later. Therefore, they are present in fewer years than the guerrillas. If we look, however, at armed groups' presence in the communities included in the sample without disaggregating by year, we find that paramilitary groups were present in 49 percent of all communities.

[10] Since less than 3 percent of all observations have at least one missing value in any of the explanatory variables, the results presented in this chapter use list-wise deletion. The results remain unchanged when I replicate the central models using ten datasets where missing values were multiply imputed.

locality–years experienced the presence of only one armed group. In other words, only in 8 percent of all locality–years, two or more armed groups were present at the same time. This is, to my knowledge, the first comprehensive and representative dataset on wartime order and institutions.[11]

My research team also created a local history for each community that contains the qualitative information that we obtained with the surveys and workshops. These local histories reconstruct several aspects of the interaction between civilians and combatants, providing detailed descriptions of several aspects of local life in the economic, social, and political realms, as well as of civilian and combatant behavior. The dataset and local histories offer a rich, detailed description of how armed groups penetrated local communities, how civilians responded, how new social orders emerged, and how new institutions operated. Chapter 6 uses this evidence to describe the process by which different forms of social order are created and how they function.

In the next sections, I use these data to test the hypotheses on the emergence of order separately from the hypotheses on the form that such order takes – that is, whether it is closer to rebelocracy or aliocracy. I start with the analysis of the determinants of order and disorder and I then turn to rebelocracy and aliocracy.

THE DETERMINANTS OF ORDER

Hypotheses and Data

This section starts by summarizing the hypotheses on the origins of wartime social order that come from the theory presented in Chapter 3, and describing the data that I use to measure each relevant variable. I then turn to the statistical models.

The dependent variable is the emergence of order, that is, the existence of a social contract between civilians and combatants in which both tend to follow a clear set of rules. As discussed in Chapter 3, order is likely to vary along a continuum from low to

---

[11] Our understanding of these dynamics will keep growing, as other scholars have recently collected – or are in the process of doing so – systematic data on local governance in contexts of civil war. For example, Keister (2011) collected data on the provision of public goods, security, and taxation in the Philippines. Sánchez de la Sierra (2015) collected data on taxation and the provision of security in the Democratic Republic of Congo. Rana Khoury and Mara Revkin are in the process of gathering data on rebel governance in Syria.

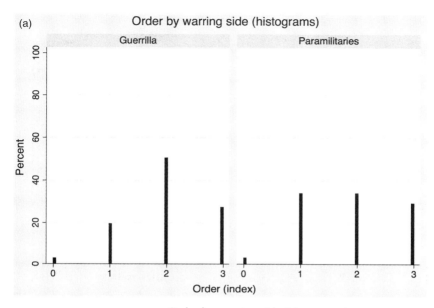

FIGURE 5.3A Order by warring side (histograms)

high predictability. I measure order as an index that aggregates three variables. The first two measure whether participants responded "yes" to the following questions: "Did people in the community know the rules of conduct that combatants had to follow?" And, "In general, did people obey the rules that the armed actor established?" The third variable captures whether respondents indicated that they lived under high uncertainty or not, based on the qualitative evidence collected with the survey and memory workshops. *Order* is the simple arithmetic sum of these three variables. As Figure 5.3a shows, order varies greatly across and within armed groups. Figure 5.3b shows that it also varies across localities.[12]

Based on the theory presented in Chapter 3, a social contract is more likely to be established between the armed group and the community when the former has a long time horizon; otherwise, *disorder* is more likely. The theory identifies two central conditions under which armed groups' time horizons are likely to be short: when the armed group faces internal problems of indiscipline, and when it competes with other armed

---

[12] See Appendix 2 for the exact wording of all survey questions.

FIGURE 5.3B Order by locality

organizations for territorial control. As discussed in Chapter 3, the state can also increase the level of disorder when its armed forces compete for territorial control.[13] Two testable hypotheses can be derived:

H1: *Disorder* is more likely than order when the armed group suffers from internal problems of indiscipline.

H2: *Disorder* is more likely than order when two or more armed forces (state or non-state) compete with each other in the locality.

I measure these explanatory variables as follows. *Indiscipline* is measured by interviewees' answer to the following question in the survey: "If a combatant disobeyed his group's rules on treatment of civilians, was it common that he was punished?" This question does not measure the unpredictability of an armed group's behavior. Rather, it aims to capture interviewees' perception of how permissive the group was with combatant behavior that people knew to be forbidden by the group. Civilians not only tend to know whether combatants can get into trouble for misconduct, but some of them actually complain about it to commanders.

---

[13] The theory also discussed macro-level changes, but I do not test their effect in this book.

Armed actors often encourage such complaints and even establish formal mechanisms for that purpose.[14] Overall, guerrilla groups showed indiscipline in about 26 percent of all observations, and paramilitaries in about 34 percent of them. As Figure 5.4 shows, the level of order is substantially lower when undisciplined groups are present. The difference is statistically significant at 0.1 percent.

Competition is a dummy that takes on the value 1 when two or more armed groups (including both non-state and state forces) were actively disputing territorial control of the area in which the community is located. This information comes from the timeline that was created for each community, and was cross-checked with the dates provided in the survey. Overall, two or more groups competed in 19 percent of all locality–years. Guerrillas competed with other guerrilla groups, paramilitary groups, and state armed forces. Paramilitaries competed with other paramilitary groups and with guerrilla groups, but not with state forces. As Figure 5.4 shows, the index of order tends to be higher when there is no competition between armed groups, and the difference is statistically significant at 0.1 percent.

In many cases, *indiscipline* and *competition* do not vary within municipalities; that is, competition is usually felt throughout the communities where any of the groups are permanently present; likewise, when a group exhibits indiscipline, it tends to be constant throughout the municipality. However, variation does exist across municipalities, and in some cases also across communities within municipalities.

A third hypothesis follows from the extension of the model discussed in Chapter 3, which aimed to incorporate the strategic value of territories. When an armed group encounters a community able to resist rebelocracy in a highly strategic territory, disorder is more probable. In such territories, armed groups are less likely to tolerate civilian autonomy and are therefore prone to harassing organized communities that wish to preserve their own institutions. According to the theory, only communities with high-quality dispute institutions are able to pose a credible threat of resistance. Hypothesis 3 can thus be stated as follows:

H3: *Disorder* is more likely than *order* in communities with high-quality institutions located in a highly strategic territory.

---

[14] This was the case in several localities in my sample. For an example beyond Colombia, see Giustozzi's (2014) detailed discussion of the Taliban's efforts to allow civilians to complain about abuse.

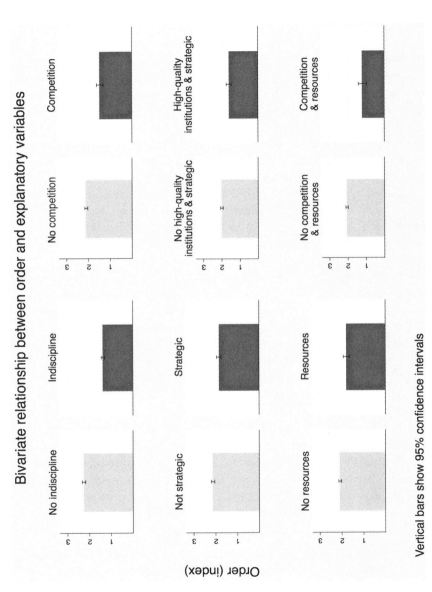

FIGURE 5.4 Bivariate relationship between order and explanatory variables

The strategic value of territories is measured with a dummy variable that captures whether any of the following apply to each municipality in a given year:[15]

- The territory was highly strategic for armed groups due to its location. For example, it was part of a corridor to move weapons, export coca, or connect key areas of the country. This variable is coded based on primary and secondary sources.[16]
- Whether there were *illegal* natural resources – coca or poppy crops – in the municipality, based on official data on crops at the municipality level, the survey, and primary and secondary sources.[17]
- Whether the municipality had valuable *legal* natural resources, such as oil or coal. This variable is coded based on official data as well as primary and secondary sources.[18]

Of all dyad-years made up of a guerrilla group, 41 percent correspond to municipalities that were strategic. The percentage is higher for paramilitaries: about 66 percent.

In order to measure the quality of preexisting local institutions, participants were asked in the survey a series of questions about the quality of the institutions in place prior to the arrival of any armed actor, especially their dispute institutions. Some questions capture the existence of clear rules; others their efficacy; and others, their legitimacy. One question asked if there were clear rules in place or, rather, people did as they pleased – a measure of the efficacy of institutions to create order. Another question asked whether it was common for people to solve conflicts using force; this is another measure of efficacy because if people are relying on established means to resolve conflicts, they do not use force. This variable can plausibly capture legitimacy as well, if most community

---

[15] These data are not available at the locality level. However, the strategic value of territories is not likely to vary greatly within municipalities, except for those municipalities that are very large.
[16] Primary sources include newspaper articles on the armed conflict on each municipality. Secondary data include reports and scholarly articles on the armed conflict in the region or municipality, and especially the reports of the Vice-Presidency's Human Rights Observatory on specific regions. These reports provide background information on each region, and mention which resources, if any, had made the territories economically attractive to armed groups. They also assess which main strategic corridors armed groups used across time.
[17] I used data collected by the UN SIMCI office and provided by the Center for the Study of Drugs and Security at Los Andes University.
[18] Data provided by Colombia's National Planning Department.

members believe that using violence is not a legitimate way to solve problems, but this is likely to vary across communities. Participants were also asked about the ways in which locals used to solve disputes with neighbors over land borders or debts. One question asked whether these problems were resolved quickly (a measure of efficacy); and another one asked whether they perceived the ways in which they were resolved to be fair (a measure of legitimacy). Finally, I use two measures that come from the qualitative evidence collected in open-ended questions: one measures the legitimacy of local institutions by capturing whether most people in the community approved of the rules in place to resolve conflicts; the other measures the efficacy of those rules based on whether people used to follow them.[19]

Theoretically, communities that are willing and able to organize and resist a guerrilla or paramilitary group should have quite strong preferences for the status quo; furthermore, their members should have internalized the rules and view them as valid, in order to be able to launch and maintain such risky collective action. Individuals in a community whose institutions give some signals of illegitimacy or inefficacy are unlikely to have the kind of preferences for the status quo that would trigger a desire to resist; likewise, they are unlikely to have a sufficiently strong capacity for collective action for it to be able to resist an armed actor. In order to capture whether a community has high institutional quality in this strong sense, I use a dichotomous variable that indicates whether *all* of the previous dichotomous variables are equal to 1. Hence, the variable *institutional quality* is calculated as the interaction of these six variables.[20] Overall, 27 percent of all communities had high-quality institutions.

As Figure 5.4 shows, the level of order is lower in strategic territories, and even more so in territories that in addition to being strategic also have

---

[19] I coded these two measures of the legitimacy and efficacy of institutions based on responses given to open-ended questions in the survey as well as in the memory workshop, which, together, provide rich details about the community. I then asked a research assistant to read all the material collected in the workshops and survey and code the same variable using the same coding guidelines I used. Our measures were exactly the same in 89 percent of the cases for legitimacy and 91 percent of the cases for efficacy. In addition, these two measures are strongly correlated with the other four measures of institutional quality, which come from the survey. A Cronbach's alpha estimate (an estimate of internal consistency of scores) is 0.77.

[20] As mentioned before, the six variables seem to be internally consistent (based on Cronbach's alpha estimate, which is 0.77). However, they do measure slightly different aspects of institutional quality. We can think of these measures as different tests. In as much as resistance requires remarkable institutions, a cleaner measure is one that identifies those institutions that pass all the tests.

high-quality institutions. These differences are statistically significant at 0.1 percent.

How about alternative explanations? As follows from the discussion of the rebel governance literature in Chapter 2, most existing accounts focus on the armed group as the unit of analysis. The explanatory variables tend to be specified at the level of the state or the armed group. Given that my goal is to explain local variation within and across armed groups, localities, and time, most of those arguments do not offer a viable explanation. One exception entails those hypotheses that identify a negative effect of armed competition and internal organizational problems on public goods provision and security (Kasfir 2004; Weinstein 2007). H1 and H2 are consistent with these arguments, as they posit that competition and indiscipline prevent the emergence of a social contract.

One argument that could help explaining variation within Colombia is Weinstein's (2007) hypothesis on the effect of the availability of natural resources on rebel governance. According to his argument, armed groups' reliance on valuable natural resources makes them less disciplined and more abusive. Metelits' (2010) argument, according to which social contracts are unlikely when control of natural resources is disputed, could also help explain the emergence of disorder (in fact, the Colombian rebel group FARC is one of her case studies). The following hypotheses can therefore be tested:

H4:   The presence of valuable natural resources increases *disorder*.
H5:   The combination of armed competition and natural resources increases *disorder*.

To test these hypotheses, I use *resources*, a dichotomous variable that identifies the presence of valuable resources (*legal* or *illegal*, as defined above). Overall, 23 percent of all dyads involving a guerrilla group corresponded to a locality with valuable resources, compared to 49 percent of dyads involving paramilitaries. To test the effect of competition over resources, I use the interaction between *resources* and *competition*, as defined before. As Figure 5.4 shows, order is lower in localities with either resources or both competition and resources. Both differences are statistically significant at 0.1%.

Statistical Models on Order

In these data, observations are clustered by locality, armed group, municipality, and year. Observations within a given cluster are likely to share similarities, suggesting a lack of independence between them. For example, all observations on a given dyad over time are likely to be similar. Likewise, observations on dyads within a given locality, or on localities within a given municipality, are unlikely to be independent. Dyads belonging to the same armed organization may be similar to each other, as are observations on guerrillas and paramilitaries. In order to account for this clustering in the data, I use multilevel models, which account for variability in predictors and residuals across clusters and for sample imbalances (Gelman & Hill 2006; Rabe-Hesketh & Skrondal 2008). I estimate four-level multilevel models where the first level is the occasion or measurement (i.e., the dyad in a given year); the second level is the locality–armed group dyad; the third level is the locality; and the fourth level is the municipality.[21] The models include fixed effects for the armed organization and its category or warring side – that is, whether the group is a guerrilla or a paramilitary. These fixed effects account for the characteristics of the armed actors and warring sides that do not vary over time and could affect social order, such as their ideological affiliation.[22]

Given that these are temporal data, there could be shocks happening in particular years that affect all observations on that year. Trends over time could also create dependence among observations. All models include year fixed effects and are robust to a linear time trend as well as to unit-specific time trends.[23]

---

[21] The model equations are presented in Appendix 2. The number of dyads, localities, and municipalities is large enough for the parameters to be estimated with little bias (see Appendix 2). As a robustness test, the models were estimated using Bayesian analysis (with uninformative priors), which provides estimates for higher-level predictors that are within 5 percent of the true population value (Stegmueller 2013:753; see also Finch et al. 2014:ch. 9). The results support the conclusions obtained with the maximum likelihood estimates, with only one exception: the model testing resistance as the mechanism. I come back to this issue later in the chapter. See Appendix 2 for a more detailed discussion of the specification of the multi-level models.

[22] There are different ways to classify the armed groups that were present in the sampled localities: by unit (for example, the specific front in the case of the guerrillas, and the specific block in the case of paramilitaries); by regional structure; and by armed organization or federation. I use fixed effects for the ten armed organizations identified before (five guerrillas and five paramilitaries), since the groups belonging to each of them are likely to share a similar internal structure or be under the same leadership. In addition, I use fixed effects for warring side (i.e., if the group is a guerrilla or paramilitary organization).

[23] Plots of the trajectories of order and rebelocracy for dyads, localities, and municipalities do not suggest any temporal trends. Plots of residuals of the models also fail to indicate clear temporal dynamics. The Bayesian models offer an additional robustness test. See Appendix 2 for a more detailed discussion.

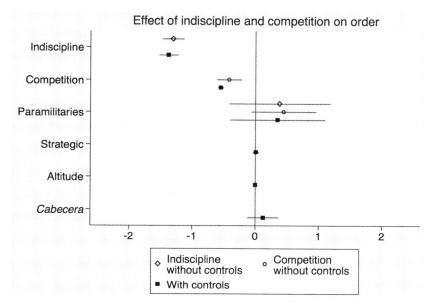

FIGURE 5.5 Effect of indiscipline and competition on order

In what follows I present the central results of a series of linear multilevel models to test the hypotheses derived from the theory on the causes of order. In addition to including fixed effects for armed organizations, warring sides and years, I control for two additional variables that may impact armed groups' incentives, or ability, to create order: *altitude*, a measure of rough terrain, and *cabecera*, which measures whether the locality is a county head.[24] For each variable of interest, I estimate a bivariate model as well as a multivariate model; the latter includes all relevant predictors and the control variables.[25]

Indiscipline has a negative and significant effect (at 0.1 percent) on the level of order, as predicted by the theory. Figure 5.5 plots the estimated parameters from bivariate models as well as from models including the control variables. Figure 5.6 illustrates the size of the effect by showing the predicted values of order when indiscipline changes from 0 to 1, holding

---

[24] I do not include proxies of the economic situation of the localities because there are no official data at this level of analysis for any year.
[25] I present plots only of the estimates of the fixed portion of the models. The full tables, including the random effects, are presented in Appendix 2.

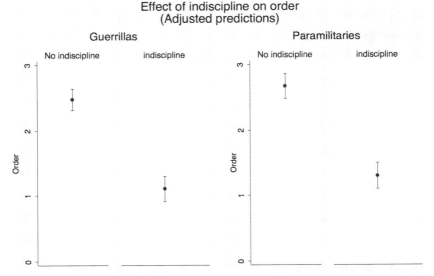

FIGURE 5.6 Effect of indiscipline on order (adjusted predictions)

competition fixed at 0 and all other variables at their mean.[26] The size of the effect is quite substantial: the level of order shows a decrease of about 30 percent due to indiscipline.

Competition between any types of armed actors also has a negative and significant effect on order at 0.1 percent (Figure 5.5). Figure 5.7 shows the effect as competition changes from 0 to 1, holding indiscipline fixed at 0 and all other variables fixed at their means. The level of order decreases by about 24 percent when two or more groups compete.

The last hypothesis that follows from the theory posits that when armed groups confront a community with high-quality institutions in a valuable territory, disorder becomes more probable as civilian autonomy is less likely to be tolerated. The results fail to support this hypothesis, as the value of order is not lower in communities that meet both conditions (Figure 5.8). This finding may suggest that armed actors do tolerate civilian autonomy even in highly strategic territories. As I discuss later in

---

[26] All predicted values are estimated with the model specification that includes control variables, and take into account the random components.

The Determinants of Order

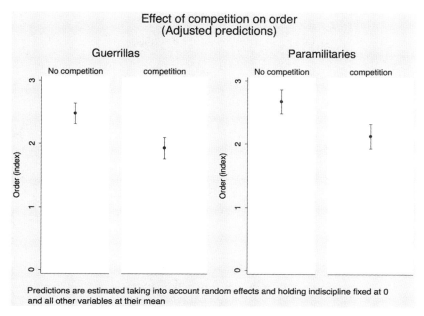

FIGURE 5.7 Effect of competition on order (adjusted predictions)

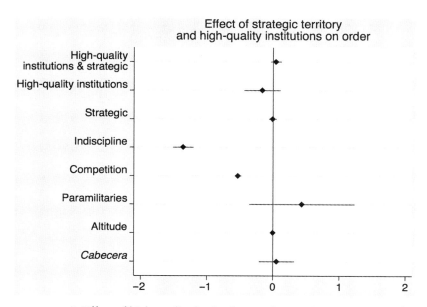

FIGURE 5.8 Effect of high-quality institutions and strategic territory on order

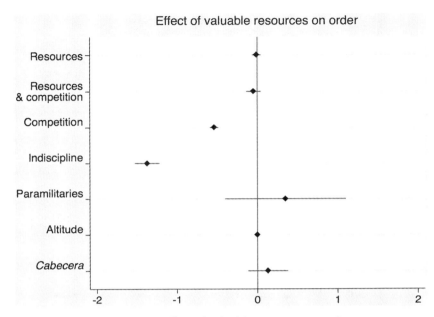

FIGURE 5.9 Effect of valuable resources on order

the chapter, results on the determinants of rebelocracy support this possibility.[27]

A final model tests the effect of two variables that have been hypothesized to prevent armed actors from providing services to civilians or establishing social contracts with them: the presence of valuable resources (Weinstein 2007) and competition over such resources (Meteltis 2010). The results suggest that neither of these variables have a significant effect on order (Figure 5.9).

Causal Inference

Could these results be explained by some other factor? One possibility is that *competition* and *indiscipline* are driven by disorder and not the other way around: disorder could lead to competition if armed groups see in a situation of disorder an opportunity to take over a territory;

---

[27] Another possibility could be that civilian cooperation is more important in certain types of strategic territories than in others. Yet, none of the types of strategic territories have a significant effect on order.

The Determinants of Order

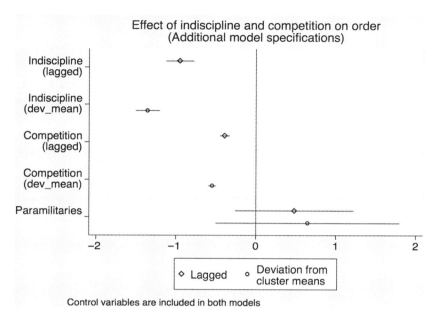

FIGURE 5.10 Effect of indiscipline and competition on order (additional model specifications)

disorder could also lead to indiscipline if combatants' tendency to follow orders decreases when facing a situation of disorder. To account for potential reversed causality, I estimate the effect of lagged competition and indiscipline. The results do not change in any substantial way (Figure 5.10).

An additional concern is the possibility of omitted variables that are correlated with both the independent variables and wartime order. In multi-level models, when the endogenous variables are nested within higher levels, it is possible to use the deviation from the cluster mean as an instrumental variable (Mundlak 1978; Rabe-Hesketh & Skrondal 2008:ch. 3).[28] This approach allows for identifying the effect of the explanatory variable on variation over time within each dyad. For competition, I use the deviation from the municipality mean; for indiscipline, I use the deviation from the armed group mean, as the indiscipline of an armed group in a given dyad-year is nested within

---

[28] This approach addresses endogeneity at the cluster level for unit-level covariates. For a discussion of this method see Mundlak (1978) and Rabe-Hesketh and Skrondal (2008:ch. 3).

that armed group.²⁹ The estimated coefficients of the deviation from the cluster mean for both competition and indiscipline are negative and significant at 0.1 percent, confirming the previous results. Furthermore, the size of the effects is very similar across models (Figure 5.10).

Overall, these results suggest that disorder tends to be higher when armed groups face internal problems of indiscipline or compete with other state or non-state armed actors. It is worth noting that the variable *paramilitaries* does not have a significant effect in any of the specifications of the model. Furthermore, the predicted effect of all the explanatory variables on order is quite similar for guerrillas and paramilitaries, as the different graphs show. Despite embracing opposite ideologies and exhibiting important differences in their organizational structure, these groups create order and disorder under similar conditions.

THE DETERMINANTS OF REBELOCRACY AND ALIOCRACY

Hypotheses and Data

I now turn to the determinants of the form that social order takes when a social contract is established, giving place to order. The dependent variable, whether order takes the form of *rebelocracy* or *aliocracy*, is likely to vary along a continuum from low to broad intervention in civilian affairs by rebels or paramilitaries. *Rebelocracy* aggregates several proxies of armed groups' influence in the economic, social, and political realms of life in the locality. This information comes from close-ended questions in the survey, which asked about the group's influence in the following realms:

- Economic: armed groups' intervention in local economic activities such as fishing, hunting or logging, and in the assignment of state subsidies to individuals (Figure 5.11). Tax collection and other forms of material contributions are not included, as taxes can also be part of a social order of aliocracy.³⁰

---

[29] I also include the cluster mean of all other clustered variables, in order to account for the correlation between those variables and the cluster-level random intercepts, therefore ensuring consistent estimation of all the within effects (Rabe-Hesketh and Skrondal 2008:119).

[30] Armed groups often regulate the production, processing, or transportation of coca or of illegal mining. I do not take into account their intervention in these markets because it involves taxation, and is therefore part of aliocracy as well.

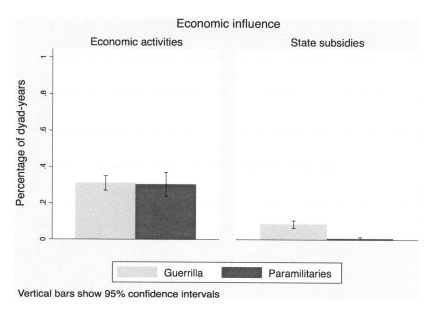

FIGURE 5.11 Economic influence

- Political: when asked, "Who ruled this locality back then?" whether respondents pointed to the armed group; if the group created an alternative justice system or conflict resolution scheme, measured by whether locals turned to the group to solve problems over land borders, debts, or robberies; and whether the group intervened in elections (by forbidding voting or asking people to vote for a particular candidate) (Figure 5.12).
- Public goods provision: whether the group provided or regulated the provision of education, health or the construction of infrastructure (Figure 5.13).
- Social: whether the group established rules to regulate domestic violence; personal appearance (like skirts for women and long hair and earrings for men); and sexual behavior (like forbidding homosexuality or regulating prostitution) (Figure 5.14).
- Three additional variables measure the social interaction between combatants and civilians by identifying whether they used to have a beer together, play pool, or play soccer (Figure 5.15).

Rebelocracy aggregates these sixteen measures in an index (a simple arithmetic sum) that varies from zero (when all items take the value "no") to

140   *The Determinants of Social Order*

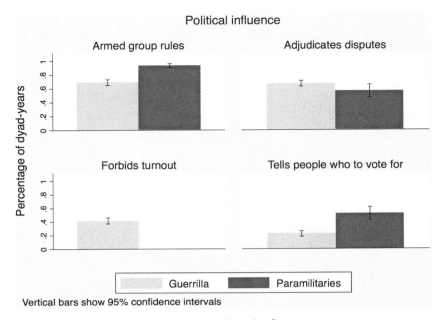

FIGURE 5.12 Political influence

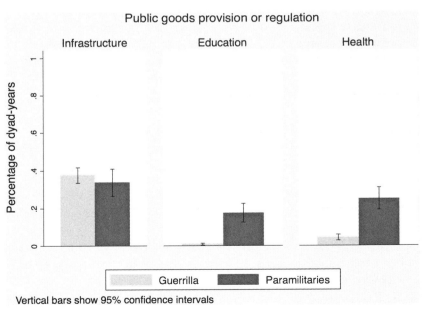

FIGURE 5.13 Public goods provision or regulation

The Determinants of Rebelocracy and Aliocracy 141

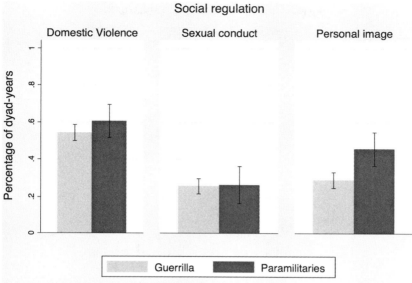

FIGURE 5.14 Social regulation

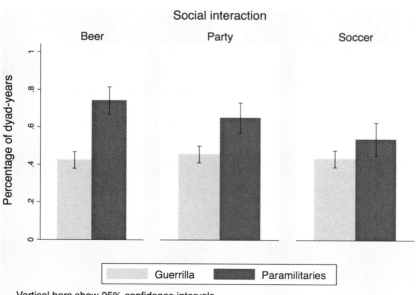

FIGURE 5.15 Social interaction

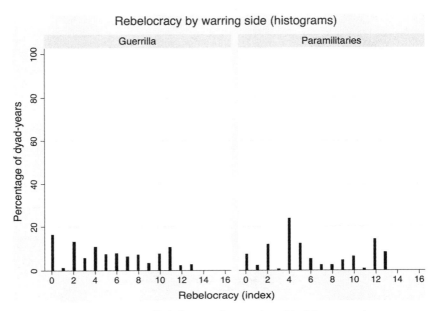

FIGURE 5.16A Rebelocracy by warring side (histograms)

seventeen (when all items take the value "yes"). Figures 5.16a and 5.16b show variation across and within the warring sides and localities.[31] Note that this index excludes taxation and the maintenance of public order because they are components of both aliocracy and rebelocracy, and the goal is to differentiate the two.

In Chapter 2 I discussed the quality of this typology by evaluating its relevance and parsimony. It is also important to assess whether this simple distinction between rebelocracy and aliocracy indeed captures distinct types that are observed in reality – ideally, it should be capturing "natural" groups: types where within-group variation is minimized, and between-group variation is maximized, while being parsimonious (Gerring 1999:380). Are *rebelocracy* and *aliocracy* capturing two distinct realities?

---

[31] These measures are not proxies of a latent variable. Rather, they are a direct measure of the theoretical concept, to wit, the scope of the armed group's influence in local affairs by establishing institutions to regulate conduct. This is why it makes more sense to use a continuous variable. Another possibility would be to create an index of intervention in each realm of life, and build the index of rebelocracy giving each realm an equal weight (as opposed to giving each item the same weight). Adopting this approach does not change the results in any substantial way.

The Determinants of Rebelocracy and Aliocracy 143

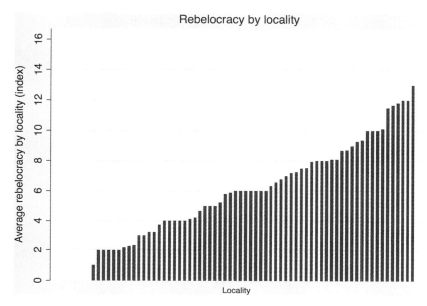

FIGURE 5.16B Rebelocracy by locality

Using k-means cluster analysis we can calculate the Euclidean distance between observations on the basis of measures of the dimension the typology is trying to capture – to wit, armed groups' influence on local institutions. Based on this distance, we can identify two groups or clusters that are homogeneous – where each cluster contains elements that are as close as possible to the other elements in the cluster. Using the measures of armed groups' influence in each realm of local life introduced before, I created scores for their economic and political influence, provision of public goods, regulation of social conduct, and social interaction. Each score is standardized to have values between zero and one. As Figure 5.16c shows, there is a strong positive correlation between all the different scores within each cluster, and a strong, negative correlation between all indexes across both clusters.[32] This means that armed groups' intervention tends to be either broad or narrow, regardless which spheres of local life we look at. These results suggest that this simple, minimalist typology successfully captures two very distinct types whose elements share many attributes.

[32] These results are not sensitive to adding or dropping variables or changing the seed. See Appendix 2 for a more detailed discussion of this test of the quality of the typology.

144   The Determinants of Social Order

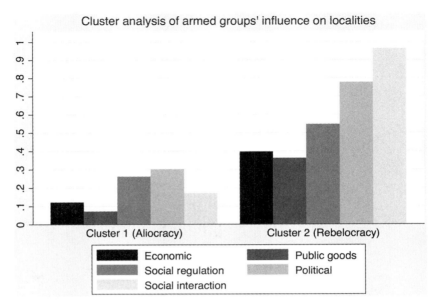

FIGURE 5.16C Cluster analysis of armed groups' influence on localities

The central contention of the theory advanced in Chapter 3 is that aliocracy is more common when the quality of local institutions is high – in particular, of dispute institutions. In such communities, the armed group prefers to abstain from establishing rebelocracy because it expects collective resistance to it. When dispute institutions are low-quality – that is, either illegitimate or ineffective – individual preferences and collective action problems prevent resistance from being organized and sustained; anticipating a low probability of resistance, armed groups are more likely to establish a social order of rebelocracy. The following hypothesis can be derived:

H6:   Rebelocracy is more likely than aliocracy when the quality of local dispute institutions is low. Likewise, aliocracy is more likely when such institutions are of high quality; that is, when they are both legitimate and effective.

As Figure 5.17 shows, communities with high-quality preexisting institutions tend to have lower levels of rebelocracy than communities with low-quality preexisting institutions. This difference is statistically significant at 0.1 percent.

It is possible that the quality of local institutions changes after the arrival of the first armed group. Imagine, for example, that a guerrilla group creates committees to adjudicate disputes. If the guerrillas leave and

The Determinants of Rebelocracy and Aliocracy 145

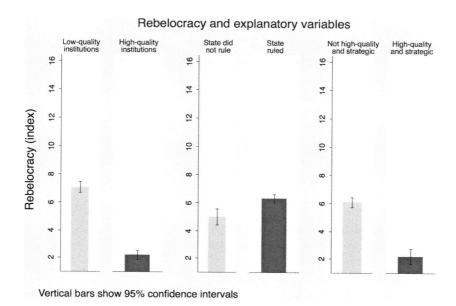

FIGURE 5.17 Rebelocracy and explanatory variables

a new armed actor arrives, wouldn't these committees operate as high-quality institutions, successfully adjudicating disputes and providing the basis of high-quality collective action? As discussed in Chapter 3, while possible, this is a rare development. Precisely because armed groups fear that civilian autonomy hurts their control over the population and, hence, of the territory, they seldom develop community organizations that are really autonomous. Some of them, especially the guerrillas, do foster several instances of community organization; but they seldom allow them to operate independently. On the contrary, it is quite common to find that all warring sides harass and oppose grassroots organizations that aim to operate outside the leadership of the armed actor. As a civilian in Itagüí, Antioquia, said about the time of paramilitary rule in his community, "we had to abandon all our leaderships, keep a lower profile .... Of all our community work, 80% decayed."[33]

As the extensions of the theory discussed in Chapter 3 suggest, state presence can also increase the likelihood of aliocracy by creating high-quality local institutions:

---

[33] Case # 40. See Appendix 1 for the list of cases.

H7: Aliocracy is more likely than rebelocracy when the state's noncoercive presence is high.

In order to capture whether state presence decreases rebelocracy, I use the variable *state rule*, a dummy variable measuring whether when asked the question, "who ruled in the community at that time?" participants responded that a state agency or public servant did (e.g., the major, the police inspector, the *corregidor*). In 62 percent of all observations, the state ruled. As Figure 5.17 shows, when the state rules rebelocracy is actually likely to be *higher* (and the difference is statistically significant at 0.1 percent), suggesting that the quality of state institutions tends to be low.

Finally, I mentioned before that, contrary to what the extensions of the theory discussed in Chapter 3 suggest, disorder is *not* more likely in communities with high-quality institutions located in highly strategic territories. I explore whether rebelocracy is more or less likely in these communities in order to help elucidate whether they avoid disorder by allowing rebelocracy to be consolidated, or whether they do have bargaining power even in highly strategic territories and therefore manage to decrease armed groups' intervention. As Figure 5.17 shows, these communities exhibit, on average, much lower levels of rebelocracy, suggesting that civilians do retain some bargaining power even in highly strategic territories.

Statistical Models on Rebelocracy

In order to test these hypotheses on the determinants of aliocracy and rebelocracy, I estimate similar linear multi-level models to those estimated for order. As before, these models have random intercepts and fixed slopes; I include fixed effects for armed organizations, warring sides, and years, and include as controls altitude and whether the locality is a *cabecera*. In addition, I control for the strategic value of the territory.[34]

---

[34] Given that the hypotheses aim to explain rebelocracy and aliocracy *conditional on order having emerged*, I estimate the models only on cases of order, based on the variable that captures whether civilians lived under high uncertainty. Cases of disorder, which based on this measure make up 19 percent of the sample, cannot, by definition, be aliocracies or rebelocracies because the latter require stable rules. Nevertheless, I make two robustness checks: (1) I use the Heckman correction for selection bias, and the results of OLS models are consistent with those of the multi-level models; and (2) I use a multinomial model (with the dependent variable being order, rebelocracy, and aliocracy) and the results are also consistent. I discuss this issue in greater depth in Appendix 2.

The Determinants of Rebelocracy and Aliocracy   147

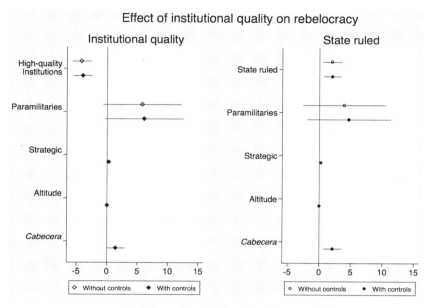

FIGURE 5.18 Effect of institutional quality on rebelocracy

As the left graph in Figure 5.18 shows, high-quality local institutions have a negative and significant effect (at 0.1 percent) on rebelocracy. The figure shows the estimated parameters of two models: one without controls and one with strategic, altitude, and *cabecera*. The size of the effect of institutional quality on rebelocracy is quite large. As Figure 5.19a shows, when holding all other variables fixed at their mean, rebelocracy decreases by 59 percent when the guerrillas interact with communities that have high-quality institutions, as compared with communities with low-quality institutions; although the decrease is lower among paramilitaries, it is still very large: 44 percent.[35]

Whether or not the state rules does not decrease the level of rebelocracy. To the contrary, it seems to facilitate armed groups' ability to rule civilian affairs (Figure 5.18). This can be explained by the stark variation that exists not only in the extent to which the state is present in localities across Colombia, but also in the quality of its institutions and its provision of services. Insofar as the

---

[35] Note that low levels of rebelocracy do not amount to disorder because I am estimating the models *only* on cases where order did emerge.

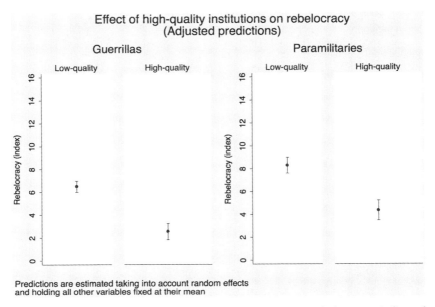

FIGURE 5.19A Effect of high-quality institutions on rebelocracy (adjusted predictions)

state provides high-quality institutions, its rule *does* hinder rebelocracy: estimating a model only on communities that were ruled by the state shows that high-quality institutions do reduce rebelocracy by approximately 51 percent for guerrillas and 40 percent for paramilitaries (Figure 5.19b). This result calls for future research that disaggregates the form and quality of state presence and investigates their impact on wartime social order.[36]

Finally, communities with high-quality institutions in highly strategic territories exhibit *lower* levels of rebelocracy, although the size of the effect is small (Figure 5.20). Recall that in the previous section the models on the determinants of order and disorder suggested that disorder is not more likely in communities with high-quality institutions that are located in a strategic territory. The data on rebelocracy suggest that when communities that meet both conditions escape disorder, they do experience slightly lower levels of rebelocracy. Together, these results indicate that armed actors are less tolerant of civilian autonomy in highly strategic territories,

---

[36] I pursue this goal elsewhere (Arjona 2016c).

The Determinants of Rebelocracy and Aliocracy 149

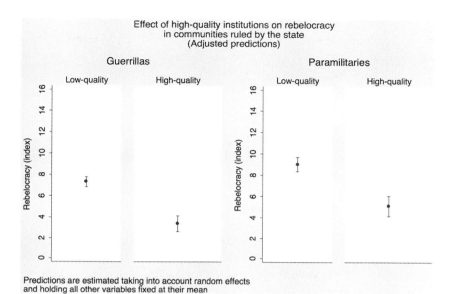

FIGURE 5.19B Effect of high-quality institutions on rebelocracy in communities ruled by the state (adjusted predictions)

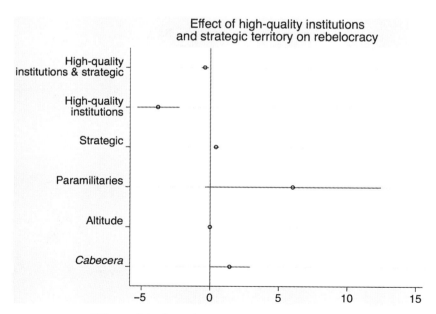

FIGURE 5.20 Effect of high-quality institutions and strategic territory on rebelocracy

but still reduce their intervention in civilian affairs. In other words, in this context armed actors are still willing to negotiate the terms of their rule but are willing to accept lower levels of civilian autonomy than in territories that are less strategic.

Causal Inference

Could these results be explained by other factors? Reverse causality is not a possibility in this case, since the quality of preexisting institutions is time invariant and captures an attribute of the localities before any armed group arrived to the area. However, it is possible that omitted variables explain the correlation between institutional quality and lower levels of rebelocracy.

There are theoretical reasons that suggest that a problem of omitted variables is less likely in this case. In Colombia, high-quality local institutions – defined as formal and informal rules – come from very different sources: the state, indigenous traditional institutions, *sui generis* organizations of peasants, and religious leaders. Figure 5.21 shows the quality of institutions by source in the sampled localities. It is unlikely that

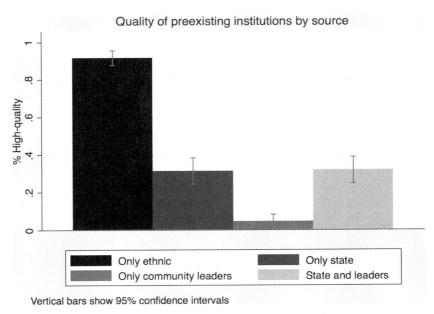

FIGURE 5.21 Quality of preexisting institutions by source

a single variable could explain these heterogeneous sources of good institutions in small geographical units throughout the country. Furthermore, such a variable would have to also be correlated with rebelocracy, but not through its effect on local institutions.

In order to improve the basis for causal inference, I rely on an instrumental variables approach. The instrument measures the potential influence of indigenous populations since the beginning of the twentieth century on the quality of institutions in each locality in the sample. In order to substantiate the relevance of the instrument, and to defend the plausibility of the exclusion restriction, I rely on key pieces of historical evidence as well as a detailed description of a single case. As Dunning (2012) suggests, detailed evidence on processes can be crucial to defend both the relevance and plausibility of instruments.

Internal migration has been a constant in Colombia since the arrival of the Spaniards in the sixteenth century (Tovar 1997). Indigenous and black populations escaped from the domination, mistreatment, and genocide of the conquerors, fleeing to remote areas throughout the colonial period. In the nineteenth century, the war of independence and several internal civil wars caused new waves of internal migration (Velandia & Buitrago 1989; Gómez 1991). Marginalized populations continued to migrate in order to escape from violence, the pressure of landowners, and poverty. Indigenous populations in many areas of the country fled in search of new territories (Gómez 1991). In many cases, they migrated in groups, bringing with them their traditions and social organization.

Over time, some of these indigenous groups mobilized to preserve their institutions by educating the youth, prioritizing the respect of their traditions, and demanding the state to respect their autonomy. In the 1970s, indigenous organizations started to demand cultural rights and the recovery of their land. Some of them achieved unprecedented forms of self-governance that allowed them to confront the state, landowners, regional elites, and multinational organizations. The 1991 Colombian Constitution recognized the autonomy of the indigenous peoples, their right to their land, and established new mechanisms for their participation in national politics. Despite the importance of these formal changes, the rights of indigenous communities are still being violated, and their struggle continues (Benavides 2009; Rappaport 2007).

Since the current armed conflict started in Colombia, several indigenous populations have exhibited highly organized forms of resistance, and have openly declared their opposition to being ruled by armed actors (Caviedes 2007). In my interviews with former guerrilla and paramilitary commanders, it became clear that they learned how hard it was to impose their rule on indigenous populations that were organized around their governance structures. A former mid-level paramilitary commander described how futile it was to try to force certain indigenous communities to submit to his group: "when you are dealing with some indigenous communities, fighting them is useless. If there are a hundred, you can kill 90 of them, and the remaining 10 will keep fighting, even if armed only with sticks. It is too costly to confront them. It is much better to strike some deal early on."[37]

As Dunning (2012) argues, qualitative methods can be extremely useful to address the validity of instrumental variables. In Appendix 2, I provide detailed evidence of how an indigenous Nasa community in the Cauca region was able to consolidate highly effective institutions to adjudicate disputes, solve community problems, interact with state agencies, and deal with threats from armed actors. This system of self-governance enjoyed broad backing by community members and was highly effective – it eventually led to some of the most remarkable instances of collective action in the country. Over the years, this community was able to obtain inalienable land ownership of more than 500,000 hectares of land, and the right to manage political and administrative affairs. Using process tracing, I show how these forms of local governance and outstanding collective action allowed them to resist the occupation and rule of the FARC. The community also demanded that soldiers of the National Army abandon its territory, and – armed only with their batons – its members even rescued victims of kidnapping by scouring the bushes until they found them and their captors. Although not all indigenous groups have achieved these outstanding forms of self-governance, some have successfully done so in different regions of the country. Hence, the presence of indigenous populations correlates with high-quality local institutions, making it a relevant instrument.

As indigenous groups migrated, they carried with them the potential to create high-quality institutions. Building on the work of España and Sánchez (2010) and Diaz-Cayeros (2011), I built a proxy of the effect that indigenous people could have had on the quality of local institutions across the national territory over the course of five decades. I use data on the total number of indigenous people living in each

---

[37] Interview conducted by the author (interview # 108; see Appendix 1 for a list of interviews).

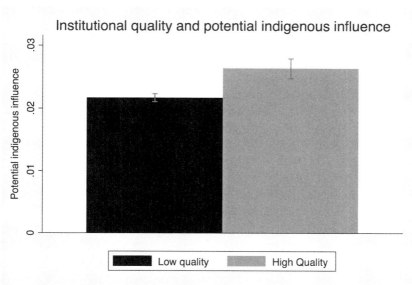

FIGURE 5.22 Institutional quality and potential indigenous influence

municipality of the country from the 1912 census. To measure the potential effect of these populations if they migrated later on, I built a distance matrix – that is, a matrix with the distance between the urban center of each municipality and the localities in my sample. I then weighted the rate of indigenous people in each municipality by the distance to each locality in my sample, which provides a measure of the potential effect of indigenous migrants on each locality. This measure captures the effect that indigenous people could have over time on other communities depending on how far and accessible they were.[38] As Figure 5.22 shows, the instrument is highly correlated with institutional quality: the potential influence of indigenous populations since 1912 is higher in communities with high-quality local institutions during the armed conflict.

There are two reasons why the "exclusion restriction" could be violated, i.e., why indigenous migration could be correlated with wartime social order through a mechanism different than its effect on institutional quality: that the potential for indigenous migration is correlated with

---

[38] For a detailed description of this measure see Appendix 2. I thank Fabio Sánchez for his insightful comments.

other factors that affect wartime social order, and that such migration could have brought something else beyond institutions that shape wartime social order. Although it is impossible to fully rule out these possibilities, there are several pieces of evidence that suggest that they are unlikely.

First, the instrumental variable captures the *potential* for indigenous influence, not its actualization. It is unlikely that the many factors that determined who migrated since the early twentieth century, and where they went, are correlated with the distance between the places where indigenous people lived and the sampled localities. It is therefore improbable that the potential for indigenous migration to a given locality is correlated with the emergence of rebelocracy through a different channel – especially given the large internal migration the country has experienced since the 1910s.

The second possibility is that indigenous influence amounts to more than institutions. In what ways could indigenous communities influence the strategies of armed actors or the response of civilians other than through their institutions? An important issue to note is that while using a proxy of ethnicity as an instrument for a variable that aims to explain rebel behavior would be clearly misleading in ethnic conflicts, the Colombian conflict has not been fought along ethnic lines. It is definitely not the case that armed actors prefer not to occupy the territories inhabited by indigenous populations, who have in fact been highly victimized in the conflict.[39] Furthermore, armed actors often do rule in areas populated by Afro-Colombian and indigenous persons.

Armed actors could have lower incentives to create rebelocracy where indigenous populations are present because some indigenous communities own collective land. Armed groups seeking to expropriate land could be less interested in ruling indigenous communities because obtaining legal property rights over their land would be more difficult. In order to account for this possibility, I control for whether the locality had collective land (owned by either indigenous or Afro-Colombian communities).[40]

Another possibility is that indigenous communities bring with them a complex bundle of institutions that impact their members' responses to rebelocracy through other channels beyond the quality of their governing

---

[39] For example, by 2013 almost 10 percent of the indigenous population had been displaced due to the armed conflict (www.semana.com/especiales/proyectovictimas/ [accessed on February 10, 2014]).
[40] I rely on official data from the *Instituto Colombiano de Desarrollo Rural* (INCODER).

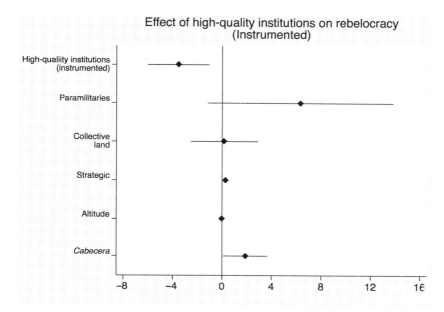

FIGURE 5.23 Effect of high-quality institutions on rebelocracy (instrumented)

institutions and, specifically, of their dispute institutions. Since there are no measures of the distinct institutions that indigenous communities have developed, I cannot rule out this possibility. However, several studies of indigenous communities that have resisted armed actors stress the former's desire to preserve their institutions as well as their high capacity to sustain collective action (e.g., Hernández 2004; Hristov 2005; Rappaport 2007; Caviedes 2007; Troyan 2008; Wirpsa, Rothschild, & Garzón 2009). The detailed evidence presented in Appendix 2 supports the contentions of this literature.

In sum, this is a clearly relevant instrument and several reasons suggest that it is highly plausible. As such, it contributes to hypothesis testing by reducing the possibility of omitted variables. I estimate again the effect of institutional quality on rebelocracy, this time with the instrumental variable. I perform a two-stage estimation with multi-level models with bootstrapped standard errors in the second stage.[41] The second stage shows that, consistent with previous models, the quality of preexisting local institutions leads to lower levels of rebelocracy, and the effect is significant at 1 percent (Figure 5.23).

---

[41] I use the multi-level bootstrap of the lme4 package in R.

Testing the Mechanism

The results presented in the previous section provide strong support for the central hypothesis advanced in this book: that, when the conditions for the emergence of order are met, the quality of preexisting institutions leads to lower levels of armed group intervention in civilian affairs. Yet, is this result explained because those communities are more likely to resist? Is the capacity to resist the underlying mechanism?

In order to test for this mechanism, I explore the effect of instances of resistance to an armed group in the past on current levels of rebelocracy. All else being equal, if communities that can resist are likely to push armed actors to establish lower levels of rebelocracy, then communities that have resisted in the past should be more likely to negotiate in the present – and, in consequence, armed groups should be more likely to limit their ruling aspirations. We should therefore find that instances of resistance to other armed actors in the past are associated with lower levels of rebelocracy in the present.

Lagged resistance is a variable that counts how many of the following forms of resistance took place in the past in a given community: locals organizing to ask an armed actor to change its behavior, uniting to protect themselves from an armed group, engaging in peaceful or armed resistance, or rescuing victims of kidnapping. The variable measures the occurrence of these events as the community interacted with the previous armed group that was present in the area, and therefore excludes the first interaction that the community had with an armed group. Although the sample size is small (209 observations), the effect is negative and significant at 0.1 percent. Holding all other variables at their mean, rebelocracy decreases by 72 percent in the case of guerrillas, and by 56 percent in the case of paramilitaries, when the community engaged in collective resistance with another armed actor in the past, as Figure 5.24 shows.[42]

While this test is suggestive, it is not robust. Theoretically, we would expect resistance to be unlikely to emerge because armed actors adapt their ruling behavior in order to avoid it – hence, the cases of resistance that we do observe are likely to be either outliers or cases of highly strategic territories, where civilian autonomy is less tolerated. Empirically, there are very few observations and the estimates of these models can be biased.[43] In Chapter 7 I come back to this mechanism

---

[42] The results of this model are presented in Table A2.4 in Appendix 2.
[43] This is the only result that is not confirmed by a Bayesian analysis.

Conclusion

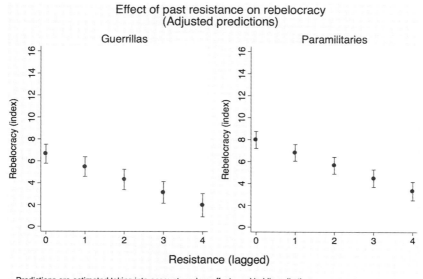

FIGURE 5.24 Effect of past resistance on rebelocracy (instrumented)

and test it using a very different approach: combining process tracing and the logic of natural experiments. I use detailed qualitative evidence to show how the quality of local institutions facilitates resistance, gives civilians bargaining power, and, in turn, leads armed groups to limit their intervention in civilian affairs.

CONCLUSION

In this chapter I provided a detailed account of my data collection process, and tested the theory developed in Chapter 3 on the determinants of variation in social order across communities in war zones. Relying on an original panel dataset of community–armed group dyads, I found broad support for most of the hypotheses developed in previous chapters on the conditions under which *disorder, aliocracy*, and *rebelocracy* are likely to emerge. Armed competition and indiscipline have a robust, positive effect on the level of *disorder*.

Turning to the factors that explain why communities and armed groups interact under different types of social contracts, the quality of local institutions has a strong effect: rebelocracy is, in all specifications of the model, less likely to emerge when the community has both legitimate and effective institutions. The presence of state institutions does not prevent rebelocracy; in fact, it tends to facilitate it. However, high-quality local institutions do hinder rebelocracy even in areas ruled by the state. These results suggest that what matters is the quality of state institutions, not its mere presence.

While these findings shed light onto the question about the determinants of variation in civilian–combatant relations and the social order in which they live, they do not say much about the dynamic aspect of their interaction. How does disorder emerge? How are aliocracy and rebelocracy consolidated? How do they function? How do civilians live within the new regulations that are established under each social order? I turn to these questions in Chapter 6.

6

Creating Rebelocracy, Aliocracy, and Disorder

Chapter 3 developed a theory that identifies the conditions under which each form of social order emerges. Chapter 5 tested the main implications of that theory. Yet, the interaction between civilians and combatants is evidently a dynamic process, where both actors shape, adapt, and respond to each other's behavior. There are several, fascinating aspects of this interaction that are relevant in and of themselves, as they speak to more general questions about the foundations of political order. This is, in the end, a story about an aspiring ruler who conquers, occupies, and (sometimes) rules a population. How that happens matters beyond contexts of civil war, as it bears on the old question of how political order comes to be. In this sense, the processes by which rebelocracy, aliocracy, and disorder emerge speak to the foundations of domination, governance, obedience, and revolt.

Analyzing these processes is also essential to understanding wartime social order: we need to grasp not only the conditions under which different forms of order emerge, but also *how* they do so. How do armed groups approach local communities when they first establish contact with them? How does the process of achieving territorial control take place? How do combatants gain deference, respect, and cooperation, or defiance and disdain? How is each type of social order consolidated and sustained over time?

This chapter explores the processes leading to rebelocracy, aliocracy, and disorder to achieve three goals. First, I aim to offer a more nuanced theoretical account of the strategies that armed groups employ towards civilians. Thinking of civilian–combatant interactions as taking place within a process where an aspiring ruler attempts to build a new order can illuminate important dynamics of war. Based on the theory on wartime social order presented in Chapter 3, I derive implications on three questions about civilian–combatant interaction: Why armed groups use violence and against whom, what kinds of alliances they seek with local actors, and what roles do community structure and social divisions play in these processes?

Second, I want to offer detailed descriptive evidence of the functioning of these local orders. By relying on different sources and kinds of evidence, I provide a nuanced account of the different stages involved in the consolidation of social order in war zones. I also describe how each social order functions with rich information on both the grand attributes of these social orders – such as who rules and what the core regulations are – and daily life within them.

And finally, I illustrate the causal mechanisms linking my central explanatory variables with the outcome. In particular, I discuss the mechanisms by which armed groups' discipline, armed competition, preexisting local institutions, and the value of local territories shape social order. While I cannot offer a systematic test of every assumption and mechanism, this evidence illustrates their plausibility. Chapter 7 tests systematically the mechanism underlying aliocracy, to wit, that the quality of preexisting institutions creates the conditions for resistance to rebelocracy, allows civilians to bargain with armed groups, and pushes the latter to settle for aliocracy. Chapter 8 offers a systematic test of one of the central microfoundations of the theory, to wit, that cooperation is higher under rebelocracy, by testing its implication on recruitment.

I start with a stylized view of the process by which new social orders are created, from the arrival of a non-state armed actor to a territory, to the consolidation of a new social order. Based on the theory presented in Chapter 3, I then theorize armed groups' strategies to approach local communities. After briefly describing the sources that I use in this chapter, subsequent sections discuss the processes leading to rebelocracy, aliocracy, and disorder.

THE PROCESS OF CREATING SOCIAL ORDER IN WAR ZONES

Although each case has its own particularities, we can think of the process by which new social orders are consolidated on the basis of the following stylized view, with three distinct stages (Figure 6.1):

The Process of Creating Social Order in War Zones 161

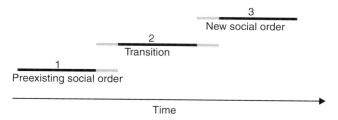

FIGURE 6.1 Stages in the process of creation of social order

In stage 1, the local community lives within a given (preexisting) social order. The gray line at the end of this stage represents the first arrival of an armed group to the locality. The group may send a small delegation to venture in the targeted territory and gather information about its residents. The delegation may stay to create ties with some locals, perhaps undercover, or go back and forth exploring the area. Combatants may also rely on a few informants to gather information, avoiding the need to visit the area more frequently. Once the group starts its activities, stage 2 begins. The divide between stages 1 and 2 can be blurry, as armed groups often initiate their activities slowly, covertly, in a manner unnoticed by locals. Yet, in some cases the change is abrupt and the group simply shows up one day in the locality and immediately undertakes multiple activities. Violence may be entirely absent, or very intense, as will be explained below.

Regardless of how open or covert the rebels' arrival is, we can analytically differentiate between the first stage, when no combatants are actively present, and the second, when they initiate their activities. In this second stage, both the rebels and the community are active players: the former adopts a particular behavior towards civilians – what I call their *entry strategy* – and the latter responds to that behavior. In this transition phase, both players may adapt their behaviors to one another as they update their expectations of viable alternatives. Over time, the transition phase ends and a new social order is consolidated, under which both civilians and combatants know which rules guide behavior. This social order may differ either slightly or radically from the order that the community experienced in stage 1, as the armed group may have caused either major changes or only minimal ones. Within this new order, locals learn what the likely outcomes of alternative conducts are, given the new organization of their affairs. If no clear rules are established, for example, because two or more groups compete with each other, the transition phase

162   *Creating Rebelocracy, Aliocracy, and Disorder*

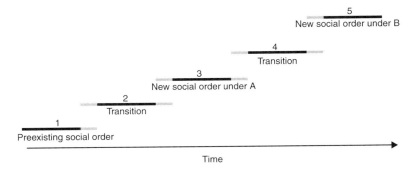

FIGURE 6.2 Example of concatenation of social orders in a community throughout the war

does not lead to a new form of order, although it does disrupt the preexisting one, bringing about disorder.

In reality, this process can take place multiple times in a given community as it interacts with several armed groups. As a result of those interactions, multiple social orders can emerge throughout the war. Figure 6.2 shows the trajectory of a community that lives through different forms of social order during its interaction with armed groups A and B.

In this example the community lives within a given order before an armed group arrives in its territory (1); armed group A arrives, and a transition phase starts (2); within some time, a new social order is consolidated in which civilian affairs are shaped by the interaction of the armed group and the community (3). When group B arrives, it finds a community living within a particular social order. For analytical purposes, this order can be depicted as a preexisting order of the community that group B has targeted for conquest, even if group A plays a key role in it. There is, again, a transitional phase (4), until a new social order is consolidated (5).

In this chapter I break this trajectory into smaller, intelligible processes by focusing on each cycle that starts with a transition, moves on to a new order, and ends with a new transition. Additionally, I take into account the key role that previous interactions with armed actors may play in shaping future ones.

COMMUNITY STRUCTURE AND ARMED GROUPS' STRATEGIES

Once we recognize that armed groups interact with civilians under different forms of social order, it becomes evident that their incentives and abilities to use different strategies are likely to vary depending on their goals, constraints, and expectations. As they play different roles within the community, expect different behaviors from civilians, and confront (or not) armed competitors, combatants are likely to make different choices regarding their interaction with civilians. In this section I explore how community structure impacts armed groups' strategies.

I start with armed groups' strategies to bring about a new form of order. Who within the community do armed groups approach in their quest for rebelocracy and aliocracy? Their choice can be inferred on the basis of the general theory presented in Chapter 3.

I argued that simply by looking at whether the community has legitimate and effective institutions, or not, we can explain the type of social order that emerges: if institutions are legitimate and effective, the armed actor opts for a social order of aliocracy to avoid triggering organized resistance; if the institutions are *either* ineffective or illegitimate, the group is better off by establishing rebelocracy. While community structure does not affect the outcome – that is, whether rebelocracy or aliocracy emerges – it does impact the process by which it happens.

An armed group faces different incentives when aiming to build rebelocracy or aliocracy. In the former case, it is an aspiring ruler; in the latter, it is an occupation army – sometimes welcomed, sometimes not. Seeking to secure military control is quite different from envisioning social, political, and economic rule. By inquiring into the particular institutional failure in a given community, we can theorize who the group approaches to penetrate a new zone in order to build one of these forms of social order, as Table 6.1 shows.

To develop this argument, I explain why armed groups would approach a different sector of the community in each case, and identify the strategies that they may use. In particular, I discuss the use of violence, private goods, and ideological mobilization. Violence entails any act of physical aggression towards a civilian in the locality. Private goods entail

TABLE 6.1 *Community structure and armed groups' strategies to build order*

		Legitimate institutions	
		No	Yes
Effective institutions	No	From below (Rebelocracy)	Through faction (Rebelocracy)
	Yes	Through faction (Rebelocracy)	From above (Aliocracy)

providing goods that only one person or family can benefit from, like groceries, as opposed to public goods for the entire community or certain members of it, like a road. Ideological mobilization consists of discussing with locals the group's political goals and appealing to the grievances or challenges that they, as members of a given group (a class, ethnic group or other collectivity) confront (Sanín & Wood 2014:215). To be sure, I do not argue that we can understand these strategies *only* by looking at the group's desired form of social order and community's structure. Rather, my point is that by taking into consideration the interaction between civilians and combatants within a particular process whereby a new form of order emerges, we can learn more about the conditions under which combatants are likely to use these strategies, and the effect they are likely to have. The purpose of this section is to lay out the logic of the argument. I offer detailed evidence later in the chapter, when I address the process by which each form of order comes to be.

Armed Groups' Strategies Leading to Aliocracy

When institutions are both effective and legitimate, the armed group has incentives to establish an order of aliocracy; the mechanism is the expectation of resistance by a cohesive community that values their current governance structure and is capable of organizing collective action. Knowing that leaders or representatives are strongly endorsed by the population at large, armed groups have incentives to approach this community *from above*, in an effort to agree on a mutually beneficial social contract in which the existing structure of governance is respected. This negotiation can have different modalities. The group may try to convince the leaders to offer spontaneous support and comply with minimal rules due to a common ideological interest; this is likely to happen when the group's stated goals overlap with the interests of the community, and no previous grievances exist against the group within the communities' leadership. Combatants may also offer material rewards, security, or protection in an effort to obtain civilian cooperation.

When armed groups have doubts about a community's capacity to resist collectively, they often use violence as a measurement instrument: they threaten or even kill the leaders to weigh the community's capacity to preserve its governance scheme once the group tries to take over. If by beheading the leadership local collective action is destroyed, the group tries to find key cooperators to bring about rebelocracy. If the community, on the other hand, remains united and resists, the group may negotiate a social order of aliocracy.

Once aliocracy has been consolidated, armed groups may use private goods, violence, and ideology in particular ways. Violence is used only to punish those whose behaviors break rules that affect the group's security and, if applicable, taxation. At the same time, combatants abide by rules of behavior of which locals are aware. The group may also provide private goods and disseminate its ideology to foster greater cooperation.

It is important to note that even though aliocracy rests on civilians' bargaining power because they can resist, not all cases of aliocracy entail tension. In fact, communities that are ideologically supportive of a group may well preserve their autonomy in terms of handling their own affairs while being strongly committed to the rebels' cause. In these cases, combatants may engage in activities to teach their ideology and mobilize locals based on it.

Armed Groups' Strategies Leading to Rebelocracy

There are two paths towards rebelocracy: *from below* and *through faction*. When institutions are both ineffective and illegitimate, the group anticipates that current rulers or leaders – if there are any – lack support among the population. In addition, the absence of working institutions makes resistance very unlikely. Anticipating a low probability that current leaders are backed up by the population at large, the armed group has incentives to approach the community from below. As will be explained later, a mix of violence, ideological appeals, promises, and public and private goods often suffice to gain sympathies and access to networks. Using violence to preserve public order tends to be essential in this quest, as it signals both might and the capacity to establish and enforce effective institutions. Ideology helps to give this power an aura of legitimacy. The provision of goods and services creates selective incentives as well as a moral obligation to reciprocate; it also shapes beliefs and emotions, which help to motivate cooperation. Once a large segment of the community is on board, rebelocracy is likely to emerge and be consolidated.

When institutions are legitimate but not effective, or effective but not legitimate, the group can expect to find a divided community where at least a sector is willing to bring about change – be it regarding class structure, ethnic prerogatives, social mobilization, or any other grievance. Likewise, it can expect that some members of the community would resent new institutions and therefore deny cooperation. In this situation, armed groups have incentives to approach that part of the community that would favor change, and portray themselves as a viable means to bring it about. By making alliances with key actors, infiltrating their organizations, or colluding with them, the armed actor penetrates the community, gains power, and eventually establishes a new social order of rebelocracy.

Such alliances can be sought with a segment of powerful elites, a union, an organization of peasants, an ethnic minority, a group of victims of another armed actor, or a political party. Ideology here plays a central role, as it is likely to determine who is the most viable candidate. A guerrilla group seeking to redress the grievances of the poor is more likely to find allies among poor peasants; and paramilitaries defending property rights and the status quo are more likely to be aided by elites.[1] In Colombia, in fact, both rebels and paramilitaries often exploit existing social conflicts in local territories to insert themselves by allying with a sector of the population, as Pécaut (1993) has argued.

Violence and private goods can be used strategically as well to form alliances. Violence is useful because it can show allies quick returns: if institutions are illegitimate, violence is used to expel or punish the elites; if institutions are ineffective, it is used to create rule enforcement. Offering private goods can also help to convince a reluctant influential sector to engage with the group.

Once rebelocracy has been consolidated, the group creates formal and informal rules to regulate different conducts beyond security. Combatants use violence not only to punish disobedience of rules related to security and taxation, as in aliocracy, but also to ensure social control by punishing noncompliance with other rules. Hence, even though the incentives to use violence against potential detractors are lower, as Kalyvas (2006) argues, the group has incentives to use it for the sake of maintaining the desired form of social order.

In rebelocracy, armed groups also have incentives to grow their influence and gain more cooperation by preaching their ideology and

---

[1] Local conditions, however, may push an armed actor to forge alliances with population groups that do not share their interests or ideological views. The FARC, for example, has offered protection to landowners in some areas of the country in exchange for material contributions (Aguilera 2013:103).

appealing to locals' interests and values. Likewise, public discourse about the group and its presence in the area is monitored. In addition, private goods are often used to push specific individuals to cooperate, and public goods are sometimes provided to the general public. I give many examples of these practices later in the chapter.

Armed Groups' Strategies Leading to Disorder

What are the strategies of armed actors with short time horizons? According to the theory presented in Chapter 3, disorder is the equilibrium when the group's time horizon is short due to high armed competition, internal opportunism, or macro-level changes in the war (such as the imminence of peace negotiations). It may also be sought as a means to eliminate (via assassination, displacement, or a combination of both) a community that aims to resist in a highly valued territory. Who armed groups approach in each case, and why they use violence against them, can also be inferred on the basis of this logic.

When a unit has a short time horizon due to competition, its goal is to secure control in the short run. I will refer to the group that used to have control and is being challenged by an incoming group as the "defending group," and to the incomer as the "attacking group." Following Kalyvas (2006), both the defending and attacking groups have incentives to use selective violence against civilians to deter defection. If information about civilian defection is gained, selective violence will be high; otherwise, armed actors will opt for indiscriminate violence. Due to the imbalance in territorial control, the attacking actor is more likely to rely on indiscriminate violence in the earlier stages, as its capacity to get information is highly restricted; the defending armed group, on the other hand, has access to the population and is more likely to use selective violence.[2]

However, this pattern may not be homogenous across communities. Combining Kalyvas' theory of violence with the underlying mechanisms of civilian cooperation discussed in Chapter 3, we could expect some communities to be more or less likely to be targeted with selective violence: since the likelihood of supplying information to either group varies across communities, so should their vulnerability to selective targeting. There are three reasons why local populations may be more

---

[2] This is the situation found in zones 2 and 4 in the model proposed by Kalyvas (2006).

or less likely to denounce other community members as collaborators under the same level of competition between the warring sides.

First, communities living under disorder have greater incentives to provide information to the attacking group than other communities would under the same circumstances. Even if the defending group can punish defection more effectively, people may see cooperation with the attacking group as a way out from an erratic and repressive ruler. Second, communities living in a social order of rebelocracy may have beliefs, emotions, and preferences that push them to cooperate with the defending group – mechanisms like ideological beliefs, the recognition of the group as an authority, and reciprocity may be at work. These communities would exhibit greater cooperation toward the defending group than other communities, all else being equal. Finally, communities with strong institutions and living under aliocracy might be better able to avoid supplying information to either group, given their greater capacity for collective action.

If this logic is correct, defending groups are more likely to use indiscriminate violence when (i) they have previously ruled the community under disorder, or (ii) the community had high-quality institutions prior to the arrival of the defending group, because in both situations civilians would be less likely to supply information on defectors. However, defending groups would be less likely to use indiscriminate violence against a community where they have ruled under a social order of rebelocracy. Attacking groups, on the other hand, are more likely to use indiscriminate violence against communities with high-quality institutions, and communities living under rebelocracy; yet, they are more likely to find denouncers in communities living under disorder, and therefore are better able to use selective violence there.

As I mentioned in Chapter 3, it is important to note that when lacking informants, armed groups can rely on alternative strategies to select their targets. As Balcells (2017) suggests for *regular* civil wars and Steele (2016) for *irregular* civil wars, group membership provides clues about who is more likely to cooperate with either side. In the Spanish civil war, Balcells finds certain individuals were more likely to be targeted by the republicans – for example, priests. In the Colombian case, Steele finds that those living in areas where voting for the Left was high were more likely to be targeted by right-wing paramilitaries. Available evidence also suggests that unionists in Colombia, who are often assumed to be associated with the Left, are more likely to be targeted by the Right.[3] Although all armed groups have incentives to use this type of group targeting when attacking an armed actor that has greater access to the population, it could be more common in communities with high-quality institutions given their lower probability of providing information about collaborators.[4]

Despite armed groups' greater likelihood of using violence when competing for territorial control, coercion is not their only strategy. The attacking group has incentives to approach in nonviolent ways members of the community that are at odds with the enemy either for ideological reasons, personal interests, or emotions. Victims of the defending group are often a key resource for the attacking group because they have strong emotions against combatants who harmed them or their families. In its quest to find a few early supporters who provide information and offer assistance in the confrontation, the attacking armed group often offers private goods to some individuals, or seeks to mobilize them based on ideology. I will offer evidence of these practices later in the chapter.

According to the theory outlined in Chapter 3, armed competition is not the only scenario in which a social order of disorder emerges. Undisciplined combatants are likely to break the social contract with local populations because such contracts impose constraints that decrease combatants' short-term benefits. Even combatants who do care about long-term outcomes have incentives to free ride in order to satisfy short-term preferences; if they are part of an organization that cannot ensure that its members comply with their rules, free riding becomes widespread and disorder emerges regardless of competition and local conditions. In this situation, the armed actor is unlikely to target specific individuals due to their identity or their leadership; rather, combatants choose their victims in order to obtain private benefits – be it economic profit or some other form of personal gain, including committing different forms of violence.

---

[3] More than 1,000 unionists were killed in Colombia between 1999 and 2009 (Vidal Castaño 2012).

[4] As I mentioned in Chapter 3, some armed groups are more violent and abusive than others, even in communities enduring disorder. Internal rules and discipline may have a great impact on the limits combatants follow in their treatment of civilians (Hoover 2011), even when no tacit mutual agreement has been established. The point is not that combatants act without following any rules under disorder, but rather that they follow *internal* rules as opposed to rules that the community expects them to comply with.

Finally, the theory of social order predicts that when an armed actor aims to control a highly strategic territory, tolerating aliocracy is costly. This is the case in areas that conceal high-level leaders or training camps, or that serve as *corridors* connecting large areas of the country or allowing for the trade of illicit goods. If communities living in these areas deny full cooperation, the armed actor has incentives to eliminate them and either leave the area unpopulated or bring in strong supporters. Approaching the local community from the beginning with violence and direct orders to flee is common in this situation. Once the community has been expelled, the group can work toward the construction of rebelocracy with newcomers or they can keep the area empty. Civilian leaders are more likely to be targeted first, in case doing so breaks local organization and makes rebelocracy feasible. However, if the community proves to be resilient, targeting is likely to be generalized.

In the remainder of this chapter, I illustrate the process by which social orders are built by providing evidence of armed groups' strategies and civilians' choices in each stage of that process.

MEASURING AND DESCRIBING ORDER AND DISORDER, REBELOCRACY AND ALIOCRACY

In the subsequent sections of this chapter I rely on empirical evidence from different sources. First, I utilize the qualitative and quantitative data I collected on the interaction between civilians and combatants over time described in Chapter 5. Using interviews, surveys, and memory workshops, I reconstructed the history of interaction of a random sample of 124 community–armed group dyads in 74 communities located in 29 municipalities throughout Colombia. More than ten different armed groups (some left-wing guerrillas and some right-wing paramilitaries) operated in these localities. This evidence allows for identifying patterns in the different social orders, while also giving a sense of why the actors involved behaved as they did. The details on the methods I used to gather this evidence are given in Chapter 5. All descriptive statistics come from these random samples.[5]

---

[5] All descriptive statistics incorporate sampling weights. I follow the Horvitz-Thompson approach to create sampling weights based on the probability that each unit is included in either of the two samples. For a discussion see O'Muircheartaigh & Pedlow (2002).

The second source consists of almost 180 in-depth interviews and focus groups conducted with former combatants of both paramilitary and guerrilla groups, civilians living in war zones, scholars, NGO staff members, and public officials. This evidence provides insights into the mechanisms that underlie both civilians' and combatants' choices at different times in their interaction with each other. They also give additional detailed accounts of how different wartime social orders work, and how people experience them.

I also use former combatants' responses to a survey that I conducted in collaboration with Stathis Kalyvas in 2005. A random sample of about 800 former combatants of both guerrilla and paramilitary groups participated in this survey, responding to questions about the places where they lived prior to enlisting in an armed group and the places where they operated as combatants.[6] These data provide additional information about how different forms of social order function as well as about both civilian and combatant behavior.[7]

As discussed in Chapter 5, both order and rebelocracy vary along a continuum. Uncertainty varies from low (*disorder*) to high (*order*); and the scope of intervention of the armed group in civilian matters varies from low (*aliocracy*) to high (*rebelocracy*). However, in order to describe each form of social order, I need to classify each dyad at a given time as a case of disorder, aliocracy, or rebelocracy.[8] In this chapter I rely on two simple measures that capture the central feature of each type.

The central attribute of order is, by definition, the existence of a social contract between civilians and combatants that gives place to predictability. I measure order based on an open-ended question that asked respondents to indicate if they ever lived under high uncertainty and, if so, when. Cases in which respondents reported that they did are classified as disorder; cases in which they did not are classified as order.

Although the social contract that underlies civilian and combatant behavior is rarely spelled out, people often learn what the rules are and can plan their lives accordingly. Although armed groups abused civilians

---

[6] Chapter 8 describes this survey.
[7] Throughout this chapter I provide the name of municipalities but not of villages and neighborhoods in order to protect the identity of my interviewees.
[8] As in Chapter 5, the unit of analysis is the community-armed group dyad. For simplicity, I use the term *case* to refer to this unit when describing the data.

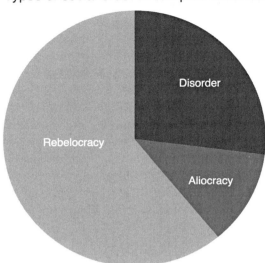

FIGURE 6.3 Types of social order in sampled localities

in almost every place studied for this project, periods of high uncertainty were less common than periods of order: overall, 27 percent of all observations are cases of disorder, while 73 percent are cases of order. Localities under guerrilla presence were more likely to face order (83 percent) than those under paramilitary presence (58 percent). This difference is likely to be explained by the fact that paramilitaries often expanded to places with guerrilla presence, and competition with them led to disorder. Guerrillas, on the other hand, often expanded to places where no other armed actors were present, and therefore built new forms of order without creating disorder first.

Turning to rebelocracy, although the level of intervention of armed actors in civilian affairs varies greatly, rebelocracy is defined as intervention beyond two essential roles of government, to wit, security and taxation. Using this measure, 84 percent of all cases of order are rebelocracies, while 16 percent are aliocracies (the difference between guerrillas and paramilitaries is not statistically significant). Figure 6.3 shows the classification of all observations based on these measures.

All descriptive statistics in the subsequent sections rely on these measures of disorder, rebelocracy, and aliocracy, and come from the random samples described before, unless otherwise noted.[9] Testimonies come from interviews or focus groups conducted in case studies. I refer to interviews as "Int. #" and to case studies as "C. #." The list of interviews and cases can be found in Appendix 1.[10] It is important to take into account that all this information comes from testimonies and, as mentioned in Chapter 5, memory can have many flaws and people may be more willing to report certain events than others. However, many clear patterns emerge from the evidence, showing stark similarities between communities located in different areas of the country, as well as between testimonies of civilians and former combatants. This consistency across sources suggests that the evidence does capture essential aspects of the wartime social orders that have operated in Colombia.

THE CREATION OF REBELOCRACY IN WAR ZONES

Following the theory presented in Chapter 3, rebelocracy is more likely to emerge in a situation where military competition is low, the armed group does not face major indiscipline problems, and preexisting local institutions are of low quality.

The first step in the construction of rebelocracy is gathering information about the local population: who they are, what are their problems and needs, who might become strong allies, and who is likely to show opposition. Going through a process of *data gathering* is therefore important for two reasons. First, this information allows the group to assess the community's capacity to resist which, in turn, determines how costly or beneficial it is to try to establish rebelocracy there. Second, having good information on which institutions are ineffective or illegitimate provides the group with a clear sense of what it could offer, and to whom, to win sympathies. Knowing whether the community is strongly divided along a cleavage, which are the relevant factions, and who can command others are also useful for rebels to identify potential allies as well as targets.

It might seem unrealistic to expect that a rebel group would invest in such a careful exploration of local societies, but existing evidence suggests

---

[9] A few descriptive statistics come from the survey with former combatants. I make this explicit every time I use this source.
[10] Every time I talk about a case or an interview, I provide the name of the municipality and department but not of the locality in order to avoid the identification of the communities that participated in this study.

that commanders do so quite often. A former member of the FARC who joined the group in 1970 and demobilized in 2007 was very clear about the importance of getting to know communities before trying to control their territory:

> To win a civilian they [the FARC] go to a house and introduce themselves. They ask how the family is doing regarding food, the harvest, etc. Sometimes combatants come back and organize a collective sowing ... If they visit a poor house, the commander orders combatants to bring food ... perhaps a bag of groceries. They may buy a cow for that family. In this way the civilian feels protected by the FARC, and in the future, is of use to the group. (Int. 99)

In a village of El Roble, Sucre, people remember that around the year 2000 members of the FARC started showing up in the town donning civilian clothes rather than uniforms. "They only came to have a beer or to buy something or at night to play pool ... they also came as street vendors or as people who offered some service gathering intelligence and looking at how people behaved" (C. 90).

Combatants often see this initial work of "intelligence" as a necessary step towards victory. Commanders and low-rank combatants that I interviewed who were in charge of "the work with the masses" or "social work," identified locals' needs as the best opportunity to gain early collaborators. To a mid-level commander of the FARC, "The best way to enter a new territory is by identifying what people need; even more, what people dream of. If the organization is able to directly work for that outcome, or pressure someone to do it, it should. Why? Because this is the best and easiest way to create a social base" (Int. 105).

Another former FARC member noted that it is essential for the group's success to be attentive to people's preferences and demands:

> There are differences across cultures. In some places you cannot arrive talking against alcohol and partying ... that goes with the culture. You have to focus on security. But if you arrive in an area where people cultivate potatoes, you need to criticize the government, the prices, the lack of help. If it is a village that is not getting anything from the local government because people did not vote in support for those holding office, the FARC stresses its support to get public services; they soon see the movement as their ally. (Int. 110)

A mid-level paramilitary commander discussed the problem of how to approach communities in non-contested areas in a strikingly similar way; "It is important to know who is who in each zone. The best is to achieve a slow *concientización* [consciousness-raising] in the area ... We arrive and ask for the president of the Communal Action Association (JAC), the

TABLE 6.2 *Entry strategies to build rebelocracy*

	Private goods (%)	Public goods (%)	Social cleansing (%)*	Ideological meetings (%)	Violence against leaders (%)
Paramilitaries	10	15	100	50	40
Guerrilla	17	35	80	75	26

* This number comes from the sample studied in 2010, not 2012. In 2012 we did not ask this question in all communities.

mayor, and we try to create a team." Even more, when I asked what happened if people denied cooperation, he said: "Well, if the FARC are not around, we try to reach them through others who have influence on them. We work on them through the people they trust." If another armed actor was previously in the community, the newcomer tries to exploit resentment against it: "If there was abuse by the subversives, it is easy to identify who to talk to. In meetings with the population, in houses, having some drinks ... People want defense (by the state or by us) and we tell them we will do it" (Int. 108). A former FARC member who operated in Cundinamarca said the same: "You look for victims, and that is the best way to penetrate networks and gain early support" (Int. 104). To another former FARC member, "the relatives of the victims of the state or the *paras* [paramilitaries] see the FARC as their friends" (Int. 110).

Once the group has a social map of the community, it sends combatants to the area either disguised as civilians or in uniform. At this point they may combine different strategies to gain cooperation from a few persons early on. Table 6.2 shows the entry strategies adopted by paramilitary and guerrilla groups in cases where they eventually built rebelocracy.

Private goods – such as giving food or helping the sick – were used in 15 percent of the cases where rebelocracy emerged under either guerrilla or paramilitary groups. Many interviewees remember that combatants arriving at their homes or public places in their communities offered help on various matters, ranging from addressing children's needs to paying debts. In a community in Itagüí, Antioquia, paramilitaries from the Metro Bloc gave small presents for Christmas (C. 45).

Private goods are often combined with initiatives to improve infrastructure or the provision of a public good. In the cases where they eventually built rebelocracy, the guerrillas were much more likely to provide some form of public goods (35 percent) than the paramilitaries (15 percent). This difference can be explained by the fact that guerrillas are much less likely to start their interaction with communities under competition than paramilitaries are, since the latter often expand to territories with guerrilla presence.[11] A former FARC member recounted how his group used to organize events to clean trails as a way to show people how things could improve under their leadership. In Cundinamarca, they even built an aqueduct during the first stage of interaction with the local population (Int. 104).

Launching "cleansing campaigns" (*campañas de limipieza social*) to clear the area of "undesirables" often follows. Rapists, thieves, and drug addicts are often targeted soon after the group arrives in the territory. Combatants seem to be well aware of the benefits that these campaigns may render: in several interviews conducted with former paramilitary and guerrilla members, it was clear that what they often call "pacification" opens up the main gateway to many local communities. As a former member of FARC put it, "bringing security to a defenseless community that is fed up with robberies and street fighting signals the benefits that our presence may bring to people" (Int. 109). Indeed, guerrillas and paramilitaries often rid the areas where they operate of delinquency.

A journalistic account of the modus operandi of paramilitary groups in Colombia depicts the situation in similar terms:

[T]heir entry to the cities is usually through the most marginal neighborhoods, where the presence of the state is weak and the provision of public utilities is insufficient. The paramilitaries start by killing thieves and drug addicts in order to provide a feeling of security to its inhabitants ... This helps to explain, in part, why in some of the poorest neighborhoods of [different Colombian cities] killings have increased while robberies have decreased.[12]

Several other studies of guerrillas, paramilitaries, and conflict zones in Colombia have found that this type of violence tends to be welcomed by residents in many places (e.g., Cubides 2005; Taussig 2003; Aguilera 2013).

Public gatherings to talk about the group's ideology and its shared interests with the community are also common. Guerrilla groups organized this type of meeting in the first stage of their interaction with civilians in 75 percent of the cases where they eventually established rebelocracy. The percentage is lower among paramilitary groups

---

[11] While ideology could also explain the difference, once order is established paramilitaries are as likely as the guerrillas to get involved in the construction or maintenance of infrastructure.

[12] *Semana*, April 23rd, 2005.

(50 percent). The difference might be explained by the disparity between guerillas and paramilitaries in the importance they give to ideology more generally. As mentioned in Chapter 4, combatants are socialized in different ways in both groups: while guerrillas often hold frequent meetings to discuss their ideology and politically train their members, paramilitaries do so much less often. In fact, in my interviews with ex-combatants the difference between former members of guerrilla and paramilitary groups in terms of their political training was usually quite evident. Those who participated in guerrilla groups knew more about the goals of their group and its underlying political position than their paramilitary counterparts.

In communities with illegitimate and ineffective institutions, combatants usually invite everyone to attend these meetings. They then try to convey their commitment to locals' interests and outline the steps that will be taken to pursue them. In a village in the Sucre department, for example, the FARC held a few meetings on a Saturday – the day when fishermen visited the main town to have some drinks. A combatant would go bar to bar announcing the meeting and emphasizing that it was mandatory to attend. All public places were closed until the meeting was over. An interviewee remembers these gatherings as follows: "The commander of the 35th front of the FARC introduced himself as the authority of the community. He talked about his ideology as that of the army of the people, and warned everyone that some issues were not negotiable with them, such as the issue of gossipers and thieves." In a rural community of Santuario, Risaralda, the paramilitaries also started by inviting everyone to attend a meeting. "Almost everyone came. It was a pacific arrival. They told us who they were, and did not mistreat anyone. On the contrary, they were polite ... They didn't yell" (C. 75).

In divided communities, combatants start with more selective meetings in order to gain backing from key individuals and organizations whose support facilitates the penetration of social networks. For example, guerrillas often approach communities where peasants see the landowning elite's rule as illegitimate by seeking alliances with unions, peasant organizations, or wage workers. Cities or towns with a large, discontented workforce are targeted in similar ways. The Popular Liberation Army (*Ejército de Liberación Popular*, EPL), for example, deeply penetrated and eventually took over some unions in the city of Barrancabermeja, where thousands of people worked for ECOPETROL, Colombia's public oil company (C. 4). The situation in rural areas where many people worked on large plantations with poor living conditions was similar.

Paramilitaries often approached those affected by the guerrillas or who had interests in opposing popular mobilization, like owners of large plantations. Furthermore, in many cases the paramilitaries arrived to a region because the elite called them. In Santuario, Risaralda, "It is a well known secret that facing the threat of kidnapping, the municipal elite called the AUC" (C. 61). Upon their arrival, the paramilitaries already had allies. In fact, they had so much help that the guerrillas did not even fight back. They quickly left the municipality.

As the group gains access to community networks, it starts to expand its influence. According to a local resident in Itagüí, Antioquia, the paramilitaries of the Metro Bloc "put their people in the JACs, we don't know if also in some NGOs, in order to investigate who were their friends and who weren't. They infiltrated the police, the city council, everyone ... They got to the youth, then to merchants. This is how they expanded" (C. 45).

In communities with illegitimate and ineffective institutions, the population tends to view the combination of private goods, public order, infrastructure projects, public goods provision, and public meetings as improvements – thus, these actions are unlikely to lead to rejection. The presence of the group is perceived as a source of organization, order, and positive change. In this sense, accepting its presence does not entail allying with a side of the armed conflict; rather, it is about allowing an actor to continue a conduct which has in some manner advanced the situation of the local population. In this early stage, many individuals welcome the presence of the group and voluntarily cooperate with its initiatives to improve local conditions. In this way, combatants penetrate local networks, get to know people, and create links with them by combining private goods, community work, and ideological appeals.

The words of a young former FARC combatant illustrate the group's success in this method of gaining early cooperation, and preparing the ground for becoming a de facto ruler:

When you arrive at one of those zones ... and help a person to build her house, or show up with groceries at a home in need, or succeed in organizing the community to build something, like a trail ..., later on these people won't deny you their help, even if they have to risk their life. And this is how, little by little, there are more, and more, until the group can arrive in the area, wearing the uniform, to really organize the community. (Int. 100)

Once the group has penetrated networks and gained sympathizers, it gradually expands its influence over other spheres of local life; it may ask for material contributions, intervene in political and social organizations, and establish a new code of behavior, making clear displays of its coercive power when misbehaviors take place.

In communities with illegitimate and ineffective institutions this rule is open and direct: the group creates new regulations and openly enforces them. However, in divided communities combatants often rule in the shadows. Power and control over the population are gained by exploiting whatever influence and command those allied with the group have. Eventually, however, people know that behind the union, the mayor, or the elite, there is a guerrilla or paramilitary commander.

In some cases, the group slowly takes over the faction that allowed it to penetrate networks, control the population, and gain power. This has often been the case with local elites that supported the paramilitaries – it was with their help that the armed actor managed to penetrate networks, gain cooperation, and regulate conducts. But once the group had enough power, it could use this influence to dominate those that were initially its allies. In Villanueva, Casanare, this is precisely what happened. The cattle ranchers and agro-industrial elites supported a local paramilitary group led by alias Martin Llanos since around 1994.[13] The group soon became abusive, threatening even those who had supported them at the beginning. They also slowly infiltrated local organizations to "take over any money available and be the authority" (C. 35). Similarly, in Puerto Gaitán (Meta), the paramilitary groups organized by emerald traders decided to strengthen the JACs. According to a local interviewed there, "the JACs were very weak and the *paras* organized them so that they could co-opt them. Many of their leaders became informants. At the same time, the *paras* gave the JACs money for parties and for food" (C. 29).

Sometimes rebelocracy also starts with violence against leaders. As I discussed before, armed groups sometimes harass leaders to assess how strong collective action can be, and to weaken the community's resolution to act united against the armed actor. I illustrate this use of violence later in the chapter when I turn to armed groups' entry strategies leading to aliocracy.

Although the process by which rebelocracy is consolidated looks quite different depending on whether the group tries to build it from

---

[13] This was actually the second group created in the area. The *Buitragueños* operated since the 1990s, led by Martin Llanos' father.

below or by seeking alliances with key actors, the outcome is similar across time: more or less overtly, the group manages to transform local institutional arrangements in ways that favor it either directly or indirectly. How do such institutions operate on the ground? What does this new order look like?

LIFE UNDER REBELOCRACY

Regardless of how armed groups begin the process of building rebelocracy – either by ruling directly or by infiltrating a sector of the population – they usually end up influencing many domains of local life, permeating the spheres of politics, economics, social relations, and even private life. An interviewee from the municipality of Granada in the Meta department described the presence of the paramilitaries in the town as follows: "They have a lot of influence in the way in which civilian life is organized. They are some sort of a state. They regulate everything and establish rules like not to rape, steal, or hit children" (C. 10). Similarly, the paramilitaries in Puerto Gaitán, led by alias Guillermo Torres, created rebelocracy with great intervention in all sorts of affairs. They established rules that banned stealing, rape, and domestic violence, and regulated social behavior in public places and even sexual conduct. Prostitutes were obliged to take medical exams often, and they shaved the heads of women who were found having sex in public places and forced them to clean public spaces for a few days. Several case studies provide detailed evidence on the regulatory practices of paramilitary groups throughout the country (Torres 2004; Gutiérrez & Barón 2006; Madariaga 2006).

Descriptions of social order under guerrilla groups are similar. In the city of Barrancabermeja, an interviewee described the presence of the ELN as follows:

At first, the Elenos [ELN fighters] came in to replace the state. They set up rules; regulated the salaries and jobs at ECOPETROL [Colombia's national petroleum company]; they were the owners of the gasoline cartel; they influenced the decisions of the local government; they were invited to all social events; organized the strikes in ECOPETROL, and with that, they paralyzed half of the country. (C. 4)

As this example suggests, rebelocracy does not emerge only in rural areas. Several poor neighborhoods of large cities, including Bogotá, the country's capital, are often ruled by armed groups. As I discuss later in this chapter, rebelocracy does not imply that the state is absent. Often, civilians still relate with state authorities even though many aspects of their lives are ruled by armed actors.

In what follows I discuss armed groups' intervention in different aspects of local life.

Security and the Use of Violence

For an armed group, the monopoly over the use of violence is crucial. Above all, it is a means to defend sovereignty, as it makes it more difficult for other armed groups to take over the territory. It also increases social control, which in turn strengthens territorial control. In 20 percent of the cases of rebelocracy, locals reported that the group protected them from other armed actors at least once.

Turning to armed groups' use of violence *against* civilians, even though combatants have fewer reasons to expect civilians to cooperate with enemy groups when they fully control the territory (Kalyvas 2006), they still use violence for another purpose: to maintain the social order that they have established. Within rebelocracy, violence is used to punish disobedience of a myriad of rules. Depending on the offense, civilians are often given two opportunities to correct their behavior before being expelled from the locality or killed. Disobedience with respect to certain rules, like those banning the provision of information to enemy forces, is often punished with death without warning.

Violence against civilians can also be used in ways that awaken sympathies, depending on who is getting killed or harmed. As with the cleansing campaigns discussed before, by becoming the prosecutor of violent actors like thieves and rapists, the armed group can win the applause of many locals. In 88 percent of the cases where rebelocracy emerged in the sample, the armed actor established clear punishments for those committing these type of crimes. In numerous interviews I conducted, civilians praised the capacity of both paramilitaries and guerrillas to keep people they saw as criminals or deviants away. Even several of my interviewees who resented the brutality of violence under the paramilitaries in the town of Tierralta, Córdoba, were quite assertive in their acknowledgement of the group's capacity to stop all delinquency: "You could leave anything on the street, during the entire night, and no one would take it. They knew they would be dead the next morning. Girls could walk around knowing they would not be abused. Now, since the demobilization, thieves are making their business again. And several girls have been raped. And nothing happens" (C. 20).

Armed actors often regulate mobility as well. In about 60 percent of the cases, they established rules about when civilians could be outside their homes or travel.[14] Locals often had to ask for permission to leave the municipality, especially if they were leaving for several days. Furthermore, in some places they needed to carry documents to be able to show the group that they were indeed residents, if stopped at checkpoints. A person in Puerto Parra, Santander, recounts that between 1975 and 1982 the FARC gave them a pass (something like an ID) that allowed them to move around the municipality. "It was uncommon for the FARC to let anyone in unless they had a pass, or they came with someone who had one." Even though the FARC controlled this locality, the army was nearby:

The army also came up with a pass in order to be able to move around and we had to carry it. We had to report to control points every two weeks or every month. If we didn't go, they would ask where we were and verified that were still living in our home. If people didn't show up, they investigated or tortured them ... People had to carry both passes, but if the army found someone carrying the pass of the FARC, they were in trouble. (C. 70)

This testimony depicts the difficulties that civilians encounter when living in a rebelocracy surrounded by another armed actor, as well as the trouble armed groups go to in order to maintain that order.

Taxation

All armed groups fighting in the Colombian conflict have demanded contributions from civilians. Who is taxed and how heavily varies across cases. In Puerto Gaitán, Meta, everyone had to pay: teachers, merchants, fishermen, and landowners (C. 29). In other cases, only the wealthier paid, like in the FARC's early years in Viotá, Cundinamarca. Overall, in 75 percent of all cases where communities interacted with armed groups under a social order of rebelocracy, combatants asked for some form of economic contributions from civilians. The percentage is slightly higher among paramilitaries (80 percent) than guerrillas (73 percent).

In addition to demanding contributions, armed groups also taxed certain activities. In Viotá (Cundinamarca), the FARC taxed the owners

---

[14] This number comes from the sample of communities studied in 2012. We did not ask this question in 2010.

of large extensions of land, merchants, and large companies that had sold their products in the area for years. At some point, they also started to tax peasants who owned small farms (C. 21, 23). According to several interviewees in Tierralta (Córdoba), the paramilitaries taxed every worker in town; from those selling coffee in carts on the street to taxi drivers to shop owners – all had to pay (C. 20).

Dispute Institutions

As discussed in Chapter 3, the backbone of rebelocracy is the armed group's ability to become the central adjudicator of disputes. By doing so, armed actors not only monopolize the use of violence but also the right to mete out justice. Overall, in 63 percent of all cases where armed groups intervened beyond security and taxation, they became the de facto court – that is, the actor people turned to in order to solve problems related to the location of land borders (i.e., property rights over land) or debts. The percentage is higher for guerrillas (68 percent) than for paramilitaries (53 percent).

Several accounts suggest that armed actors strive to become the de facto court in areas under their control. García Villegas' (2008) fascinating study of judges in Colombia's conflict zones provides several examples. In some cases, armed actors expelled judges from the municipality in which they worked (p. 111); in others, the commander allowed the judge to stay in as far as he did not do his job (p. 97).

The evidence collected in my fieldwork overwhelmingly shows that once an armed group becomes the main adjudicator of disputes, it becomes a central figure in the life of the locality. For example, in Pasca, Cundinamarca, a local recounts that the FARC "became like an office of complaints: everyone would go there to solve all the problems" (C. 64). In Puerto Parra, Santander, a civilian said that the FARC solved all kinds of conflicts, "because everyone wanted to get rid of bad things .... And without knowing who else to turn to, we looked for the FARC" (C. 85). In Pasca, another civilian states that

> the FARC became indispensable to people because they always looked for the group to resolve problems, and [the group] would scold those responsible. People were calmed and they hung onto [the FARC] because there was no law there, and [the FARC] started to fulfill the role of authority. In this way, it was common that people asked [the group] to threaten or execute someone, or for its support to collect a debt. When someone wanted [the FARC] to intervene, they simply went up to look for them. (C. 65)

In a rural community of Casabianca, Tolima, turning to the paramilitaries became so common that people would use the threat "or else, I will let the paramilitaries go after you!"[15] (C. 94).

Economic Activities and Labor

Both rebels and paramilitaries display attempts to regulate economic activities, including labor, in some of the areas they control. It is common for both groups to forbid fishermen to use nets in high parts of the river so that fishermen down the river are not left without fish. Armed actors regulated fishing in many of the places where they operated (36 percent of all observations, with little difference between the two warring sides). Often, they also regulated activities to preserve endangered species. In a rural community of Puerto Parra, Santander, the paramilitaries regulated fishing and hunting: "They said that people couldn't fish with a drag-net, they forbade fishing at night ... In hunting, it was forbidden to kill [certain animals]" (C. 83). The protection of natural resources was particularly widespread among the FARC. According to one of my interviewees in Viotá (Cundinamarca), "at least, what we have all gained with this is the re-emergence of the beautiful woods we used to have here. Both flora and fauna bloomed after years of strong regulations [by the FARC] ... No one dared to cut or move a piece of wood without the approval of the commander" (C. 21–23). Likewise, in Córdoba, where exotic wood was exported for some time, the FARC regulated peasants' felling of trees.

Armed groups also regulated certain activities. Taxi drivers affiliated with different companies in Tierralta, Córdoba, were only allowed to operate on certain days of the week by the paramilitaries in order to, they said, allow everyone to have their share of the market (C. 209). In 65 percent of the cases where rebelocracy emerged, armed groups intervened to set minimum wages, improve the conditions for workers, or regulate other aspects of labor. Of these, most were cases under guerrilla rule (85 percent), and only a few were under paramilitary rule (15 percent).[16]

Direct intervention in profitable economic activities was not uncommon. Perhaps the best documented examples are the activities related to the cultivation, production, and transportation of coca. Although

---

[15] In Spanish, they used an expression that is used to warn someone that they would let their dog loose on them: *"le voy a echar a los paras."*

[16] This statistic comes only from the sample of 2010. The question was not asked in 2012.

these practices have varied across time and space, both guerrillas and the paramilitaries got involved in every step of the production chain, either by creating a monopoly over the activity, or by taxing those who participated. Overall, armed groups regulated the coca market in 25 percent of the cases of rebelocracy. Paramilitaries regulated mining in 43 percent of the cases, while guerrillas did so in less than 1 percent of them. Illicit mines became an important source of income to illicit groups late in the conflict; in the cases I studied, it occurred in the late 1990s or early 2000s.

Private Behavior and Social Interaction
In most cases of rebelocracy, armed groups regulate several aspects of the private behavior of locals. Domestic violence is regulated by both warring sides in most localities where they established rebelocracy (67 percent of all observations, with little difference between guerrillas and paramilitaries). According to several interviewees, both warring sides were quite vigilant of infidelities, and particularly strict about physical abuse of family members.

Personal appearance was regulated by armed groups in about 40 percent of the cases where they established rebelocracy. In these cases, long hair and earrings on men were usually forbidden, and transgressors of this rule often faced physical punishments. In some places it was prohibited for women to wear short skirts.

Sexual conduct was also regulated in about 30 percent of the cases. According to interviewees, homosexuality was forbidden and adultery would be punished most of the time, by both sides. Most interviewees also mentioned regulations of prostitution, although the specific ways in which armed groups deal with it vary across regions.

Some measure of freedom of speech was also guarded by both sides in most of their areas of influence. Different interviewees who lived under the rule of the FARC or the paramilitaries said that sometimes there were no formal or explicit rules over what could be said and discussed and what couldn't. Yet, people knew there were some topics they should not comment on, and everyone was aware of the danger of sharing political views and opinions that were opposed by the ruling group. It was quite telling that in many interviews across the country people often used proverbs or sayings to describe the situation: "the law of silence rules" (C. 65), "a closed mouth gathers no flies" (C. 63), and "people had to make sure their tongue didn't go loose" (C. 75). Overall, people report rules on what could and could not be said in about 90 percent of all cases of rebelocracy.

Both guerrillas and paramilitaries also established other rules to regulate social interaction. Banning the excessive use of alcohol and gossiping are examples of these rules. Although these often allow the groups to gain some sympathizers, they are particularly useful as tools for controlling civilian conduct more generally. This is what regulation of social interaction is all about for a former FARC mid-level commander: "The FARC creates rules for living together. But this is not with the goal of creating ideological consciousness, but rather to increase their social control" (Int. 105).

Which realms of local life an armed group regulates varies across time and space. The ideology of the group plays an important role because, as mentioned earlier, while armed groups are strategic and often establish a rule because it benefits them, sometimes their only goal is to put into practice their ideology. For example, the influence of the Catholic Church on the ELN was evidenced in their explicit ban on polygamy. Guerrilla groups often defended the interests of workers – for example, by enforcing minimum wages – while paramilitaries quelled workers' demands on landowners and plantations. In addition, armed groups choose how to insert themselves in communities in response to cultural differences, local idiosyncrasies, and civilians' requests.[17]

Finally, combatants often become quite familiar to civilians. In 59 percent of the cases where rebelocracy existed in the sample, people said that locals used to play soccer or pool with combatants, and 50 percent said that they attended parties together.

Political Participation and the Capture of Democracy

Armed groups also intervene in local politics and shape political participation. Influencing elections is quite common: in 50 percent of all cases of rebelocracy, interviewees reported that combatants intervened in local, regional, or national elections. The guerrillas banned turnout 40 percent of the time – a practice not found among the paramilitaries in the municipalities under study. Sometimes the guerrillas or paramilitaries decided who could run for mayor or council member. In Puerto Parra, Santander, the paramilitary group Los Masetos once called a meeting with the candidates in a different municipality. There, the political advisers of the AUC decided who was the most viable candidate, and selected him (or her) as the winner, way

---

[17] Later in the chapter I argue that armed groups have incentives to allow for some expression of dissent.

before the elections took place. "They made us all vote for him. We were given meat and a soda .... After the election, the winner had to follow their orders" (C. 85). Telling locals for whom they should vote was actually quite common in many other places: overall, this happened in 44 percent of all cases of paramilitary presence and 22 percent of cases of guerrilla presence. In relation to the so-called *para-politics* scandal, researchers have shown systematic evidence on armed groups' involvement in national elections, and the judiciary has investigated hundreds of politicians for striking deals with armed actors to win elections.[18]

The capture of democracy in conflict zones has been substantial, not only due to armed groups' influence on elections but also due to their influence on how elected officials rule. In many cases, civilians reported that guerrillas and paramilitaries told the mayor what to do, made council members vote for specific projects, and even decided who should take posts in public agencies. By relying on coercion, alliances or both, armed actors often managed to influence how local governments were run.

Combatants' intervention in politics does not stop at the ballot box. They often organized, infiltrated, or supported political protests and strikes. For example, in San Bernardo, Toledo (North of Santander), the ELN forced everyone to attend a demonstration in another locality to protest against the abandonment of the state (C. 34). In other cases, however, they supported, and often exploited, protests organized by civilians. This is what the FARC did in San Benito Abad, in Sucre, where they infiltrated a protest in the municipality's urban center (C. 36).

Finally, in many cases of rebelocracy community associations lost their autonomy. Sometimes they became weak and dissolved, and sometimes they worked as the intermediary between the armed actor and the community. This was particularly the case of the JACs: in many cases they simply disappeared; in other cases, they ended up being co-opted by armed actors, as happened in a rural community in Aquitania (Boyacá), where the FARC and the ACC operated. According to a peasant, "the JAC never worked in the same way. It fell apart" (C. 50).

This is not to say, however, that community leaders necessarily side with the armed actor. In many cases, the presidents of the JACs were

---

[18] See Romero & Valencia (2007) and López (2010). As mentioned in Chapter 4, by 2012, 200 members of congress and 470 public servants nationwide had been implicated in this scandal (Verdad Abierta 2012).

simply trying to maneuver in a very difficult situation. They often tried to deal with the group and still work for the community, without comprising their security or that of their neighbors. In some cases, however, leaders did abuse their power and their proximity to armed actors to obtain privileges or advance their interests. In some other cases, the group simply decided who should be the president of the JAC, and acted as his boss. It is important to stress, however, that community leaders cannot be assumed to be allies or collaborators. In many cases they are heroes who continue to fight for the wellbeing of their communities, but have to adapt to whoever is in power. The history of community organization and leadership in conflict zones is complex and escapes stereotypes.

It is also important to stress that the state was present in some way in most of the communities studied for this project. While at the beginning of the conflict some communities were really far away from an urban center and did not interact with any state official for long periods of time, in more recent years the state has expanded the presence of its security forces (especially the police) and of some of its central agencies. However, the *quality* of state presence remains poor in many areas. In consequence, civilians living in rebelocracy often do interact with the state while being ruled by an armed actor. What is more, they turn to the state for several services and comply with some of its demands. But the quality of this interaction is deeply tainted by the armed conflict for many reasons.

In some of the places where I conducted fieldwork the extent of collusion between public servants and armed actors was simply astonishing. In a municipality in Córdoba, I was introduced to a former *personero* (the local ombudsman) only to learn later on that he had been a paramilitary commander *while* being the *personero*. To state this more clearly: the state official responsible for defending human rights in the municipality *was* a paramilitary commander – in a municipality that endured very intense and gruesome violence. In many cases the mayor was described as a puppet of the armed group; in others, as an astute politician who got elected after making an alliance with the armed group and, as mayor, had to keep the commander happy. In other cases, people saw their political leaders maneuver very difficult environments, obeying an armed actor to some extent while trying to advance the wellbeing of the population. As these cases of co-optation, collusion, and coercion repeated themselves over and over, many civilians developed a deep mistrust of formal politics, democracy, and, more generally, the state. The political wounds of the war run deep.

The Provision or Regulation of Public Goods

There seems to be great variation both in the extent to which armed groups provide public goods when establishing rebelocracy, and in the strategies they choose to do so. Sometimes public goods are regulated in formal ways – through clear and enforced rules – while in others they are taken care of via informal procedures.

The different armed groups that operated in my field sites engaged in both formal and informal regulation of public goods. While there is no evidence that they directly engaged in the construction of schools or hospitals, they often pressured local authorities to build them or improve their services. In a few instances, civilians or combatants reported that the FARC built houses for peasants – about 150 in Planadas, Tolima (Int. 105), and a neighborhood in Apartadó, Antioquia (C. 2).

Paramilitary groups also occasionally helped civilians in need of health services (about 27 percent of the cases). In Puerto Gaitán, Meta, interviewees reported that people asked the paramilitaries for money to pay for doctor's appointments or to buy prescribed drugs (C. 15). Although the guerrillas were much less likely to do so, several interviewees in my case studies in Córdoba reported instances where the FARC helped wounded peasants by bringing the nurse that worked with the organization; interviewees in Viotá, Cundinamarca, said it was common for FARC commanders to find a vehicle and cash to take pregnant women and the sick to nearby health centers – even when these facilities were located in areas considered to be controlled by the enemy (e.g., C. 21). The accounts, however, always referred to a few cases, and seldom described these practices as systematic. Many civilians claimed they never saw or heard of the groups' involvement in these matters.

In about 18 percent of the cases where paramilitaries ruled under rebelocracy, combatants interfered somehow in the provision of education. Most of the cases entail providing children with school supplies, although on a few occasions armed actors paid the salary of the school teacher. As with health services, however, these practices are far from being systematic and only entailed the sporadic offer of aid.

In several areas, armed groups took on other public goods like the construction and maintenance of roads. They did this either by bringing in machinery or by "pulling strings" in the local administration. Several interviewees remembered instances when the FARC stole the municipality's machinery in order to build a road or repair it. Sometimes combatants would "retain" (the FARC's term for kidnapping) the operator of the machine during the days it took for the road to be built or improved. In some areas where the FARC had direct authority over the members of the council or the local administration, this was not necessary, as they would just order the work to be done. The paramilitaries, on the other hand, relied on their ties with the local administration, and usually managed to get local authorities to devote resources to this type of public project. For example, in Santuario, Risaralda, the coordination between the paramilitaries and the municipal authorities was obvious to civilians: the paramilitaries organized a day of compulsory work, and established a fine for those who did not show up. "People arrived first, they worked, and then the machinery of the municipality arrived to finish the work" (C. 61).

Getting public works done by organizing the community and making collective action compulsory is actually common among both guerrillas and paramilitaries. The maintenance of dirt roads, for example, is mostly organized via collective work. In Tierralta, Córdoba, both the FARC in the 1990s and the paramilitaries in the early 2000s set the rule of "Saturday community work": every Saturday all members of the community (or at least one representative per family) were expected to work on a local public good such as cleaning a trail. To be sure, this not only benefits civilians but, often, also armed actors themselves, as improving road conditions facilitates moving combatants, weapons, and illicit goods. There are also cases where armed groups organized collective work to take care of the town or its public spaces. In a rural community of Magangué, Bolívar, the AUC ordered civilians to keep the cemetery clean (C. 48). In many cases, the armed group ordered people to keep the front of their homes and sidewalks clean. Overall, armed actors intervened in the construction or maintenance of infrastructure in 43 percent of the cases. The percentage is somewhat higher for guerrillas than paramilitaries. In some cases, armed groups directly provided private goods to large numbers of people. They often helped with donations during festivities and in a few cases with gifts for children during Christmas.

I only found one case in which the groups provided club goods – goods to be given only to their supporters (Berman & Laitin 2008). In a rural community of a municipality of Sucre, the FARC created a cooperative to raise pigs and chicken, providing infrastructure and training. However, those who participated had to do certain things in return, like delivering packages and messages for the group (C. 92). Being part of the cooperative without offering cooperation to the armed actor was not possible.

The Costs and Benefits of Rebelocracy

Even though these different forms of intervention might seem to require substantial resources, the evidence suggests that often armed groups are able to control the behavior of the civilian population without permanently deploying many combatants to the locality. In a rural community of Santuario, Risaralda, civilians noted that the paramilitaries did not deploy members to the area but, rather, designated two locals as militiamen (*urbanos*, as they were often called) to be in charge of controlling the community. They would patrol the community once per day. Although many in the community felt uneasy with them at first, over time many people acquired their cell phone numbers and called them if they had problems or if they saw anything outside of the ordinary. Locals also noted that they had access to the commander because everyone knew where they could find him every Saturday (C. 75). In another community of the same municipality, a civilian noted that the paramilitaries did not settle in the community but visited it twice or three times every week. Despite that, they had great influence in the community and established rules to regulate many conducts, including robberies, domestic violence, and personal appearance (C. 74).

In most cases, civilians recounted that someone in the community communicated with combatants, and that gave the group the capacity to rule. People knew that information would be passed along, even if combatants were not actually living in the locality. In addition, all armed groups strived to create clear precedent early on, punishing disobedience, often with severe sanctions. The process is very similar throughout cases of rebelocracy: the group penetrates the community and gets at least some people on board, designates militiamen or allies, shows the community that it has the willingness and capacity to enforce its rules, and then maintains its new order by relying on the information provided by its local contacts.

The benefits of rebelocracy for the group cannot be overstated. Most civilians obey and a few offer spontaneous support. Some are only motivated by fear, but many are also motivated by other aspects of rebelocracy. For example, some value the group's success at eliminating delinquency; others believe in its political goals; others simply want to be on good terms with the ruler to continue with their economic activity or just to be safe; others want to gain status locally, and being an ally of the group helps. The testimony of a civilian in a town in Puerto Parra, Santander, is quite telling of the extent to which cooperation grows despite violence: "It was a relationship of respect especially because they had the weapons. But it was a pacific relation ... They protected us from other armed groups and outsiders ... They brought us calm, at least we could sleep calm. They also killed, but they didn't kill just anyone. If you hadn't done anything, they didn't touch you" (C. 85). I come back to the effect of rebelocracy on civilian cooperation in Chapter 8.

Needless to say, cooperation is not absolute. Civilians express their disagreement, make small demands on the armed actor, and even sabotage some of its orders. As I argue elsewhere (Arjona 2015), armed groups actually have incentives to tolerate, to some extent, individual opposition to certain aspects of rebelocracy. Such expressions of discontent are important for rebelocracy to be maintained, as they allow the armed actor to hone its practices and, in the long run, maintain civilian cooperation. Offering some space for dissent is essential for the stability and longevity of rebelocracy. It is indeed quite common to find instances of small acts of resistance in any locality living under rebelocracy.[19]

It is important to note that even though civilians have multiple reasons to cooperate with combatants under rebelocracy, many of those reasons disappear as soon as the group loses control. As Kalyvas (2006) points out, cooperation is usually as fluid as territorial control. Once the group's influence on local life fades away, so do the incentives to comply. Beliefs about the group can change – sometimes quickly – when a new group comes in. And new dynamics lead, once again, to a new social order where reasons to cooperate with the new ruler abound. This shift in civilian obedience and spontaneous support – again, not necessarily ideological – has been noted by many scholars working on the Colombian conflict. Romero (2003:267–71), for example, details how workers of banana plantations in Urabá cooperated with the guerrilla groups for years. However, when the war between the FARC and ex-EPL fighters and paramilitaries started, civilians had to change sides and cooperate with the latter, despite years of a close interaction with the FARC. In times of war, cooperating with an armed actor is often nothing other than a survival strategy.

---

[19] For a theoretical discussion of individual and collective resistance and empirical evidence see Arjona (2015, 2016a).

COLLECTIVE RESISTANCE, BARGAINING, AND THE PATHS TO ALIOCRACY

According to the theory presented in Chapter 3, a social order of aliocracy[20] is more likely to emerge when the group does not face armed competition or internal indiscipline – that is, when it operates with long time horizons – and local institutions are both effective and legitimate. In this situation, combatants give up their ruling aspirations in order to avoid fuelling resistance. The outcome is a social order where civilians obey rules about security, and make material contributions to the group while armed groups limit their intervention in other civilian affairs.

Civilians' capacity to make demands on armed actors, and even more, to resist, is usually assumed to be minimal. How can unarmed peasants confront an army? However, I found at least one case of aliocracy in most of the municipalities where I conducted fieldwork; in most of these cases, civilians were able to limit the intervention of the armed actor. Given that these municipalities were randomly selected within the country,[21] this evidence suggests that civilian bargaining with armed actors is not as rare as is often assumed.

The theory presented in Chapter 3 is agnostic about the sources of good institutions. These can be tradition, religion, the state, ethnic authorities or local organization for self-governance. The cases where I conducted fieldwork at the community level support this claim, as aliocracy was usually consolidated where legitimate and effective institutions were in place, regardless of their source. In some cases it was indigenous traditional governance; in others, civil society; and in others the state. I provide detailed evidence on the mechanisms by which high-quality local institutions, particularly dispute institutions, drive civilians' preferences for self-governance and enable collective action in Chapter 7. In this section, I briefly describe several cases where civilians expressed their opposition to being ruled by armed actors and engaged in collective action either to bargain with combatants or to resist them.

---

[20] Consistent with the measurement that I use of rebelocracy in this chapter, I consider a locality to live under aliocracy if the armed group did not intervene beyond security and taxation.
[21] As I explained in Chapter 5, I did not include the large, unpopulated areas of the southeast of the country – that is, the departments of Amazonas, Vichada, and Guainía. In these areas the presence of armed groups has traditionally been quite low, although in recent years it has increased.

Several testimonies suggest that civilians often have strong preferences against being ruled by an armed group, and that when they have a strong capacity for collective action they have bargaining power to limit combatants' intervention in civilian affairs. I found examples of this dynamic in different areas of the country, and among peasant, indigenous and Afro-Colombian communities alike. Furthermore, the ideological position of the community members does not seem to change its desire to preserve its form of governance. There are, for example, several cases where civilians sympathized with the Communist Party but resisted the rule of the communist FARC.

This was the case in a rural community in Pasca, a municipality that has long been a stronghold of the FARC. A civilian stated that even though he is a communist, his union condemns both the army and the FARC because "the FARC also does wrong. They come to treat the peasants as if we were part of a military group, and no, we are not their subalterns" (C. 66). In this same community, another peasant said that the relationship between the FARC and the civic leaders of the community was "clear and direct ... We talked to the FARC in strong terms, and we told them the truth."

In another community of peasants in Casabianca, Tolima, people welcomed the FARC's intervention to end robberies. But they disliked the group's influence in community matters. Interviewees recounted that when people had a problem they tried to find a solution within the community quickly, so that the FARC would not interfere (C. 94). The same happened in a town in El Roble, Sucre. Civilians appreciated that the ELN limited the robbery of cattle, but they did not want a new system of governance. They had always turned to the police inspector whom they saw as a legitimate authority, and they continued to do so (C. 90).

In other communities, civilians did not sympathize with the armed group's activities nor its goals, and simply wanted to be left alone. In Caimito, Sucre, the ERP (a smaller guerrilla group) asked peasants to attend a meeting. At the meeting, combatants offered their help with several matters and asked locals to cooperate. But several peasants told them that they were not going to help them. An interviewee recounts that "the message was: do not count on me. I work independently and I do not work with you." A woman proudly states that "people organized a meeting in order to coordinate and not cooperate with the guerrillas for anything; all united. Hence, those people [the guerrillas] feared the community." Civilians stressed that if they said yes to anything, they would have given guerrillas the opportunity to consolidate their power (C. 87). While this rebel group did build a social order of rebelocracy in the neighboring town, it only developed aliocracy in this community.

The first stage of the process by which aliocracy is built resembles that of rebelocracy because the group tries to gather information on the community. As discussed before, this is sometimes done with informants, sometimes with infiltrators, and sometimes by directly showing up and asking questions. Once the group has realized that local institutions are backed by most of the population, it decides to approach the leaders and consolidate a social order of aliocracy from above. However, as with rebelocracy, there are different paths to aliocracy.

In some cases, the quality of institutions and the strength of cohesion are so obvious that armed groups do not need to inquire much about them. I found several examples of local populations where negotiation with the armed actors was peaceful, and even straightforward. In Puerto Gaitán (in the Meta department), for example, the paramilitaries disputed territorial control with the FARC near the land of an indigenous community. Interviewees reported that the arrival of the paramilitaries was quite peaceful, as the FARC did not have a permanent presence there. The paramilitaries asked the leaders to avoid any relation with the guerrillas, and promised to respect their government and way of living. Later on, the group established rules on the use of violence, which were usually followed by members of the indigenous community. But in the case of disobedience, the paramilitaries talked to the indigenous authority (the Major Captain) who was in charge of imposing sanctions. "He always respected our territory," said an indigenous governor about Guillermo Torrres, the paramilitary commander. "He always said that he was not going to pick on us in as long as we did not deal with *guerrilleros*."

Over time, however, the paramilitaries did try to penetrate the community and extend their influence over it. The community governor recounts that the paramilitary commander suggested that they create a cooperative, while offering his help and advice; he also offered weapons for defense. However, the community always managed to reject these offers. The governor says they knew that if they said yes, their autonomy would have been lost. Aliocracy lasted for more than fifteen years (C. 30).

Similarly, in an Afro-Colombian community in Medio Atrato, Chocó, the FARC came peacefully to the locality and told the community that they were there to protect it. They assured locals that they respected the local authority – in this case, the Community Council (*Consejo Comunitario*). Later on, when the 43rd Front established a permanent presence in the area – day and night – the local Council sought the commander to inform him about the statutes that ruled the community. These statutes made it clear that the community was neutral in the conflict and did not have a position in favor of or against any armed actor. The statutes also stated that the community had well-defined rules for solving problems among its members, and that everyone should follow them. The presence of any armed actor, including the national army, was forbidden in the houses of this village, as well as in the school. The demands of the community even included that FARC combatants abstain from getting personally involved with community members, in particular, abstaining from romantic relations with local women. The FARC reacted by promising to abide by all these rules, which they did for some time, allowing a social order of aliocracy to be consolidated (C. 24).

The interaction between the FARC and an indigenous community in Caño Mochuelo (Arauca), in the southwest of the country, was similar. The FARC arrived in the area in 1987. They held several meetings inviting the indigenous community to join them. But local authorities were emphatic about preserving their own politics and organization. The FARC accepted the decision of the community for about three years. During this time, a social order of aliocracy, marked by little violence, disciplined combatants, and minor civilian contributions, functioned without problems. Yet, around 1990 and 1991 a new FARC commander tried to gain greater cooperation, this time by threatening the indigenous community. The local leaders sought a meeting with the commander and described, again, their way of living. The FARC responded by trying to ally with some members of the indigenous community and affect voting behavior through these members. However, the community realized this was happening and expelled the collaborators from political organizations. Soon they recovered the FARC's respect of their autonomy and interacted with the group under a social order of aliocracy for many more years (C. 17).

When the armed group realizes early on that the community will resist rebelocracy, it is better off approaching the leaders on good terms from the beginning. In this way, cooperation may not only consist of obedience to minimal rules but also of acts of spontaneous support. This is more likely to happen when the group can easily exploit some shared identity or interest with the community. When the community does give ideological support to the group, the interaction between civilians and combatants is more similar to that of a social movement and its followers. However, even then, minimal rules to protect security and sometimes to ensure locals' material contribution to the organization are likely to be established.

In other communities, however, good institutions are the outcome of a unique process, often invisible to an outsider; for this reason, the group doubts the strength of local governance. In these cases, the community has to show the armed group that it is determined to remain united and resist rebelocracy in order to gain bargaining power. This was the case of a small community of peasants in the region known as Nudo Paramillo in the north of the country (Córdoba). In order to keep the FARC at bay, peasants had to endure a difficult negotiation with the rebels. This is a community created by migrants in a remote, rough-terrain land, where there was no state presence whatsoever. Despite this, the community was very organized. It had a large cooperative that was very productive, had clear rules to solve problems, and engaged in many collective efforts to provide public goods and build infrastructure. According to one of its leaders, "at the beginning [the FARC] tried to rule over everything. They came to our meetings. They told us what we could do, where we could go, and when. We could not let this happen. We had been our own rulers for years" (Int. 57).

Determined to stop the FARC from seizing power over their local cooperative, the community decided to talk to the commander. Aware that it was a risky enterprise, they requested a meeting, and a few days later met with him.

We told [the commander] very clearly that we did not want militiamen in the area. That it was not needed. "If what you need is some information, we will give it to you. But we do not need orientation or guidelines to know what we need to do. We don't need any of that. We know very well what we need to do." And in the end, the commander agreed. (ibid.)

After a long discussion that included threats and insults, the group agreed to respect the cooperative and to avoid intervening in its affairs. It would still require some contributions, and if cooperation with the national army was discovered, the deal would end. The group even agreed to issue a written agreement to be signed by both parties. Soon after, however, the paramilitaries arrived, burned the village, and displaced the entire population (Int. 57).

As mentioned before, when the group is dubious about the collective action capacity of the community it may use violence both to test the community's resolution, and to behead a potential resistance movement. Overall, in 39 percent of the cases where aliocracy emerged, the armed group threatened or harmed the leaders soon after arriving to the area. In some cases, the community grows stronger, as in some of the examples that I describe below. In other cases, however, violence does weaken collective action. For example, in Itagüí, Antioquia, "a female leader told members of the paramilitary group that the community did not need them and that they should leave ... A few days later, the man who had held the meeting shot her son as well as another community leader ... With this they silenced the leaders and stayed in the territory" (C. 98). This is one of the most somber patterns of violence in Colombia. The country is full of stories of assassinations of courageous leaders who represent their communities in their defiance to rebel and paramilitary rule. In some cases, the communities have the mechanisms in place to continue the struggle; in others, however, the group hurts the leaders, wins, and brings about rebelocracy.

A very telling example of armed groups' opposition to civilian organization comes from the early years of the indigenous movement in the Cauca department. One of the first political documents of this movement, called *Jambaló 81* and written in 1981, recounts the FARC's opposition to their organization and their mobilization for land – goals that would be consistent with FARC ideology. In the document, the indigenous movement states the following:

Since we started our fight with more strength, three years ago, the FARC started to oppose our fight. When we were fighting to recover our land, they came to call us to their elections. When we were holding our meetings, they came to try to take over them to talk about their strange policies. On many occasions, they opposed our land recovery ... This is why we ask: is it that all people of the FARC, of the M-19, are against our rights and our fight?[22]

The reasons why armed groups agree to limit their ruling aspirations when expecting a high probability of resistance were clear in conversations with both civilians and combatants. When asked about their interactions with well-organized communities, ex-members of both sides often spoke about indigenous populations. Many of these communities rely on well-defined, embedded mechanisms of social order. Furthermore, since the 1970s several organizations of indigenous groups have worked specifically on strengthening their autonomy.[23] This is why several

---

[22] Document shared with the research team in Silvia, Cauca.
[23] The first was the National Indigenous Organization of Cauca, ONIC, followed by the Indigenous Organization of Antioquia (OIA), and then by others throughout the country.

indigenous communities have become emblematic examples of self-governance and civilian resistance in the country. Pedro, a FARC ex-combatant captured by the army, said the following in an interview: "when you are patrolling [indigenous' territories] they pretend they don't speak Spanish ... They would just not talk to you; they can stay there, staring at you without saying anything, without even nodding. It is impossible to get anything from them" (Int. 110). Likewise, as I mentioned in Chapter 5, a former mid-level paramilitary commander described how useless it was to try to force indigenous communities to submit to his group: "when you are dealing with indigenous communities, fighting them is useless. If there are a hundred, you can kill 90 of them, and the remaining 10 will keep fighting, even if armed only with sticks. It is too costly to confront them. It is much better to strike some deal early on" (Int. 108). Commanders on both sides made it clear that many indigenous communities value their self-governance like a treasure they would defend with their lives. For Pedro, the FARC commander, "you should not touch their culture and their traditions because that is untouchable ... You should not harm them in any way. Only negotiate. You can buy, sell ... but not rule them" (Int. 102).

Former paramilitary combatants in Tierralta (Córdoba) gave a similar response when asked about their group's strategy to enter territories of indigenous communities: "With the Indians [sic], we used to arrive and ask for the *cacique* [indigenous authority]. If they said it was a territory of peace, that was respected" (Int. 58). Another former paramilitary member interviewed in Tierralta gave a similar response, although not specifically about indigenous communities but generally about well-organized populations: "You go and talk to the leaders. You get the community together for a talk, and explain the objectives. Sometimes they said they were neither with us, nor with the guerrillas. Some commanders said that if they followed the rules, we should leave them alone. But sometimes the FARC killed the leaders to blame us [paramilitaries]" (Int. 59).

A former FARC member recounted his experience with an indigenous community in the Amazonian region:

When the Amazonian Front [of the FARC] was created, there was no previous presence of the organization in the area. The indigenous population is very difficult because they have their beliefs, their ideology, their governor. It is difficult for them to see people with weapons, wearing a uniform. It was very hard. We tried to penetrate their consciousness, but we didn't succeed. One day they would hide, and the next day burned their hamlet and left. They also hid the trails that the FARC needed to move around in the jungle. (Int. 100)

Although combatants tried to convince the indigenous people that they would help with public goods and security, the community kept avoiding them and fleeing, moving around in the Amazonian jungle.

Although several of the emblematic cases of resistance come from indigenous communities, peasant communities have also relied on high-quality institutions to unite and reject the intervention of armed groups in their territories. Combatants are also aware of this possibility. To a former FARC member, "when you encounter resistance from a leader you see him as a potential enemy. He is monitored and if he makes any mistake, he is expelled or killed. But if that leader has a lot of *mando* [popular mandate], then you cannot touch him. People may revolt [*se levanta la gente*]. But there are only a few cases" (Int. 106).

Civilians also proudly stress that their capacity to preserve their ways of running things in their communities relied on community cohesion and organization. Having the capacity to coordinate and stand by their collective decisions was useful in every meeting and encounter with combatants. In a rural community of Caimito, Sucre, civilians said that, "because the community stood up together, firm, united around the same position, the group was not able to have action and a strong presence with the population of [this community]." This was, to them, their "greatest achievement" (C. 87).

Aliocracy does not emerge simply because civilians have what it takes to resist collectively. Rather, it often follows a bargaining process in which civilians signal their capacity to remain united and sustain collective action. Often, armed groups keep trying to increase their influence, and civilians have to show their determination to keep combatants at bay, as demonstrated by previous examples. Small demands, negotiations, and incipient forms of resistance were widespread in aliocracy, even if confrontation was ultimately avoided, and organized, sustained resistance did not emerge.

It is quite interesting how clear this sequence of events is to civilians in some communities. Locals from a community made up mostly of displaced persons in Buenaventura, a city in Valle del Cauca, repeatedly said that they knew that the only way to avoid some of the horrors of war was to keep the armed actors away from community matters. "They [combatants] said that they did not like women who were dating someone else's husband, and they said many things; but since we did not let them in, they could not impose and make demands. If we were to turn to the group to solve our problems, that would give them space" (C. 99). Civilians in many other places stated in similarly clear terms how important it was for them to deny space – space for *ruling* – to the armed actors.

Some communities aiming to limit the activity of armed actors in their territory decided to make their position public. A few emblematic cases have been well documented by scholars and journalists[24]. Many of them were instances of resistance to violence more than resistance to rebelocracy, although some involved both. There were several cases of public declarations of neutrality, peace, or resistance.[25] One of them took place in an indigenous community in Apartadó, Antioquia. In 1994, the leaders of the community made public a declaration of neutrality in which they stated that armed groups could cross their territory and drink water, but could not stay in it. They delivered flyers to the paramilitaries as well as to the FARC. All members of the community stood by their declaration and denied cooperation to all the warring sides. When the paramilitaries accused a community member of being an informant of the guerrillas and took him to the municipality's main urban center, the women and children of the community marched there to bring him back. They found the paramilitaries, requested his release, and brought him back home (C. 40).

Given the centrality of this causal link between the quality of local institutions, on the one hand, and civilians' preferences against rebelocracy, collective action, and resistance, on the other, I revisit this issue in Chapter 7. Using process tracing, I offer a detailed account of the ways in which high-quality local institutions enabled collective resistance in a peasant community and, in turn, led to aliocracy. In addition, Appendix 2 presents evidence on high-quality institutions and collective resistance in an indigenous community.

THE PATHS TO DISORDER

According to the theory developed in Chapter 3, there are three paths to disorder. In the first path, two or more armed actors compete for territorial control. In this situation, both sides focus their energy on winning the territory, without thinking much about what comes next. In the second,

---

[24] There is an excellent, growing literature on peace communities and civilian resistance in Colombia. Several references are included in the references list and in Appendix 3.
[25] Some communities, like the indigenous *resguardo* of Guambia, in Silvia, have stressed that their position is not one of neutrality but, rather, a political position in which they, as an authority, demand respect to all actors, including the state (C. 59).

the group has problems of indiscipline that allow combatants to behave opportunistically. In this case, private goals may lead the group to rely on coercion to take what it wants, regardless of its effects on future civilian cooperation. Finally, on the third path, a territory is highly strategic for the group and it cannot tolerate aliocracy because it needs full cooperation. If resistance emerges, the group responds with coercion, rather than by establishing a social order of aliocracy.

Disorder under Armed Competition for Territorial Control

When two or more warring sides compete for territorial control, disorder emerges due to the behavior of both contenders. The defending group tightens its control over the population and redirects all available resources to defend itself. This implies that any provision of goods or services is likely to stop, while abuse of civilians becomes more common as the group tries to prevent cooperation with the enemy. Preexisting rules regulating combatant behavior towards community members are often violated.

The attacking group, on the other hand, is likely to have less access to information on civilian behavior and, therefore, is more likely to rely on indiscriminate violence (Kalyvas 2006). These incursions accentuate disorder, as uncertainty increases and civilians ignore where violence is coming from and why.

In the communities where I conducted fieldwork, there was not even one instance of armed competition where disorder did not emerge. Locals described periods of dispute between warring sides as the worst episodes in their interaction with armed actors. Violence was high and even commanders that people considered benevolent often treated civilians badly. According to a former FARC member, "in areas of bad public order or contestation, what you need are warriors; a purely military approach" (Int. 110).

In Villanueva (Casanare), for example, different paramilitary factions fought with each other at different times over territorial control. Until 2003, the ACC (Self-defense Forces of Casanare) had been in control and ruled over many communities – sometimes under a social order of rebelocracy, and sometimes under aliocracy. In 2003, the Centauros Bloc, a faction of the AUC, arrived in the area with the goal of taking over. The ACC tightened its control over the population, forbidding anyone to move within certain areas of the municipality. For example, only some taxis could go to certain nearby villages. At the same time, the AUC made incursions at night, killing civilians accused of being strong supporters and allies of the ACC.

Disputes lasted about six months, during which time civilians suffered great uncertainty and intense violence. A Colombian think tank that studies the history of the paramilitaries described the situation as follows: "Two paramilitary bands, supposedly created to fight the guerrillas, killed each other for control of drug trafficking, oil revenues, and thousands of hectares of land in the Casanare department. Their cruel war ... left 3,000 victims, or perhaps more, in only a few months between 2003 and 2004" (Verdad Abierta 2009a). Ironically, after the AUC had won the battle, it established in the urban center and in many of the rural areas a social order of rebelocracy that looked quite similar to that imposed by the ACC a few years earlier. As the ACC had done before, the AUC infiltrated local politics, controlled the mayor's office, infiltrated and monitored all social organizations, and regulated civilian life in the economic, political, and social domains.

Even the relationship between an armed group and civilians in areas that have been strongholds for years turns sour upon the arrival of a new armed actor. In Pasca, Cundinamarca, the FARC have been present since their formation. For years, the relationship with the civilian population in most rural areas was fluid and largely positive. Yet, according to a peasant, "At first the difference between peasant and guerrilla member was not big, because the guerrilla was above everything else about revolutionary ideas and it existed here as a social movement. The difference came when they had to take their weapons and shoot, which was in the 1990s" – that is, when the army started to fight them there (C. 56).

Sometimes armed groups attack communities, not with the intention of taking over their territory, but to eliminate what they consider a support base for their enemies. Combatants often attack these communities using gruesome and widespread violence. Civilians often respond to these types of incursions by fleeing. Two communities in Tierralta that lived under aliocracy with the FARC were targeted in this way by the paramilitaries. In one, the attack was brutal and lasted four days. The entire community left, leaving the town empty for years (C. 18). In the other, the paramilitaries killed people, burned houses, stole animals, and warned everyone that they should leave within three days (Int. 56).

During times of disorder, some people try to be as little involved as possible with any group to avoid being targeted. Some try to protect themselves by fleeing, and some join one of the warring sides. Often, people's reactions depend on their history of interaction with the competing groups. When they have been mistreated by one of them, they have incentives to aid the enemy, hoping things will be better if it wins. This was the case in Tierralta, Córdoba, where many locals supported the paramilitaries, after growing tired of abuse from the FARC (C. 29). On the contrary, strong supporters of a ruling group are likely to fear persecution if the enemy wins; they prefer, therefore, to help the ruling group to preserve its control over the area, enlist in its ranks, or flee. Staying if the enemy wins is often tantamount to a death sentence.

Despite how violent and strenuous disorder can be, civilians adapt to changes in control and power quite quickly. Disorder does not preclude other social orders from being established later. Once a group is victorious and gains control over the territory, it changes its behavior and interacts with civilians either under rebelocracy or aliocracy. Most people learn what the new rules are and follow them. Over time, incentives, beliefs, and even preferences change, favoring both obedience and spontaneous support to the new ruling actor. It is this adaptability of civilian behavior that allowed the paramilitaries to fight the guerrillas in many areas of the country and, once victorious, establish a social order of rebelocracy.

It was striking to find many cases where locals recounted horrible acts perpetrated by an armed group while disputes over territorial control lasted, but then reported a "good" interaction with those same combatants later on. In some cases, they even praised the positive actions and interventions of combatants in this later stage. In a village in Tierralta, Córdoba, the incursion of the paramilitaries was extremely violent. Testimonies of people being killed in the middle of the night in front of their families were common; witnesses were often also eliminated. Several interviewees recounted that children were killed with machetes (C. 20). However, once the guerrillas had been pushed away, the paramilitaries changed. People remember behaviors that they appreciated, like large parties for families during Christmas time, with presents for the children, and the provision of public goods. Despite the horrific first interaction with the paramilitaries, most people later obeyed them and some even engaged in acts of spontaneous support. It is important to stress, once again, that in most cases this cooperation was not political or ideological in any sense. However, given how the group permeated every corner of social and economic life, locals had many incentives to behave in ways that allowed them to be on good terms with combatants. This reminds us, once again, of how fluid and changing civilian–combatant relations and local dynamics can be in war zones.

The evidence also suggests that different armed groups can coexist within the same region or even within the same municipality without competing with each other. Sometimes one group rules over a village or a neighborhood while its enemy rules in the next bloc or town. As discussed by Kalyvas (2006), civil war fragments the space in geographic units controlled by different armed actors. In some cases, this coexistence of the warring sides is stable as they make a credible commitment to respecting each other's jurisdiction. Under these circumstances, disorder is avoided and rebel and paramilitary rebelocracy may function in parallel within a few miles of distance. However, as soon as competition starts, social contracts are likely to be broken, giving rise to disorder.

Disorder under Undisciplined Armed Actors

The second reason for the emergence of disorder is the opportunistic behavior of combatants. As Weinstein (2007) argues, controlling their members is one of the key challenges that armed organizations face. When groups have internal organizational problems, the opportunities for mid-level commanders or the rank and file to act in a predatory manner are greater. If combatants can get away with not abiding the group's rules, disorder is likely to emerge.

Armed groups facing major internal organization problems are not the norm in Colombia. As noted in Chapter 4, both guerrillas and paramilitaries have been relatively well organized, although the guerrillas tend to be especially hierarchical and disciplined. There is variation within paramilitary factions as well. Some commanders were able to socialize combatants under tighter rules of behavior than others. In addition, some units operated in their hometowns, and others had to make incursions from far away which seem to have given combatants greater leeway to use coercion for private ends. Yet, overall, both guerrilla and paramilitary groups in Colombia are armies that successfully overcame many internal organizational problems.

Former combatants of both groups gave strikingly similar testimonies about the severity of internal discipline. Cases of commanders who abused the population and were punished by their superiors were common, for example, in Caquetá, Puerto Gaitán, Apartadó and Santuario. In several cases, civilians remember how commanders clearly stated what the rules of behavior for combatants were, often at public gatherings. In a rural community of Santuario, Risaralda, the AUC made it clear to civilians that it was forbidden for combatants to engage in certain types of behavior (C. 76).

In the survey with former combatants, 89 percent said that a member of the group that killed a civilian without having been ordered to do so would face severe punishment, and over 90 percent said that raping a civilian would lead to a death sentence. A few testimonies suggest that sometimes such punishments were delivered publicly to let people know that combatants were supposed to behave well. In a town in Apartadó, for example, a paramilitary combatant threatened to kill a woman unless she left the town within twenty-four hours, because she had had a dispute with another woman who happened to be his girlfriend. The victim managed to talk to the commander who reviewed the case and found the expulsion to be unfair. The commander took the combatant's weapon away and punished him (C. 40). Similarly, in Puerto Gaitán, people could denounce abuses committed by paramilitary members. Several interviewees recount instances where exemplary actions were taken to punish indiscipline. For example, on one occasion a drunk paramilitary stopped a bus and heckled passengers, ultimately hitting and killing one of them. People complained, and the day after, the paramilitary was found drowned in the river (C. 29). In San Vicente del Caguán (Caquetá), the area that was de-militarized for peace negotiations by President Pastrana, the FARC even had an office of complaints open to the public (*Semana* 1999); the same happened in La Macarena (in the Meta department) (*El Tiempo* 1999).

Despite these trends, instances of opportunistic commanders were identified in some case studies and interviews. For example, as will be explained in Chapter 7, in the municipality of Viotá the 42nd Front of the FARC relied heavily for some time on untrained militiamen. These youngsters started to abuse the population by duplicating tax collection and stealing. Civilian reactions quickly followed, as the FARC's social base was weakened, and fear and resentment spread among the population. After interacting for about ten years under rebelocracy, civilians and combatants started to live under widespread disorder. People did not know what to expect from combatants. Some complained of being taxed after having paid their mandatory contributions; others said militiamen were stealing and the FARC let them do so as long as 10 percent went to their coffers; merchants complained about militiamen showing up on their motorcycles, giving orders as they pleased, and taking what they wanted. Testimonies from locals in the nearby municipality of Pasca show a similar pattern (C. 63–66).

In a rural community of Magangué, Bolívar, the AUC treated civilians in an abusive and erratic manner. Sometimes they would show up at parties, where they "pressured women to dance with them and they did not pay for their drinks." Another person said that "if at a party [combatants] wanted a woman, no one could oppose them. Women feared them. It was subjugation. They subdued the men, who could do nothing about it" (C. 48).

In the municipality of Toledo (in North Santander department), locals remembered how particularly violent and abusive a female commander of the FARC, who operated there around 2003, was. She punished minor misbehaviors with death, overlooking previously established rules that gave locals two or three chances to improve their behavior before being expelled from the area or killed. Under her rule, combatants were often drunk, partied on the streets with loud music late at night, and wantonly fired their weapons into the air. According to different interviewees, FARC combatants came to the town one day in their jeeps, entered each house, and took fridges, televisions, and other valued goods from locals (C. 28).

Several ex-combatants from both warring sides also mentioned that certain decisions depended fully on the "quality" of the commander. When asked about how his group approached communities that claimed to be neutral in the conflict, a young former paramilitary member in Tierralta, Córdoba, simply responded that, "it depends on the commander. Sometimes there is respect, sometimes there isn't" (Int. 53). A mid-level paramilitary who was collectively demobilized said the following when interviewed in Bogotá: "When there is resistance, the response depends on the commander. If he is a true *autodefensa* (member of the self-defense forces), he respects it. It is there where they [the commanders] reveal who they are. Political work is more effective than leaving lots of deaths" (Int. 107).

Civilians also reported that a change of commander could mean a change in abuses. In Puerto Gaitán, for example, interviewees reported that when Gilberto Torrez took on the leadership of the *Carranceros* (a paramilitary group), creating the group AMV (Self-defense Forces of Meta and Vichada), he stressed internal discipline much more than Carranza, an emerald trader and previous leader of the group, had done. Combatants became much more accountable, and people knew abuses were likely to be punished quickly and with exemplary actions (C. 29).

Disorder in Highly Strategic Territories Inhabited by Organized Communities

The third path to disorder takes place when communities resist a group's attempt to establish rebelocracy in a highly strategic territory. As mentioned before, certain localities are targeted to serve a particular purpose within the war that requires high levels of civilian cooperation. This happens when high-level commanders live nearby and security rings are needed to protect them. It also happens in territories used to train combatants or heal the wounded. Strategic corridors may also require full cooperation, depending on how much competition with other armed groups is anticipated. When the particular use of the territory requires full obedience and high support, but civilians deny them, violence is used to eliminate the population by displacing it (or even killing many of its members).

In the cases included in the samples, armed groups confronted a few communities who were able to resist rebelocracy in highly strategic territories. For example, the municipality Toribío in the Cauca department – where Nasa indigenous resistance is well known – has been and still is targeted by the warring sides. This region of the country became highly strategic in the early 2000s due to its location. Writing in 2005, an analyst stated that the group "who dominates the Colombian Massif [where Toribío is located] will determine the course of the war" (FIP 2005:26). As the FARC fought intensely to control the area, they attacked Toribío more frequently, aiming to keep the police away. The FARC also sought to subdue the population, as a Nasa leader put it, "because of the autonomy that we have expressed – an attitude that they have not liked and for which they have always seen us as a threat" (García 2005). But despite this violence, resistance prevailed.

In 2004, Vitonás Noscué, the mayor of Toribío and a prominent indigenous leader, traveled to the Southern department of Caquetá. On his way back to Cauca, a FARC commander stopped him. "Why haven't you quit your post as mayor since we, the FARC, gave the order that all mayors quit?" Noscué replied: "Precisely for that reason. Because you do not give us orders. You are wrong because you were not the ones who elected us, it was the community and it is the community we obey." The commander decided to kidnap the mayor, who assured the guerrilla that the Indigenous Guard would soon rescue him (Neira 2005).

The Indigenous Guard was a nonviolent, civil defense organization created in 2001 by indigenous peoples in Cauca to protect their communities and territories from armed actors.[26] Community members of all kinds – men, women, teenagers, and elders – volunteered to join the Guard. It was supervised by the *cabildo*, and had about 6,000 members. It alerted communities when armed actors were present, recovered bodies, and rescued kidnap victims (Ballvé 2006). After Noscué was kidnapped, about 400 members of the Indigenous Guard scoured the mountains until they found the FARC and Noscué. Armed only with their ceremonial canes that symbolized the authority of the Guard, they surrounded the FARC and demanded the immediate release of Noscué. The FARC had no choice: killing 400 people would have been too politically costly, and it would have probably triggered a draconian response from the state. They let Noscué go (Neira 2005). What is more, he was not the only person the Guard saved. It impeded kidnappings and recovered kidnap victims on many occasions, including some who were not members of their communities (e.g., Caracol 2011).[27]

The sustained resistance of this community led the FARC to harass its members for years, preventing the emergence of a social contract. The community continued being the victim of attacks and selective killings. Even while negotiating peace with the government in Cuba, the FARC killed two leaders from Toribío in 2014 (*El Tiempo* 2014).

COLLECTIVE CIVILIAN RESISTANCE

Throughout this chapter I have given several testimonies and descriptions of cases that illustrate the link between institutional quality and resistance. Some of the cases illustrate the absence of civilian cooperation to confront armed actors in communities with significant institutional gaps. Other cases illustrated collective action vis-à-vis armed actors, often within a process of bargaining. The cases discussed in the last section illustrate

---

[26] The Nasa movement, the Indigenous Guard, and Toribío have been awarded several prizes, including the National Peace Prize and the Equator Initiative Prize of the United Nations.
[27] I provide a more detailed description of the process of civilian resistance led by the NASA movement in Appendix 2.

resistance to prolonged periods of violence. Two additional pieces of evidence support my theory of collective civilian resistance.

First, we asked participants in the structured interviews whether people in their community ever resisted the group peacefully. Communities with high-quality institutions were ten times more likely to do so than communities with low-quality institutions (13 percent and 1 percent of the cases, respectively).

As an additional plausibility test, I reviewed the literature on local resistance in Colombia and coded whether the author mentions that the territory where the community is located was highly valued by armed groups for some strategic reason.[28] Out of thirty-seven sources, twenty-seven explicitly mention that the territory where the community lived was highly strategic for the armed group. That is, 72 percent of the cases of resistance reviewed by this literature took place in areas that were highly valuable for armed groups. Although these studies do not look at a random sample of cases of resistance, they serve as a simple plausibility test of these hypotheses. Appendix 3 provides a summary of these sources.

Chapter 7 relies on process tracing to isolate the effect of high-quality institutions, especially dispute institutions, on collective action and, in turn, on aliocracy. Together, these pieces of evidence support my contention about the causes and effects of collective civilian resistance.

CONCLUSION

This chapter analyzed the different stages involved in the process of creating rebelocracy, aliocracy, and disorder. It explored how the interaction between civilians and combatants evolves through time in different contexts. In so doing, it discussed the behavior of armed groups, local communities, and individuals. The empirical evidence helped to illustrate how these interactions actually work. In addition, it offered evidence of two important contentions about civilian behavior: that rebelocracy leads to high civilian cooperation, and that collective resistance is more likely to emerge against rebelocracy and sustained disorder in communities with high-quality institutions.

These findings have important implications. For some civilians living in conflict zones, interacting with an armed group entails paying taxes and

---

[28] I thank Andres Felipe Aponte for his research assistance.

obeying some rules regarding their involvement with other warring sides, while others interact with combatants on a daily basis and have parts of their private life regulated by the group's rules. This variation is not only illustrative of the great differences in armed groups' behaviors across territories, but also of the diverse ways in which life is organized in war zones. In particular, institutions can change greatly in the midst of war. Assuming that chaos reigns and that war is best approached as an absence of governance is wrong-headed. Governance structures change, institutions are redefined, and people learn to live with them. Anarchy is rare, while different configurations of civilian–combatant governing structures are common.

It follows that inferring armed groups enjoy wide political support when they rule or control a locality for a long period of time can be largely misleading – and so is the assumption that cooperation is mostly coerced. Civilians decide to obey rules or even to offer spontaneous support for myriad reasons that are often shaped by war itself, as well as by the history of their communities. Trying to understand civilian choice abstracting from the contexts in which that choice is made can only lead to misguided simplifications. On the contrary, we need to better theorize civilian choice within the distinct realities that war brings about. Furthermore, by delving into the conditions in which civilians and combatants interact across social orders, and over time within them, we can develop hypotheses to explain other aspects of the conduct of war. I develop some ideas in this direction in the conclusion of the book.

The empirical evidence also suggests that war transforms the social and political fabric of local communities in drastically different ways across time and space. As armed actors colluded with, coerced, or co-opted local politicians and state agencies, they transformed people's attitudes towards democracy, formal politics, and the state. We know little about the long-term consequences of these changes, but the literature is moving towards some answers (e.g., Wood 2008; Bellows & Miguel 2009; Blattman & Annan 2009; Shewfelt 2009; Cassar et al. 2013; Gilligan et al. 2013; Grosjean 2014; Rohner et al. 2013; Balcells 2017). This chapter suggests we should take local variation in wartime institutions more seriously in that quest.

7

How Local Institutions Matter

A Process-Driven Natural Experiment[1]

One of the central arguments in this book is that aliocracy and rebelocracy are the outcome of a process in which an aspiring ruler – an armed group – expands the scope of its rule as much as possible, unless civilians push back. I have argued that rather than being always at the mercy of armed actors, civilians have bargaining power if they can credibly threaten combatants with collective resistance, and that high-quality local institutions are the key enablers of such resistance.

Chapter 5 used quantitative data to test the central implication of this argument – to wit, that aliocracy is more likely to emerge in communities with high-quality preexisting institutions, while rebelocracy is more likely where institutional quality is low. Chapter 6 offered evidence of the processes and mechanisms that underlie the construction of aliocracy and rebelocracy. These analyses point to a link between preexisting local institutions, on one hand, and civilian and combatant behavior, on the other.

This chapter aims to supplement previous chapters by providing additional evidence for the hypothesis on the causal effect of institutional quality on social order, as well as for the underlying mechanisms. The chapter presents an in-depth study of three rural communities in Viotá, a municipality located in Central Colombia. The three villages were very similar until the 1950s when, due to a fortuitous event, their institutional paths changed. This divergence offers a unique opportunity to trace the effects of institutional quality on the form of social order that emerged three decades later when the

---

[1] A shorter version of this chapter was published as a journal article in Arjona (2016c).

FARC took over the municipality. The evidence comes from primary and secondary sources as well as fieldwork conducted in 2007 and 2008, when I interviewed local residents and FARC ex-combatants who operated in Viotá.[2]

The study entails two components. First, I use within-case process tracing to show that several "observations about context, process, or mechanisms," also known as causal process observations (CPOs) (Brady et al. 2010:24), are consistent with the mechanisms by which, according to the theory, institutional quality affects wartime social order. Specifically, I show that in *each case*, several facts as well as the sequencing of events are consistent with the proposed hypotheses on the effect of institutional quality on civilian resistance, armed group behavior, and, in turn, wartime social order. Furthermore, I discuss why alternative logics that emphasize ideology and the provision of selective incentives are not consistent with the evidence.

Second, I compare CPOs across three cases that are very similar but differ on the independent variable due to a fortuitous event. I provide two sets of evidence to claim that the cases are indeed very similar. First, I show that the three villages were formed in the early 1950s when two coffee haciendas (plantations) within a single, small municipality, were parceled off after years of highly organized peasant mobilization throughout the municipality. Such mobilization led to the creation of autonomous peasant institutions, which operated in all three villages. Hence, I claim that they shared the same social, economic, and political history through the 1950s. Second, I show that the quality of their local institutions diverged in the 1960s due to a fortuitous event, making it even more likely that the villages did not differ on any other relevant domain.

The study therefore invokes the logic of natural experiments in terms of an as-if-random event affecting units independently of their attributes. However, causal inference is based not on comparing averages between treated and nontreated units in a large sample, but on processes across a small set of cases – an approach that I have called elsewhere "process-driven natural experiments" (Arjona 2016b). As Bennett & Checkel (2014:29) argue, combining within-case process tracing with a case comparison strengthens inferential claims, especially when there are few differences between

---

[2] To protect the identities of participants, all the names of villages and interviewees have been changed.

the cases. In addition, the more similar the cases are, the more it simplifies "the task of process tracing since some (ideally all but one, but hopefully many or even most) mechanisms are being held constant" (Lyall 2014:192). In this study, a natural experiment provides a strong basis for such controlled comparison by reducing the number of mechanisms that may underlie the causal effect of the main explanatory variable.

The chapter provides evidence of several components of the argument. It shows that the FARC preferred to establish rebelocracy to aliocracy, and that civilian obedience and voluntary cooperation were indeed higher where rebelocracy emerged. The evidence also shows that where the FARC encountered a community that was willing and able to resist collectively, they limited their rule, establishing aliocracy instead. I argued that this concession is based on the expectation that collective resistance will preclude civilian obedience and spontaneous support in the long run, therefore endangering territorial control. By establishing aliocracy, in contrast, rebels give up some of the benefits of rebelocracy but preserve their primary goal of territorial control. The evidence in this chapter substantiates this claim about armed groups' strategic calculation about when to limit their ruling aspirations. The fine-grained evidence also shows that locals' preferences to defend their institutional status quo or embrace rebel rule varied drastically across communities with different institutional quality. Furthermore, the study shows how a community with legitimate and effective institutions united to bargain with the FARC and how, when combatants violated the social contract that sustained aliocracy, that community organized to resist.

Conducting this study on Viotá has several advantages. First, as I explained before, the shared history of the communities and the sudden variation in their institutions offers a unique opportunity to compare processes across them. Second, Viotá is a hard case for my theory given the most plausible alternative explanations. If political ideology, identity, and economic interests could explain resistance to rebelocracy, Viotá is *the* place where we should not expect to see widespread opposition to the FARC. For decades, this municipality was one of the strongholds of communism in the country. And even though the FARC and the Communist Party eventually distanced themselves from each other, their ideological proximity remained. In fact, many people in Viotá did recognize the social and political goals of the rebels as close to their own.

In addition, if successful land reform precludes the expansion of rebel movements as is often argued (Albertus & Kaplan 2013),[3] Viotá is the place where rebelocracy should never emerge because it is one of the few cases where land reform did happen in the country. Finally, I chose to focus on a peasant community as opposed to an indigenous community to show that what has made some Colombian indigenous communities so successful in their resistance to armed actors is not their cultural distance to these organizations. Rather, it is their strong desire to preserve their institutions and their astonishing capacity to organize and sustain risky collective action. By focusing on Viotá, I show that peasants who are not members of any ethnic minority group, were just as willing and able to organize resistance in order to preserve their autonomy.

The chapter is organized as follows. I start by describing the situation of the peasants in the haciendas where the three villages come from in the 1920s. I then reconstruct the history of the agrarian movement and the institutions it created, from the 1930s to the 1950s. I then turn to the event that altered their institutional paths, and discuss the evidence that suggests that it was indeed fortuitous. I then trace the effects of institutional quality on wartime social order in each village in the 1990s. In a separate section, I specify the ways in which the different pieces of evidence support my claims, or fail to do so, while also assessing rival explanations. The last section concludes.

LIFE IN THE COFFEE HACIENDAS

Viotá is a mountainous municipality in the Cundinarmaca Department in the center of Colombia (Map 7.1). It is spread over 80 square miles and is composed of about forty rural villages and four small towns. According to the 2005 census, the total population is about 13,000, of which 4,000 live in the *cabecera* (the main urban center of the municipality and seat of the local government), and the remaining in the rural areas. Founded in the nineteenth century, Viotá became home to one of the strongest revolutionary agrarian movements in Colombia. Between the 1930s and 1950s, the peasantry of Viotá was able to dismantle the coffee haciendas and implement a successful agrarian reform despite decades of persecution by the hacienda owners, the army, and the police.

---

[3] As Albertus and Kaplan (2013) note, land reform has been linked to the onset of rebellion in many cases, including El Salvador, Peru, the Philippines, Vietnam, Zimbabwe, and South Africa.

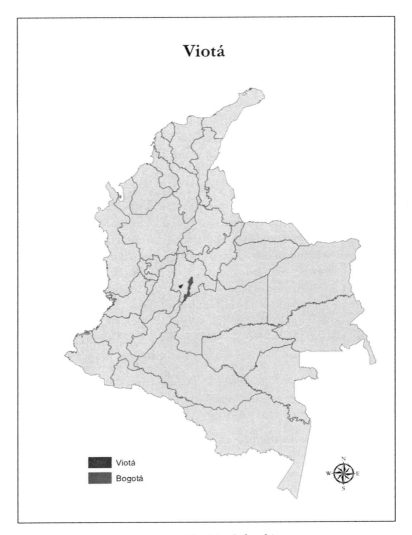

MAP 7.1 Viotá in Colombia

By the early twentieth century, the municipality was a rural area at the service of the haciendas, dedicated to the cultivation of coffee (Acero 2007). Unlike other areas of Colombia at that time, most land in the region had owners (Palacios 2002:156). According to imprecise records, in 1930 about twenty families owned all the land – an area of approximately 160,000 acres (Merchán 1975:106). Since the possibility for peasants to acquire land was minimal, locals and migrants worked in the haciendas.

The pre-capitalist inner structure of the haciendas in Cundinamarca entailed two different forms of labor: temporary wage earners and tenants. Temporary wage earners did not live in the hacienda and were paid a salary for their work. Tenants lived on the hacienda and had an agreement with the planter (hacienda owner) by which the former rented a small portion of land; tenants and their families could build a hut on the plot and plant any crops, except *root crops* such as coffee (Palacios 2002:219). If found growing root crops, peasants were imprisoned (Merchán 1975:108). In exchange for the right to live on the plot of land, the workers owed labor hours to the planter, called an "obligation." Peasants – and their families – had to work on the hacienda from five in the morning until sunset, sometimes receiving in exchange, "very bad food ... sometimes with beef but from cows that were sick or had been found dead on the haciendas" – according to Victor J. Merchán, one of Viotá's most famous agrarian leaders (Merchán 1975:108). When a worker had fulfilled his obligation, his work would be compensated by 50 percent of the salary that was paid to temporary workers. It was also common to receive food, or a combination of money and food as payment (Sánchez 1977:31). Some peasants were not allowed to buy certain goods at the market; they were obliged to buy the goods at the local store on the hacienda, at inflated prices (FG. 170). [4] When taking the produce from their plot to sell at the local market, tenants had to pay tolls and duties to the hacienda. As late as 1930, a Secretary of Government in Cundinamarca denounced the fact that peasants were still subjected to *derecho de pernada* – a landlord's right to have sex with women living on their haciendas (usually the workers' wives and daughters). A woman leader asserts that this was still happening as late as 1950 and adds that, "if the husband or father complained, he would lose his job" (Int. 34).

Overall, tenants were not as poor as temporary wage earners, and in many cases they were able to save money (Palacios 2002:221). However, tenants were often forced to do the most difficult jobs without receiving the same payment as temporary workers for these activities, which led to tensions between both types of laborers (Palacios 2002:224).

---

[4] I refer to interviews as "Int. #" and to focus groups as "FG. #." A list of interviews and focus groups is presented in Appendix 1.

Regardless of their "status" on the haciendas, peasants' living conditions were poor, to say the least. Most *Viotunos*, as people from Viotá are called, describe that period of their history as a time of slavery, entailing mistreatment like unfounded incarceration, sexual abuse, and physical punishment. Clara, a tireless leader who worked for land acquisition and women's rights, recounts that, "everyone worked for a very low salary, and in addition had to work for free on Sundays in order to pay rent, since they lived on the estates. It was very hard slavery" (Int. 5). Jorge, another leader, discussed how easy it was for his father and his co-workers to be arrested: "the administrator of the estate decided who should be arrested and which punishment should be implemented. The mayor obeyed the words of the administrator as if he were the law. There was no due process back then" (Int. 7). Peasants were punished even for failing to greet the owners properly – "My master, how are you?"[5] (FG. 1). Usually, the administrator would ask the worker to deliver a note to the police officer; "not knowing how to read and write, the peasant would deliver it, only to find out that the note asked the police to incarcerate the messenger for days or weeks" (FG. 1).

Tensions among tenants and temporary workers, hacienda owners, and administrators intensified in the early twentieth century. Peasants demanded better conditions on different fronts, from compensation for their work and the quality of food rations, to the size of their plot and their right to plant coffee. They complained about mistreatment by administrators, the local government, and the police (Palacios 2002:224). The first explosion of this conflict took place in 1918, when peasants burned public buildings and refused to work unless salaries were increased and housing and living conditions were improved (Machado 1977:247).

Despite these early signals of collective protest, competition between permanent and temporary workers made it difficult for them to unite and mobilize on a larger scale. In his analysis of the inner structure of the hacienda in Cundinamarca, Palacios (2002) finds convincing evidence that tenants had economic incentives to care for the wellbeing of the hacienda – the better the hacienda did, the better was their economic situation. At the same time, they were subject to harsh rules, and their subsistence was often threatened by macro-economic changes. As a result, they were simultaneously plantation workers aiming to subvert the labor demands of the planters, and tenants seeking to "protect and expand the peasant household embedded in the estates." This explains why the

---

[5] "Mi amo, cómo está?."

relationship between planter and peasant "was at once symbiotic and deeply conflictive" (Jiménez 1988:20).

The national economic crisis of the 1920s exacerbated the local socioeconomic conflict, as it pushed planters to cut down labor costs, restrict tenants' autonomy within the estate, and change the conditions of tenancy contracts (Jiménez 1988). National politics also aggravated this tension. "Liberals and revolutionary syndicalists were in a peculiarly symbiotic relationship as opposition to the Conservatives escalated after 1926" (ibid.:29). Supported by the local bourgeoisie and liberals, tenants engaged in various forms of resistance against the planters. For example, by 1933, the Ministry of Industry had received petitions by tenants from seven haciendas in Viotá demanding that they be allowed to grow coffee on their plots (Sánchez 1977:41–42). "Neither Church campaigns to resocialize the lower classes, nor repression could assure social order and discipline." The emerging "culture of peasant resistance" was "usually individual, occasionally collective, though seldom politically articulated"; nevertheless, it kept "the state and the planters on the defensive" (Jiménez 1988:22).

These were the early signs of mobilization in the 1920s. However, political guidance and more severe economic conditions would be necessary for the different strata of peasants to unite and pressure the haciendas and the state. Such mobilization would give rise to an agrarian movement that eventually created institutions, which not only enabled peasants' mobilization for land, but also transformed the very pillars of social order in rural Viotá.

AN AGRARIAN MOVEMENT IS BORN

In the late 1920s the Socialist Movement in the Colombian capital of Bogotá noticed the dissatisfaction of the peasantry in Viotá, and offered its guidance and support. Peasants quickly embraced this offer, and within a few years Little Moscow (*Moscucito*), as Viotá was later called, became one of the focal points of communism and agrarian mobilization in Colombia.

Why were peasants in Viotá able to organize such a powerful movement? Perhaps they were eager to embrace socialist ideas because "the haciendas [had] achieved a level of social conflict that was only lacking political expression" (Palacios 2002). According to Jiménez (1988), other factors were crucial too. Migration in the 1920s impeded the creation and preservation of paternalist bonds between the lord and the peasant. Since the type of patron-client relations common elsewhere in Colombia did not take root in Viotá, peasants there had greater autonomy. At the same time, cohesion across family units was facilitated by the breakdown of traditional gender roles. Viotá escaped the patriarchal structure of the household that was common elsewhere, in part because migrants were mostly single men and women rather than families. The weak presence of the church and the state, and even of the landowners, could only help to strengthen this multifaceted autonomy.

Socialist ideas first arrived in Viotá when Maria Cano and Ignacio Torrez Giraldo, leading activists of the Revolutionary Socialist Party, visited the municipality in 1926 (Merchán 1975; Jiménez 1988).[6] Under Cano's leadership, meetings were held to discuss the problems of the peasantry; they even organized a public demonstration in Viotá's urban center (Merchán 1975). According to Viotá's oral history, although the police surrounded the town to impede Cano's participation, peasants managed to get her in by hiding her in a coffin; when the police finally realized it, "there she was: speaking in the middle of the plaza" (FG. 1). Since then, multiple events signaled the emergence of an "effervescent but spontaneous class struggle" against what peasants saw as a "feudal system of exploitation [in] the haciendas" (Merchán 1975).[7]

On July 17, 1930, the Colombian Communist Party (CP hereafter) was created in Bogotá. One month later, a group of peasants founded the first branch in the hacienda Buena Vista in Viotá. In 1932 Victor J. Merchán, a former unionist at a major brewing company in Bogotá, was commissioned by the CP to support the peasants in Viotá. Under his leadership, between 80 and 100 cells (small working groups) (FG. 1) and several agrarian unions and peasant leagues were formed in the municipality (Merchán 1975:105). The party grew so quickly that it soon evolved into a massive agrarian movement.

It is not clear whether the CP allied with the wage earners first or the tenants (Jiménez 1988; Palacios 2002). In either case, the party became the key institutional supporter of the tenants' mobilization and land tenure became the central issue in the struggle. Temporary

---

[6] The Revolutionary Socialist Party was the first Marxist party founded in the country. Created in 1926, it was renamed as the Communist Party in 1930.
[7] Whether the system of the coffee hacienda was indeed closer to feudalism or capitalism is debated in the literature. For Palacios (2002:347) the term "Andean pseudo-servitude," introduced by Martínez Alier, is more accurate, as the tenant could leave the hacienda if he liked.

Institutional Innovations in the Struggle for Land   221

workers were asked to join forces with the tenants in exchange for the movement's promise to obtain land for them as well (Palacios 2002). The movement grew so fast, and reached so deep into Viotá's peasantry, that in the following decades it would sponsor several members to travel to the Soviet Union, China, Cuba, and other communist countries to pursue higher education. Peasants say that around 200 people studied abroad, fully sponsored by the CP (Int. 37). Although this fact is difficult to confirm, pictures with Asian communist leaders abound in the cadres' homes and several of their children are professionals who received their college degrees in these countries. The municipality became such a focal point for the movement that it hosted some national-level meetings (like the Tenth Congress in 1966) and by 1947 seven out of nine council seats in the municipality government were won by the communists.

In line with the guidelines of the Communist International at the time (Third Congress of the International Communist 2015), the movement was structured on the basis of three organizational principles: first, there was mandatory participation in collective work, which included small study groups, meetings to discuss pressing issues, and undertaking legal and illegal activities; second, leaders were to have the closest ties with the masses; and third, party decisions were to have broad popular support and be strictly observed. This organizational structure allowed the movement to develop institutions to address different needs and challenges in the years to come.

INSTITUTIONAL INNOVATIONS IN THE STRUGGLE FOR LAND

The first institutions were developed to organize the struggle for land. The unions and associations were in charge of formalizing peasants' demands to the haciendas, as well as of coordinating their many illicit activities such as building houses as opposed to huts on their plots, growing root crops such as coffee, and refusing to pay their "obligations" to the hacienda owners. The "invasions" – occupations of land without legal ownership – proved particularly effective. This practice was initiated and, as the cadres say, "oriented," by the CP through the unions, especially the union of the Buena Vista hacienda. The process took advantage of Law 200 of 1936, which recognized ownership of land that had been worked by the settler, even if someone else had legal ownership of it. This was a risky and demanding practice that required highly coordinated collective action. The unions were responsible for explaining the process to the peasants and supporting it.

As peasants recall, an invasion usually consisted of twenty to forty families who would get together at around 8 p.m. to build a hut and sow trees and crops that had already grown elsewhere. In the morning, when the police and the administrator of the hacienda arrived, it appeared as if these few small plots had been inhabited by peasants for a long time. According to Law 200, these families could not be evicted. The police often arrested the men (and if there were no children to take care of, the women as well), but other peasants used to show up en masse when administrators or police forces tried to vacate a family (Merchán 1975; FG. 1). Women and children often stood in front as human shields (Int. 34). Sometimes even the night-guards would help the peasants because they sympathized with their fight. "They were poor too," cadres say, "and some of them ended up getting their parcel with the aid of the movement" (FG. 1).

These actions first took place on two haciendas and were soon replicated elsewhere. Viotá's emerging peasant leaders even visited haciendas in nearby municipalities to spread the word, mobilize the peasantry, and reinforce the struggle (Merchán 1975). Writing in 1934, the Secretary of the State of Cundinamarca reported that in Viotá "workers were living in a state of permanent belligerence" (Palacios 2002:336).

Threatened elites sought to whip Viotá into submission by persecuting, incarcerating, and even killing peasants. But the peasants did not retreat; rather, they responded by intensifying their legal and illegal resistance. Some led the legal fight, reporting all forms of mistreatment to the courts and the police, and demanding better conditions. Others worked clandestinely to protect the peasantry, forming self-defense groups with machetes, knives, and a few homemade and second-hand shotguns (Merchán 1975). These groups were often called "The Red Guard" – in contrast with the Official Guard, as the police of the department were called.

As conflict escalated, peasants organized several (at that time, illegal) protests in the main square of Viotá's urban center. They "took the square by assault, in military formation, from the four corners, surprising the enemy" (Merchán 1975). Peasants also organized strikes, usually during the most important harvesting seasons. "Entire harvests were lost" (Int. 38). In addition, they established new rules to support those who paid the highest costs of the struggle. For example, imprisoned peasants returning to Viotá after serving their sentence found their plots in better conditions than when they had left them: other peasants had kept them in good shape by dividing the labor among them (Merchán 1975).

The movement scored significant gains early on. Seeing that their repression was fomenting backlash, the planters started to concede to some demands. In the mid-1930s, they agreed to improve working conditions for the peasants. According to Jiménez (1988:36), by 1935 "a significant group of tenants had ceased paying either labor dues or rent to large landowners." Tenants and planters also reached agreements about other institutions within the hacienda, such as making labor voluntary – that is, abolishing obligations as part of the tenancy – as the hacienda Florencia did in 1934 (Palacios 2002:339). Furthermore, some planters negotiated with tenants to parcel their haciendas and sell the plots to them. Although four haciendas were partially or fully parceled between 1934 and 1936 (Palacios 2002:171), most peasants had to continue their fight for two more decades before they could own land.

In the late 1930s, the national climate for agrarian reform turned sour. What had seemed to be an unstoppable agrarian reform under President López Pumarejo in the 1930s was reversed by Conservatives and moderate Liberals. But the political climate in Viotá was different. The CP had won the municipal elections of 1937 with 65 percent of the vote, which symbolized "an institutionalization of peasant gains" (Jiménez 1988:37). In the late 1930s, "while uprisings throughout most of the Magdalena basin had been crushed or co-opted, Viotá remained a major arena of conflict where service tenants challenged planters and government authorities" (Jiménez 1988:9). Throughout the 1940s and 1950s, the agrarian movement worked hard not only to give land to more peasants but also, as we will see, to meet the organizational needs of the peasantry.

Mobilization paid off. By 1960, all haciendas but two had been parceled (Palacios 2002:348) and, according to Merchán (1975:115), divided into more than 4,000 small farms. This outcome has no other parallel in Colombia: Viotá's agrarian reform was exceptional (Palacios 2002:362). To be sure, there were some drawbacks as well. The parceling sometimes benefitted the planters, who were able to sell defective properties at market price. In addition, while planters were compensated, tenants were charged for the financial and administrative costs of the parceling process. Furthermore, the land sold to tenants was sometimes of poor quality, and the costs of the necessary improvements were often not taken into account, forcing them to pay additional expenses (Palacios 2002: 351–356). Bureaucratic problems also complicated the parceling; different agencies were in charge of the process, leading to inefficiency and disorganization (Palacios 2002:357).

Some peasants struggled to make their payments, and not doing so sometimes led to eviction and loss of property rights. The community responded, once again, with the force of unity, by collecting money for those who needed assistance. "It didn't matter if they were Liberals or Conservatives," says Felipe, one of the leaders (Int. 29). "The goal was that peasants were not expelled from their land."

Although Palacios (2002:341,362) concluded that several haciendas of the region were likely to have escaped conflict, he also found evidence that most ended up parceling off and selling the plots, at least partially due to the pressure of the agrarian movement. Most Viotunos I interviewed in the rural areas of the municipality say that they owe their land – or that of their parents – to the work of the communist leaders of the 1930s–1950s. Even a Liberal interviewee, who stressed the role of the Liberal Party in defending peasants' rights in the 1920s and 1930s, believes that they "owe to the CP the change in the property of land in Viotá" (Int. 36). And the cadres' pride of the role they (or their parents) played in this fight can still be felt in every conversation with them: "After much effort ... the land was bought by the peasants who worked it. It was a tremendous fight" (Int. 5).

SELF-GOVERNANCE: INSTITUTIONS TO PRESERVE PUBLIC ORDER AND ADJUDICATE DISPUTES

As unique as Viotá's successful agrarian reform was, acquiring land was not the peasants' sole achievement. They also developed institutions to ensure public order and adjudicate disputes.

Viotá's record of organized self-defense is impressive. In addition to creating the Red Guard in the 1930s, the peasants formed self-defense forces during *La Violencia* – the brutal civil war fought between Liberals and Conservatives between 1948 and 1959. During the war, the Conservatives' resolution to dismantle peasant unions and leagues led them to launch a military attack against Viotá, which they saw as one of the most threatening agrarian movements in the country. The Liberal Party called on the people to unite and defend themselves, facilitating the formation of self-defense groups that came to be known as liberal guerrillas. The director of the Communist Party, Gilberto Vieira, also asked the party to secure the defense of the peasantry by creating self-defense committees (Medina 1980:557). Viotá's rural population quickly organized. Peasant leaders asked the entire population, both communists and non-communists, to join forces to repel the attackers in what they called a "united front." According to my interviewees, almost everyone joined the movement. "The poor peasants and the agrarian wage-earners organized the armed front ... The wealthy peasants and merchants of the urban center were in charge of supplying goods, drugs, and clothes. Finally, the neighboring land-owners were in charge of the 'diplomatic front,' combining resistance with negotiation" (Merchán 1975:118).

Self-defense groups consisted of between fifteen and twenty people (Int. 4). Using cow horns as trumpets, they were able to alert the entire population about suspicious activities within minutes. Thanks to well-organized resistance, "the municipality was sealed off early on from the surrounding maelstrom," keeping bandits, partisan gangs, and the police away. "The chulavitas [Conservatives] did try, but peasants responded fiercely. One attempt to enter the mountains would result in thirty-five policemen dead," says a Liberal leader with pride.

In 1953, when General Rojas Pinilla took control of Colombia with a coup d'état, he offered amnesty to the small guerrillas that had proliferated throughout the country. The communist self-defense forces agreed to demobilize without disarming. Fearing a sudden attack, the peasants of Viotá preserved a fine-tuned scheme with permanent vigilance posts for identifying newcomers and mobilizing their units quickly. History would prove the peasants' suspicions right.

President Rojas banned the CP in 1954 and launched a violent campaign in the areas where the party had led the agrarian struggle, labeling them as "small communist revolutions." More than a third of the army was deployed to the region where Viotá is located to "conduct massive summary executions, bombardments of the civil population, and [to create] the first concentration camp" (Zambrano 1998:242). Yet, the peasants' self-defense forces of Viotá were well prepared in the mountains, and the army was never able to take over the municipality. The population was so capable of defending itself that the central committee of the CP relocated there for a while to avoid persecution in Bogotá (Int. 36). Peasants still take pride in their relentless unity in defending themselves: "Can you believe it? Twice, the army tried to erase Viotá from the map, and twice they failed!" (Int. 183, FG. 1). Their success made the municipality one of the few in the interior of the country that only witnessed a few killings throughout *La Violencia*.[8]

And yet, defending themselves from violence was only one of the challenges that peasants confronted in that period. Since their local system of self-defense required them to remain in the hills, isolated from the urban centers, some system of governance was needed to avoid social conflict and hunger. Once again, the peasantry of Viotá excelled. They set up institutions to organize production in the farms and haciendas, and preserve public order. For example, they created "control and solidarity commissions" and "popular tribunals" that were in charge of settling disputes among peasants. For Merchán (1975:119), this was essential for daily life to go on without neglecting military defense: "it was mandatory to put an end to disputes and disorders, [and to] stop thugs and spies." The community also solved problems related to education and roads (Int. 4).

Delegates of the unions, peasant leagues, and self-defense groups formed these popular tribunals. Both members and non-members of the CP participated in the tribunals, which came to be recognized as legitimate, de facto courts not only by the peasants but also by the hacienda owners, the mayor, and even the police inspector, who referred people to the tribunals to solve all kinds of disputes. At some point, they even performed marriage ceremonies (Merchán 1975:119; Int. 4). Viotunos remember this stage in their history as a unique example of popular rule, as well as a testament to their unity and organization.

Rojas Pinilla's dictatorship ended with his resignation, forced by massive protests and riots, opposition from the church, and the defection of army generals. Leaders of the Conservative and Liberal parties agreed to share power by rotating administrations every four years – a deal known as the National Front. In 1958, voters confirmed the National Front as an amendment to the Constitution, which paved the road for sixteen years of shared power between the traditional parties. Although this pact succeeded in putting an end to the war between Liberals and Conservatives, persecution of Communist bases continued (Jiménez 1988:2). Viotá remained alert for a while, but over time, it was able to recover a sense of normality. Peasants were able to return to the urban

---

[8] In Chacón's dataset of violence during *La Violencia*, Viotá had intensity 1 in a range from 0 to 4 in the early years, and 0 in a range from 0 to 8 in the late years (Chacón 2004).

center and gradually escape their state of isolation. The permanent vigilance posts were dismantled, but the self-defense groups continued their work to ensure the security of peasants. A CIA report estimated that Viotá had fifty "armed militias" in 1966 (CIA 1966). Until the 1970s, they were in charge of public order. For example, if a thief was caught, the self-defense forces would capture and turn him into the police.

The union, which existed in every village, was still recognized as the key authority by the community after the war had ended. For many peasants, like Jorge, "the union was like a local government" (Int. 6). In one union, representatives used to meet the first Monday of every month: "The meeting started with roll call; then we discussed disputes over land borders, damages by animals, and marital problems. Then we turned to the socio-economic problems of the community ... Then we partied" (Int. 16). The popular tribunals continued to be the preferred system for adjudicating disputes years after the war had ended. The union was in charge of reviewing the cases and appointing commissions to resolve them. Hilario described the process as follows: "People would seek our help – and if they did, it meant they would accept the decision of the commission. We created a commission made of persons who could be impartial and also discreet – so that things didn't get out of the commission. That created a good reputation, and trust on the commission" (Int. 4).

According to some of my interviewees and one historical source, Viotá was also home to one of the first women's organizations in Colombia, the Feminine Alliance, and in 1953 women from Viotá actively participated in the Democratic Women Association (Acero 2007:74). Although there were earlier efforts to advance women's rights elsewhere in Colombia (González 2000:704), Viotá was home to local associations that played a leading role. These associations were formed, according to one of their founders, because "we realized that our situation was similar to slavery. We were not able to have land titles; we didn't have *cédula* (ID cards)" (Int. 5). The associations fought for equality in representation, and were linked to women elsewhere in the country. Despite not knowing how to read and write, a woman from Viotá named Rosa Domínguez became one of the national leaders of the movement. "When she intervened in protests or manifestations, people went crazy. The CP sent her later on to study abroad," says one of the elder cadres (Int. 15). The women's movement also took on Viotá's own gender problems. In 1980, they designed a program to educate women about their rights, as well as those of children. "In some places men were angry," Cecilia remembers, and then adds with a smile: "maybe it was our fault; we were very harsh" (Int. 34). Women in Viotá were so enthusiastic – "we thought our time had arrived," says Cecilia – that they created their own drama, music, poetry, and dance groups. More than 2,000 women from the municipality would get together for their movement's celebrations.

The effects of the agrarian movement and the institutions it developed on Viotá's rural population cannot be overstated. With their organization, peasants not only revolutionized the system of land tenancy, but also the different "forms of political and social domination that were part of the structure of the hacienda" (Sánchez 1977:17). At the same time, they created a truly self-governing scheme in charge of security, adjudication of disputes, contract enforcement, and securing property rights, as well as mechanisms to undertake collective action.

A unique signal of the community's recognition of the profound impact of this movement is the fact that many people still call each other "comrade," regardless of their partisanship – "that reveals that a strong identity was created around the agrarian struggle," says a Liberal (Int. 36). A leftist, non-Communist leader agrees; to him, "the Communists are part of Viotá's identity" (Int. 37). People still say that the second language in Viotá is Russian, perhaps a symbolic local myth, and one can find a Spanish/Russian dictionary in the traditional bar of the main square.

To Jiménez (1988:41), the movement "promoted the formation of an oppositional culture favoring smallholder interests and yet breaking the intracommunal competition for resources" that was so common in the region. Viotá came to be characterized by a "radically democratic, anti-oligarchic vision, as well as a strong, cooperative spirit" (Jiménez 1988:54). The autocratic character of the municipality endured so much, that in 1961 a senator called Viotá an "independent republic,"[9] and visitors sensed its particular collective unity: "It is different from the rest of the Colombian countryside. It has its own history, its epic songs, its heroes, its pioneers in the struggle for land, its own general concerns, its own means of communication, its rituals, its messianism, which practically constitute an entire culture."[10]

---

[9] In a Congressional debate, Senator Alvaro Gómez Hurtado denounced the existence of "independent republics" in rural areas – communities that were organized around their own governing schemes, claimed land ownership, and denied access to the National Army. Viotá was one of them.

[10] Gutiérrez, José. 1962. *La Rebeldía Colombiana: Observaciones Psicológicas Sobre La Actualidad Política*. Bogotá: Tercer Mundo. pp. 85–90. Cited by Jiménez (1988:42).

ZAMA, TELLUS, AND LIBREA: DIVERGENCE IN LOCAL INSTITUTIONS

As the haciendas were being parceled, small villages were formed. This study focuses on three of them: Zama, Tellus, and Librea. Zama and Tellus belonged to "Florencia," and Librea to "Los Olivos." Both haciendas were created in the late nineteenth century and went through different partitions (Palacios 2002:170), until disappearing. By 1960, there were no haciendas in Viotá. The three villages have always belonged to the same politico-administrative unit, the municipality of Viotá. The local government is located in the *cabecera*, also called Viotá, where the office of the mayor and the city council operate.

Florencia was one of the four haciendas where the agrarian conflict was most intense within Viotá (Palacios 2002:345). The highly organized community surprised many, including a public official of the Institute of Colonization and Migration, who stated, "in the parceling of Florencia ..., in Viotá, where I spent a few months in charge of its administration, I had the occasion to observe, despite their infamous rebelliousness, the strict observance of those people. You can't find there the deplorable demoralization of this parceling."[11]

Librea served as an important long-time crossroad in rural Viotá. Although the level of conflict was lower in Los Olivos, Librea became a central place for the CP, and the very first peasant union was founded there. "The CP in Viotá actually comes from what today is Librea," says Dario, from the village of Permia. As in Florencia, the partition of what used to be Los Olivos was the result of strong pressure from the CP (Int. 15).[12]

Yet, during the 1960s, the strength of the agrarian movement and its institutions decayed in Tellus and Librea, but not in Zama. "It goes back to 1946," says Felipe, a cadre from Zama, "when the community had a collection to buy a plot and give it to Victor J. [Merchán] as a gift in gratitude for his community work." The most important leaders were at that point dispersed throughout the villages because as land was being parceled, they got their plots in various parts of the municipality just as everyone else. But, with Merchán there, in the following years Zama became a focal point: the "communist house" was built there, serving as

---

[11] Abraham Aldana, general secretary of the Institute for Colonization and Immigration, Silvania, March 3, 1946 (quoted by Palacios 2002:360).
[12] Librea comes from two haciendas that were created after the first partition of Los Olivos: Los Olivos and La Magdalena.

the headquarters of the CP in the 1950s; in 1966 it hosted the party's 10th Congress (FG. 1).

As time went by, several leaders sold their plot and bought one in Zama: the first moved in 1950 (FG. 1), and many others followed. By 1960, the leadership of the CP was concentrated in Zama. "That's life, [the leaders] just ended up together ... to see each other more, to meet more often," says Felipe (Int. 29). Over time, this concentration of leaders allowed Zama to preserve many of the governance structures that had flourished in the previous decades. But in the rest of the municipality, things changed.

The peasantry of Viotá entered the 1960s with full legal ownership of land, a strong grassroots organization, and autonomous institutions responsible for preserving security and adjudicating disputes. Yet, victory backfired: peasants eventually lost interest in preserving the movement that had given them so much.

Hilario, one of the most important leaders of the village of Zama, is admired by most peasants even today. He began his activism at an early age, during the last years of the land struggle. In 1960, he went to Moscow to study with thirty other young, communist leaders, and became one of the most important members of the CP upon his return. He was one of the most recognized figures in Viotá, not only by the peasantry but also by the estate owners and state officials. Everyone I interviewed for this project portrayed him as an honest, principled man who devoted his life to the movement – although a few took issue with his intransigence.

Now in his 80s, living in a small house on a plot of land that the movement he helped lead gave him, Hilario speaks with a mix of pride and nostalgia. After dedicating most of his life to his community's struggle for land and progress, his disappointment with the general peasantry in Viotá is evident: "The peasant is revolutionary only when he lacks land – as Lenin rightly said" (FG. 1). "Here the great movement was for land ... While [it] was strong and alive almost everywhere in Viotá until the 1960s, it faded away in most places after that ... It took us much effort to keep the movement alive in our village [of Zama]" (Int. 4).

In addition to land ownership, improved economic conditions fueled a sense of completeness. Between 1967 and 1980, the coffee sector experienced sustained growth in Colombia, which led Viotá to a period of prosperity. "We all had everything. Parties, cows, money, work. Peasants thought everything was resolved. The state and the Federation of Coffee Growers (FCG) started to give money for roads, schools, everything ... so people felt they did not have to battle any more" (FG. 1).

As the state increased its presence in Viotá and improved its provision of public goods, services, and infrastructure, the rural areas became more integrated into the state. In addition, in 1958 the national government created a new form of local organization, the Communal Action Association (*Junta de Acción Comunal*, JAC), to serve as the formal interlocutor between citizens and the state. Since the JACs were the formal means to access a more powerful – and wealthier – municipal government, they soon became the dominant form of local-level participation. At the same time, the state offered an alternative to the schemes that peasants had developed in previous decades to deal with problems of public order and dispute adjudication, leading many to see the autonomous institutions that used to deal with basic order superfluous.

But the communist cadres were still convinced of the importance of preserving a grassroots organization and popular rule. To them, the institutions that had allowed their communities to be in charge of their security and dispute adjudication were still crucial to their safety and their development. Regarding safety, they were still distrustful of the state. For example, Dario recounts that when the JACs first obtained resources to build roads, some cadres showed opposition because they were afraid that these roads would allow the army to enter the villages (Int. 16). Also, they saw the police as much less capable of stopping delinquency than the community organizations had been. In fact, as late as 1970, when there was a robbery people would turn to local organizations to look for thieves and turn them in to the police.

In terms of development, the cadres also saw the old institutions and their participatory character as the building blocks of their unity, which, in turn, was essential to push for development. To Hilario, the fight "could not die with land, because now we needed progress: roads, aqueducts, schools. And community work was the only means to get these things" (FG. 1). Popular rule and the "work with the masses," as they call it, was to them the only way for the peasantry to put pressure on the government and keep progressing.

In sum, the old communist cadres were committed to fighting for the preservation of their grassroots organization and autonomous institutions. This was the vision of peasant mobilization they had learned as members of the CP, and their experience had proved that vision right – this is how they got their land, and how they escaped violence.

But this time, their work met many difficulties. There were no pressing problems to address – no abusive planters, no armies, no extreme poverty; to most peasants, attending community meetings was not as important. Furthermore, those meetings couldn't even offer the space for socialization that they did in the past: "These meetings used to be like people's break, but with T.V. no one had time anymore" (FG. 1), says a cadre. In addition, the communists were not the only ones trying to spur participation. "Now the discourse was not for land but for other goals – goals that were also stressed by the traditional parties; so the CP competed directly with them" (Int. 36). Others blame clientelism: "the new ways of doing politics – those mayors giving people groceries ... one pound of rice is enough: people show up" (FG. 1). It was hard for the CP to compete under those circumstances, because "with no money, there is no party" (Int. 36). What is more, as many peasants now owned land and hired workers, the communist ideology no longer fit their profile.

To make things worse, the CP had neglected training the new cadres, and young leaders did not stand by the principles of popular participation and self-governance as the old ones did (Int. 36). A non-communist interviewee stresses the apathy of the cadres' sons and daughters. "They left," he says. "They did not continue their parents' fight, and now only the old leaders are here." And one of the key cadres even places the blame on himself and his comrades: "the old leaders feared that the new ones wanted to take over; and the young ones, returning from Moscow, perhaps assumed they had a place that they were not entitled to yet" (Int. 8).

All these changes made the job of the cadres who wanted to preserve local, autonomous institutions very difficult. The cadres of Tellus and Librea tried hard, but they did not have a critical mass to resist the expansion of the state and the apathy of the peasants. They joined the JACs, and often served as presidents, but as time went by, fewer and fewer people participated. While a few key cadres stayed in Tellus, the movement was generally weakened. Elsa, a leader who left later, recognizes that "all the leaders in Tellus were either communists or non-partisans. When most of us [the communists] left, it led to a big vacuum. The communitarian process decayed" (Int. 33).

Things were even more difficult in Librea. "Why have a meeting if [the principal leaders] were not going to attend?" says a leader from another village, who tried to revive the movement in Librea at that time (Int. 15). In addition, once the CP was weakened in Librea, the Liberal Party gained much power in the village, but could not organize the community as the agrarian movement had done before. Even Liberals themselves acknowledged their weaknesses in Librea: "it was a Liberal stronghold ... but [the leaders] were not well-organized" (Int. 173). A sustained confrontation between them and the few communist leaders that stayed in the village contributed to these failures. By the late 1970s, Librea had lost the cohesion and organization that had characterized it before.

Over the years, the JACs in both villages preserved their function as an intermediary between the peasants and the state, and played a key role in obtaining resources to build schools and roads. Yet, they stopped adjudicating disputes and intervening to preserve public order. They also lost legitimacy. As in other Colombian municipalities, they often became used for clientelistic purposes, where the traditional parties would seek votes in exchange of favors and resources (Borrero 1989). In the 1970s, "in Viotá the sign of stagnation permeated all social and political activity. The strength that the peasant movement had in previous periods faded away." (Ruiz 1983:59).

By the 1980s, the pillars of order in both villages were in the hands of the state. But the police and the other agencies responsible for adjudicating disputes were never as effective as the popular tribunals and unions had been. Furthermore, security was getting worse, and the police was unable to keep public order as well as the old peasant organizations. The region was experiencing high levels of "common and quotidian violence that the newspapers registered daily," often called "the rural insecurity" (Ruiz 1983:57). The incapacity of the state to deal with these issues further undermined its legitimacy. Interviewees from all villages reported this downturn in local institutions and peasant participation.

In Zama, in contrast, the JAC remained for years the platform to hold meetings; keep locals informed about current events; make demands to the municipal government and the FCG; adjudicate disputes among neighbors; and solve problems of public order (FG. 1; Int. 6). Many of the most respected leaders had moved to Zama and they made every effort to preserve the forms of self-governance that had characterized Viotá in the past. Despite how dormant participation was elsewhere, the people of Zama remained active. When walking around Zama, the cadres proudly pointed to everything we encountered – "Do you see this aqueduct? This school? These trails connecting every single farm to the road? We did it all!" (Int. 6).

In the 1980s the JAC in Zama, run by the cadres, continued to play a central role in community life. According to a local resident, "at that time, the communists were in charge of security and of managing everything. They were very organized" (Int. 29). To be sure, the villagers did not participate in meetings as much as they used to, but they still regarded the JAC as a legitimate institution and turned to it to solve many issues.

By 1990, the differences between Zama and other villages were fully accentuated. In Zama the community was active, and the leaders remained highly involved. Local dynamics were still deeply shaped by traditional, local institutions that were ingrained in locals' identities. In most other villages, however, the agrarian movement – and, along with it, community organization – was history. People delegated leadership to a new class of politicians, rather than participating directly. The ties between communities and peasant leaders had weakened, and seldom were the operating institutions seen as effective as those from the past. This deviation between the villages would prove to be crucial again two decades later under renewed violence.

COMPARING PROCESSES ACROSS VILLAGES

This divergence in local institutions provides a unique opportunity to trace the effect of institutional quality on the form of order that emerged in the 1990s, when the FARC took over the entire municipality of Viotá.

I argue that the three villages were historically very similar, and that subsequent differences in their local institutions were due to a fortuitous event. As related above, the agrarian movement and its local institutions flourished throughout all of Viotá. Zama did come from one of the haciendas where the conflict for land had been most intense, but so did Tellus. What is more, the strongest union was not located in Zama but in Librea, and many of the most famous leaders did not live in Zama prior to the 1950s. Furthermore, when I asked my interviewees why Merchán was given land in Zama and not elsewhere, they said there was no specific reason – the plot they found just happened to be in Zama. In addition, in interviews with the leaders who now live in Zama, it was very clear that the only reason they moved to Zama was to be near their comrades.

The evidence also suggests that the incidental concentration of leaders in Zama had a direct effect on local institutions. Different primary and secondary sources show that the communist leaders supported the institutions that allowed peasants to defend themselves, adjudicate disputes, and organize collective action to obtain land from the 1930s to the 1950s. Once most of those leaders were in Zama, it became easier for them to preserve those institutions despite the pressures from the state and the growing apathy from the peasantry. My study suggests that the movement of leaders *did* entail a change in ideology and leadership. Nevertheless, I offer both theoretical reasons and empirical evidence that suggest that neither of these factors could alone explain the events that took place when the FARC ruled Viotá.

THE FARC IN TELLUS AND LIBREA

Many assert that the FARC had some presence in Viotá since the group's creation in the 1960s. In fact, some news sources mention the FARC's influence in the region since the 1960s (e.g., *El Tiempo* 2003a). A CIA report from 1966 describes the municipality as an area of FARC influence, and claims that there was no armed struggle because of Viotá's strategic value for the CP as a safe stronghold (launching attacks would have attracted the army) (CIA 1966). Most locals, however, assert that they did not actually see combatants until the late 1980s or early 1990s. Many of the communist leaders that I interviewed say that, at first, FARC troops established territories up in the mountains, far away from people. "There was no presence in Viotá proper. The CP actually denied those accusations and emphasized several times that Viotá was no home for armed struggle, but for something else" (FG. 1). When the FARC did extend its presence to different areas of the municipality in the early 1990s, some communist leaders demanded an explanation, and, according to the cadres, sent a letter to the FARC's 42nd Front asking it to leave the area. The front sent it to the Secretariat, "but the members [of the Secretariat] were mad and ordered the front to stay" (Int. 29). In any case, it seems clear that the FARC did not have full control of Viotá until 1990, when combatants started to show up around the villages. A former combatant interviewed in Bogotá confirmed this perception: "The FARC arrived to Viotá in 1991 to rule" (Int. 28).

There are several hypotheses on the FARC's decision to shift from a sporadic to a more permanent presence in the area. To some, the group was responding to the invitation of the communist cadres. One interviewee said that they did so to counter the liberals who illegally brought in voters from Bogotá to steal the elections (Int. 17). Yet, the high-level communist cadres deny this and offer as proof their early independence from the FARC, as well as outright opposition that crystallized later. One of them, however, believes that a central cadre did invite the FARC to Viotá, without discussing this decision with others. He explained: "the FARC were not in our land in 1980 because we didn't let them. But one day this cadre told us that eight FARC members were coming for a few days. But then they stayed longer, and after two months announced that they were here for good. They had everything planned in advance" (Int. 4). It seems clear that some rejected the FARC early on. Others welcomed them for ideological reasons; the FARC, after all, embraced communism and formed in response to the government's attack on their agrarian movement.

Other hypotheses point to national conditions as opposed to any local dynamics in Viotá. The state's bombing of Casa Verde, an attack that was directed at the Secretariat of the FARC, led the guerrilla group to disperse and expand to new municipalities. Others in the municipality think that the FARC used the remote territory (the highlands) before, but did not need to rule or have any stronger presence because the communists ruled; as sympathizers of the FARC, they would make sure people did not denounce the group. In their 7th Conference held in 1982, however, the FARC decided to expand their territorial control and surround Bogotá. Viotá became a target. Yet another hypothesis points to the coffee crisis in the 1990s: "The prices went down, Coffee Berry Borer (a beetle harmful to coffee) came, and production fell 50%. This was important because the FARC could come and offer something" (Int. 37).

Finally, relations between the CP and the FARC could also help to explain why the guerrilla group decided to take over Viotá only in the 1980s. The CP and the FARC had close ties in the 1960s and 1970s. However, the CP declared many times that it only supported the armed struggle as a means for defense. As time went by, the two organizations became more distant and by the 1980s they broke their ties more openly (Pizarro & Peñaranda 1992:202). In the 1980s the FARC decided they could now control the municipality as part of their expansion plan without losing too much on the political front, because their relations with the CP had been damaged anyway.

Two FARC fronts operated in Viotá: the 42nd and the 22nd; it was the 42nd Front that was in charge of Tellus, Librea, and Zama. As elsewhere in Colombia, the rebels carefully planned how to penetrate social networks, gain sympathizers, and finally take over Viotá. The first stage entailed the visit of small "commissions" of combatants to the rural areas. According to a former combatant, they went door-to-door, asking how many people lived there and introducing themselves, as well as explaining why they were there and their ideals (Int. 117). They were, for the most part, peaceful. They talked to people, contacted leaders, and explained their goals. One local says that they "entered softly, having meetings with one, and the other ... until they were established" (Int. 20). A Liberal politician from another village told me, "well, you know, they came and interviewed me, exactly like you are doing now: they asked about the community, its problems, its people ..." (Int. 9). Dario, a leader of another village in Viotá, recounts how the commander, alias Alfredo, held a meeting right after arriving at the village for the first time:

> As the president of the JAC, I attended. He said they were going to do guerrilla work in the area. "We need people like you to work on the political front," said Alfredo. He offered me a cell phone, a motorcycle, and a gun. But I told him that I have a structure here. I belong to that structure. A structure of the leadership of the CP. I can't suddenly change the language with the people. And Alfredo said, "Fine, so you are of no use to me," but we were on good terms. He didn't try to convince or force me. (Int. 15)

As they penetrated networks, talked to leaders, and won allies, the FARC slowly created its own social web. Initially they did not coerce anyone, and displayed "benevolent" behavior. For example, they offered money or goods to families in need, and helped communities with local projects. Selective and public incentives were broadly used. To gain greater acceptance, the rebels also "cleansed the area of undesirables," as they usually did elsewhere in the country: "They started going to places that had robberies, so that they could control them" (Int. 11). At some point, they even put up a huge billboard announcing their presence; some interviewees said it was 20 feet long.

At the time, the situation in Tellus was similar to that in other places in Viotá. The leaders who did not move to Zama maintained a strong presence, but local organizations were weak. Juan was the president of the JAC in Tellus. He was a well-recognized, elite member of the CP. Yet, he became a marginal figure in his own community. Although he remained active in the movement after other leaders had left for Zama, his own community was not active. While people focused on their plots, their children, and their lives, Juan tried to maintain his work with the leaders of Zama from a distance.

The FARC arrived to Tellus with a similar dual strategy: a gradual penetration of the social fabric, and courting the CP leaders. Combatants arrived slowly, making ties with a few peasants. They first approached a few individuals, and stressed their ideology and their promise to work for the wellbeing of the community. Then "they used the entire discourse; with trust – you know, 'I know this *compadre* (buddy), and this other' – and they slowly created a social network that rapidly advanced" (Int. 16), says Juan. Romantic relationships between rebels and civilians apparently helped facilitate the process. Some also received material support: "For those who didn't have money to buy groceries, there were the FARC: 'here you go, for the groceries'; and also to pay debts. They helped many people," adds Juan. The FARC also promised to deal with thieves and quickly eliminated petty crime, a change many welcomed. Similar to the tactics used by politicians, they were even ready to chip in when parties or celebrations took place. "One day they paid for an orchestra to play for 2 days . . . they killed two cows to give meat to everyone at the party. Who wouldn't gain support in that way?" (ibid.).

Communist leaders from other villages describe their comrades from Tellus as "good," well-trained cadres who were victims of the apathy that consumed most of Viotá. With only a few remaining leaders in Tellus, it was very difficult for them to work to preserve their community's organization. According to Felipe from Zama, "Some of the leaders cooperated openly [with the FARC]. Some just tried to stay still. And the FARC were able to take over" (Int. 29). The FARC also promised the leaders that, together, they would make the JACs take over power in the municipal government and beyond. "Many fell for it," says Clara (Int. 5), including some of the CP leaders. Outsiders have the same impression. A worker of SENA (the National Service for Learning), who spent years visiting Viotá, remembers that "the FARC entered Tellus with the support of the leaders . . . The FARC know that if they rule the one on the top, following down the hierarchy they could rule the ones below" (Int. 11). And they did. Soon, the FARC became the de facto ruler of Tellus. The peasantry turned to the rebels to solve all sorts of private disputes, and the FARC regulated many of their conducts. A Liberal summarizes the situation bluntly: "the FARC became in Tellus judge, police, and state – all at once" (Int. 36).

The arrival of the FARC in Librea was somewhat different from Tellus. While liberals had triumphed over the communists, competition was still harsh, and the community was divided along partisan lines. The FARC exploited this division and sought the support of the communists, while declaring the Liberals their enemies. A few Liberals openly opposed the arrival of the FARC, and they were killed or expelled.[13]

---

[13] In 1995, a liberal commission estimated a death toll of 60 liberals in Viotá (*El Tiempo* 1996). This estimate is unlikely to be true, though. Locals say that at most ten liberals were assassinated in Viotá as a whole, two of which came from Librea. I was not able to find any reliable estimate of the death toll of the conflict in Viotá, let alone by party membership.

As for the communists, they were low-rank cadres with weak popular support. According to an outsider who worked for a state agency in Viotá for over a decade, these leaders "were not members of the elite of the CP; they didn't have as much power and authority. And in their disputes with the liberals, their capacity to lead was even more jeopardized" (Int. 11). Soon, they were fully co-opted by the FARC, who even brought in their own people to serve as presidents of the JACs. With neither liberal nor communist leaders pulling them down, conditions were ripe for the FARC to take over. Using the same mix of ideological appeals, offers of help, and social interaction to gain support that it used in Tellus, the FARC managed to gain many sympathizers, including CP cadres.

Many welcomed the FARC in both Tellus and Librea. The low coffee prices and the decrease in production due to coffee berry borer (a harmful pest to coffee crops) had deeply affected the daily life of the peasantry, and people did not think the state was doing much to solve their problems. Thus, many were optimistic about the FARC's promise of better social conditions. Others were simply thankful for the rebels' help, and eagerly returned their favors when asked. Juan, perhaps the most influential leader in Tellus, acknowledges that he welcomed the FARC for ideological reasons. He believed in their cause because he saw it as a natural extension of his own cause. "I believed in their promise of social justice," he says (Int. 16). Many others simply accepted the FARC's offer to help with community projects, families in need, and victims of robberies or abuses. As civilians who were pleased with these conducts engaged in conversations with the rebels, joined their projects, and attended their meetings, they opened their networks to the FARC. Cooperation consolidated, and as it did, the FARC had a free path to rule.

Despite the different ways in which their interactions with the FARC began in Tellus and Librea, the process by which rebelocracy was built was very similar in both places. After offering people monetary assistance and guidance, they began demanding obedience of some rules. The rebels first regulated delinquency and behaviors that could compromise their own security. For example, moving around by car was forbidden after 6 p.m., and whoever was walking around after the curfew was required to use a flashlight, even if it were not necessary. "If you were found walking around without a flashlight, you could get killed. It was the way to let them [the FARC] know that you were from the area" (Int. 20). Freedom of speech was also limited early on. "They prohibited speaking out against the armed movement or complaining about it," says a politician (Int. 23).

Informing the police or the army about the FARC, or providing them shelter or food, resulted in a death sentence. Those who threatened public order were also punished: "thieves were usually warned twice, and if they reoffended, were expelled or killed. Rapists and assassins were killed directly" (Int. 23).

The creation of an alternate system of justice was central to the consolidation of rebelocracy. The most well-known FARC commander in the area, alias Negro Antonio (*Black Anthony*), managed to establish his front (the 42nd front) as the people's preferred court. When someone had a dispute over a land border or a debt, or was victim of a robbery, or even of domestic violence, they would say they needed to go to the *42nd Court*. "They used to run everything – from separations to sessions, inheritances, and bigamy disputes" (Int. 16). Furthermore, "lawyers used to litigate both with normal law, and with Negro Antonio. They would go up there [to the camp] to process papers. Even the notary went there. Entire processions climbed up the mountain to see him" (Int. 37). Clara, another leader, says that even the police inspector turned to the FARC when "a case was way over his head" (Int. 6). To many, this was not only a convenient way to handle disputes, but also one that met moral standards – as a Liberal leader says, the FARC "became a valid interlocutor" (Int. 35).

The 42nd Court was recognized enough that people even knew about it in nearby municipalities. In La Mesa, a neighboring county, a merchant says that over time, people no longer formally sued anyone in court. "Lawyers stopped coming to Viotá [the main town]. Everything was solved up there" (ibid.). A young politician says that the FARC "became like a center to mete out justice; like a court, and Negro Antonio was the judge" (Int. 23).

The FARC also influenced local organizations. "There were militiamen [part-time FARC members] working at the JACs," says a demobilized woman who operated in the area. "When I arrived in Viotá, people were very organized, and they worked well with the guerrillas." Some people in Tellus say that the FARC simply told the president of the JAC what to do. Another local states that "5 years after the FARC arrived, the CP [in Tellus] was nothing" (Int. 32). In both Tellus and Librea, when the community had a problem, it had to talk to the FARC commander before adopting a solution. Even when planning local festivities, consulting the FARC was a must (Int. 23). In sum, the role that the union and the JAC had formerly played was now in the hands of the rebels. Although the JAC was still operating, it followed the FARC's decisions (Int. 32). A liberal councilman summarizes the situation in one sentence: "there were no teachers, no parent associations, no JACs ... only FARC" (Int. 35). This epitomized the extent of intervention into quotidian relations that occurs under rebelocracy.

While serving as president of the JAC in Tellus, Juan realized the FARC did not merely want mobilization of the community; they wanted submission. At first, he thought the community would work hand in hand with the rebels, but he soon realized that was not the power dynamic that the rebels had in mind; the latter ruled, while peasants followed. By the time he came to regret his choice of supporting the rebels, it was too late: the FARC had consolidated its power. Something similar happened to many locals, as Blanca recounts: "At the beginning people thought that the FARC were the best – but they were tricked. And when combatants had settled, they tightened up" (Int. 32).

The group also regulated economic activities in many ways. Selling certain brands of beer or soda was forbidden: "It was a strict rule. Merchants could not buy it, and their trucks did not come to deliver anymore" (Int. 35). Some were blessed by this rule, as they enjoyed a monopoly over the distribution of the only brand allowed in the area, "Polar Beer." A young politician in the main town recounts that "a militiaman was the only one who could distribute the beer for the entire municipality" (Int. 17). Another interviewee explains the origins of the prohibition: "if they didn't pay the *shot* [bribe], the group would ban their trucks and all stores from selling their products" (Int. 23).

Furthermore, the FARC also controlled some individuals' private economic decisions. If someone wanted to open a store, he or she had to seek permission from Negro Antonio. Wealthier peasants and merchants had to pay their dues on time to avoid harassment, kidnapping, or death. The FARC regulated salaries for wage earners in the farms and, according to a young right-wing politician, they intervened to "make more humane the job of day laborers" (Int. 23). Those involved in trading exotic wood had to find another job, as cutting down trees for commerce was severely punished. So was the hunting of endangered species. The preservation of fauna actually seems to be one of the few positive consequences of the FARC's presence in the area: "Now I see species that I had not seen in my entire life in Viotá," says Luis, who has traveled to every corner of the mountains of the municipality. "The change in the flora and fauna with the FARC was enormous. This is a gain that has no price ... Pumas, ocelots, 'Talla X' [snakes], monkeys ... At least we have that" (Int. 37).

Regulating domestic life was also part of the FARC's ruling agenda. Those who mistreated children or women were sanctioned. "For example, [violators of the rule] would work to improve the condition of the roads for a day, or carry the 'remittances' of the town up to the FARC's camp" (Int. 117).

The FARC did not only rule over so many realms of inhabitants' lives; they also captured local democracy and took over the municipal government. Popular election of mayors was established in Colombia in 1988. The FARC saw in this change an opportunity to seize the resources of the municipal government for its coffers (Sánchez & Chacón 2006), as well as to direct subsidies, services, and contracts to reward supporters or convince potential ones. The local government of Viotá was no exception. The group's capture of the local government was comprehensive. "All the state institutions in Viotá collaborated with the FARC," says a former combatant. "The commander had them all organized. The mayor spent a lot of time with Negro Antonio, and the notary did too" (Int. 117).

This infiltration was achieved with various strategies. One entailed direct involvement in local elections, as described by an interviewee: "There were several mayors imposed by them [the FARC]. The technique was very effective: they put the word out that they preferred a particular candidate, and on the day of the elections sent buses to pick up voters, brought them to vote in town, and then drove them up again" (Int. 12). The winning candidate owed his mandate to the FARC, and thus followed their directions.

Another strategy consisted of designating their own members or delegates as candidates for councilmen. A former Liberal councilman named Mario recounts how the local council used to discuss problems:

> When the Council had a meeting, all the councilors attended: the members of the Liberal, Communist, and Conservative parties. Some were collaborators of the guerrilla, and others were guerrillas proper. They had all won their seats in the elections. When an important matter was being decided, the guerrillas would stop the meeting and call the commander, Negro Antonio, to ask whether he agreed with what was being decided. When it was about awarding a contract, they decided everything and none of us could say anything. (Int. 12)

From elections to council debates, the rebels had captured "democracy." Furthermore, according to several interviews, even politicians campaigning in Viotá to get elected at the departmental level had to pay the FARC and bend to its will. Other studies have found evidence of this practice elsewhere in Cundinamarca (Peña 1997).

Decisions about how to run the local government and public agencies were also under guerrilla control. A young, former councilman says that the FARC "asked the manager of the hospital, the principal of the school, the secretary of public infrastructure, and many more, to report to the commander ... and he let them know about his approval or disapproval of their performance as public servants" (Int. 23). While this influence benefitted some communities and sectors, public funds often found their way to the FARC's private coffers. Several interviewees believe that contractors of public works always gave a share to the group (Int. 23). Negro Antonio made decisions about appointments and firings alike.

Coercion was certainly used as a complementary strategy to ensure full power over the administration. "Since 1994, mayors had to learn to deal with the FARC and rule with it – enduring bombs, deaths, and threats" (Int. 23). The group even killed councilmen and mayoral candidates for allegedly violating FARC rules. As a communist leader puts it, "either by hook or crook, at city hall everything was done as [the FARC] wanted. All the agencies functioned in the way they wanted, and with whom they wanted" (Int. 16). In sum, the FARC fully permeated Viotá's political life, establishing a rebelocracy.

Parallel to its institutions to regulate civilian conduct, the FARC provided private and collective incentives. "It used to steal from trucks and give the food away, or sell it very cheap to people" (Int. 18). Providing and caring for public goods was also part of its agenda. The group maintained roads, forcing people to clean them once every month. Sometimes whoever did not show up to work on the roads had to pay a fee (Int. 9). Planning parties for the locals always provided good opportunities for the rebels to gain more sympathizers. As Hilario says, "the FARC organized parties with lots of drinks and free food. They did this, and won people in that way. In the parties of the CP you didn't see this – we didn't have money, so people were not convinced in that way" (Int. 4). According to some interviewees, Negro Antonio also lent money to people (Int. 9). Others say that people often went to see Negro Antonio to cash checks and bills for collection (Int. 24). The group thus became every local institution: court, police, party-organizer, ideologue, and bank.

The FARC also relied on ideological appeals. In Tellus and Librea, ideology was stressed repeatedly at meetings, as well as in private conversations. Some people report meetings taking place as often as every two weeks, with mandatory attendance. In those meetings, the FARC presented its views on national and local politics and recounted their deeds. This constant affirmation of their discourse could only help to consolidate the FARC's control over the communities.

Last but not least, rebels achieved social control with strict monitoring and punishment. They relied on informants and allies in each village, who would communicate instances of disobedience and opposition. Some infractions were mildly punished, while others were considered serious and were dealt with by expulsion or death.

How did civilians behave once the FARC had consolidated rebelocracy in their village? Cooperation – in the form of both obedience and spontaneous support – was widespread. Most people obeyed the myriad rules established by the group. Many volunteered to provide information and other kinds of help. For example, most interviewees described how individuals would denounce each other to the group as collaborators of the enemy (Int. 23). Many sought ways to please combatants in order to be on good terms with them. As one local recalls, "[t]he Viotuno was proud to be having a beer with those people [the FARC], and [women] of dating combatants" (Int. 23). A young politician running for a right-wing party goes even further: "People dedicated themselves to deifying the FARC and Negro Antonio" (Int. 23).

Although cooperation was widespread, adolescents were particularly fond of the FARC. To them, combatants were "someone to emulate, people with power, an option to imitate" (Int. 23). The FARC knew their attraction to the youth was one of their best assets, and worked hard to win them over: "They were very good friends [with the youths], often partying together" (ibid.). Adolescents and people in their twenties were their strongest allies. To Hilario, from Zama, their support for the FARC was a sign of immaturity (FG. 1). And Blanca, from Tellus, agrees: "they liked the cars, the cell phones ... and girls were crazy about dating them" (Int. 32). Recruitment of this age group was therefore common.

Juan estimates that in the nineties, about 30 percent of the youth in Tellus went to live in a big city; 30 percent migrated to work in the coca fields; and 30 percent joined the FARC. Hilario recognizes that the community's history of heroic, armed defense may have somehow contributed to this: "that idea of self-defense, of the way of weapons, was misused." He believes that the youth fell into that trap more easily because of the glorified memories of the community's self-defense forces. "But that was a wholly different story: we had the support of the entire community, we were defending ourselves from brutal attacks" (Int. 4).

Sometimes parents pushed their sons to join the FARC. "They said 'go and see what you can help them with, son'" (Int. 16). But in many cases, the youths would enlist against their parents' will. In fact, many families are said to have left Viotá in order to prevent their sons from joining the FARC. "People would send their kids to Bogotá during the night," remembers one leader (Int. 4), and another goes even further: "those who were not astute in taking their sons out [of Viotá] when they finished school, eventually saw them joining [the rebels]" (Int. 6).[14]

Behind cooperation, there were many stories of ideological positions, material interest, fear, and ambition. In every village, there was an amalgam of motivations. A few were truly convinced of the importance of defending the revolutionary project in Viotá, but, as other scholars have found, these were a minority (e.g., Petersen 2001; Wood 2003). In most cases, cooperation stemmed from the multifaceted power that the FARC had accumulated – consisting of weapons, veto power in politics, and regulation of economic activities, private conducts, and public discourse. The FARC's power over virtually every aspect of life in most of the municipality created the conditions for people with a wide range of preferences to cooperate. Youngsters were enchanted with the power that teenage combatants exhibited, as well as with their uniforms and guns. Families and workers appreciated the maintenance of the roads, the investment in public works, and the possibility of having efficient "judges" and "police" to impart justice. Displays of coercion clearly added an essential ingredient to this decision-making process. In the words of a former FARC combatant who operated in Viotá, "the guerrilla was in charge of people; some liked it, others didn't ... but people had to obey ...; otherwise, it would be bad for them" (Int. 117).

In addition to this power were the ideological appeals for a society with a history of oppression, resistance, and agrarian reform. The FARC had been born in a community of peasants that, like Viotá's, were fighting for land – only that the former had been bombarded by the army. Despite Viotá's desire for a different path to agrarian reform, embracing the FARC's discourse was easy. This idea of a just fight – or even of its possibility – certainly appeased many

---

[14] FARC leaders have been indicted for more than sixty cases of recruitment of minors in Viotá (Verdad Abierta 2013).

whose cooperation was primarily founded on personal interest, and led others to assume their participation was a righteous act.

This subtle mix of fear and respect, benevolence and abuse, produced an equally complex web of incentives, beliefs, and motivations that favored cooperation. People list the many ways in which the FARC controlled life, and wonder how they could not help but cooperate: "They ruled on everything. Private life, public life, the finances of the local government," says Dario. Slightly surprised by my question about why people cooperated with the FARC, another leader responds: "well, everyone supported them – you know, they were the government" (Int. 190).

THE FARC IN ZAMA

But in the village of Zama, things were different. Despite the FARC's decisive influence over virtually all spheres of life elsewhere in the municipality, the community managed to retain its autonomy on several fronts.

Unlike in Tellus and Librea, upon arrival to Zama, the FARC had a meeting with the leaders, entering the village "from above." Combatants explained why they were there and offered their help to protect the community and improve people's living conditions (Int. 4). Some leaders were supportive, some weren't, but when the FARC tried to gain influence by offering to partake in the meetings of the JAC, all denied these offers. At the same time, combatants approached the common residents of Zama here and there. But, according to Felipe, "it was very difficult for the FARC to win over the masses. They did so in other places but not in Zama. People didn't follow" (Int. 29).

As time went by, a tacit arrangement was consolidated in Zama. The rules that the FARC had imposed on security, mobility, and collaboration with the state armed forces elsewhere in Viotá were also strictly observed in the village. However, many aspects of daily life remained under the regulations of the old peasant institutions. The meetings of the JAC continued to take place without the presence of FARC members; decisions were made without consulting the commander; and problems were adjudicated as before. Most locals turned to the JAC to solve problems, trusted the judgment of the committees appointed to solve conflicts, and followed their resolutions. A peasant who arrived in Zama in the 1970s states that he "never noticed the FARC's presence in the JAC of Zama. They [the FARC] did take some power away from the communists, but in general in [the municipality at large]. In Zama [the communists] were still in charge of many things" (Int. 190). In addition, interactions with combatants were not as close as elsewhere. For example, a local from Zama says that the FARC "only came in passing; they did not come to parties, or to play soccer, or anything like that" (Int. 190).

The CP leaders kept doing their work at the Municipal Council sessions, where they had about 50 percent of the seats. They said what they thought and opposed decisions of the FARC that they viewed as harmful to the community. A former Liberal councilman confirms this: "I always saw the difference between the councilmen of the CP and those of the guerrilla ...; I was aware that they never interceded for the guerrilla in the council" (Int. 3). According to a FARC ex-combatant, "[the CP leaders] did not want to be with the FARC or against them; they were part of the community. And when they did not agree with something that the FARC were doing, they went to see the commander and blocked things" (Int. 27).

This is not to say that the FARC always tolerated Zama's autonomy without any pushback. In fact, there were several moments where the FARC probed the community and its leaders. Felipe recounts that "[rebels] came and told us to our face that the CP was a hindrance for them, that our authority was a hindrance" (Int. 6). Hilario remembers a time when there were rumors that the FARC wanted to kill him. "The CP leadership in Bogotá asked me to leave Viotá. But I was not going to! Instead I went to see Negro Antonio" (Int. 4). Fortunately, the FARC commander did not kill him.

There were also instances in which civilians were forced to obey rules beyond security. For example, one resident says that the FARC held meetings to talk about its ideology every two months, and the people of Zama had to attend (Int. 22). He also recounts that sometimes Negro Antonio would call someone to go up to the camp in order to solve a problem raised by another civilian. There were also many negative changes in daily life: a few people from Zama were killed by the FARC, locals didn't organize parties anymore, and some youngsters supported the group (FG. 1).

As these events unfolded, the community met, discussed the options, and decided to remain united and decline the FARC's attempts to intervene in their affairs. Social interaction with combatants remained distant, while people in Zama tried to keep their lives together and avoid fueling tensions with the FARC – until they had had enough. In the years to come, the FARC started to break its social contracts with all the villages, and the peasants of Zama stood against it.

CIVILIAN RESISTANCE

To control Viotá in general, and Zama, Librea, and Tellus in particular, the FARC relied on both combatants and militiamen – the former being full-time members of the FARC, and the latter locals working with the group. At the beginning, both were disciplined. In some villages, people usually saw only "two armed men, always dressed in civilian clothes. They passed by all the time, up and down" (Int. 9). Those two men were enough to control the village. The commander would stop by once in a while, and everyone knew what the rules were. In other villages, visits were more frequent, and combatants sometimes stayed there for long periods of time. And in others, combatants were permanently present. In all cases, interaction was based on a mutual understanding of both civilian and combatant conduct.

In the late 1990s, the FARC started to recruit youngsters as militiamen throughout Viotá who had no experience and did not receive training, jeopardizing the group's discipline. "They spent their days riding motorcycles around town. People knew who they were. They were pretending to be *guapos* (brave and cool). They delivered messages from the guerrilla" (Int. 17). These new members started to abuse the population and to demand money without orders from the commander. A merchant who owns land in Viotá says that when farm owners received a ticket – the FARC's note demanding payment – they wondered if it was really the FARC authorities or someone else taking advantage of the situation. In many cases, they asked for an "audience" with Negro Antonio to clarify whether or not it was really a ticket from the FARC. Robberies also became common, and people felt certain the militiamen were behind them.

The FARC had used violence before, to be sure. But combatants had generally been disciplined, and, for the most part, people knew what to expect from them. Violence was usually "justified" on the grounds of some misbehavior, and material contributions to the rebels were stable and regulated with the *shots* – formalized taxes demanded mostly from the wealthier sectors of the population. As its name suggests, if people paid the shot, they could trust that no other demands would be made, just as a vaccine promises to keep the illness away.

Now it was different, and these behaviors did not go unnoticed. People resented the abuse of power that aimed for the personal enrichment of FARC members. "They messed things up," says a leader in Viotá's main town. "They relied on the lumpen – kids who did not know how to do anything. And their values changed" (Int. 37). Some noticed, for example, that only certain thieves were punished. "I had a few cows stolen," says a farmer, "but I didn't complain because I knew who did it – they were militiamen, and I knew nothing would happen to them" (Int. 17). According to a person from Librea, "if someone tried to go to the commander, he or she was punished" (FG. 1). A former demobilized combatant, however, fully denies these accusations: "There were no swindlers there; the FARC killed anyone who introduced himself as a FARC member and asked for money" (Int. 117). To locals, however, it was clear that the group was either losing control of its own members or failing to monitor impostors or both.

This climate of uncertainty and fear took its toll on economic and social life. "People were not motivated to work anymore," said a Liberal leader. "They [the FARC] came to take what they wanted – so why bother?" (Int. 9). There was a clear shift in people's ties with the FARC: "Before violence started, people were fine with the rebels; they were thankful for them." When the abuses started, people resented their presence and felt trapped, as it was too late to deny cooperation (FG. 1). An ex-FARC fighter who operated in the area agrees: "Everything was ruined because we did not take care of the social base. The commander gave too much power to the squad commander (*comandante de escuadra*), and they did not take care of people" (Int. 27).

In addition to the indiscipline of the militiamen, the FARC were dealing with the threat of military confrontation. The paramilitaries were disputing FARC control in nearby municipalities, leaving in their wake many deaths. Everyone knew Viotá's turn would come soon. In 2000, the mayor, an alleged FARC puppet, was assassinated, presumably by paramilitaries; a mayoral candidate was also killed shortly thereafter (*El Tiempo* 2000). The FARC started to screen the population, searching for defectors. Civilians felt the rebels tightening control over them, and had no one to turn to. In the streets, people denounced a close collaboration between paramilitaries and state forces in the region (*Semana* 2003). The institutions that the FARC had created were crumbling, insecurity was widespread, and Viotá could not expect the police or the army to protect its citizens. Viotá was now living under disorder – the social contracts that the villages had with the FARC had been broken.

The people of Zama decided that they had had enough. Civilians had suffered mistreatment. Politicians had watched as their colleagues became murder victims. Public resources were extracted. This was not a form of governance that they could tolerate. Trusting their capacity to organize and stand together, they decided to respond with collective action – once again.

The mayoral elections of 2000 were coming up and the FARC, as usual, had their own candidate. Seeing that in other villages people's preferences were not with the FARC anymore, the communist cadres decided to put forth their own candidate – a move that involved a direct confrontation with the FARC. Knowing it would be hard, they trusted that with the support of the people of Zama, they could turn things around and become, once again, a viable alternative for the peasantry of Viotá.

Ricardo, one of the most famous and beloved leaders from Zama, was chosen as the candidate. He brought together both communists and non-communists. "It was a civic movement," says Dario, from another village (Int. 15). But suddenly, Ricardo died of a heart attack one month before the elections. The FARC asked the communists to support their candidate, but the communist leaders decided to hold a primary election to select another candidate. "Everyone who came to hold a wake for Ricardo, casted a vote... communists and non-communists voted – almost 3,000 people [about 25 percent of the population of the municipality]," says Clara. Adelia Benavidez, a sharp young cadre, won the election. "She was crying. She didn't want to... She was scared," says Felipe (Int. 6). But she went on to run in the mayoral campaign.

Two weeks before the election, Negro Antonio called fifteen communist leaders to a meeting. With a list in his hands, he accused them of many things – from informing the army, to corruption, to gossiping. "He tried to scare the leaders, but they didn't let him" (Int. 5). Negro Antonio made it clear to the leaders that the FARC had already decided who the mayor should be, and carrying out their campaign would be a frontal aggression to the organization. "The candidacy of Adelia was an act of braveness; an open opposition. We were convinced that we were right, and that gave us courage. We wanted to show our point of view. To show the town and the army the position of the CP leaders, and to the FARC that they were wrong" (ibid.). The leaders went back to their homes and continued the campaign.

On the day of the election, "the FARC were very mad. They were furious," recalls Clara. "They threatened us and ordered everyone to vote for their candidate. While people said they would, most ended up voting for Adelia, and we won" (Int. 5). The leaders had to hide in a house for a few days after the results of the elections were made public.

It turned out that 2,277 people had voted for Adelia against the FARC's orders.

This electoral result shows that many in Viotá did not want the FARC to rule anymore. By bringing disorder about, the rebels lost cooperation among many civilians, and the election offered those dissatisfied an opportunity to express their preferences. But not everyone was convinced yet – the candidate of the FARC did get many votes and, according to one of Adelia's aides, six of the council members were FARC allies. While it is impossible to know who voted for Adelia and who didn't, it is likely that those who still benefitted from FARC rule, or strongly identified with the group's cause, continued to support it.

While disorder changed many civilians' preferences towards FARC rule, it did not suddenly create the conditions for collective action everywhere in the municipality. Voters defied the FARC when casting their vote, but this was not a very risky enterprise because the FARC did not monitor who voted for Adelia. The real risk was faced by those who campaigned for her. In 2015 I went back to Viotá to better understand the way in which Adelia's candidacy was advanced.[15] While many people say that everyone supported her – "the conservatives, the liberals, the communists, the non-communists, those who pray and those who do not" (Int. 40), they also said that people were really afraid to express their support in public. "It wasn't a big campaign because it was a short period of time, and we couldn't kick up a racket (*hacer bulla*), it was all under the table" (ibid.). The leaders of Zama carried out the most dangerous work for Adelia's candidacy. Leaders in other villages did support her, from all the political parties, but "it was support, not active work" (ibid.). "The leaders were all in a waiting mode ... everyone had to protect themselves." For example, they were the ones that usually went with her to meetings – typically small, clandestine meetings of five to seven people. "We would call for a meeting, but then people wouldn't show up." Sometimes the persons who agreed to hold the meetings at their home would not attend. These testimonies suggest that although many supported Adelia, those who came together to engage in dangerous collective action to sustain her candidacy were, for the most part, the leaders of Zama.

After the election, the FARC organized a rally against Adelia and forced everyone to attend; they also threatened her and asked her to

---

[15] I conducted interviews in Viotá in the summer of 2015. I thank Sara Zamora for conducting additional interviews early in the fall.

leave the municipality. But Adelia did not give in. She stayed and fulfilled her service, and asked the central government for protection. She had to work from other municipalities on certain occasions due to threats, but she did not permanently move her office outside of Viotá, and she did not quit. When asked about who helped Adelia during these difficult times, one of her close aides said the leaders of Zama were in constant communication with her, and worked with her. The Municipal Council also refused to be intimidated. Several councilmen met clandestinely because the FARC tried to infiltrate the council to block Adelia's rule. And even though the rebels were threatened with a bomb once for not obeying the FARC, they continued with their work.

Despite its many threats, the FARC did not retaliate against any of these leaders. What protected them? Why did the FARC abstain from killing them, as they had done with so many civilians who stood in their way? I asked these questions to my interviewees over and over. Some point to their communist ideology; others to the ties of Ricardo, who was dead by then, with high-level FARC commanders. Yet, they also point to their popular backing. Clara, for example, says: "I think perhaps they couldn't kill the communist leaders because of the command that we had." Another cadre says, "maybe the FARC thought that if they killed the leaders the masses would revolt" (Int. 16). The election of Adelia was a very clear sign of where the people of Zama stood. In a way, it had been a plebiscite on the FARC – and they lost. According to rumors, even Negro Antonio himself acknowledged his defeat: "War is war and he who loses has to leave; people here showed that they do not want us anymore, so we are leaving" – these were his words, according to a politician who met with him a few days after the elections (Int. 23). While such humility is hard to believe, Antonio left Viotá for good.

Some say that Negro Antonio was transferred to another area due to his failure in controlling the elections and was replaced by a commander known as Shirley. In any case, the military control of the FARC did not last long, as a new wave of violence hit Viotá when the paramilitaries arrived.

A NEW WAVE OF VIOLENCE: THE PARAMILITARIES ATTACK IN VIOTÁ

The Self-Defense Forces of Casanare, paramilitary group, arrived in Viotá in 2003, although they had made smaller incursions before. "They came in

A New Wave of Violence: The Paramilitaries Attack in Viotá 253

two ways: politics and violence. The politicians stayed here. The violence was fast and severe" (Int. 16). Some say that trucks with about 300 armed men entered the municipality in daylight, passing through several army posts. Others say that the paramilitaries did not need to bring so many combatants, since they were well-prepared – a lot of people were willing to cooperate, and they already had lists with the names of FARC collaborators. In one village, people realized retrospectively that an outsider had come a few months before the paramilitaries showed up. "He made friends, played *tejo* (hopscotch), had drinks with people, and did his research. Then the paramilitaries came with someone wearing a hood who pointed out who should get killed, and who shouldn't" (Int. 9). They also used to patrol the municipality in a truck with armed men ready to shoot. "If they saw someone on the road, they stopped them to see who they were, and if they had them on their list, they took them" (Int. 17). The group also threatened and killed politicians, local leaders, and common citizens. In some cases they dismembered their victims.

The army allegedly worked alongside the paramilitaries. Army Captain Édgar Arbeláez, who arrived in Viotá in 2003, was sentenced a few years later for killing at least two people in collusion with the paramilitaries (*El Tiempo* 2008; *Semana* 2015). The evidence that the prosecutor used against him included conversations he had with paramilitaries to plan killings of innocent civilians. Captain Arbeláez would then claim that the targets were paramilitaries as proof to his superiors that he was acting against them (Verdad Abierta 2010b). The attorney also found a list of names under the heading "guerrilla collaborators" in the captain's personal notebook. All of the people listed had been killed in Viotá in the years he served there (*El Tiempo* 2008). My interviewees also recounted horrible cases of torture and extortion perpetrated by Captain Arbeláez. Army Colonel González Medina and two other officers of the Colombia Battalion were also indicted for several crimes, including killings, kidnappings, displacement, and terrorism (*Prensa Rural* 2008).

When the first large operation of the paramilitaries took place in April of 2003, the rebels ordered all the presidents of the JACs to tell everyone to leave their homes. "To protect us, they said. But for me it was their way to use us so that they could flee," says Clara (Int. 5). More than 2,000 peasants went to Viotá's urban center while running away from the threats. They waited for ten days before they could return to their villages. It was the largest displacement registered so far in the Cundinamarca Department (*El Tiempo* 2003a). Many say that while civilians were heading to the main town, the FARC were leaving Viotá for good.

During those days, many people disappeared. As Juan recounts: "Those who had close ties with the FARC did not come back. In the meantime, lots of people were killed up in the mountains" (Int. 16). Clara adds: "Most of the presidents of the JACs who had helped the FARC did not go back to their homes. They either fled or were killed ... The [paramilitaries] did not kill in masses. Their killings were mostly selective: one here, one there" (Int. 5). According to all my interviewees and available primary sources, the paramilitaries did not face resistance from the FARC.

After the displacement ended, the paramilitaries killed those accused of being marijuana consumers or informants of the guerrilla. Some say that they brought thieves from other places for the purpose of capturing and killing them, in order to gain popular support (Int. 11). However, after a few months the paramilitaries were rarely seen again in rural Viotá. As Clara recounts, "the worst of the paramilitaries lasted about six months. After that, they did not come back here" (Int. 5). Hilario agrees: "As far as I know they only killed people. They didn't want to infiltrate the JACs; they didn't rule over our issues. They only killed" (Int. 4). One source cites 32 killings by paramilitaries during 2003 (CCJ 2006), but people believe the toll to be much higher.

In the *cabecera*, however, the paramilitaries did establish some rules of behavior, and residents had to interact with them in one way or another. "Many people turned to the sun that heats the most: when the FARC were here, they were with the FARC. When the paramilitaries came, they helped them right away" (Int. 5). In general, many welcomed the paramilitaries after having endured the FARC's abusive behavior for the last years. Comparing them, a farmer and merchant says that the paramilitaries "ticketed people more moderately, and with more protocol. They explained to us that they were here to protect us from the guerrillas. 'That entails costs, of course,' they said, and they expected our support" (Int. 17). Others denounced their neighbors as collaborators of the guerrillas to exact revenge upon personal enemies, as often happens in civil wars (Kalyvas 2006). For example, one person recounts that once "in broad daylight, [the paramilitaries] arrived at the city hall and ordered several public servants to leave. Then other people were either expelled [from the municipality] or shot – some due to gossip by others" (Int. 5). Most people simply found a way to obey the new rules and stay away from trouble.

Despite the violent campaign of the paramilitaries and the state forces in many areas of Viotá, Zama was not targeted. A news report described the police's incursion to the municipality, listing the villages where they raided houses looking for the FARC's allies and materials. The report includes many villages, including Tellus and Librea, but not Zama (*El Tiempo* 2003b). Many presidents of the JACs were killed, but in Zama not even one communist was attacked, despite being open members and militants of the CP.

In 2004, the national army created a permanent base in the municipality. Since then, people say that paramilitary presence has been subtle and weak. The most common explanation seems to be that they came to Viotá fulfilling a deal with the National Army, with whom all the operations were coordinated (CAJAR 2008), and left when the job was done. It is possible that a few militiamen stayed, but combatants were not seen again. The army, on the other hand, has been permanently present in different areas of the municipality. Although security improved afterwards, the paramilitaries made incursions into the municipality and perpetrated additional crimes. In 2007 fourteen people were massacred, of which three allegedly had ties to the FARC (*El Tiempo* 2008). By 2012, the situation had improved dramatically. However, locals report the presence of small armed groups, instances of extortion (Ministry of Interior 2012), and harassment of union members by the army (CINEP 2015).

CAUSAL INFERENCE: THE EFFECT OF INSTITUTIONAL QUALITY

In this section I discuss how the aforementioned evidence supports the theory advanced in this book, while accounting for alternative explanations. Given the previous discussion of how the evidence supports my claim that the three villages had been quite similar, and that the event that changed local institutions was accidental, I focus on the village characteristics that are not held constant by design.

The first hypothesis that this study aims to test is that civilian resistance to rebelocracy emerges where the quality of preexisting local institutions is high. Two mechanisms underlie this hypothesis. First, the quality of institutions explains civilians' *desire* to resist. This is supported by the fact that in Tellus and Librea, where institutional quality was low, most locals welcomed not only FARC presence, but also the institutions the group offered. In particular, people not only obeyed rules, but also *turned* to the FARC to adjudicate disputes and solve problems. To be sure, a few leaders did resent the expansion of FARC rule, but they were a minority. In Zama, in contrast, while some people welcomed the presence of the FARC due to ideological reasons, most continued to turn to the old governing institutions to solve their problems.

The second mechanism is the effect of the quality of institutions on civilians' *capacity* to resist. When FARC members started breaking their social contract and abusing locals, everyone wanted to oppose them. But it was in Zama that locals launched resistance and bore the highest costs. Adelia Benavidez was a mayoral candidate from Zama. While disorder did change the preferences of many civilians towards FARC rule – and this is why Adelia won the election – voting was not in itself a costly act. It was being a candidate, campaigning for her, and holding secret meetings that was extremely dangerous. And this was mostly a task that people in Zama took up.

The second hypothesis contends that when confronting communities that can resist, rebels adapt their strategies insofar as civilians' demands do not compromise territorial control. The underlying mechanism is that civilians' potential for resistance gives them bargaining power: if civilians want the terms of rebel governance to change *and* can resist, rebels make concessions. Several facts show that Zama had bargaining power that Tellus and Librea lacked. In Zama, people denied intervention in subtle ways – for example, declining offers to hold their JAC meetings with FARC members – while the leaders spoke up at the Municipal Council meetings, and talked to the FARC commander when they disagreed with the group's decisions. The rebels, in return, tolerated demands and did not impose their institutions on Zama.

Another fact that supports this hypothesis is that, when Zama resisted, the group still did not hurt the leaders. The FARC didn't know the paramilitaries and the army would soon force them out, so the group was probably still concerned about its ability to control the territory in the long run. It is therefore highly plausible that rebels did not hurt the leaders because they feared it would backfire, given the leaders' support within the population.

Several events also show that in the cases where collective resistance was unlikely, Librea and Tellus, rebels did not tolerate opposition to their rule, and established rebelocracy. The few liberals who opposed the FARC in Librea were killed or expelled; and the communist leaders who *wanted* to resist rebelocracy in Tellus did not think they could voice their opposition – and thus didn't. In both villages, a full-fledged rebelocracy operated for years.

How do alternative explanations compare? As I argued earlier, the evidence suggests that these three villages were historically quite similar and that Merchán's settlement in Zama was an accidental event that led to variation in the quality of local institutions. By comparing previously similar cases that diverged due to an unexpected event, my research design limits the possibility of alternative explanations although, of course, it cannot rule them out. In particular, there are two concerns. First, other events could have taken place between 1950 and 1990 that impacted only Zama (or only Tellus and Librea), and in turn shaped social order when the FARC ruled the village. However, it is unlikely that different pieces of evidence support the mechanisms connecting institutional quality with wartime social order when some other factor was in reality the cause. Still, it is worth assessing whether the differences that did emerge between the three villages prior to the arrival of the FARC could explain the observed outcomes.

I have identified two such differences. First, members of the Liberal Party had large farms in Librea, and they gained power there, while not in Tellus and Zama. Yet, these events cannot explain rebelocracy because Tellus did not experience them and rebelocracy was also established there. Furthermore, the evidence I presented shows that the presence of the Liberals impacted the ways in which the FARC approached the village at the beginning – by targeting the Liberals and exploiting internal divisions in the community. However, once the Liberals were gone, the FARC built rebelocracy in very similar ways in both Tellus and Librea.

Second, it was very difficult to acquire land in Zama for people who did not have a good relationship with the cadres. Hence, Zama became quite homogeneous over time, which may have contributed to its capacity for collective action regardless of its institutions. Yet, the same process happened in Tellus. Indeed, according to a person from the urban center, Tellus was actually more homogenous than Zama (Int. 37). This factor cannot, therefore, explain why Tellus and Zama experienced different outcomes.

The second concern about alternative explanations has to do with the possibility that the gift of Merchán impacted other factors that, in turn, would shape locals' relations with the FARC. Again, while the different CPOs that support the underlying mechanisms address these concerns to some extent, it is important to ask whether such evidence could still be consistent with alternative explanations.

A first possibility is ideology: does communism have something to do with the outcomes? The cases actually contradict the most obvious hypothesis, which would claim that civilians resist rebel rule when they dislike rebels' political goals. Given that both the FARC and the CP are communist, Zama is the least likely of the cases for civilian resistance. We could focus instead on the ideological differences between the FARC and the CP – there were tensions between the two organizations nationwide since at least the 1980s[16] – and argue that the leaders of Zama led the resistance due to their ideological differences with the FARC. But then, why did communist cadres in Tellus and Librea not oppose rebelocracy?

Ideology could also potentially explain the FARC's tolerance of Zama's autonomy: perhaps they were fine with it, only because the leaders shared their ideology. Yet, the fact that the FARC at some point did probe and harass the leaders, even before Adelia's campaign, suggests that the group was at least bothered by that autonomy. Furthermore, there were cadres in Tellus and Librea too, and the FARC did not give them any autonomy.

Another plausible explanation suggests that leadership enables resistance, as opposed to institutions. There are theoretical reasons and empirical evidence against this alternative. Theoretically, collective resistance requires two conditions: the willingness to resist and the capacity to do so. While leaders could facilitate collective action, it is not clear how they would convince people who either do not believe in the legitimacy of the institutions, or see them as ineffective, to organize to defend those institutions from an armed actor. Empirically, in both Tellus and Librea there were communist leaders when the FARC arrived; their mere presence was, however, not sufficient to spur resistance. To be sure, this failure could signal weak leadership, or that there were not enough leaders. Yet, while it is possible that in Tellus and Librea people *could not* resist because leadership was not good enough, the evidence suggests that in those villages people were not *willing* to resist in the first place, as locals not only obeyed the FARC, but also actively used its system of dispute adjudication. That said, leadership may play an important role in these processes as a key igniter of collective action, and as an important force to sustain it, especially in highly

---

[16] Even though both embraced communist ideals, there were tensions between the FARC and the CP, and the former became increasingly independent from the latter since the 1980s (Medina 2009).

dangerous situations. One of the contributions of this study of Viotá is that it opens up interesting questions about the relationship between leadership and informal governing institutions. I return to this issue in the conclusion of this book.

Turning to other potential explanations, it is worth pointing out that the research design rules out the theories of peasant resistance, on one hand, and of rebel governance, on the other, that point to social, political, and economic conditions such as the previous presence of the state (Wickham-Crowley 1991; Mampilly 2011), threats to peasant subsistence (Scott 1977), economic conditions (Paige 1975), and communal ties (Wolf 1969), because all villages shared the same social, economic, and political history. A theory of selective incentives also fails, because the people of Zama did not receive any selective incentives from the state or CP leaders to oppose the FARC.

Finally, variation in wartime social order cannot be explained by different levels of intensity of the armed conflict, or by variation in the FARC's interest in controlling the different villages. Indeed, in a recent study, locals from different villages of Viotá identify Zama, Tellus, and Librea as three of the seven villages that were most affected by the conflict (Tejidos del Viento 2014).

Another potential source of concern is that the persons that I interviewed in Zama were biased. The reality could have been the same everywhere, but those in Zama simply remember it differently. It is important to recognize that while the history of the villages from the 1930s to the 1960s is based on historical accounts as well as on oral testimonies, most of the evidence for events since the 1960s is based on interviews and focus groups. Unfortunately, I found little written evidence on the evolution of these villages after the glorious years of mobilization for land, and no record of how the FARC ruled them in the 1990s. While oral testimonies have many limitations, the unavailability of documents should not preclude our investigation of these important questions. In order to avoid bias in my evidence on the different villages, I interviewed leaders in many villages, not only in Zama, Tellus, and Librea, and asked them about the dynamics in all three villages. While I did interview several communist leaders – most leaders in Viotá were communists – I also interviewed leaders from other parties. Additionally, I conducted several in-depth interviews with persons from the urban center who knew the leaders and the history of the villages well, without being themselves communists. The testimony of two persons from other municipalities – one is a merchant, the other did work in rural Viotá for a state agency – were very useful to corroborate the accounts I received from *Viotunos*. I also interviewed civilians who were not leaders, and former members of the FARC who operated in Viotá. While I recognize the limitations of oral testimonies, I believe that it is unlikely that people from different villages and with different backgrounds incorrectly portrayed these three villages in similar ways.

In sum, the history of these villages offers evidence consistent with the hypothesis that institutional quality affects the form of wartime social order through its effect on communities' capacity to resist collectively. Alternative explanations do not seem to hold, even if leadership plays an important role. These villages also provide detailed evidence on the process by which new forms of order emerge in warzones and, importantly, on the mechanics of nonviolent resistance. The validity of these findings strongly supports results obtained from analyzing evidence collected in other areas of the country with other methods. Each piece of the research design tests a specific component of the theory; altogether, they provide broad support to its claims about the origins of various forms of social order in war zones. This design supports the use of multiple methods at different levels of analysis to further causal inference.

CONCLUSION

The controlled comparison of micro-historic processes presented in this chapter offers an intimate look at the ways in which the quality of local institutions impacts communities' preferences for new rule as well as their ability to organize collective action. It also shows that communities that can organize collectively can have bargaining power even in the wake of enormous asymmetries in power. Furthermore, it shows that combatants respond differently to demands for autonomy depending on civilians' resolution to stand together. In addition to presenting the evidence, I discussed the specific ways in which several causal process observations are consistent with my theory and inconsistent with rival explanations. I also suggested new theoretical possibilities that emerge from these cases, in particular about the role of leadership and its relation to informal institutions.

But testing my theory is not the only contribution of this chapter. The history of Viotá is about much more than wartime order. It is also about the mechanics and effectiveness of sustained nonviolent resistance – a type of resistance that is usually studied in the context of massive mobilization against the state (e.g., Schock 2005; Chenoweth & Stephan

2011). As the history of Zama shows, small-scale nonviolent resistance can be quite successful against non-state armed actors in conflict zones as well.

The history of Viotá is also about the resilience of human agency in political contexts defined by powerful structures. Where there is domination and coercion, so too is there popular mobilization and social solidarity, be it in the realm of war, state building, development, or regime change. Society interacts with state and non-state actors at the local and national levels, and communities found institutions in times of peace and times of war.

And this is, at the same time, the story of a country that has experienced horrible forms of exploitation, coercion, and domination of vulnerable populations by the state, elites, insurgents, and paramilitaries, all while giving birth to amazing forms of collective action, solidarity, social movements, and self-governance. Herein are breathtaking efforts of heroic individuals and communities to defend human dignity.

8

Testing the Microfoundations

Social Order and Recruitment

> *Whether individuals come to act as rebels or collaborators, killers or victims, heroes or cowards during times of upheaval is largely determined by the nature of their everyday economic, social, and political life, both in the time of the upheaval and the period prior to it. The extraordinary is inextricably linked to the ordinary.*
>
> Petersen (2001:1)

The evidence presented in the previous chapters suggests that preexisting civilian institutions, armed groups' internal organization, and the value of local territories shape the form of social order that emerges in a given locality. The logic behind this causal relationship relies on a set of assumptions that have been well established by the literature, to wit, that armed groups seek to control territory and that civilian cooperation is essential for that quest. I also assumed that armed groups want to maximize the byproducts of territorial control. While this is a novel statement, it is far from counterintuitive and several empirical facts have been widely documented that support it. For example, the fact that armed groups organize labor to obtain profits in areas under their control or influence local governments suggests that they do try to use their control in order to strengthen their organization.

But the argument is also built on an additional assumption that is not well established in the literature, to wit, that civilian cooperation is higher where rebelocracy emerges. This is a crucial assumption in the theory: I argued that rebels have strong incentives to establish rebelocracy mostly *because* it leads to higher civilian cooperation. If civilian cooperation is not higher under rebelocracy, the foundations of my theory falter.

Testing the Microfoundations: Social Order and Recruitment

Furthermore, this theory of wartime social order has an important implication for civilian cooperation with insurgents that opposes a long tradition in the study of rebellion and civil war. For decades, a central contention of studies of peasant rebellion, civilian support for insurgents, and recruitment has been that civilians capable of solving collective action problems are likely to join rebellions because rebelling is, above all, a collective action problem: given that participating in a rebellion is costly, why would rational individuals do so when they can benefit from it even if they do not participate? (Gurr 1970; Popkin 1979; Paige 1983; Taylor 1988; Wood 2003; Trejo 2012) Under this view, it is the members of societies that can solve collective action problems in some way who are likely to participate in rebellion. While this is likely to be the case for the early stages of a rebellion – when a new armed group is initially mobilizing (Lewis 2010; Trejo 2012) – I argue that it does not explain the decision of many of those who to enlist once the rebellion is already under way.

If the theory of social order that I propose is correct, communities with a high capacity for collective action should exhibit lower levels of civilian cooperation. Those communities should be more likely to value their institutions and desire to limit rebel rule, and thus use their high capacity for collective action to bargain to live under aliocracy instead of rebelocracy. Civilians living under aliocracy can certainly cooperate with rebels, perhaps motivated by selective incentives, moral or political commitments, or emotions; these forms of cooperation exist in rebelocracy as well. But in rebelocracy there are also many other reasons to cooperate because being on good terms with the armed group can be quite consequential, given its power over so many aspects of people's lives. Furthermore, as I argue elsewhere, the armed actor that rules can impact not only civilians' available alternatives, but also their beliefs, expectations, and emotions in ways that tend to favor cooperation.[1] For this reason, civilian cooperation should be more likely under rebelocracy than under aliocracy and, by implication, in communities with low capacity for collective action.

This chapter tests these contentions by focusing on the ultimate form of civilian cooperation: joining the armed group as a full-time member. Relying on the community-level data presented in Chapter 5, I estimate the effect of rebelocracy on recruitment. In addition, I provide evidence of the indirect implication of theory, to wit, that high-quality preexisting

---

[1] I investigate the local dynamics that are triggered under disorder, rebelocracy, and aliocracy and their impact on civilian decision-making elsewhere (Arjona 2016a).

institutions are negatively correlated with recruitment. Relying on descriptive data on about 800 former members of guerrilla and paramilitary groups as well as more than 500 civilians, I also show that micro-level evidence is consistent with these findings: civilians are more likely to join an armed group while living in a locality where such a group rules under rebelocracy.

I start with a discussion of how my argument relates to current theories of recruitment. I then present the empirical findings at the community level, followed by the descriptive evidence on joiners and nonjoiners.

I use interchangeably the terms recruitment and enlistment, and in both cases I am only referring to voluntary recruitment. By "voluntary" I mean that the combatant can make the choice to join without facing direct punishment if he or she refuses to do so. For example, if an armed group threatens to harm a person's family if she refuses to join, her decision is not voluntary. To be sure, the concept of voluntary recruitment can only be controversially applied to minors, who account for a large portion of recruits by armed groups in most conflicts. Still, given that so many youngsters decide not to enlist in these groups, I assume there is a decision to be made.[2]

WHO JOINS REBEL MOVEMENTS?

A large literature on peasant rebellion, revolution, and civil war has sought to understand why people participate in these struggles. Some of the arguments aim to explain why new rebel groups are formed and who are the early joiners, leading to the onset of a new revolution or civil war; others seek to explain specific forms of participation that fall short of enlistment, such as engaging in risky actions to aid the rebels; and others specifically address civilians' decision to enlist as full-time members once war is already underway. Although these questions refer to distinct phenomena, arguments designed to explain one of these processes are often invoked to explain the other two.

The hypotheses that follow from these different accounts can be classified into four approaches. The first states that individuals dissatisfied with the status quo join rebel groups to bring about change and

---

[2] I do not seek to explain coerced recruitment. The hypothesis that I test in this chapter is that rebelocracy makes it more likely that civilians *decide* to enlist. In the Colombian case, most recruitment seems to have been voluntary. In the survey of former fighters introduced below, less than 3 percent of them said that they were forcedly recruited.

redress grievances. Some variants of this argument emphasize economic hardship, while others focus on political exclusion and domination (Davies 1962; Gurr 1970; Hobsbawm 1971; Scott 1977; Kaldor 1999; Gates 2002; Weinstein 2007). The main limitation of this theory was identified by Olson (1965). In his seminal work on the logic of collective action, Olson argued that individuals lack incentives to engage in costly activities in order to obtain collective benefits. Rather, each person prefers that others face the potential risks while he or she enjoys the benefits if others are successful. In the case of a rebellion, if both participants and non-participants would equally benefit from its success, why would anyone decide to bear the costs? The other three approaches address this problem by identifying additional motivations that drive participation.

The second approach also claims that socioeconomic difficulties lead individuals to join rebel groups but invokes a different mechanism: rather than pursuing a collective good, those who are disadvantaged have low opportunity costs and respond to selective material incentives. Rewards can be delivered upon joining, like a salary, during the insurgency by looting, or at the end of the conflict if victory is achieved, for example, in the form of land property (Popkin 1979; Lichbach 1995; Collier & Hoeffler 2001; Gates 2002; Weinstein 2007; Dube & Vargas 2013). Under this view, individuals only gain the benefits of collective action if they directly participate.

The third approach emphasizes security and the logic of military contestation as important determinants of recruitment. Some proponents of this view argue that civilians decide to join armed groups in an effort to seek protection when security conditions deteriorate (Dube & Vargas 2013; Kalyvas & Kocher 2007; Nillesen & Verwimp 2009; Goodwin 2001; Humphreys and Weinstein 2008; Eck 2010); others, however, argue that, in areas of intense state repression, civilians are likely to seek safety by *not* joining a rebellion (Trejo 2012). Kalyvas (2006) emphasizes the logic of military confrontation rather than violence, and argues that civilian cooperation with an armed actor grows with that actor's level of control over the locality in which the person lives.[3]

---

[3] In Arjona and Kalyvas (2007) we test hypotheses on the differences between the profiles of recruits of guerrillas and paramilitaries. We find that, indeed, guerrilla members tend to come from areas where guerrillas are present but paramilitaries are not; paramilitary recruits, on the other hand, usually come from areas with exclusive paramilitary presence.

The fourth approach argues that moral, emotional, and social motives also explain people's decision to participate in rebellion.[4] Moral commitments (Wood 2003; Parkinson 2013), the desire to bolster the status of the group a person identifies with (Sambanis & Shayo 2013), or preferences to follow social norms (Viterna 2006; Wood 2008; Parkinson 2013) can also propel civilians to enlist. In addition, violence often awakens emotions like hatred, fear, outrage, and resentment, which ignite the desire to partake in the struggle (Petersen 2001; Wood 2003; Pearlman 2013).

Several authors emphasize not only individuals' motivations to enlist, but also the conditions that facilitate recruitment. Rough terrain makes it easier for rebel groups to recruit because it is more difficult for the state to fight them in remote, inaccessible areas (Fearon & Laitin 2003). Social ties, interpersonal trust, and social networks both between civilians and between civilians and insurgents facilitate cooperation with the rebel group (Gould 1995; Petersen 2001; Wood 2003; Trejo 2009; Parkinson 2013); furthermore, depending on their structure, social networks can make recruitment safer or riskier for rebels, impacting their decision about where to seek recruits (Trejo 2012). Rebel indoctrination can also spur recruitment (Eck 2010).

While all of these arguments highlight important motivations for participating in rebellion, as well as conditions that facilitate recruitment tactics, they overlook the fact that war transforms the institutional context in which civilians make choices. These transformations need to be incorporated in our studies of recruitment to understand how it may vary throughout a conflict (Arjona 2014). Once a war is underway, the rebel group has been able to consolidate a particular internal structure and expand throughout the territory.[5] As discussed in Chapter 3, throughout this expansion armed groups often fight with their enemies, control territory, and lose it. Insofar as the presence of armed actors transforms the institutional context in which civilians live – and this book shows that it does – it is important to take such transformation into account in order to understand when people enlist in armed organizations and why.

---

[4] Some of these studies do not aim to explain full-time enlistment but, rather, high-risk participation such as providing food or information to rebels, offering shelter to them, or lying about their presence to government soldiers.
[5] To be sure, these transformations are irrelevant for recruitment taking place prior to the onset of civil war and, in fact, many of the arguments discussed above aim to explain the origins of rebel groups or the initial stage of their mobilization (e.g., Trejo 2012).

This is particularly relevant if most recruits enlist when war is already underway. There are several factors that suggest that most recruitment takes place after the war has already started. First, as time goes by, combatants that desert or die need to be replaced. In addition, if the group expands organizationally or territorially, it needs to recruit more members. This is certainly the case of guerrillas and paramilitaries in Colombia: the FARC, for example, started as a group of a few dozen peasants in the late 1960s and in the 1990s were estimated to have nearly 20,000 members (Gutiérrez 2008). The paramilitaries also began as small, local groups in the 1980s, and by the early 2000s had consolidated as a federation of larger groups of about 13,000 members (ibid.). To be sure, Colombia's is a very long conflict. But there is also evidence of recruitment taking place mostly *after* the onset of war in very short civil wars. In the civil war in Kosovo (1998–1999), for example, 78 percent of all recruits joined after the war escalated (Kraja 2011). Rapid recruitment also occurred in the Syrian civil war, where over 5,600 armed groups and 100,000 fighters emerged between 2011 and 2014 (Romanow 2015). My argument would be less relevant in cases where most recruitment takes place before the war starts and armed groups control territory, but the expansion of armed groups during a civil war – and hence recruitment – is a common and intuitive phenomenon.

WARTIME SOCIAL ORDER AND RECRUITMENT

How does social order shape recruitment? If the foundations of the theory of social order presented in Chapter 3 are correct, recruits should mostly join groups that establish *rebelocracy*. Under this form of social order combatants enjoy a privileged situation that allows them to transform available alternatives and their associated payoffs, and even locals' beliefs and preferences, in ways that make obedience and spontaneous support more likely. Within rebelocracy, combatants may inspire respect and admiration in those who believe in their cause; they may live extraordinary lives in the eyes of youngsters who crave adventure and novelty; they can even be the only authority some villages have known for years, providing a means for solving disputes, certain public goods, and public order; and they can, too, be powerful individuals with guns who have the capacity to harm. In sum, combatants may be surrounded by the aura of fear, respect, and deference that often accompanies those who rule.

Civilians living in this context may decide to enlist in order to achieve a myriad of goals such as to be part of a just struggle; impress the opposite sex; gain status in their communities; be with a loved one; seek adventure; obtain power; gain material rewards and privileges; be safe; honor norms of reciprocity; or enact emotions like indignation and revenge. To be sure, most of these motivations *have* been identified by the existing literature on recruitment. What has been overlooked is the importance of local wartime institutions as key triggers of these motivations.[6] In this way, my account allows for making sense of what seemed to be contradictory hypotheses, by identifying *when* specific factors are more likely to trigger recruitment.

It is worth noting that some of these motivations can also push people to join armed groups when they are *not* living in a social order of rebelocracy. I am not claiming that these paths to recruitment are exclusive of rebelocracies. The point is, rather, that the range of motivations that are consistent with joining the group is much broader under rebelocracy, due to the role armed groups play and the consequent transformation of local dynamics. If more mechanisms favoring cooperation in general – and spontaneous support in particular – are triggered under rebelocracy compared to other social orders, recruitment should be more likely in communities living under rebelocracy.

The theory advanced in this book on the origins of wartime social order has an additional implication on recruitment. If the theory is correct, rebelocracy should be more likely in communities where institutions are either illegitimate or ineffective. In these communities, preferences to preserve the status quo are weak, and the capacity for collective action is low. When communities are unwilling or unable, or both unwilling and unable, to oppose armed groups' rule, they are likely to live under rebelocracy. Thus, recruitment should be positively correlated with prewar institutional failure and negatively with collective action.[7]

---

[6] The specific ways in which rebelocracy triggers these motivations entail complex mechanisms. Discussing them in detail, and testing them empirically, is beyond the scope of this book. I pursue these goals elsewhere (Arjona 2016a).

[7] I remain agnostic about which communities are most likely to launch a rebellion, form a new armed group, or cooperate with a nascent movement. I argue that communities with low capacity for collective action are more likely to exhibit recruitment into an existing armed group fighting a war that is *already underway*.

EVIDENCE ON COMMUNITIES IN WAR ZONES

I use the data described in Chapter 5 to test these hypotheses at the community level. These data were gathered on a random sample of seventy-four communities throughout the country, where different guerrilla and paramilitary groups have operated. Using surveys, semi-structured interviews and memory workshops, I reconstructed the history of interaction between these communities and each armed group that was present in their territory for more than six months. Using this evidence, I built a database with detailed information on the characteristics of local communities, armed groups' strategies, and the form of social order that emerged.

One of the difficulties involved in estimating the effect of rebelocracy on recruitment is that many attributes that impact armed actors' abilities to control a territory militarily, therefore enabling rebelocracy, could also impact recruitment. For example, if localities with lower state provision of services are more likely to be ruled by armed groups and are also more likely to join armed groups due to their grievances, it would be difficult to separate the effect of rebelocracy from that of poor provision of state services. In fact, in Arjona and Kalyvas (2007) we found that territorial control by an armed actor does correlate with higher recruitment. Identifying the effects of rebelocracy on recruitment requires separating the determinants of control from the determinants of rebelocracy. Furthermore, there could be time-invariant attributes of local communities that impact both rebelocracy and recruitment. Omitting these variables would bias the results.

In order to isolate the effect of rebelocracy on recruitment, I adopt two strategies. First, I focus on those cases where only one armed actor was present in the area. This design allows me to hold constant all the time-varying attributes of localities that may impact armed groups' ability to control a territory militarily. In this way, the analysis explores the effect of rebelocracy on recruitment conditional on the armed group having already controlled the territory militarily. Overall, 90 percent of the community–armed group dyads interacted at least one year without the presence of another armed actor. The unit of analysis is therefore the locality–year.[8] There are 1,042 observations in the dataset that meet this

---

[8] In Chapter 5 the unit of analysis was the community–armed group (dyad)–year. Since in this chapter I am using observations on locality–years where only one armed group was present, there is only one dyad in each locality–year.

condition. Overall, 39 percent of all locality-years correspond to a paramilitary group and the remaining 71 percent to guerrillas.

The second strategy is to estimate the models using the difference between the level of rebelocracy in each community and the average level of rebelocracy in the municipality it belongs to as an instrumental variable. This allows for accounting for the time-invariant attributes of the locality. I explain this approach later in the chapter.

The survey asked respondents if it was common for people to enlist in the group that was present in the locality. Overall, recruitment was common in 36 percent of all observations. The percentage is higher in localities under the presence of guerrillas (46 percent) than those involving paramilitaries (20 percent). In most cases, civilians reported that recruitment was stable throughout the years when the group had territorial control. This means that once a group controlled the territory, recruitment tended to be either high or low across the years until the group left or another group arrived to the area. However, recruitment did vary greatly across and within municipalities. Figure 8.1 shows the percentage of observations with low and high recruitment in each municipality.

To test the hypothesis on the effect of social order on recruitment, I use *rebelocracy* – the same index used in Chapter 5 – which aggregates the following measures of armed group influence on local affairs in a given year: whether the armed group intervened in local economic activities such as fishing, hunting or logging, and in the assignment of state subsidies to individuals (*economic*); adjudicated disputes, intervened in elections, and was perceived to be in charge of local affairs (*political*); established rules to regulate private conduct like domestic violence, personal image, and sexual behavior (*private conduct*); provided education, health or infrastructure, or intervened in their provision (*public goods*); and its members used to play soccer, have a beer, and attend parties with civilians (*social*). As Figure 8.2 shows, every indicator of rebelocracy is higher in communities where recruitment was common compared to communities where it was not. In all the cases the difference is significant at 0.1 percent. Figure 8.3 shows that recruitment by both guerrillas and paramilitaries follow this pattern.

To adjust for the economic situation of the communities, I use *resources*, a dichotomous variable that measures whether the locality had valuable natural resources in that year such as oil, coca, gold, and coal. Localities where such resources are present can benefit in different

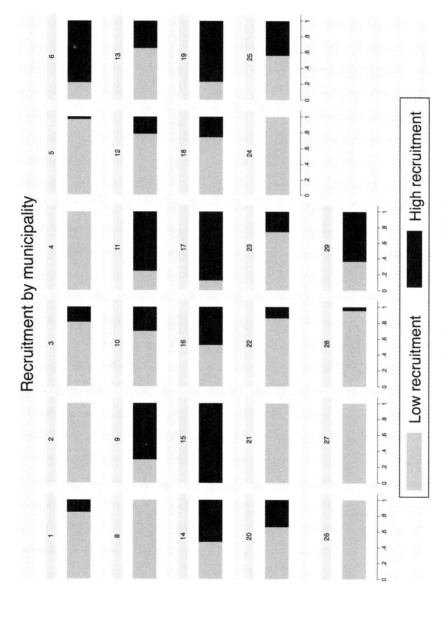

FIGURE 8.1 Recruitment by municipality

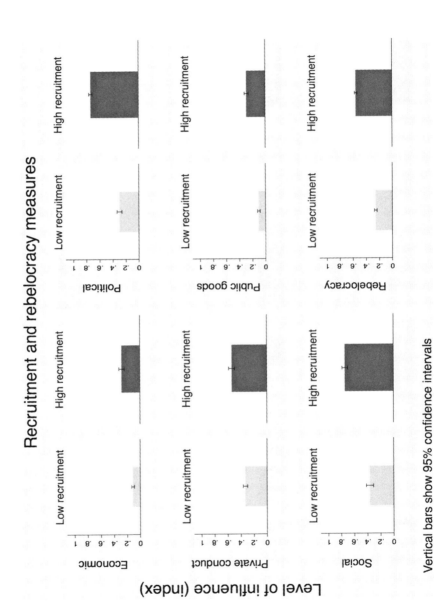

FIGURE 8.2 Recruitment and rebelocracy measures

Evidence on Communities in War Zones

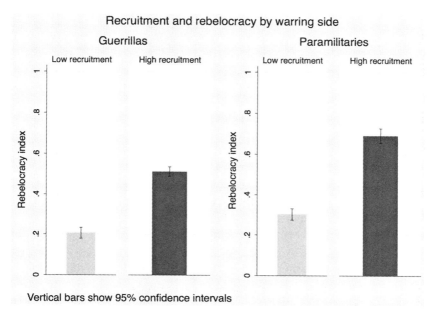

FIGURE 8.3 Recruitment and rebelocracy by warring side

ways, depending on the type of resource. In some cases, locals may be paid higher wages than in other localities, and unemployment may be lower; in the case of oil and other fossils, municipalities obtain transfers from the central government based on their production of these resources. The variable *paved*, a dummy variable measuring whether there was a paved road connecting the locality with other localities or the municipality's urban center, captures the level of development of the municipality as well as state presence.

The variable *state* is an index of the provision of public goods in the community prior to the arrival of the first armed group to the locality. The index measures how many of the following existed in the locality at that time: primary school, secondary school, and health center. Hence, it does not capture the decrease or increase of state services due to violence or the presence of armed actors. Rather, it captures the historical presence or absence of the state in each locality.

I also account for other behaviors of armed groups beyond establishing rebelocracy, which could impact recruitment. *Massacres* measures whether there was at least one massacre in the municipality, perpetrated by any warring side, during the year.[9] *Ideology* measures whether the armed group held meetings to discuss its ideology with civilians soon after it arrived to the locality. Finally, I include proxies for two factors that can facilitate armed groups' operations in a given area: *altitude*, a measure of rough terrain (Fearon & Laitin 2003), and *cabecera*, which indicates whether the locality is the county head or not, which can make insurgent activity more difficult (Kocher 2004). Figure 8.4 shows the bivariate relationship between these variables and recruitment.

Localities with high recruitment do not significantly differ from those with low recruitment in terms of state presence (based on the presence of schools and health centers), violence (as proxied by massacres), and being the county head of the municipality. Communities with high recruitment are less likely to have valuable natural resources, which could signal a higher opportunity cost for joining when such resources are present. High recruitment is also associated with the community *having* a paved road. Based on the existing literature, this would be an unexpected result for the guerrillas, which are expected to succeed more in isolated, rural places. However, given that the data are only looking at localities where the armed actor has been able to establish control, it might be that these armed actors devote especially high efforts to gaining civilian cooperation in well-connected towns. At the same time, recruitment is higher in territories with higher elevation, which tends to correlate with remote, inaccessible places. Recruitment is also associated with the community being exposed to ideology talks by the armed actor. However, in the models most of these variables are either not significant or have a negative effect on recruitment, as I discuss below.

Statistical Models on Recruitment

In these data observations are clustered within the locality, armed group, municipality, and year. I use the same type of linear multilevel models used in Chapter 5, but without the dyad as a level. Hence, in these models observations are nested within localities, and localities are nested within municipalities.[10] As in Chapter 5, I use fixed effects for years, armed

---

[9] The data come from Colombia's Historic Memory Commission. I use data on the municipality because data on violence at the level of the locality are not available.

[10] Given the number of random effects, a multilevel logit model that incorporates all the fixed effects does not converge. However, I obtain very similar results with different specifications of multilevel logit models that do not include armed group- and year-fixed effects. In all models the effect of rebelocracy on recruitment is positive and significant at 1 percent.

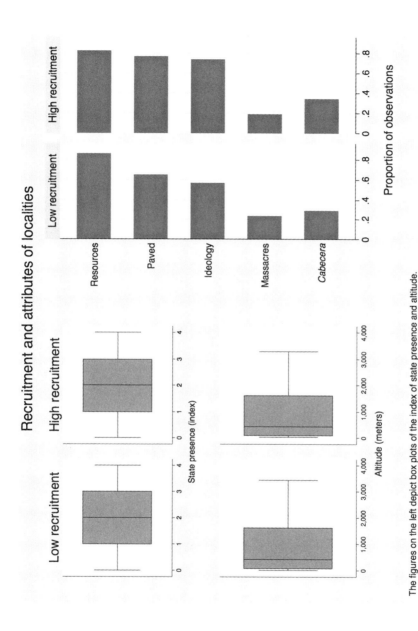

FIGURE 8.4 Recruitment and attributes of localities

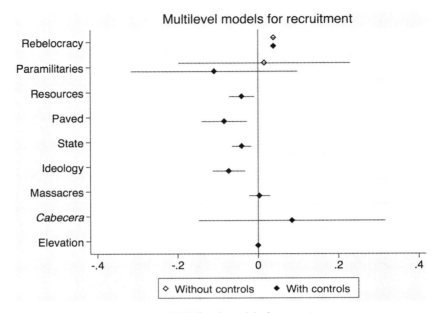

FIGURE 8.5 Multilevel models for recruitment

organization, and warring side. The models are robust to time trends as well as unit-specific time trends.[11]

The dependent variable is recruitment and the explanatory variables are attributes of the localities, armed groups, and municipalities. The first model estimates the effect of rebelocracy on recruitment. As Figure 8.5 shows, rebelocracy has a positive and significant effect on recruitment with and without controls. Figure 8.6 shows the predicted effects on recruitment for different values of rebelocracy, while holding other variables constant. The effect of rebelocracy on recruitment is substantial: the probability of high recruitment in a community with a value of 3 in the index of rebelocracy is about 21 percent; the probability in a community with a value of 8 in the index of rebelocracy increases to 45 percent; and in a community with

---

[11] As with the models of Chapter 5, I also estimate the standard errors using the multilevel bootstrap of the lme4 package in R. The substantial results do not change. Also, there are only forty-eight observations (out of 1,042) with missing values. Hence, I use list-wise deletion. The results are consistent with those obtained with ten datasets where missing values have been imputed.

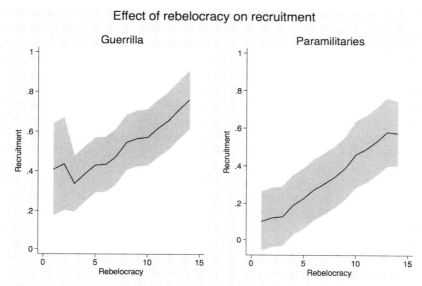

FIGURE 8.6 Effect of rebelocracy on recruitment

extreme levels of rebelocracy (13 or 14), that probability increases to about 70 percent. All the variables that are correlated with recruitment (as discussed in the previous section) are either not significant or have negative coefficients.

In order to account for potential endogeneity due to omitted attributes of the localities and armed groups, I employ the same approach explained in Chapter 5: I use the deviation from the cluster mean as an instrumental variable for rebelocracy (Rabe-Hesketh & Skrondal 2008:115–118). I estimate the effect of *rebelocracy dev_mean*, which measures the difference in the index of rebelocracy between the locality and the average of all localities in the same municipality and under the same armed group, in a given year. This approach allows for identifying the causal effect of rebelocracy on recruitment *within* locality–armed group dyads, accounting for locality-level and armed group-level omitted variables that may be correlated with the cluster-level random intercept.[12] The full table of results is presented in Appendix 4.

[12] The estimated coefficient of the cluster mean captures the effect of rebelocracy on variation *across* communities under a given armed group, although it does not account for potentially omitted variables. The models also include the cluster mean (municipality–armed group

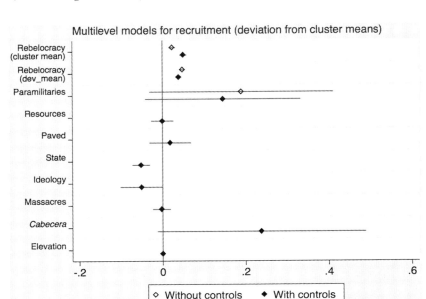

FIGURE 8.7 Multilevel models for recruitment (deviation from cluster means)

The deviation of rebelocracy from the cluster mean also has a positive and significant effect (at 1 percent) on recruitment. The estimated coefficient for the cluster mean is also positive and significant, suggesting that rebelocracy also explains variation across dyads (Figure 8.7). The size of the effect is similar to that of previous models, and again varies little across localities controlled by guerrillas and paramilitaries.

In order to provide an additional indirect test of the theory, I test whether high-quality preexisting institutions are associated with lower recruitment. I rely on the same proxy of *institutions* used in Chapter 5, which measures whether or not all of the following describe the community prior to the arrival of the first armed group: there were clear rules in place; it was uncommon for people to solve conflicts using force; locals used to solve disputes with neighbors over land borders or debts quickly and in ways they deemed to be fair; most community members approved of mechanisms to resolve conflicts; and rules were effective – that is,

mean) of all variables that are clustered at the municipality or armed group levels, in order to account for the correlation between those variables and the cluster-level random intercept (Rabe-Hesketh & Skrondal 2008:119).

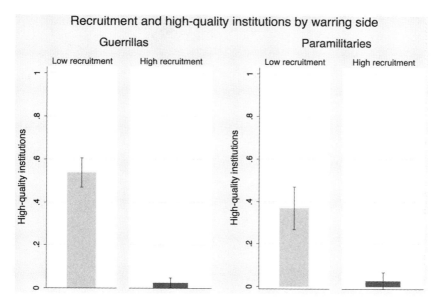

FIGURE 8.8 Recruitment and high-quality institutions by warring side

people used to observe them.[13] Overall, 37 percent of all localities had high-quality preexisting institutions. As Figure 8.8 shows, the percentage of communities where recruitment was common is about fifteen times lower when institutions were of high quality than in communities when they were of low quality.

I estimate the effect of high-quality institutions on recruitment with a linear multilevel model that includes the same control variables of the previous model. Institutional quality has a negative and significant effect at 0.1 percent on recruitment (Figure 8.9a).[14] Figure 8.9b shows the predicted values of recruitment for low- and high-quality institutions, in localities under guerrillas and paramilitaries.[15] Although this model does

---

[13] All of these measures come from close-ended questions except the last two, which come from open-ended questions in the survey as well as from the memory workshop. Details on how these measures were collected and coded can be found in Chapter 5 and Appendices 1 and 2.
[14] The full results are presented in Appendix 4.
[15] Given the small variation in recruitment over time within dyads, as a robustness check I estimate a linear model with the data aggregated at the level of the dyad – that is, I estimate the effect of the average level of rebelocracy and institutional quality for each dyad on the average level of recruitment. This aggregation reduces the number of observations to 106. The effect of rebelocracy on recruitment remains positive and significant at 1 percent.

280 *Testing the Microfoundations: Social Order and Recruitment*

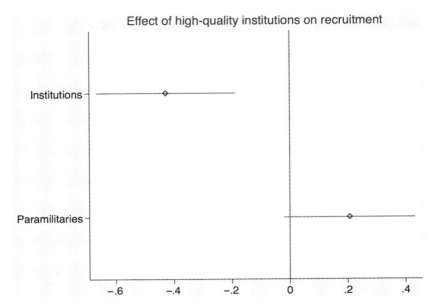

FIGURE 8.9A Effect of high-quality institutions on recruitment

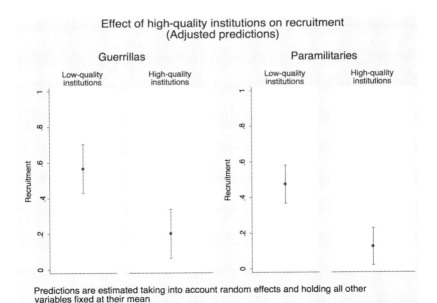

FIGURE 8.9B Effect of high-quality institutions on recruitment (adjusted predictions)

not account for potentially omitted variables, the results offer additional support to my contention that preexisting institutions and rebelocracy are associated with higher recruitment.

Alternative Explanations

Could these results be explained by other accounts? The design contributes to isolating the causal effect of rebelocracy on recruitment in two ways. First, it rules out time-varying attributes of local communities that favor territorial control by exploring the effect of rebelocracy within cases where a single group controlled the territory. And second, by using the deviation from the municipality mean, it accounts for all the time-invariant attributes of localities. Furthermore, the evidence supports the indirect implication of the hypothesis, to wit, that high-quality institutions should be associated with lower recruitment. The likelihood that omitted variables can explain both of these results is low.

Measurement error could also be a concern. Communities that lived under rebelocracy could have exaggerated the extent to which recruitment took place in their communities, while communities that did not live under rebelocracy could have understated recruitment among their members. If rebelocracy leads civilians to support an armed group, it is possible that their responses were biased.

Based on my fieldwork and the qualitative evidence that I collected on these communities, this does not seem to be the case. People often portrayed recruitment as a negative phenomenon; a sad fate for the youth. Furthermore, when asked about the reasons people joined an armed group, respondents often pointed to the allure of weapons and power, the desire for social status, material needs, and even the immaturity of young people. Only in a few places did people portray enlistment as a commendable act. Nevertheless, it is plausible that other reasons could lead to a systematic bias in people's responses, for example social desirability bias.

In the next section I turn to the profiles of joiners and nonjoiners. In this case measurement error of recruitment is not an issue because I do not rely on people's perception of whether recruitment was common in their community but, rather, on whether the respondent had recently demobilized from an armed group or not. The likelihood of interviewing a combatant who portrayed him or herself as a civilian is very low. Furthermore, measurement error in the variable that measures rebelocracy seems unlikely. Combatants do not seem to have tried to portray their organizations in a solely positive way because they reported on their groups' use of violence and mistreatment of civilians. In addition, many of them reported that other enemy armed groups had a high influence on civilian affairs. The fact that half of respondents decided to leave their groups also suggests that they may not be strongly motivated to defend them.

EVIDENCE ON JOINERS AND NONJOINERS

By comparing joiners with nonjoiners, as well as joiners of different groups, this section shows that recruits are more likely to come from communities where the armed actor they joined ruled under rebelocracy.

I use data on individuals coming from a survey with former members of guerrilla and paramilitary groups as well as civilians that I conducted in collaboration with Stathis Kalyvas in 2005 and 2006. In what follows I briefly describe the sampling strategy and the survey. Additional details can be found in Appendix 1.[16]

Survey of Former Guerrilla and Paramilitary Combatants

The survey was conducted in 2005 with 821 ex-combatants, of which 436 had demobilized voluntarily from the guerrilla groups FARC ("IFARC") and ELN ("IELN"), as well as from paramilitary groups ("IPARAS"). We also conducted 387 interviews with collectively demobilized paramilitaries ("CPARAS") – that is, those who did not make the choice of demobilizing, but did so following their commanders' order to turn in their weapons. The survey instrument was designed to gather evidence on three main areas: joining, group organization and practices, and demobilization; it includes 255 questions, of which the majority are close-ended and a few are open-ended, which allowed us to collect both quantitative and qualitative evidence. Participation was voluntary, and interviews lasted on average 1.5 hours.

The sampling strategy was different for individually and collectively demobilized ex-combatants. At the time of the survey, 7,131 members of guerrilla and paramilitary groups had voluntarily decided to quit arms and join the government's demobilization and reintegration program (DRP). After demobilizing, fighters chose a city or town to settle in, and the government provided them with a place of residence in that locality, usually in houses that hosted several former combatants. More than half

---

[16] All results presented in this chapter include sampling weights. Some of the results of the survey with former combatants are discussed in Arjona and Kalyvas (2011).

Evidence on Joiners and Nonjoiners 283

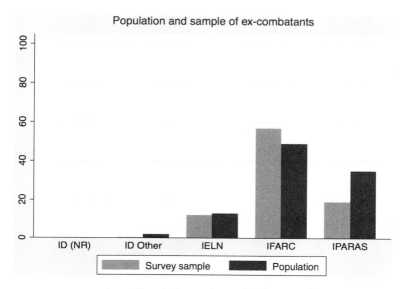

FIGURE 8.10 Population and sample of ex-combatants

selected Bogotá (56 percent), while most of the rest opted for other large cities and a few for rural areas. Given that 56 percent of all individually demobilized ex-combatants (IDEs) had chosen Bogotá, we selected a random sample among individuals who were living there. Although we cannot control for potential differences between those who chose to move to Bogotá as opposed to elsewhere, the wide variation in our respondents' place of origin suggests that our sample includes ex-combatants from all over the country. In fact, the 439 IDEs in our sample came from 185 different municipalities located in twenty-eight of the thirty-three departments of the country.

We randomly selected a sample of 450 former combatants within Bogotá following the procedure described in Appendix 1. Over 95 percent of those invited to participate responded to the survey. We stratified our sample in order to over-represent former FARC members, given that all collectively demobilized fighters belonged to paramilitary groups. Data provided by the Ministry of Defense in December 2005 suggest that our sample is representative of the IDE population in terms of group membership (Figure 8.10).[17]

---

[17] However, according to the data of the Ministry of Defense, 13 percent of all IDEs at the time were women. For reasons that remain unclear, women are underrepresented in our survey, as only 8 percent of interviewed IDEs were women.

Even though we are confident about the quality of our sample of individually demobilized combatants, it is important to stress that it is not representative of the universe of guerrilla combatants in Colombia, since respondents are selected from the population of combatants who voluntarily joined a demobilization program. Given that the FARC and ELN had not signed a peace agreement to demobilize its fighters, it was impossible to identify a representative sample of fighters of these organizations who had not demobilized.[18] However, given the large numbers of persons who have demobilized from these groups – so far close to 13,000 of FARC and 2,000 of ELN,[19] which is said to correspond to between 35 percent and 50 percent of their troops in 2000 – we believe that our respondents represent a substantial portion of these organizations, and hence their responses provide valuable information.

Turning to the CPARAS, the universe of this population consisted of 4,433 individuals at the time of the survey, living in seven towns or cities throughout the country. We decided to focus on two paramilitary factions: the *Cordoba Bloc* and the *Catatumbo Bloc*, whose former fighters were living mostly in the cities (or nearby locations) of Montería and Cúcuta, respectively.[20] At that time, 925 fighters had demobilized from the Cordoba Bloc, and 1,425 from the Catatumbo Bloc.[21] We randomly invited 500 members of these organizations to attend a meeting. We completed 387 interviews – 162 with former members of the *Catatumbo Bloc* (11 percent of the entire population), and 222 of the *Cordoba Bloc* (24 percent of the entire population) with those who attended.[22] Overall, our sample includes persons who enlisted in 187 municipalities throughout the country, as Map 8.1 shows.

---

[18] This may change soon, as the FARC and the Colombian government seem to be close to signing a peace agreement. Negotiations with the ELN may soon be initiated.
[19] Data as reported by Colombia's High Commission for Reintegration's website www.reintegracion.gov.co/Es/proceso_ddr/Paginas/balance.aspx [last accessed January 25, 2010].
[20] Even though we focus on these two factions, our sample is drawn from the cities where almost half of all CPARAS were living at that time: 32 percent were in Montería, and 13 percent in Cúcuta.
[21] Séptimo informe trimestral del secretario general al consejo permanente sobre la misión de apoyo al proceso de paz en colombia (MAPP-OEA) www.mapp-oea.org/documentos/informes/Trimestrales%20MAPP/7mo%20inf-colombia-MAPP.pdf [Accessed February 20, 2006]
[22] As discussed in Appendix 1, it is unlikely that those who did not come induced bias in our results because they did not know about the purpose of the meeting when deciding not to attend.

Municipalities where former combatants lived at the time of joining an armed group

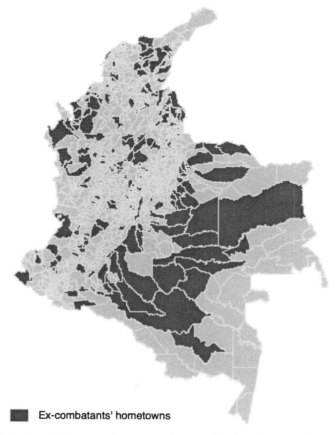

MAP 8.1 Municipalities where former combatants lived at the time of joining an armed group

As with any other survey, the responses of former combatants could be affected by a number of problems due to memory, motivation, or communication issues (Sudman & Bradburn 1982). We tried to minimize these in designing our questionnaire, for example, by trying not to ask about the frequency of events or their specific timing. Nonetheless, survey data have limitations.

Survey of Civilians

In 2006 we conducted a survey of civilians to build a control group for surveyed recruits. As mentioned earlier, recruits in our sample were living in 187 different municipalities one year prior to joining an armed group for the first time. We randomly selected a sub-sample of these municipalities by stratifying them by the kind of armed group presence they had, creating four strata: (1) municipalities with both guerrilla and paramilitary presence; (2) municipalities with only guerrilla presence; (3) municipalities with only paramilitary presence; and (4) municipalities with neither guerrilla presence, nor paramilitary presence. We then randomly selected four municipalities from each stratum. Map 8.2 shows the selected sample of municipalities per stratum.

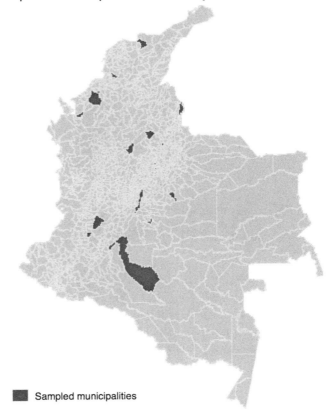

MAP 8.2 Sample of municipalities for survey with civilians

Within each municipality, we relied on cartographic information to randomly select a few blocks in the urban areas and a few units in the rural areas. Within each block and rural unit, we randomly selected households. Interviews were conducted with one randomly selected person in selected households who were born between 1973 and 1987 – the range of birth year of most ex-combatants in our sample. In total, 565 civilians were surveyed. Additional details on the sampling strategy can be found in Appendix 1.

Joiners and Nonjoiners

Former combatants were asked about their personal situation and that of their family and community in the year prior to their enlistment in a non-state armed group for the first time.[23] Who should these joiners be compared to? Most studies of recruitment using systematic micro-level data rely on civilians' responses to survey questions about their situation either at the time of the survey (which is often once the war has ended), or prior to the beginning of the war. Geography is usually taken into account, as most samples try to include civilians living in the same places where combatants used to live; however, time is usually overlooked. This approach does not allow for identifying good control groups, as most recruitment takes place once the war has started, not at its onset or right before its termination. Ideally, we should compare the profiles of recruits at the time of enlisting with the profiles of civilians who did not choose to join at that time.

For example, the ideal control for recruits who joined, say, the guerrillas in 1995 would be civilians of similar age in 1995, living in the same place, who did not choose to join the guerrillas. Assuming that civilians' profiles in 1995 were the same as before the war started neglects the many ways in which war can affect a person, her family, and her community. Relying on their profiles after the war ended is also misleading, as joiners may have joined during the war, before their civilian counterparts had experiences that affect their profile at the time of the survey. In order to assess the differences between joiners and nonjoiners, greater efforts should be made to measure the situation of nonjoiners in the places where, and at the time when, others decided to enlist.

---

[23] Some respondents demobilized and joined another group later on, and some switched sides. The analysis only includes their first recruitment.

The problem is, of course, the absence of baselines. To counter this problem, the survey asked interviewees about four different time periods, which allows for obtaining information on civilians of different ages at different points in time. This design allows for the creation of refined control groups that take into account the place and time when recruits enlisted, as well as their age. In what follows, I compare recruits and civilians who were living in the same municipalities at the time when recruits enlisted. This is only doable for recruits who enlisted in any of the seventeen municipalities where civilians were surveyed. This subsample has a total of 2,491 observations.

Using retrospective measurement with surveys of course brings up issues due to recall, telescoping, and nonrandom censoring errors (Groves 2004). However, the alternative is to rely on data that, even if well measured, do not constitute a good control group of recruits. In addition, most studies of recruitment ask respondents about their situation when the war started, which makes them vulnerable to the same problems associated with retrospective measurement.

Recruitment is measured by whether the person was part of the demobilization program or not. While it is possible that we interviewed a combatant or former combatant in the survey with civilians, given the low percentage of joiners among the population, this probability is low.

I start by showing that the data fail to display many of the differences that we often expect to find between joiners and nonjoiners. By design, all respondents have similar ages: the average joiner was born in 1984 and the average nonjoiner was born in 1982. Hence, most of them were in their twenties at the time of the survey.

Figure 8.11 shows how respondents differ regarding several individual-level attributes. *Poor* measures whether the person reported her family to be poor as opposed to middle class or rich. Joiners are not significantly more likely to be poor than nonjoiners. *Party* indicates whether the person indicated that he or she identified with a political party, and is therefore a measure of political representation. Joiners are indeed more likely to report that they did not identify with a political party prior to enlisting. *Others joined* indicates whether the person had relatives or friends joining in the past, and is a measure of networks. The difference between joiners and nonjoiners is not significantly different from zero. *Victim* measures whether at least one relative or friend was harmed, threatened, or killed by any armed group in the past. Civilians are actually *more* likely to know victims of armed actors. Overall, only the hypothesis that points to political representation is consistent with these data.

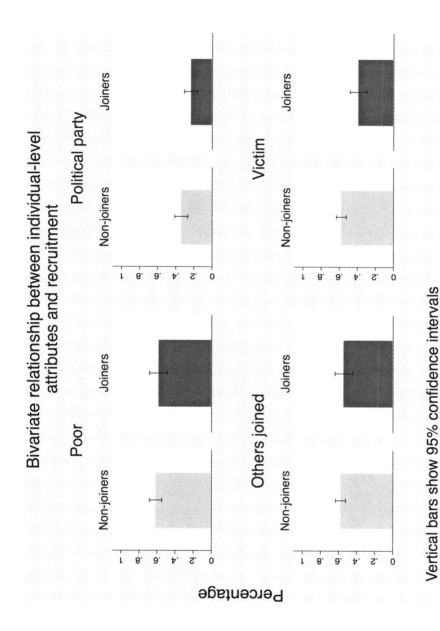

FIGURE 8.11 Bivariate relationship between individual-level attributes and recruitment

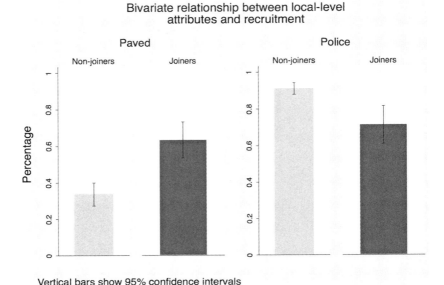

FIGURE 8.12 Bivariate relationship between community-level attributes and recruitment

How about the characteristics of the communities? *Paved* measures whether a paved road connected the locality to nearby locations, and is a proxy of local development; *police*, which measures whether a police station existed in the locality, is a proxy of the state's coercive power at the local level. Joiners tend to come from localities that had a paved road and lacked a police station, suggesting that the effect of state presence is more complex than often assumed. (Figure 8.12).

It is important to remember that civilians lived in the same municipalities where joiners were right before enlisting. They lived under the same local government and local economy. A comparison between joiners and the average Colombian would probably yield different results. For the purpose of this chapter, comparing respondents who lived in the same municipality allows me to hold constant factors that explain the presence of armed groups, permitting a better examination of the differences in the form of social order in which they lived.

I now turn to the attributes of the social order in which respondents lived, the predictor of interest in this book (Figure 8.13). I use several indicators of armed groups' influence in civilians' matters. *Dispute institutions* measures whether the group tended to solve private conflicts among locals in a given year. As I argued in Chapter 3, institutions for adjudicating disputes

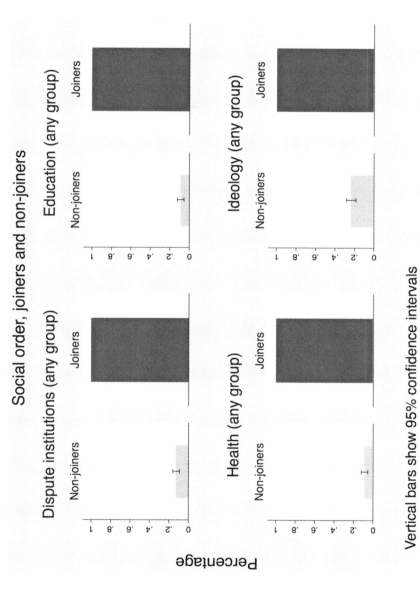

FIGURE 8.13 Social order, joiners, and nonjoiners

are the backbone of rebelocracy. Armed groups' provision of *education* and *health* services (or their influence on its provision) are also shown, as are *talks*, a measure of whether the armed group gave talks to civilians about their ideological goals.

Every single indicator of armed groups' influence on civilian affairs is higher among joiners than nonjoiners, with all differences being significant at 0.1 percent. Joiners are more likely to live in places where an armed actor adjudicated disputes, gave ideological talks, and intervened in the provision of education and health services. This supports the argument that joiners were more likely to live under rebelocracy than nonjoiners.

As Figures 8.14a and 8.14b show, disaggregating joiners by group membership shows that, for the most part, they joined the group that was behind rebelocracy in their community. Although many joiners of paramilitary groups lived in places where the guerrillas had been present in the year prior to their enlistment, in those places the guerrillas did not tend to exert a high influence in locals' lives. The opposite is true for the guerrillas: while a portion of them lived in areas where the paramilitaries were present, very few came from "paramilitary rebelocracies." These results are based on data on all 821 former combatants, not just those who enlisted in the municipalities where civilians were surveyed.

Overall, the data suggest that armed actors influence civilian behavior through mechanisms other than violence, ideology, and the effect of the war on people's material situation. While these are just descriptive statistics and do not allow for making causal claims, they are highly suggestive.[24] When taken together with the theoretical discussions and empirical evidence offered in the other chapters of this book, the characteristics of joiners and nonjoiners suggest that civilian cooperation with armed actors is deeply shaped by the form of social order in which they live.

To be sure, my argument *is not* that personal and family attributes do not shape recruitment. My claim is, rather, that taking into account different behaviors that rebels adopt, and the new social orders that they bring about while interacting with civilians, is essential to better understanding where people join armed actors and why. Rather than claiming that existing hypotheses lack explanatory power, I argue that incorporating the variation in

---

[24] I investigate the effect of rebelocracy on individuals' choices in a more systematic way elsewhere (Arjona 2016a).

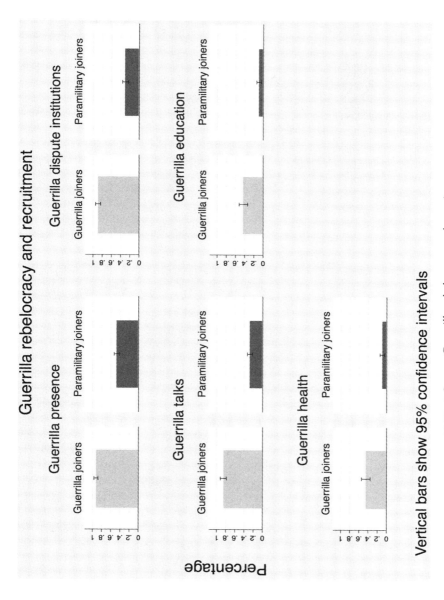

FIGURE 8.14A Guerrilla rebelocracy and recruitment

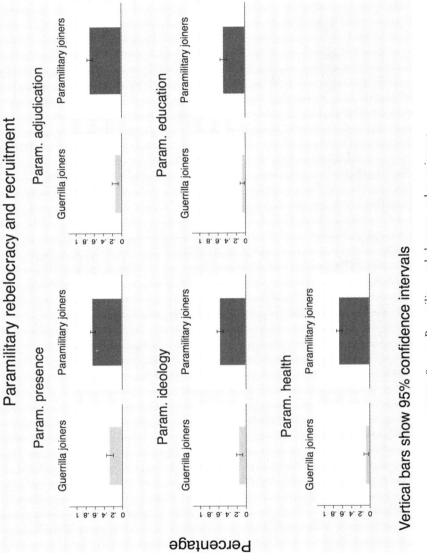

FIGURE 8.14B Paramilitary rebelocracy and recruitment

wartime institutions across localities should allow us to better theorize why specific mechanisms are triggered, and why certain individuals are likely to enlist given the context in which they make that choice.

CONCLUSION

In this chapter I proposed a new theoretical approach to recruitment in civil war by focusing on the terms of civilian–combatant interactions and, in particular, the form of wartime order in which they live. Following this approach, I argued that people are more likely to join groups that consolidate a social order of *rebelocracy* because combatants are able to greatly influence locals' lives, triggering multiple mechanisms that make enlisting an attractive option. The analysis of data on communities in war zones shows a robust link between *rebelocracy* and recruitment. The association between the quality of preexisting institutions and recruitment, and the descriptive evidence on joiners of guerrillas and paramilitaries as well as nonjoiners, provided additional support to my approach.

These findings suggest that the study of rebellion and civil war needs to consider time more carefully. We often merge together phenomena occurring at different stages of civil war, ignoring the tremendous variation that takes place as war evolves. The very nature of the phenomena may change, as the conflict evolves from early mobilization to full-fledged war. For example, while creating a rebel group or joining it in its early stage may entail a crystal-clear collective action problem, enlisting in an existing organization may be an entirely different consideration. As a war evolves, armed groups develop a reputation; they engage in a myriad of activities that were not previously in their mandate; they ask different things from individuals and communities; they offer different benefits to those who join them; and they may even be more or less able to invoke certain ideals, given their own behavior. The act of joining a group is qualitatively different at these different stages of the war.

The findings also reveal the importance of theorizing individual agency as well as structural conditions at different levels. Instead of approaching recruitment by focusing either on the individual or on communities as is usually done, it is essential to investigate how both levels interact (Trejo 2012). Furthermore, we need to document and theorize the ways in which different actors transform local conditions, and how those transformations may in turn impact individuals differently. Paying attention to wartime institutions and the ways in which they impact the social, political, and economic life of people is central to this quest. War is not a homogeneous shock – it shapes regions and local communities differently; and by so doing, it transforms the very pillars of social order in ways that are consequential. Understanding civilians' involvement with armed groups, their relation with the state, their decision to flee or resist, and even their survival strategies requires theorizing more carefully the varying situations in which those decisions are made.

9

Conclusion

The association between war and anarchy has deep roots in political theory. Hobbes' defense of the authority of the Leviathan was based on his assessment of civil war as the worst possible human condition – and on the Leviathan's ability to avoid it. Without a sovereign, Hobbes argued, fear of death would lead humans to a war of all against all; a situation of widespread chaos where prosperity, science, arts, justice, and law cannot exist (Hobbes 2010[1651]:77–9).

Hobbes was absolutely right about the misery of war. It is a profoundly destructive process whose legacies we still don't fully grasp, nor comprehend. But his characterization of civil war as a situation of anarchy and permanent uncertainty does not fit the reality of the most common form of war of our times: irregular civil war. In this type of conflict, armed groups strive to control territory and, in their quest, often establish rules to regulate the behavior of civilian populations as well as of their own members. Furthermore, such rules give place to distinct forms of social order in which the patterns of being and relating are deeply different.

This book sought to explain the conditions under which different types of order emerge in the midst of war, and how the underlying formal and informal rules that sustain it arise and operate. In so doing, it challenged the view of war zones as situations rife with uncertainty, and made the case for a research agenda on wartime institutions. In line with literature that has questioned the existence of ungoverned spaces and failed states, this book presented detailed evidence on Colombian localities in conflict zones, revealing complex patterns of political and social order. Yet, while most studies of wartime governance emphasize the differences across armed actors, this book showed that rule by both insurgents and counterinsurgents varies across time and place.

Approaching order through this lens, the question that this book sought to answer is, therefore, not only about the emergence of order, but also about the emergence of *distinct* forms of order. More specifically, my goal has been to explain why armed groups choose to create different kinds of social contracts with local populations, why the latter abide or resist, and how the interaction between non-state armed actors, state forces, and civilian populations give place to the emergence, functioning, and collapse of new forms of social order. Thus, this book deconstructs the notion that civil wars are anarchic and, instead, traces the development of order as an interactive process between civilians and combatants.

The emergence of order in a given locality and at a particular time depends on the time horizon of armed actors. When their organizational structure or the vicissitudes of territorial competition or peace agreements privilege short-term goals, combatants are unlikely to follow rules on their treatment of civilians. Disorder is therefore likely to emerge. When, on the contrary, armed actors have long time horizons, they are both willing and able to create institutions under a social contract with the local population and honor it, giving place to order.

While this view is based on Olson's (1965) account of how the opportunity for long-term benefits creates incentives to establish social contracts, it makes a contribution by specifying the conditions under which time horizons are likely to shrink, making long-term benefits much less relevant. Furthermore, while other studies have found that competition between armed actors prevents the establishment of social contracts, this book explains why group discipline is also important for order to emerge even when combatants do care about long-term benefits.

When order emerges, armed actors prefer to establish *rebelocracy* – that is, a social order built on a comprehensive intervention of the armed actor in civilian affairs. Their choice, however, is mediated by their expectations of civilian resistance. Since the quality of preexisting local institutions shapes the likelihood of resistance, armed groups create rebelocracies in communities where such institutions are weak. On the other hand, armed actors create *aliocracies* – where they intervene minimally in civilian affairs – in communities that have strong preexisting institutions.

In this way, rather than focusing on the armed actors alone, this theory privileges the role that civilians come to play in shaping the institutions under which they live. While one of the tenets of decades of research on guerrilla warfare and insurgency is the centrality of civilian support for rebel survival and success, the bargaining power that such a position proffers civilians has been widely ignored. This book recognizes this possibility and theorizes the conditions under which civilians can work together to make demands and impose their terms of the social contract. In so doing, it brings politics to the center of civilian–combatant relations. However, the theory is not naïve: it recognizes that negotiating with an armed actor is difficult and risky, and that the heroic efforts of civilians are often met with violence. Just as violent opposition is dangerous, so is nonviolent resistance.

In addition to providing a story about civilian agency, this is also an institutionalist account. I argue that the real collective action problem in many conflict zones is not supporting an armed group but resisting it. Civilians cannot threaten armed actors with resistance unless they are able to overcome serious collective action problems – and preexisting institutions, I argue, are the key enablers of such enterprise. Dispute institutions – those for adjudicating disputes, securing property rights, and enforcing contracts – are particularly relevant, as they are a central pillar for the functioning of society.

To be sure, I do not expect institutions to give civilians bargaining power under all conditions. In certain places armed groups cannot afford to tolerate civilian autonomy. This is usually the case in highly valued territories where tight population control is necessary. Communities that resist rebelocracy in these territories are likely to be harassed by the group, and even forcibly displaced. This explains why resistance is triggered in some cases – that is, why armed groups do not adapt their behavior to avoid it.

Furthermore, I do not argue that high-quality institutions allow civilians to expel combatants from their territories. In fact, armed actors have incentives to negotiate insofar as they get to stay in the territory. Instead, by enabling collective action, institutions allow civilians to limit combatants' influence in their community.

Whether civilians have more or less autonomy has critical implications. Evidently, the most important one is that war may hurt them less and have a lower impact on their social and political reality. In addition, the broader the scope of rule by an armed actor, the more it controls the population and its territory; the more it recruits; and the more difficult it is for other warring sides to gain control over that territory. This has repercussions for many dynamics of war.

The empirical basis of these contentions comes from various tests of the theory's components. My research design took advantage of the strengths of different empirical methods and types of evidence that supplement each other. Using surveys, interviews, and memory workshops with civilians and combatants throughout Colombia, I gathered detailed information on many aspects of rebel and paramilitary behavior, civilians' choices, civilian–combatant interactions, and wartime governance. I combined statistical analysis, process tracing, and a natural experiment to test the central hypotheses on the emergence of different forms of order over time and space; to describe and test the underlying causal mechanisms; and to validate the assumptions about civilian behavior that underlie the theory.

To my knowledge, this book presents the first collection of systematic accounts on the nonviolent behavior of armed groups and local governance in conflict zones. It thereby offers not only multiple tests of my argument, but also describes systematic patterns and nuances of social order in the midst of war that we simply did not know about. By offering this new evidence, the book not only offers an account of wartime institutions, armed group behavior, and civilian choice, but also raises new questions about the conduct of war and its legacies.

In the remainder of this chapter, I address the three central questions that follow from the theoretical discussion and the empirical analysis that the book offers. First, what are the limitations of the theoretical approach, and what could restrict the validity of the results? Second, are the findings applicable beyond Colombia and, if so, what are the scope conditions? And third, what are the implications of this book on our understanding of other phenomena?

CAVEATS

The theory developed in this project takes into account several characteristics of armed groups, communities, and the context in which they interact. However, a few factors that are important in shaping this interaction require further discussion.

The first factor is the state. I do argue in Chapter 3 that the state matters enormously in this theory but it does so via the independent variables: the state can increase armed competition, and it can be the source of effective and legitimate institutions. I also argued that in many cases, the state is part of aliocracy and rebelocracy. Its practices, its interaction with the local population, and its relation with non-state armed groups influence attributes of social order.

However, the role of the state warrants further research. In Colombia and elsewhere, guerrilla groups have not only fought against the state but have also used it to grow, gain legitimacy, and rule. The same applies to the paramilitaries, although they were supposedly fighting on the side of the state. Although I explored some of these parasitic relations between state agencies and armed actors in Chapter 6, they have to be more thoroughly researched. Similarly, the state may matter in shaping civilian–combatant relations by creating ideologies, a sense of belonging, grievances, and habits. Some of these effects are captured by my argument about institutions: if the state has succeeded in creating legitimate and effective institutions, people are more likely to stand up to defend them. In contrast, when institutions do not satisfy these criteria, locals have weaker preferences for them, and may even welcome a non-state armed group's proposed solution. Yet, there are other ways in which the state can shape people's reaction to the presence, demands, and rule of non-state armed groups that are not explored in this project.[1]

A second factor that my theory did not discuss in depth is the role of armed groups' ideology. Chapter 6 argued that ideology shapes *how* social orders are built: it can impact combatants' treatment of civilians at times of disorder, and it can also infuse the content of social contracts when they are established. But ideology does not affect the outcome itself, that is, whether the group brings disorder, aliocracy, or rebelocracy about. I do not grant ideology a more important role based on the premise that groups that do not adapt their strategy to the logic of irregular warfare die out quickly. However, it is possible that ideology matters in shaping the actual outcome in at least two ways.

To start with, ideology may directly affect the likelihood that a group creates a particular form of social order. Some groups may believe in the importance of governing civilian affairs in a broad sense beyond strategic considerations. Others may not even consider ruling a given population due to their ideology – for example, insurgents inspired by a religion may not even consider ruling a population with

---

[1] I thank Francisco Gutiérrez for reminding me of the importance of clearly specifying the role of the state in these processes. While the theory does provide a clear argument about when and how state presence may shape social order, it nonetheless leaves other possible mechanisms through which it may matter unexplored.

a different religious identity. This choice is perhaps most probable in civil wars where the insurgents aim to cleanse the country (or a particular region or group of people).

Ideology may also affect armed groups' expectations of civilian cooperation and resistance. Communities that are more proximate to the group's ideology may be allowed to have some autonomy even in high-value territories because the group anticipates high cooperation to stem from ideological proclivities. Likewise, as discussed in Chapter 3, those communities perceived to be long-time supporters of the enemy may be targeted regardless of the contextual conditions, as Balcells (2017) has shown for regular civil wars, and Steele (2016) for irregular wars.

Besides the state and ideology, a final factor that I did not incorporate into the theory is the possibility that collective action develops during war, even when local institutions are not effective or legitimate. As discussed in Chapters 3 and 6, violence itself may have what I called an awakening effect by making people react; the work of NGOs and even state agencies in fostering collective action might work, creating the conditions for civilian bargaining with armed actors and greater autonomy. Understanding the conditions under which collective action can change in the midst of war is an important question that deserves attention.[2]

Turning to the empirical analysis, although I made every effort to collect systematic data to compare cases, fine-grained evidence on specific communities to explore processes, and individual-level data to analyze the microfoundations, most of the evidence is based on people's recollections. It is difficult to think of alternative ways of collecting evidence since almost no data are available in archives or other records that would allow one to reconstruct the history of interaction between small communities and armed groups in a warzone even superficially, let alone in greater depth. While we should pursue research on these phenomena despite these difficulties, the results of data collected by asking people to remember – and to share their memories – have to be assessed with caution.

SCOPE CONDITIONS AND EXTERNAL VALIDITY

As discussed in Chapter 3, this theory is expected to apply to all irregular civil wars where armed actors seek to control territory. The cleavage of

---

[2] For a study of successful bargaining with armed actors by a community without a history of successful collective action see Kaplan (2013b).

Scope Conditions and External Validity 303

the war and the goals of rebels do not contradict any of the arguments; center-seeking, secessionist, and ethnic-based wars are expected to follow the same logic in so far as they wage an irregular war.

This is not to say, however, that variation in the type of war does not matter. Some outcomes can be more or less likely in some contexts than others via the explanatory variables identified in the theory. If any of these types of conflict affect armed groups' internal organization, armed competition, the value of territories, or the quality of preexisting local institutions, then *disorder, aliocracy*, or *rebelocracy* may be more likely there than elsewhere.

Moreover, there are alternative ways in which these differences could shape social order that are not accounted for by the theory. The ideological proximity of the group to the local population is one, which I discussed above. Another factor that may lead to outcomes not anticipated by the theory is the prevalence of locally based groups, as opposed to armed groups that expand into new territories. This was actually the case in a few communities included in my sample in Colombia, where paramilitary groups primarily recruited, and were sponsored by, locals. The logic in those cases seemed to be the same. It might be, however, that this is largely due to the existence of other groups that were expanding into new territories, as armed organizations often mimic each other. It is possible that different dynamics arise when the group is fully local, for example, when bringing on board other members of the community, bargaining with powerful factions, or devising new forms of governance. Further research is needed to assess whether these cases follow a similar logic to the one advanced in this book.

Overall, it is difficult to validate the theory and findings of this project in other cases with available data. Comparative data on social order or wartime institutions is quite scarce. Based on the qualitative evidence that I was able to find on a number of civil wars, however, I can assert that the theory travels across many cases in three ways.

First, as I showed with many examples in Chapters 2 and 3, *rebelocracy* is not rare. When presenting the theoretical approach for this project several years ago, I often encountered experts on civil war who asserted that this was a marginal phenomenon, perhaps unique to Latin America. I was told that in African civil wars rebelocracy was definitely the exception rather than the norm. Perhaps because these practices vary so much on the ground, and there is no easily identifiable pattern, they are often unnoticed. But despite how much the literature on civil war overlooked for long rebels' nonviolent behaviors in general, and their creation of institutions in particular, anthropologists and journalists have recorded numerous cases of rebelocracy. The list of armed groups that have been reported to provide public goods or serve as a parallel court is quite long.[3] Furthermore, the growing field of rebel governance has recently produced a large number of studies that present detailed evidence of the many ways in which armed groups are involved in the creation of institutions beyond security and taxation in several contexts (Keister 2009; Metelits 2010; Mampilly 2011; Arjona et al. 2015). What is more, the current situation in Syria and the growth of ISIS in the Levant has propelled researchers and journalists to pay unprecedented attention to rebel governance. The more we inquire about the phenomenon, the clearer it is that rebelocracy is quite widespread.

Second, civilian demands and organized resistance against armed groups are more common than often assumed. As mentioned in Chapter 2, both peaceful and armed resistance have been documented in many armed conflicts in Africa (e.g., Mozambique, Kenya), Latin America (e.g., Peru, Guatemala), and Asia (e.g., Indonesia, The Philippines). Likewise, many forms of bargaining between local communities and armed groups have been documented in numerous civil wars.

Third, there is evidence of the positive effect of *rebelocracy* for civilian cooperation with non-state armed groups – a key premise on which the theory is built. That is, rebels have long benefited from rebelocracy. I gave some examples from Afghanistan and Sri Lanka in Chapter 3.

Finally, some studies suggest that local institutions have played an important role in preventing the success of rebel groups. As I discussed in Chapter 3, several scholars have argued that the rebel group Shining Path was unable to expand to certain regions in Peru because of the collective action capacity fostered by strong local institutions(Lair et al. 2000; Picolli 2009; Heilman 2010; La Serna 2012). Yet, new research is needed to further evaluate the explanatory power of this theory beyond Colombia. Although a sub-national design cannot investigate external validity in any way, my findings can be compared in the future with similar projects in other contexts.

---

[3] See examples in Chapters 1, 2, and 3. These include non-state armed actors in many places of Latin America (e.g., Venezuela, El Salvador, Nicaragua, Cuba), Africa (e.g., Eritrea, Somalia, Sudan, Uganda, Cote d'Ivoire, DR Congo), and Asia (e.g., Sri Lanka, Nepal, India).

IMPLICATIONS

The theory and findings presented in this book have implications for a variety of questions about civil war, post-conflict situations, nonviolent resistance, local governance, state building, institutions, and the foundations of political order.

The first implication is related to the validity of common assumptions in theories of different civil war phenomena. Even though civilian agency is increasingly recognized, theories of civil war tend to assume that civilians' choices are constant, and constantly constrained, across local communities. Similarly, variation in the nonviolent strategies that armed groups adopt towards civilians is often overlooked. The interaction between a given armed actor and local populations is, therefore, often assumed to be static. This project challenges these views and, by doing so, calls for rethinking the premises on which many existing theories are built.

To illustrate, recent studies have found that civil war violence increases collective action (e.g., Bellows & Miguel 2009; Blattman & Annan 2009; Gilligan et al. 2013). The theory advanced in this book suggests that the opposite direction of causality is possible: communities with high-capacity for collective action can be more susceptible to violence because they demand autonomy. These communities are more likely to be victimized than communities with low collective action capacity for two reasons: first, when armed groups identify some capacity for collective action but have imperfect information on its strength, violence is used as a measurement tool; second, when a community demands autonomy in a highly strategic territory where it is too costly for the group to tolerate it, armed actors use violence to repress the community or expel it from the territory. If these hypotheses are correct, we should expect to find a correlation between collective action and violence – not because the latter causes the former, but because communities with a high capacity for collective action are more likely to be victimized. This case highlights why opening the black box of civilian–combatant relations is so important to theorize civil war dynamics and to interpret empirical facts.

Moreover, the argument has implications for armed groups' use of violence more generally. Kalyvas (2006) has convincingly argued that violence at the local level is to a great extent shaped by the distribution of territorial control between the warring sides. As mentioned in Chapter 5, Kalyvas posits that violence should be higher in areas of disorder (unless control is evenly shared). Yet, since some communities may be capable of collective action, they may be more likely to deny information on defectors to all armed groups, preventing selective violence from occurring. An implication of my theory is, therefore, that communities with high-quality institutions – which are therefore capable of collective action – are less likely to be targeted with selective violence than communities that are not, and more likely to be the victims of indiscriminate violence. Put differently, the logic of violence is likely to vary within disputed territories depending on the collective action capacity of the community.

There is another implication for the use of violence: when a group has territorial control, violence serves other purposes beyond punishing cooperation with the enemy. Under rebelocracy, it may be used to enforce rules that are not directly related to territorial control. Understanding the use of violence in these cases requires treating it as a tool for governing, as opposed to a weapon used only to deter cooperation with the enemy.

The theory advanced in the book also has important implications for our understanding of civilian choice in war zones. A parallel between the existence of distinct social orders and regime types is useful to think about the effects that such variation may have on civilian behavior. As with any regime – like democracy or dictatorship – the specific characteristics of these social orders have far-reaching consequences on their inhabitants. These wartime orders determine forbidden behaviors and individual rights; the actor or organization that civilians seek for solving their conflicts; the persons and institutions they have to obey; the existence of channels to communicate with those who command them; and the availability of procedures to defend themselves when accused of misconduct. Even civilians' private lives – how they dress, what their sexual choices are – can be subjected to strict regulation.

One of the shortcomings of the literature on civilian choices in conflict zones has been abstracting the very contexts in which such choices are made.[4] This neglect is consequential for our study of civilian cooperation, recruitment, and displacement. For example, this book offers evidence showing that recruits are more likely to enlist in communities living under a social order of rebelocracy. I also presented evidence suggesting that resistance is higher in communities living under disorder. Whether a social contract exists between a community and a group, and what specific behaviors the group adopts, should be taken into account when trying to understand why civilians behave the way they do in war zones.

---

[4] As mentioned in Chapter 2, Wood (2003) and Petersen (2001) are important exceptions.

Furthermore, while armed groups' behaviors seem to be mostly strategic, understanding civilian choice requires a more complex approach that goes beyond interests and rational calculations. In particular, it is important to ask about the ways armed groups, by influencing local life in so many ways, awaken emotions, transform shared beliefs, and create new ways of reading the local (and national) status quo. Violence, discourse, institutions, and selective and public goods transform local life and individual conduct; their combination shapes how civilians experience war, and how they react to its different situations.[5]

Turning to the conduct of war, one of the key implications of this project is the importance of the community in shaping the dynamics of civil war. Consistent with arguments made by other researchers (Pécaut 2001; Petersen 2001; González 2003; Wood 2003; Kalyvas 2006; Balcells & Justino 2014), an understanding of the macro-level dynamics of war requires theorizing and observing the ways in which war unfolds across the territory. In so far as we want to understand how wars are fought – how armed groups behave, how they gain territories and maintain them, and what these processes mean to civilians – taking this variation into account is important. For example, the theory advanced in this book has implications for war duration. In its early stages, an insurgency needs civilians to participate, but supporting a nascent movement entails a collective action problem. While insurgents may initially find fertile ground in communities highly capable of collective action (Lewis 2010; Trejo 2012), my argument suggests that they are most successful expanding to territories inhabited by communities with a low capacity for collective action. Strong communities, on the other hand, are more likely to limit armed groups' control over their territory and population. An implication of this hypothesis is that disaggregating the study of war is important not only in terms of geography but also in terms of time. Several phenomena that take place in the midst of war are endogenous to the ways in which the conflict has evolved up to that point (Pécaut 2001; Kalyvas 2006).

Another implication of the theory has to do with democracy in contexts of civil war. Whenever institutions are illegitimate or ineffective, non-state armed groups are likely to co-opt or capture existing authorities. Elections are often manipulated by combatants, as well as by politicians who ally with coercive groups in order to get elected. Based on the theory, we can expect the capture of electoral politics to be likely in countries where

---

[5] For an approach to these questions see Arjona (2016a).

democracy preceded civil war, which leads to normative and empirical questions about politics in times of war. Furthermore, the argument implies that the capture of democracy is more common, and more salient, in communities with low-quality institutions, implying that local regime type can vary widely within a single country.

There are also implications on the validity of measures that are commonly used in the micro-dynamics of civil war literature. For example, violence is commonly used as a proxy of the presence of armed groups (Sánchez & Chacón 2006; Acemoglu et al. 2013; Dube & Vargas 2013). But such a measure is likely to capture only places with *certain* type of presence: places where people denounce acts of victimization and where the state or NGOs report them. Places ruled under rebelocracy, in contrast, are likely to be missed. In those places armed groups may use lower levels of violence because they do not face competition with other armed actors, and civilians have learned to obey the rules; furthermore, the victims of violence of this powerful ruler are unlikely to denounce, and the capacity of the state to record events may be hindered. Hence, using violence as a proxy may lead to systematically coding cases of rebelocracy as cases with no presence of armed actors whatsoever.

Similarly, inferring that civilians identify with insurgents based on the existence of an insurgent stronghold can be misleading; the same applies to measuring civilian support for an insurgency on the basis of the amount of territory that the insurgents control. Armed groups may establish strongholds via different arrangements with locals. Cooperation may consist of passive obedience alone, with little spontaneous support. Furthermore, even when civilian cooperation entails voluntary support, most locals can cooperate for a myriad of reasons that have nothing to do with politics – or at least with *national* politics (Kalyvas 2006).

As the study of the micro-dynamics of civil war continues to grow, this book suggests that we not only need to gather more data but also advance theory. A theoretical understanding of the local context in which civilians and combatants interact is essential to explain outcomes as well as to interpret empirical facts. Our knowledge about the conduct of war definitely needs that we find ways to isolate complex causal effects; but it also requires the careful elaboration of *theory* as opposed to isolated *hypotheses*.

Turning to the macro-level, further research is needed in order to assess how patterns in the behaviors of armed groups and civilians identified in this book aggregate. A first possible implication is that armed groups are more capable of sustaining a war and posing a real threat in countries where local institutions – be they formal or informal – are weak. Several processes can weaken institutions. Industrialization and mass migration, for example, can erode traditional forms of governance and, by so doing, make non-state armed groups more capable of creating strongholds. In contrast, where institutions are legitimate and effective, either because of successful state building or the preservation of traditional norms, armed groups have more difficulty establishing rebelocracy and creating secure strongholds. This argument would be consistent with theories of peasant rebellion that stress the effect of systemic economic changes on the likelihood of rebellion (e.g., Scott 1977) – although it provides a different mechanism.

Another implication has to do with the role that state capacity plays in making civil war more likely. In the literature on civil war onset, weak state capacity (as proxied by GDP) has been found to increase the likelihood of civil war. The logic of the argument suggests that there is a supply of aspiring rebels, but only when the state is weak can they become viable because the state lacks the capacity to deter them (Fearon and Laitin 2003). The theory advanced in this book suggests an alternative mechanism: state capacity matters because it can create good institutions, which facilitate collective resistance to rebel rule. We might therefore be overlooking the key role that civilians' reactions play in the expansion of rebel groups. State capacity may deter conflict not only with its weapons but also with its *institutions*. It makes sense, therefore, to inquire about the *forms* of state presence that make civil war less likely.

By the same token, the argument also has implications for our understanding of development programs, humanitarian action, counter-insurgency, and peacekeeping – where theorizing civilians' responses to alternative interventions is essential. One implication is the importance of disaggregating the study of interventions, as they may have different results depending on the institutional reality of each locality. A uniform strategy, thus, is inherently problematic (Arjona 2009). For example, the type of state presence that decreases the expansion of armed actors may vary across geography within the country. In communities with high-quality institutions, bringing services, infrastructure, and development programs may well help to limit the insurgents' capacity to control and influence the local territory. However, in communities with low-quality institutions, public goods might be important, but the vacuum of institutions may still give insurgents an opportunity to penetrate the community, offer its services, and gain power over it. This has been illustrated by the Taliban's success in offering an alternate court system in areas of Afghanistan where the formal justice system is slow and inefficient (e.g., Giustozzi et al. 2013; Ahmed 2015) – even in areas that had been under the control of coalition forces (*NYT* 2010c). Taking local institutions into account could, for example, help explain why recent studies have found contradicting findings about the effect of development programs on violence in conflict zones (e.g., Beath et al. 2013; Crost et al. 2014; Weintraub 2016).

Turning to post-conflict situations, by identifying variation in civilians' experience of war, this book calls for a more disaggregated approach to post-conflict outcomes. The presence of armed groups brings about profound changes to local communities, shaping not only how war affects them (as victims) but also how they react to it (as agents). Variation in wartime social order is, therefore, likely to transcend the war, creating challenges and opportunities for reconciliation, reconstruction, and development. Furthermore, as Justino (2013) argues, insofar as institutional outcomes tend to be persistent, the wartime transformation of institutions may impact the very possibility of durable peace.

To illustrate, whether the return of former combatants to their hometowns is desirable may well depend on its location and war history. In those communities that interacted with an armed group under a social contract, the challenge of reintegrating former combatants may be different than reintegrating former members of a group that operated under *disorder*. Similarly, in areas where armed groups created a social order that improved local conditions, the presence of former combatants may not be as problematic as it would be elsewhere (Arjona 2009). Even the difficulties for displaced populations to return to their homes after the war may well vary depending on how the communities they left interacted with armed groups. In cases where local support for an armed group was widespread, displaced persons may have been stigmatized when they left, and thus their return not welcomed.

More generally, different kinds of institutions, including those coming from state agencies or traditional institutions, can be deeply transformed by the rules that operated during the war. If fostering trust in the state, recovering the authority of traditional institutions, or promoting community cohesion are among the challenges that post-war societies face, understanding the ways in which the war transformed social and political organization is necessary. Ignoring the different forms that war takes across local territories and civilians' experiences under completely different social orders can lead us to overlook important ways in which war shapes individuals' beliefs, the working norms in their communities, and their relation with different state and non-state institutions. In sum, many social processes are transformed by war (Wood 2008), often in radically different ways across local communities (Arjona 2009). Investigating how this variation travels into the post-conflict period is important to evaluate priorities and alternative responses to the needs of war-torn societies.

The role of local institutions in the transition to peace is crucial (López 2016), especially dispute institutions. Not only are they essential to implement peace agreements, as García-Villegas and Espinosa (2013) argue, but also to decrease the opportunities for criminal groups to become new de facto rulers in areas formerly ruled by rebels or paramilitaries (Arjona 2016c). How to create those institutions is a difficult question on which we still have few answers. Creating legitimate and effective institutions is challenging, and perhaps both goals cannot be achieved simultaneously (ibid.). Furthermore, the state is not able to develop such institutions quickly throughout its territory, and top-down approaches are plagued with problems (e.g., Autesserre 2009; David Mason et al. 2011; Castañeda 2014). Empowering existing legitimate and effective dispute institutions that do not come from the state is a possibility that should be explored, although devising ways to ensure that those institutions respect human rights is essential as well.

My theoretical approach to civilian resistance and the astonishing forms of opposition to rebel and paramilitary rule described in this book have a strong connection to the literature on nonviolence resistance. Although civilians in Colombian territories may not have studied the principles and strategies of nonviolent resistance, they have successfully put many of them into practice. This book offers a micro-level study of nonviolent resistance, and suggests that it may be effective not only against repressive states but also against non-state armed actors.

The theory that I propose in this book is, at its core, a theory of how aspiring rulers come to power: how they approach communities, how the communities respond, and what the outcome of this interaction is. It is, in this sense, a theory of how order is created, preserved, and destroyed. As such, the book also has implications for our understanding of state-building and the sociology of power. On one hand, the book shows that different forms of order can coexist within a region where no one owns the monopoly of the use of violence – rather, small monopolies coexist, sustaining different forms of order. In those monopolies, actors need to devise ways to gain influence in many spheres of local life in order to engender the type of cooperation that can make their rule stable. But such strategy needs to be tailored to local conditions to avoid backfiring. On the other hand, the evidence shows that Colombia has had a functioning state in some parts of the country while enduring a civil war for fifty years, challenging common views on the relation between the state, political order, and violence.

The theory and empirical evidence also emphasize the importance of understanding local state building and local political regimes. In particular, it suggests that local dispute institutions can deeply shape these phenomena. This book suggests that creating legitimate and effective dispute institutions is key to the consolidation of power – a contention that is consistent with new macro-historical accounts of the creation of the state (Boucoyannis 2017). In sum, this book joins many other studies in the social sciences that reveal the need to theorize the state in new ways.

My goal when I started to research civil war was to produce knowledge that could help us understand the wounds that war leaves behind, and what we could do about them. I soon realized that I could not address those questions without understanding first what happens *during* war. Focusing on wartime institutions and the type of social order that emanates from them promised to offer some answers. Although the book questioned Hobbes' portrait of civil war as chaos, it concludes, with him, that institutions play a significant role in preventing war and resolving it. However, these institutions need not come from a Leviathan in the form of a state but can be rooted in alternative sources of order. My hope is that this research sparks attention to the important role that local institutions and civilian collective action play in the evolution of civil war – and that they become an essential ingredient of its remedy, especially as Colombia finally transitions from war to peace.

APPENDICES

Appendix 1
Fieldwork and Sources of Empirical Evidence

The sources that I use in this book are described in Chapters 5 and 7. In this Appendix, I present additional details on the ways in which the data were collected.

DATA ON COMMUNITY–ARMED GROUP INTERACTION (2010, 2012)

The data on local communities alluded to in Chapters 5, 6, and 8 were gathered in two waves of fieldwork: one in 2010 and one in 2012. In order to include cases in the different regions of the country, I stratified the Colombian territory in four regions in 2010 and three regions in 2012. Each region had the same number of municipalities. These regions included twenty-seven of the thirty-three departments of the country (the equivalent to US states). I excluded five departments located in the Amazonian region, which are highly unpopulated and where the armed conflict has only recently arrived: Vichada, Guainía, Guaviare, Vaupés, and Amazonas. I also excluded San Andres and Providencia, the islands located in the Caribbean Sea, where armed groups had not been present until recently.

In 2010, each region was further divided into two subregions with the same number of municipalities to decrease costs. I randomly chose one of the sub-regions in each region, and then two municipalities in each subregion to include in the sample. In total eight municipalities were chosen. In 2012, the selection was a bit more complicated. I wanted to ensure variation across municipalities in state presence, ethnic composition, and population distribution in rural and urban settlements. I selected a random sample of twenty-two municipalities stratifying by these variables using official data as proxies.[1]

Since the universe of cases consists of localities that have had ongoing interaction with at least one non-state armed group, I excluded from the sample the municipalities where no armed groups had ever been present for more than six continuous months. Measuring *presence* is, to be sure, a difficult task. Whereas there are available data on violence, it does not necessarily work well as a proxy of presence. To avoid this potential selection bias, I only excluded from the sample the municipalities where our contacts in the field confirmed that no armed group had been present for at least six months. In a few cases, we kept in the sample municipalities only to find out when we arrived to conduct fieldwork that none of the armed groups had ever been present there. In those occasions, the municipality was either replaced by another one or simply excluded from the sample with no replacement. Overall, we only excluded about 10 percent of all the municipalities that had been randomly selected.

When conducting fieldwork in the spring of 2010, congressional and presidential elections were close and violence peaked in different areas of the country. Due to security problems I had to replace one selected municipality, Planadas in the Tolima department, by another, Coello, in the same department.[2] Also, fieldwork had to be interrupted in North Santander, where two municipalities were selected: Toledo and Tibú. While the work on Toledo was completed, data collection was not possible in Tibú. Due to time and monetary constraints, it was not possible to replace this municipality with another. The final sample consists, therefore, of seven municipalities instead of eight.

The sample is not likely to be biased due to these changes as violence prior to the elections took place in 38 percent of all municipalities in the country (MOE 2010). Furthermore, several analyses show that violence was linked to current dynamics – such as the corridors for drugs – rather

---

[1] The sampling design, and the fact that the data come from two different samples, were taken into account to calculate all the descriptive statistics presented in the book. Since the samples were independently drawn, when combining the two samples new sampling weights were calculated based on the Horvitz-Thompson approach, where the probability for a case to be in either sample is calculated as the sum of the probabilities of being in each sample (O'Muircheartaigh and Pedlow 2002). See the section on the statistical analysis for a discussion of incorporating sampling weights into the models.

[2] Armed attacks by the FARC took place in Planadas, and four bombs were deactivated by the police, in the week prior to the elections (May 22–30), when we were doing fieldwork [www.vanguardia.com/presidente2010/noticias/nuevo-balance-de-orden-publico-en-elecciones] [accessed on December 12, 2010].

than to long-term trends. With respect to the previous electoral campaign in 2007, violence shifted to the Pacific coast and the transversal corridor from Chocó to the Venezuelan border in North Santander (MOE 2010:8).

In 2012, we were not able to finalize our work in the municipality of Ricaurte, in Nariño, due to security concerns. However, we were able to conduct fieldwork in other municipalities in the Pacific zone, where the situation has been similarly difficult in recent years.

The sample is quite diverse. It includes municipalities near the Caribbean coast, as well as the Pacific coast. It has municipalities in the south, north, east, and west of the country. There are municipalities with historic presence of one of the armed groups (since the 1970s) as well as municipalities where the guerrillas, the paramilitaries, or both arrived as late as 2000. The sample is also ethnically heterogeneous: some are predominantly populated by Afro-Colombians, others by indigenous communities, others by non-minorities, and others are mixed. The sample includes municipalities that were populated by internal migrants in the mid-1900s, as well as municipalities created and populated in colonial times.

The sample is also diverse regarding economic activities: some municipalities are rich in natural resources like oil (e.g., Villanueva, Casanare), while others have cattle (e.g., San Benito Abad, Sucre). The presence of illegal crops like coca also varies across time and space. The structure of land tenure also varies, with some municipalities exhibiting high inequality, and others low inequality. The sociopolitical structures are also diverse across municipalities, as some were formed by migrants who escaped violence in the 1950s and 1960s, or migrated for economic reasons after 1960, while others are more traditional societies based on a patron–client relation with landowners. Figure 5.1 in Chapter 5 presents descriptive statistics of many of these attributes.

In each municipality I followed two parallel approaches with the help of outstanding research assistants. First, several persons who were likely to know well the history of the municipality were interviewed; they were asked about as many localities within the municipality as they knew well enough in order to respond to questions about local institutions and interaction with armed groups. Some interviewees were chosen prior to visiting the municipality, as contacts in the municipality or in NGOs or state agencies suggested they knew well different places within the area. Others were contacted in situ, following suggestions of locals. On average, five persons were interviewed in each municipality. It is worth stressing that I did not aim to create a representative sample of *individuals*, but rather to gather high-quality evidence on *communities*. As with any study of territorial units, interviewing *anyone* was not the goal, but rather interviewing those who were likely to have information on the variables of interest.

The number of localities that exist in each municipality vary greatly across cases.[3] Large municipalities can have thirty localities, whereas smaller ones can have only three. Interviewees were asked about all localities in the municipality, although not everyone was able to give information on all, especially in large municipalities. Some localities had never experienced the presence of a non-state armed group; since they were not part of the universe of cases, they were left out of the analysis.

In the survey, the interviewer read two vignettes that described community life under the presence of an armed group. The first described in plain words a social order of rebelocracy, where the armed group intervened in several spheres of life. The second vignette described a social order of aliocracy, where the group was present and ruled over security but did not intervene in other aspects of local life. The interviewee was then asked to report which vignette resembled more the situation in each locality, and for which periods of time. The question was then asked again about each locality within the municipality that the interviewee reported to know well. The specific wording of these questions are provided at the end of this section.

Based on the responses given to this survey, I coded the type of social order that emerged in each locality year by year and identified which type had been more common over time. I then selected between two and four localities, preserving the distribution observed in the survey when possible.

In each selected locality, we invited four persons from the community to participate in the semi-structured interviews. In 2012, they were also invited to participate in the memory workshops. When possible, participants included a civil leader, a teacher, a merchant, and an elder who did not have any leadership role. In most cases, there was at least one woman in the group. Once again, the idea was not to invite a random sample of persons but rather a diverse group of experts who knew the history of their communities. We strived to avoid finding all our contacts only through one person or organization to ensure heterogeneity; however, we were able to reach out to more persons in some places than in others.

Chapter 5 presents the map with the final sample of communities where we conducted the memory workshops and the survey.

---

[3] I am referring to Colombia's statistics office's definition of "populated settlements."

Instrument Used in Survey with Vignettes

English version

Local Social Order

I would like to talk about the way in which the population and these armed groups lived together in the different areas within this municipality. Let me tell you what happened in two villages in a municipality like this one after the arrival of [*name of first armed group to arrive to the municipality*] to the zone.

In the first village, [*armed group*] became the ruler. It forbade giving information to the enemy and other things that could affect security; they also established rules to maintain order, like forbidding robberies and rape. It was common that people had to give them money, animals, or food. In addition, [*armed group*] established rules on different conducts: for example, regarding family life, they forbade mistreatment of partners; they also established norms on sexual conduct like prostitution and infidelity; and they also created rules on economic activities. When there were problems among neighbors, for example over land borders, harm caused by animals, or debts, it was common for people to seek [*armed group*] to solve them. In general, [*armed group*] had a great influence over how things were done in the community.

In the second village, [*armed group*] also established rules over security, like forbidding giving information to the enemy. It also asked that people give them money or food. But there, [*armed group*] did not establish all those rules on family life, fidelity, and all those things. When there were disputes among people due to land borders, debts, etc., they were not resolved by turning to [*armed group*]. In general, [*armed group*] did not get involved with the organization of the community. It could be said that it had military power, but did not get to rule over people's daily life.

Please try to remember how things were in [*village X*] after the arrival of [*armed group*]. To which of these two villages I just told you about does it resemble more?

Spanish version

Orden Social Local

Ahora quisiera que hablemos sobre la manera en que la población y estos grupos armados convivían en las distintas zonas de este municipio.

Quisiera contarle lo que pasó en dos veredas vecinas en un municipio como este después de la llegada de [grupo armado] a la zona:

En una vereda, [grupo armado] se convirtieron en los que mandaban. Prohibieron dar información al enemigo y otras cosas que podían afectarles la seguridad; también pusieron reglas para mantener el orden, como prohibir robos y violaciones. Era común que la gente tuviera que darles dinero, animales o comida. Además, [grupo armado] pusieron reglas sobre diferentes conductas: por ejemplo, en la vida familiar, prohibieron el maltrato a las parejas; también pusieron normas sobre el comportamiento sexual como la prostitución o la infidelidad; y crearon normas sobre actividades económicas. Cuando había problemas entre vecinos, por ejemplo por linderos, daños causados por animales o deudas, era común que la gente acudiera a [grupo armado] para resolverlos. En general, [grupo armado] tenían una gran influencia sobre cómo se hacían las cosas en la comunidad.

En la otra vereda, [grupo armado] también establecieron reglas sobre la seguridad, como prohibir dar información al enemigo. También pedían que la gente les diera dinero o comida. Pero allí [grupo armado] no pusieron todas esas normas sobre la vida familiar, la fidelidad y todas esas cosas. Cuando había disputas entre la gente por deudas, linderos, etc, no se resolvían acudiendo a [grupo armado]. En general, [grupo armado] no se metían en la organización de la comunidad. Se podría decir que tenían el poder militar, pero no llegaron a mandar en la vida diaria de la gente.

Por favor trate recordar cómo eran las cosas en la cabecera municipal de este municipio después de la llegada de [grupo armado]. A cuál de estas dos veredas de las que le acabo de hablar se le parece más?

Memory Workshops

As I explain in Chapter 5, the memory workshops consisted of three activities: a reflection on memory, building timelines, and creating institutional biographies. In this appendix I provide more details on these activities.

Mind Mapping

Mind mapping is a technique used in many different contexts to visualize a thinking process. By activating both hemispheres in the brain, mind mapping is believed to spur a more creative reflection than that of a purely lineal thinking process. Using a mind mapping technique, workshop

Data on Community–Armed Group Interaction (2010, 2012)

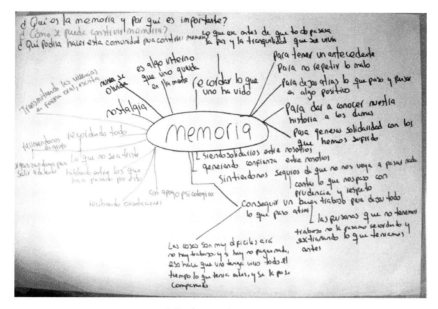

FIGURE A1.1 Mind mapping exercise on memory

participants were asked to share the ideas they related to three questions: What is memory? Why does it matter? And, how can memory be built in this community? All ideas were written on a board following a tree structure, and participants were asked to share new associations they made with what was already on the board.

I came up with the idea of conducting the mind mapping exercise while trying to find a way to contribute to the communities that participated in the study. Questions about the construction of memory were heatedly debated in Colombia at the time, as a new Center for Memory was being created and decisions had to be made about what kind of initiatives should be endorsed, the balance between top-down and bottom-up memory, and the actual role that memory can play in the stability of peace, and the quality of reconciliation. A memory workshop, I thought, could provide a space for locals to think about memory and come up with ideas about what could be done in their communities. At the same time, I wanted to invite them to reflect on what participating in the workshops could mean to them. Figure A1.1 shows an example of the mind mapping component of the workshop. In most cases, participants appreciated this activity and interesting ideas came up about what the community could do in the future to create their own memory of the conflict. This component of the workshop also helped everyone – interviewees and interviewers – to feel more comfortable about talking about the past.

Timelines

The second activity consisted on creating timelines of the history of the community. The central goal was to address a challenge that I experienced in previous fieldwork getting the dates right. To understand the local histories of communities and to create a longitudinal dataset, I needed to have reliable information on dates. However, in interviews and surveys, it is often hard for people to accurately situate events in time. In the data that I collected in 2010, I had to rely on primary and secondary data and pay great attention to every testimony to organize the information I had along a time continuum that made sense. Although I found that the survey provided fairly consistent information on each locality in terms of *what* happened, there were many discrepancies across testimonies regarding *when* events occurred.

We first created a timeline of the history of the community, going back as far as participants wanted. We identified the most important events that took place in the past. We then created a more detailed timeline of the history of the locality since the arrival of the first non-state armed group. The goal was to clearly identify which armed groups were ever present in the area and when. We also identified the major events that people remembered throughout the years in which they interacted with combatants. Chapter 5 shows the image of one of the timelines that were built at the workshops.

Institutional Biographies

Institutional biographies sought, as their name indicates, to reconstruct the "life" of institutions in each community. The underlying logic is explained in Chapter 5. This tool proved to be very useful to capture "snapshots" of local institutions that are comparable across cases. I found them to be quite insightful in the sense that they convey much about the communities without asking for much information from participants.

Survey or Structured Interviews

Each workshop participant responded to a long survey that contained both open- and close-ended questions. The survey asked specific questions about the quality of local institutions prior to the arrival of any armed actor to the locality, as well as about every stage of interaction between the community and the armed actor. Close-ended questions gathered specific data about the institutions that regulated conduct during war, as well as about specific characteristics of the armed groups that operated in the area. Open-ended questions elicited much more detailed accounts of daily life and the ways in which different sectors of the population interacted with combatants.

Outcomes

The data collected with these different tools allowed me to create a large dataset with very specific information on the interaction between localities and armed groups over time. Although the responses to the interviewees did not always coincide, most of the time they did. When we obtained different answers, the interviewer tried to obtain more details. The memory workshops were very useful to make difficult decisions, but, overall in most cases the patterns were clear. One of the reasons why I use indexes as opposed to dichotomous variables is precisely to avoid relying on a single measure that could reflect bad coding. Instead, I rely on multiple indicators of my central variables, to wit, order, rebelocracy, and the quality of preexisting institutions. Competition and indiscipline were quite easy to code, as people had a very clear idea of when multiple armed actors were present in their locality and when combatants could not get away with disobeying orders from their commanders.

SURVEY WITH EX-COMBATANTS AND CIVILIANS IN COLOMBIA

I conducted these surveys in 2005 and 2006 in collaboration with Stathis Kalyvas. Most of the sampling strategy was described in Chapter 8. In this section I provide additional details.

Sampling Individually Demobilized Ex-combatants

I explained in Chapter 5 why we decided to conduct our survey of individually demobilized combatants in Bogotá. To select our sample of respondents, we randomly selected a set of safe homes where the ex-combatants lived. Given that newly demobilized fighters were assigned to safe homes according to availability of spots, and that there were no other criteria for assigning them to a specific safe house, the distribution of ex-combatants across safe houses can be considered to be random. In each safe home, we initially gave a short presentation of the project to all ex-combatants, and we then asked for their voluntary participation, which was over 95 percent. We targeted 17 safe houses randomly selected out of 32, and conducted 315 interviews.

Due to security issues, we were forced to stop our visits to safe houses.[4] We completed 124 additional interviews at a public office that handled all requests and paperwork of the IDEs. All beneficiaries of the Reintegration Program had to visit these offices in order to solve a variety of issues related to their training, family situation, and job placement – which means that those who visit this facility do not share particular characteristics. We stratified our sample in order to over-represent former FARC members, given that all collectively demobilized fighters belonged to paramilitary groups. We randomly selected a number of former guerrilla and paramilitary beneficiaries every day, gave them a short presentation of the project, and asked for their voluntary participation in a private location. Again, participation was over 95 percent. We do not find any significant differences between the responses of the IDEs we interviewed in safe houses, and those interviewed at the public office.

As I mentioned in Chapter 8, data provided by the Ministry of Defense in December 2005 suggest that our sample is representative of the population of IDE in terms of group membership (Figure 8.8).

Sampling Collectively Demobilized Paramilitaries

I explained in Chapter 8 why we decided to focus on two paramilitary factions: the Córdoba bloc and the Catatumbo bloc. Given that collectively demobilized paramilitaries did not live in safe houses but in independent homes, and since their contact information was highly protected, we had to rely on the cooperation of the local offices of the Ministry of Interior in both cities. Through them, we invited about 500 ex-combatants to attend a meeting at a secure place, without giving any information on the purpose of such meeting. To our surprise, around 400 out of the 500 came and, after attending a presentation on the project, 99 percent agreed to participate in the survey, of which 387 completed the

---

[4] On July 15, 2005, a bomb exploded in front of one of the safe houses. The government then decided to close all the safe houses within a few weeks and relocate ex-combatants.

survey. Even though we cannot control for the possible bias derived from the fact that respondents had to select themselves to attend, the fact that only 20 percent refused to come and that they did not know about the purpose of the meeting makes us confident about the sample. We interviewed 162 former fighters of the Catatumbo bloc (11 percent of the entire population), and 222 of the Córdoba bloc (24 percent of the entire population).

Survey with Civilians

As explained in Chapter 8, we selected a sample of municipalities where ex-combatants lived prior to joining in order to conduct a survey with civilians that could work as a good control group. The strategy for sampling civilians was straightforward, as explained in Chapter 8.

LOCAL HISTORIES

In the municipalities where we conducted the survey with civilians, we also conducted interviews to build local histories. These interviews tried to reconstruct important aspects of the presence of armed actors in the municipalities. The interviews were not conducted with a random sample of civilians but, rather, with local experts who knew well the history of their municipalities. These were the first wave of interviews I conducted on the interaction between civilians and combatants. While the unit of analysis was the municipality – which is too aggregated to understand the nuances of wartime order – the interviews provided detailed evidence of the dynamics in the *cabeceras* of these municipalities. In Chapter 6 I rely on some of the testimonies that we collected with these interviews, referring to each municipality by its case number (the list of cases is provided later in this Appendix).

IN-DEPTH INTERVIEWS AND FOCUS GROUPS

In addition to the interviews conducted in the localities referenced above, I conducted almost 200 interviews with civilians, former combatants, public servants, scholars, and workers of NGOs and think tanks. These interviews were conducted in different places. Many were conducted in Bogotá, Colombia's capital. I also conducted many in Viotá (Cundinamarca) and Tierra Alta (Córdoba), two municipalities where I conducted extensive fieldwork at the initial stages of this project.

I conducted additional interviews in other places for various reasons. For example, I once traveled to Casanare to meet a sixty-year-old former member of the FARC who had demobilized after being part of the group since its formation in the late 1960s.

I also conducted focus groups in Viotá, where I invited the persons I had interviewed many times to a focus group and drew a timeline of the history of their municipality. We also discussed openly many aspects of that history.

LIST OF INTERVIEWS

TABLE A1.1 *List of interviews and focus groups (conducted by the author 2007–2015)*

No.	Category	Municipality
1	Non-communist resident	Viotá
2	Non-communist leader	Viotá
3	Former councilmember, Liberal Party	Viotá
4	Communist leader	Viotá
5	Communist leader	Viotá
6	Communist leader	Viotá
7	Communist leader	Viotá
8	Communist leader	Viotá
9	Local resident, Liberal Party	Viotá
10	Local leader, Liberal Party	Viotá
11	Former public servant	Viotá
12	Local resident	Viotá
13	Local resident	Viotá
14	Local resident	Viotá
15	Communist leader	Viotá
16	Communist leader	Viotá
17	Merchant	Viotá
18	Merchant	Viotá
19	Merchant	Viotá
20	Local resident	Viotá
21	Local resident	Viotá
22	Politician, non-communist	Viotá
23	Politician, non-communist	Viotá
24	Politician, non-communist	Viotá
25	Local resident	Viotá
26	Communist leader	Viotá
27	Former FARC member	Viotá

(continued)

TABLE A1.1 *(continued)*

No.	Category	Municipality
28	Former FARC member	Viotá
29	Communist leader	Viotá
30	Local resident	Viotá
31	Communist leader	Viotá
32	Local resident	Viotá
33	Communist leader	Viotá
34	Communist leader	Viotá
35	Former councilmember, Liberal Party	Viotá
36	Local leader, Liberal Party	Viotá
37	Non-communist resident	Viotá
38	Non-communist leader	Viotá
39	Non-communist leader	Viotá
40	Adelia's aide	Viotá
41	Communist leader	Viotá
FG1	Focus Group	Viotá
42	Public servant, Colombian Reintegration Agency	Tierralta
43	Evangelic leader	Tierralta
44	Scholar	Montería
45	Civic leader, displaced	Tierralta
46	Displaced	Tierralta
47	Evangelic pastor	Tierralta
48	Civilian	Tierralta
49	Indigenous leader	Tierralta
50	Civilian	Tierralta
51	Civilian	Tierralta
52	Fromer FARC combatant	Tierralta
53	Displaced	Tierralta
54	Civilian	Tierralta
55	Civilian	Tierralta
61	Civilian	Tierralta
62	Civilian	Tierralta
63	Civilian	Tierralta
64	Civilian	Tierralta
65	Civilian	Tierralta
66	Civilian	Tierralta
67	Civilian	Tierralta
68	Civilian	Tierralta
69	Civilian	Tierralta

(continued)

TABLE A1.1 *(continued)*

No.	Category	Municipality
70	Civilian	Tierralta
71	Civilian	Tierralta
72	Civilian	Tierralta
73	Civilian	Tierralta
56	Civilian	Tierralta
57	Civic leader	Tierralta
58	Former paramilitary combatant	Tierralta
59	Former paramilitary combatant	Tierralta
60	Former paramilitary combatant	Tierralta
74	Former paramilitary combatant	Tierralta
75	Displaced	Tierralta
76	Displaced	Tierralta
77	Displaced	Tierralta
78	Displaced	Tierralta
79	Displaced	Tierralta
80	Catholic priest	Tierralta
81	Former council member	Tierralta
82	Indigenous leader	Tierralta
83	Indigenous leader	Tierralta
84	Civic leader	Tierralta
85	Former police inspector	Tierralta
86	Civilian	Tierralta
87	Civilian	Tierralta
88	Civic leader	Tierralta
89	Civilian	Tierralta
90	Civilian	Tierralta
91	Civilian	Tierralta
92	Civilian	Tierralta
93	Civilian	Tierralta
94	Displaced	Tierralta
95	Public servant (Ombudsman's office)	Montería
96	Former EPL member	Bogotá
98	NGO worker	Bogotá
97	Priest	Bogotá
99	Former FARC member	Bogotá
100	Former FARC member	Bogotá
101	Former FARC member	Bogotá
102	Former FARC member	Bogotá

(continued)

TABLE A1.1 (continued)

No.	Category	Municipality
103	Former FARC member	Bogotá
104	Former FARC member	Bogotá
105	Former FARC member	Bogotá
106	Former FARC member	Bogotá
107	Former paramilitary member	Bogotá
108	Former paramilitary member	Bogotá
109	Former paramilitary member	Bogotá
110	Former FARC member	Bogotá
111	Former FARC member	Bogotá
112	Former FARC member	Bogotá
113	Scholar	Bogotá
114	Scholar	Bogotá
115	Scholar	Bogotá
116	Scholar	Bogotá
117	Scholar	Bogotá
118	Scholar	Bogotá
119	Scholar	Bogotá
120	Scholar	Bogotá
121	Scholar	Bogotá
122	Scholar	Bogotá
123	Scholar	Bogotá
124	Scholar	Bogotá
125	Scholar	Bogotá
126	Scholar	Bogotá
127	Member of Colombia's army	Bogotá
128	Member of Colombia's army	Bogotá
129	Member of Colombia's army	Bogotá
130	Scholar	Bogotá
131	Scholar	Bogotá
132	Public servant (Ombudsman's office)	Bogotá
133	Scholar	Bogotá
134	Scholar	Bogotá
135	Think tank staff	Bogotá
136	Scholar	Bogotá
137	Think tank staff	Bogotá
138	Think tank staff	Bogotá
139	Think tank staff	Bogotá
140	Think tank staff	Bogotá

(continued)

TABLE A1.1 *(continued)*

No.	Category	Municipality
141	Public servant (Ombudsman's office)	Bogotá
142	Public servant (Ombudsman's office)	Bogotá
143	Public servant (Ombudsman's office)	Bogotá
144	Public servant (ACR)	Bogotá
145	NGO worker	Bogotá
146	Scholar	Bogotá
147	Scholar	Bogotá
148	Scholar	Bogotá
149	Scholar	Bogotá
150	Staff, Colombian Federation of Municipalities	Bogotá
151	NGO staff	Bogotá
152	Public servant (Ombudsman's office)	Bogotá
153	Scholar	Bogotá
154	Scholar	Bogotá
155	Scholar	Bogotá
156	Public servant, Vicepresidency of Colombia	Bogotá
157	NGO staff	Bogotá
158	World Bank worker	Bogotá
159	NGO staff	Bogotá
160	NGO staff	Bogotá
161	Scholar	Bogotá
162	Public servant, Vicepresidency of Colombia	Bogotá
163	Colombian Federation of Municipalities staff	Bogotá
164	Scholar	Bogotá
165	Journalist	Bogotá
166	NGO worker	Bogotá
167	Public servant (DNP)	Bogotá
168	Scholar, NGO worker	Bogotá
169	Scholar	Bogotá
170	Public servant (Ombudsman's office)	Bogotá
171	NGO worker	Bogotá
172	Public servant (Ombudsman's office)	Bogotá
173	Scholar	Bogotá
174	NGO staff	Bogotá
175	Scholar	Bogotá
176	NGO staff	Bogotá
177	Public servant (Acción Social)	Bogotá

LIST OF CASES

TABLE A1.2 *List of cases*

Case No.	Local histories (2006) Municipality	Department
1	Algeciras	Huila
2	Apartadó	Antioquia
3	Barichara	Santander
4	Barrancabermeja	Santander
5	Bogotá	Bogotá D.C.
6	Cereté	Córdoba
7	Ciénaga	Magdalena
8	Cúcuta	Norte de Santander
9	Granada	Meta
10	Montería	Córdoba
11	Ovejas	Sucre
12	Puerto Berrío	Antioquia
13	Rioblanco	Tomila
14	Toribío	Cauca
15	Villa de Leyva	Boyacá
16	Villanueva	Casanare

Case No.	In-depth case studies Municipality and Village	Department
17	Tierralta, village 1	Córdoba
18	Tierralta, village 2	Córdoba
19	Tierralta, village 3	Córdoba
20	Tierralta, village 4	Córdoba
21	Viotá, Zama	Cundinamarca
22	Viotá, Librea	Cundinamarca
23	Viotá, Tellus	Cundinamarca

* Fake names are given for villages in Viotá and Tierralta to protect the identity of the interviewees.

Appendix 2
Supplemental Materials for Chapter 5

CODING

This section presents the wording of the questions asked in the survey that the variables used in Chapter 5 rely on, in Spanish and English (Table A2.1).

In addition to the variables described in Table A2.1, I used two additional measures of the quality of preexisting institutions: whether most people approved of the rules in place to resolve conflicts among community members (a measure of legitimacy); and whether most people tended to observe those rules (a measure of the efficacy). I coded these variables based on responses given to open-ended questions in the survey as well as in the memory workshop, which, together, provide rich details about the community. I then asked a research assistant to read all the material collected in the workshops and interviews and code the same variable using the same coding guidelines I used. Our measures were exactly the same in 89 percent of the cases for legitimacy and 91 percent of the cases for efficacy. In addition, these two measures are strongly correlated with the other four measures of institutional quality, which come from the survey. A Cronbach's alpha estimate (an estimate of internal consistency of scores) is 0.77.

The variable *indigenous* was built using the following procedure. I first created a measure of the minimum adjusted distance between each sampled community and each county head in the country (the main urban center of a municipality) that existed when the census was conducted in 1912. Using these data, I built a matrix of spatial distance as follows:

TABLE A2.1 *Coding of variables used in Chapter 5*

Variable	Survey question in Spanish	Survey question in English
Order	¿La gente conocía las normas de comportamiento que [el grupo armado] tenía para los combatientes? ¿Diría usted que la mayoría de la gente obedecía las normas que [grupo armado] estableció?	Did people in the community know the rules of conduct that [the armed group] had established for combatants to follow? Would you say that most people obeyed the rules established by [the armed group]?
Rebelocracy		
• Economic intervention	Diría usted que [el grupo armado]… – ¿Exigía contribuciones de comida o víveres? – ¿Regulaba la pesca, caza o extracción maderera? – ¿Decidía quién recibía subsidios del estado o del gobierno como madres comunitarias?	Would you say that [armed group]… – Demanded contribution of food or provisions? – Regulated fishing, hunting or wood extraction? – Decided who were to receive subsidies from the state or the government, like "community mothers"?
• Political intervention	Diría usted que [el grupo armado] influenció las elecciones… – ¿Diciendo por quién votar? – ¿Prohibiendo votar?	Would you say that [armed group] influenced elections by … – Telling people who to vote for? – Forbidding people to vote?
• Social intervention	¿[El grupo armado] puso normas sobre… – …sobre violencia domestica? – …comportamiento sexual, por ejemplo prostitución? – …imagen personal, como pelo largo, aretes o faldas?	Did [armed group] establish rules on … – …domestic violence? – …sexual behavior, for example prostitution? – …personal appearance, like …long hair, earrings or skirts?

(continued)

TABLE A2.1 (continued)

Variable	Survey question in Spanish	Survey question in English
• Public goods provision – infrastructure	Algunas veces los grupos armados logran mejoras en la infraestructura. Recuerda que [grupo armado] buscara mejoras… – Presionando a las autoridades – Organizando a la comunidad para que trabajara en las mejoras de manera voluntaria – Obligando a algunas personas de la comunidad a que hicieran las mejoras – El mismo GR haciendo las mejoras por ejemplo con su maquinaria o poniendo a sus combatientes a trabajar	Sometimes armed groups improve infrastructure. Do you remember that [armed group] tried to improve infrastructure by… – Pressuring the authorities – Organizing the community to work voluntarily – Forcing some community members to work – Working itself on improving infrastructure, for example, with its machinery or making its combatants work.
• Public goods provision – health	Recuerda que alguna vez GR interviniera en salud… – Pagando el salario al personal médico o dotaciones para el centro de salud – Ofreciendo los servicios de médicos o enfermeros del grupo a la comunidad	Do you remember [armed group] ever intervening in the provision of health services by… – Paying the salary of medical personnel or resources for the health center – Offering the services of doctors or nurses of the armed group to the community

(continued)

		– Pressuring the authorities
• Public goods provision – education	Recuerda que alguna vez GR interviniera en educación… – Pagando el salario a los maestros o útiles para la escuela – Poniendo un maestro en la escuela – Presionando a las autoridades	Do you remember [armed group] ever intervening in the provision of education by… – Paying the salary of teachers or resources for the school – Appointing a teacher for the school – Pressuring the authorities
Quality of preexisting institutions (all questions ask about one year prior to the arrival of the first non-state armed actor to the locality)	¿Diría que en esa época había reglas claras? ¿O cada uno hacía lo que quería? Ahora quisiera que hablemos sobre cómo se resolvían en esa época diferentes tipos de problemas en la comunidad. Si había un problema por linderos o por deudas… – ¿Diría usted que el problema se resolvía rápido? – ¿La gente sentía que esa manera de resolverlo era justa?	Would you say that back then there were clear rules, or did people do what they wanted? Now I would like to talk about how different kinds of problems in the community were solved at that time. If there was a conflict over land borders or debts… – Would you say that the problem was resolved quickly? – Did people feel that the way of solving it was just?
	¿Qué tan común era en esa época que la gente resolviera los problemas con la fuerza o violencia?	How common was it back then that people resolved conflicts using force or violence?

(continued)

TABLE A2.1 (continued)

Variable	Survey question in Spanish	Survey question in English
Indiscipline	¿Era común que si un combatiente desobedecía las normas sobre el trato a los civiles, fuera castigado?	If a combatant disobeyed his group's rules on treatment of civilians, was it common that he was punished?
State presence		
• Institutions	Quién diría usted que mandaba en esta localidad en esa época?	Who would you say ruled your community at that time?
• Armed forces	¿Había ejército presente en este municipio o los municipios vecinos?	Was the army present in this municipality or in nearby municipalities?
	Si había ejército, ¿en qué municipio y centro poblado estaba?	If so, in which municipality and locality was it present?

$$W_{ij} = X_{ij} / \sum_{j=1}^{n} X_{ij}$$

Where X_{ij} is the inverse of the adjusted distance between community i and the county head of municipality j, except when $i = j$, in which case X_{ij} equals zero. Matrix W is then multiplied by a vector containing the percentage of people who were indigenous in the municipalities in 1912. We thus obtain a measure of the potential influence of indigenous persons from other municipalities, depending on how distant they were:

$$\text{Potential indigenous}_i = W \times \textbf{indigenous}_{1912}$$

This approach builds on España and Sánchez (2010) and Diaz-Cayeros (2011).

CLUSTER ANALYSIS OF MEASURES OF REBELOCRACY

Since this typology was developed in 2009 (before collecting the data), the data can test whether this theoretical construct indeed captures "natural" groups. Using k-means cluster analysis we can calculate the Euclidean distance between observations on the basis of measures of the dimension the typology is trying to capture, to wit, armed groups' influence on local affairs. In other words, we can use an algorithm to find which cases are most similar to each other in terms of armed groups' intervention, therefore identifying two distinct sets or clusters.

To identify the clusters, I use different measures of armed groups' influence on local life including whether they offered dispute institutions, provided public goods, regulated legal or illegal economic activities, established rules over private conducts, and influenced political behavior. All variables are standardized to have values between 0 and 1. By graphing the mean of these variables by cluster, we get a sense of how similar is the intervention of armed groups across distinct dimensions within each cluster, and how different they are when compared to the other cluster. The graph shows that there is a strong positive correlation between all the different scores within each cluster, and a strong, negative correlation between all indexes across both clusters. This means that armed groups' intervention in local institutions tends to be either broad or narrow, regardless which spheres of local life we look at. The results are not sensitive to adding or dropping specific measures of armed groups' influence on local affairs, nor to changing the seed. These results suggest that this simple, minimalist typology

336   *Appendices*

successfully captures two very distinct types whose elements share many attributes.

STATISTICAL ANALYSIS

In this section I provide a more detailed discussion of the models estimated in Chapter 5, address potential issues, and present additional results.

Multilevel Models

As explained in Chapter 5, given that in some localities several armed groups were present at the same time – sometimes establishing different institutions – the unit of analysis is not the locality–year, but the locality–armed group–year. Structuring the data in this way allows for assessing what different armed groups did when operating at the same time in a given locality.

Observations are clustered by locality, armed group, municipality, and year. Observations within a given cluster are likely to share similarities, suggesting a lack of independence between them. For example, all observations on a given dyad over time may share similarities. Likewise, observations on dyads within a given locality, or on localities within a given municipality, are unlikely to be independent. In order to account for this clustering in the data, I use multilevel models, which account for variability in predictors and residuals across clusters and for sample imbalances (Gelman & Hill 2006; Rabe-Hesketh & Skrondal 2008).

I estimate four-level linear models where the first level is the occasion or measurement (i.e., the locality–armed group dyad in a given year); the second level is the locality–armed group dyad; the third level is the locality; and the fourth level is the municipality. Since observations on a given armed organization may be similar to each other, and observations on guerrillas and paramilitaries might also share similarities, I use fixed effects for the armed organization as well as for whether it is a guerrilla or paramilitary group.[5]

Multilevel models account for dependency across the error terms for observations in a given cluster by decomposing them in two parts: an observation-specific random shock and a cluster-specific shock. The models for each level are the following:

---

[5] For a similar formulation combining fixed and random effects, see Rabe-Hesketh and Skrondal (2008:436–438).

$$Y_{tglm} = \gamma_{glm} + B_1\chi_{tglm} + \zeta_1 Z_{t1} + \cdots + \zeta_{t-1} Z_{t-1} + e_{tglm} \quad (1)$$
$$\gamma_{glm} = \pi_{lm} + B_2\chi_{glm} + \delta_1\Sigma_{g1} + \cdots + \delta_{g-1}\Sigma_{g-1} + \tau\Lambda + u_{glm} \quad (2)$$
$$\pi_{lm} = \eta_m + B_3\chi_{lm} + v_{lm} \quad (3)$$
$$\eta_m = B_0 + B_4\chi_m + \gamma_m \quad (4)$$

The four-level model can be written in reduced form as follows:
$$\begin{aligned}Y_{tglm} = {} & B_0 + B_1\chi_{tglm} + B_2\chi_{glm} + B_3\chi_{lm} + B_4\chi_m + \zeta_1 Z_{t1} + \cdots \\ & + \zeta_{t-1} Z_{t-1} + \delta_1 \Sigma_{g1} + \cdots + \delta_{g-1}\Sigma_{g-1} + \tau\Lambda + u_{glm} \\ & + v_{lm} + \gamma_m + e_{tglm}\end{aligned} \quad (5)$$

where the dependent variable Y (order or rebelocracy) in year t, for the combination of armed group g and locality l, within municipality m, is explained by a set of fixed coefficients B, time-varying and time-invariant explanatory variables at the level of the armed group in that locality (χ_{glm}), the locality (χ_{lm}), and the municipality (χ_m); $t-1$ year fixed effects (Z) and their corresponding coefficients (ζ); $g-1$ fixed effects for the armed organization (Σ) and their corresponding coefficients (δ); and a dummy indicating whether the group is a paramilitary organization, as opposed to a guerrilla one (Λ), together with its coefficient (τ). The random part of the model is given by a residual term for each level, one for the armed group–locality dyad (u_{glm}), one for the locality (v_{lm}), and one for the municipality (γ_m), together with the level-1 residual term for each observation (e_{tglm}).

Number of Clusters

The asymptotic assumption of maximum likelihood methods in multilevel models requires the sample size to be sufficiently large. Both the number of clusters within each level and the sample size of each cluster are relevant. However, there is no consensus in the literature regarding the lower bounds for these sample sizes, with rules of thumb ranging from 8 or 10 to 30, 50, and even 100 groups (e.g., Afshartous 1995; Kreft & de Leeuw 1998; Rabe-Hesketh & Skrondal 2008; Austin 2010; Bryan and Jenkins 2016). Several studies find that there is very little bias in the estimates of both coefficients and standard errors for level-1 predictors (e.g., Van der Leeden et al. 1996; Maas & Hox 2004; Stegmueller 2013; Bryan and Jenkins 2016). However, sample sizes matter for level-2 predictors.

Recent studies that rely on simulations find that level-2 predictors are estimated with little bias when the number of clusters is higher than 20, 25 or 30, depending on the study (Bryan & Jenkins 2016; Stegmueller 2013:753–754; also Maas & Hox 2004:135). Since there are 124 armed group–locality dyads, 74 localities, and 29 municipalities, the results presented in Chapter 5 are unlikely to be affected by large bias. Nevertheless, as a robustness check, the central models were estimated using Bayesian analysis which, according to Stegmueller (2013:753), provide estimates for the level-2 predictors that are within 5 percent of the true population value (see also Finch et al. 2014:ch. 9). The posterior means obtained with Bayesian regression (using noninformative priors) support the conclusions obtained with the maximum likelihood estimates, with only one exception: the model where I indirectly test the mechanism, that is, the effect of prior resistance on rebelocracy. Given that this model can only be estimated on the observations corresponding to localities where armed actors had already operated in the past, the sample size is very small and the maximum likelihood results are not robust. However, the mechanism is tested in a more direct way in Chapter 7, combining the logic of natural experiments and process tracing. Chapter 6 presents additional qualitative evidence on several cases that supplement these tests.

The literature on dyadic analysis often recommends using cross-nested or cross-classified multilevel models (CCMLM), which take into account the kind of non-hierarchical clustering that is typical of dyads (Rabe-Hesketh & Skrondal 2008; Rasbash & Browne 2008:ch. 11; Gooty & Yammarino 2010). The data analyzed in this chapter exhibit such a structure because a given municipality can be home to different armed groups, while an armed group can be present in several municipalities. However, given that there are only about twenty armed groups belonging to ten organizations or federations, the sample size is too small to include a random effect for the armed group. As a robustness test, all models were estimated using CCMLM. The substantive results do not change.

Temporal Dynamics

As with any longitudinal data, time shocks and dynamic effects are a source of concern in this analysis. All models presented in Chapters 5 and 8 as well as in this appendix include year fixed effects. The models are robust to including a linear time trend as well as unit-specific time trends.

Statistical Analysis

Plots of the trajectories of order and rebelocracy for each dyad, locality, armed group, and municipality, suggest that there is no clear trend in the data. Plots of the residuals also fail to show any obvious trend. As a robustness check, I estimated bootstrapped standard errors using the bootMer function for multilevel models of the lme4 package in R, and the substantial results do not change. Given that there is no consensus in the literature regarding how bootstrapping should be done in multilevel models (Hox & van de Schoot 2013), in the tables and graphs I present the results of the models without bootstrapped standard errors.

Selection Bias

In Chapter 2, I defined order as the existence of stable rules that give rise to predictability; rebelocracy and aliocracy are defined on the basis of the scope of the armed actor in defining those *stable* rules. Based on this conceptualization, rebelocracy and aliocracy cannot exist under disorder. For this reason, I approach the question of whether order or disorder emerges as a separate question from whether order takes the form of aliocracy or rebelocracy, conditional on order having emerged. There are reasons to believe that there is not a problem of selection bias. To give an intuitive example, if we investigate the effect of a treatment for cancer we would only compare patients with cancer who received and did not receive treatment; we would not compare them to the general population. Given the complexity of multilevel models, estimating separately the determinants of order and the determinants of rebelocracy is a better strategy.

However, as a robustness check I estimated a multinomial model where each observation is classified as either disorder, rebelocracy, or aliocracy, using the dichotomous variables described in Chapter 6, and with standard errors clustered at the level of the municipality. The results do not change in any substantial way. Likewise, I estimate a linear model on rebelocracy using Heckman's correction for selection into order, again with standard errors clustered at the level of the municipality. The results are consistent with those presented in Chapter 5.

Missing Values

Overall, less than 3 percent of all observations have at least one missing value in any of the explanatory variables. The results presented in Chapter 5 use list-wise deletion. However, the results remain unchanged when I replicate the central models using ten datasets where missing values were multiply imputed.[6]

Sampling design

There is a large debate about whether sampling weights should be used in regression analysis in general, and in multilevel models in particular (e.g. Gelman 2007; Aitkin et al. 2009:112; Rabe-Hesketh & Skrondal 2008). The models presented in Chapters 5 and 8 do not include sampling weights. However, I estimated the same models with sampling weights for each stage (the municipality and the locality) and the results do not change in any substantive way.[7]

ADDITIONAL RESULTS OF THE STATISTICAL ANALYSIS

This section presents additional results of the statistical analysis discussed in Chapter 5. Table A2.2 shows the results of all the multilevel linear models on order.

Table A2.3 shows the results of the Bayesian multilevel models for order.
Table A2.4 presents the results of the multilevel models for rebelocracy.
Table A2.5. presents Bayesian multilevel models for rebelocracy.
Table A2.6 presents the instrumental variable estimation of the effect of high-quality institutions on rebelocracy.

---

[6] Missing values were imputed using the Amelia software in the R package.
[7] As explained before, the weights of the two samples were used to create new sampling weights using the Horvitz-Thompson approach (O'Muircheartaigh and Pedlow 2002).

TABLE A2.2 Linear multilevel models for order

		Dependent variable: Order (index)							
	(1)	(2)	(3)	(4)	(5)	(6)	(7)	(8)	(9)
Fixed portion									
Indiscipline									
Indiscipline	−1.299***		−1.339***	−1.373***	−1.359***	−1.374***			
	(0.087)		(0.077)	(0.078)	(0.07)	(0.078)			
Lag_indiscipline							−0.951***		
							(0.090)		
Indiscipline_dev_mean								−1.331***	−1.354***
								(0.078)	(0.077)
Indiscipline_mean								−0.397	−0.317
								(2.085)	(1.972)
Competition									
Competition		−0.414***	−0.546***	−0.547***	−0.529***	−0.538***			
		(0.102)	(0.024)	(0.024)	(0.025)	(0.0268)			
Lag_competition							−0.388***		
							(0.031)		
Competition_dev_mean								−0.545***	−0.545***
								(0.024)	(0.024)
Competition_mean								−0.887	−1.504***
								(0.454)	(0.436)

(continued)

TABLE A2.2 (continued)

		(1)	(2)	(3)	(4)	(5)	(6)	(7)	(8)	(9)
						Dependent variable: Order (index)				
Institutions & Strategic	High-quality institutions & Strategic					0.044				
						(0.041)				
	High-quality institutions					-0.164				
						(0.141)				
	Strategic				0.008	-0.00561				
					(0.025)	(0.0300)				
Resources	Resources						-0.010			
							(0.028)			
	Resources & Competition						-0.046			
							(0.046)			
	Paramilitaries	0.836	0.450	0.432	0.352	0.437	0.48	0.487	0.734	0.648
		(0.407)	(0.262)	(0.396)	(0.384)	(0.407)	(0.385)	(0.379)	(0.623)	(0.588)
Controls	Altitude				0.000**	0.000**	0.000**	0.000*		
					(0.000)	(0.000)	(0.000)	(0.000)		
	Altitude_mean									0.000***
										(0.000)
	Cabecera				0.125	0.055	0.131	-0.018		
					(0.126)	(0.137)	(0.127)	(0.125)		

(continued)

Cabecera_mean									0.509
									(0.279)
(Intercept)	2.411***	1.647***	2.435***	2.306***	2.409***	2.331***	2.099***	2.067*	1.840*
	(0.375)	(0.236)	(0.362)	(0.346)	(0.363)	(0.347)	(0.347)	(0.907)	(0.859)
Random portion (variance)									
Municipality	0.0471***	0.173***	0.0470***	0.019**	0.009	0.020**	0.042***	0.043***	0.00891
	(0.039)	(0.046)	(0.037)	(0.029)	(0.026)	(0.029)	(0.036)	(0.036)	(0.0257)
Locality	0.0626**	0.000***	0.0577***	0.055***	0.051**	0.057***	0.059***	0.054**	0.0573***
	(0.053)	(0.000)	(0.050)	(0.048)	(0.052)	(0.049)	(0.045)	(0.050)	(0.0489)
Dyad	0.257***	0.300***	0.247***	0.246***	0.251***	0.244***	0.199***	0.249***	0.243***
	(0.055)	(0.038)	(0.052)	(0.052)	(0.058)	(0.056)	(0.045)	(0.053)	(0.051)
Armed organization fixed-effects	Yes	Yes	Yes	Yes	Yes	Yes	Yes	Yes	Yes
Year fixed effects	Yes	Yes	Yes	Yes	Yes	Yes	Yes	Yes	Yes
Observations	1221	1248	1221	1221	1165	1221	1104	1221	1221

Note: *p<0.05; **p<0.01; ***p<0.001
Standard errors in parentheses.

TABLE A2.3 Bayesian multilevel models for order

	(1)	(2)	(3)	(4)	(5)	(6)	(7)	(8)	(9)
Indiscipline									
Indiscipline	-1.34*** (-1.55; -1.14)		-1.41*** (-1.601; -1.232)	-1.43*** (-1.622; -1.25)	-1.44*** (-1.60; -1.23)	-1.44*** (-1.59; -1.26)			
Lag_indiscipline							-0.944*** (-1.177; -0.737)		
Indiscipline_dev_mean								-1.40*** (-1.57; -1.22)	-1.43*** (-1.60; -1.25)
Indiscipline_mean								-0.71 (-5.45; 4.670)	-0.66 (-5.72; 3.948)
Competition									
Competition		-0.54*** (-0.60; -0.49)	-0.543*** (-0.591; -0.494)	-0.54*** (-0.59; -0.48)	-0.542*** (-0.589; -0.490)	-0.53*** (-0.58; -0.47)			
Lag_competition							-0.392*** (-0.459; -0.334)		
Competition_dev_mean								-0.54*** (-0.58; -0.48)	-0.54*** (-0.59; -0.48)
Competition_mean								-0.89* (-1.72; -0.07)	-1.48** (-2.40; -0.57)

(continued)

		(1)	(2)	(3)	(4)	(5)	(6)	(7)	(8)	(9)
Institution & Strategic	High-quality institutions & Strategic					0.046 (−0.02; 0.134)	0.000 (−0.06; 0.053)			
	High-quality institutions					−0.16 (−0.47; 0.082)				
	Strategic				0.029 (−0.02; 0.082)	0.014 (−0.051; −0.066)				
Resources	Resources						−0.05 (−0.15; 0.034)			
	Resources & Competition						−0.06 (−0.15; 0.06)			
	paramilitaries	0.547 (−0.362; 1.538)	1.088* (0.188; 2.061)	0.558 (0.374; 1.429)	0.46 (−0.370; 1.298)	0.344 (−0.52; 1.271)	0.471 (−0.37; 1.322)	0.786* (0.0017; 1.521)	0.919 (−0.38; 2.359)	0.639 (−0.49; 2.055)
Controls	Altitude				0.000*** (−0.02; 0.084)	−0.0002*** (0.000; 0.000)	0.000*** (0.000; 0.000)	0.000*** (0.000; 0.000)		
	Altitude_mean									0.000*** (0.000; 0.000)

(continued)

TABLE A2.3 (continued)

	(1)	(2)	(3)	(4)	(5)	(6)	(7)	(8)	(9)
Cabecera				0.095 (−0.21; 0.371)	0.0733 (−0.216; 0.388)	0.104 (−0.17; 0.389)	−0.009 (−0.278; 0.268)		
Cabecera_mean								2.018 (0.167; 4.110)	0.598* (0.055; 1.252)
(Intercept)	2.339*** (1.527; 3.245)	1.393*** (0.598; 2.197)	2.440*** (1.362; 3.191)	2.274*** (1.577; 3.014)	2.432 (1.555; 3.199)	2.281*** (1.526; 3.039)	1.944 (1.271; 2.638)	2.018 (0.167; 4.110)	1.963 (−0.039; 3.974)
Armed organization fixed-effects	Yes	Yes	Yes	Yes	Yes	Yes	Yes	Yes	Yes
Year fixed effects	Yes	Yes	Yes	Yes	Yes	Yes	Yes	Yes	Yes
Observations	1000	1000	1000	1000	1000	1000	1000	1000	1000

Note: Uninformative priors used; table shows posterior means first and 95 percent confidence intervals in parentheses.
*p<0.05, **p<0.01, ***p<0.001.

TABLE A2.4 *Multilevel linear models for rebelocracy*

	Dependent variable: Rebelocracy (index)					
	M1	M2	M3	M4	M5	M6
Fixed portion						
High-quality institutions	−4.171***	−3.954***			−3.799***	
	(0.784)	(0.787)			(0.785)	
State ruled			2.053**	2.097**		
			(0.770)	(0.718)		
High-quality institutions & Strategic					−0.391**	
					(0.132)	
Strategic		0.296***		0.289***	0.431***	−0.0534
		(0.087)		(0.083)	(0.098)	(0.075)
Lagged resistance						−1.165***
						(0.130)
Paramilitaries	5.791	6.115	3.988	4.712	6.033	7.655***
	(3.297)	(3.280)	(3.367)	(3.388)	(3.268)	(0.537)
Altitude		−0.000		−0.000	−0.000	0.000
		(0.000)		(0.000)	(0.000)	(0.000)
Cabecera		1.457		2.138**	1.443	1.826
		(0.760)		(0.750)	(0.757)	(1.389)
(Intercept)	3.895	2.922	3.224	1.451	2.925	1.401
	(3.052)	(3.220)	(3.187)	(3.323)	(3.208)	(1.265)

(continued)

TABLE A2.4 (continued)

	Dependent variable: Rebelocracy (index)					
	M1	M2	M3	M4	M5	M6
Random portion (variance)						
Municipality	0.938	0.803	0.000***	0.000**	0.751	1.832
	(1.251)	(1.684)	(0.000)	(0.000)	(1.296)	(3.277)
Locality	0.000***	0.000**	2.544	1.103	0.000***	10.97***
	(0.000)	(0.000)	(1.966)	(1.750)	(0.000)	(4.071)
Dyad	8.173***	7.725***	7.917***	8.379***	7.704***	0.0428***
	(1.554)	(2.773)	(2.390)	(2.000)	(1.591)	(0.0348)
Armed organization fixed-effects						
Year fixed effects						
Observations	963	963	1010	1010	963	212
t-statistics in parentheses						

Note: *p<0.05; **p<0.01; ***p<0.001
Standard errors in parentheses.

TABLE A2.5 *Bayesian multilevel models for rebelocracy*

	M1	M2	M3	M4	M5	M6
High-quality institutions	-4.23***	-4.09***			-3.99***	
	(-5.86; -2.39)	(-5.81; -2.38)			(-5.75; -2.43)	
State ruled			2.31**	2.43***		
			(0.453; 4.030)	(0.783; 4.222)		
High-quality institutions & Strategic					-0.39***	
					(-0.63; -0.10)	
Strategic		0.32***		0.32***	0.44***	-0.02
		(0.146; 0.507)		(0.134; 0.489)	(0.237; 0.641)	(-0.24; 0.177)
Lagged resistance						0.77
						(-0.62; 2.137)
Paramilitaries	3.44	3.50	5.94	5.28	3.57	-0.23
	(-4.33; 10.16)	(-3.31; 11.03)	(-0.96; 13.58)	(-3.01; 12.17)	(-4.04; 10.06)	(-8.77; 7.031)
Altitude		-0.00	-0.000	-0.000	-0.000	0.00
		(-0.00; 0.000)	(-0.00; -0.000)	(-0.00; -0.000)	(-0.00; -0.000)	(-0.00; 0.001)
Cabecera		1.33		2.26**	1.34	0.12
		(-0.47; 3.013)		(0.525; 4.128)	(-0.39; 3.018)	(-3.23; 3.747)
(Intercept)	6.18	5.64	1.86	1.44	5.49*	9.43*
	(-0.27; 12.89)	(-1.03; 11.98)	(-4.83; 8.457)	(-4.93; 8.347)	(-1.09; 12.13)	(1.928; 16.84)
Observations	951	951	951	951	951	185

Note: Uninformative priors used. Table shows posterior means first and 95 percent confidence intervals in parentheses.
* p<0.05; ** p<0.01; *** p<0.001

TABLE A2.6 *Multilevel linear models for rebelocracy using an instrumental variable*

	Second-stage
Fixed portion	
High-quality institutions (instrumented)	−3.53**
	1.28
Collective land	0.18
	(1.43)
Paramilitaries	6.33
	(3.85)
Strategic	0.29***
	(0.09)
Altitude	−0.00
	(0.00)
Cabecera	1.88
	(0.90)
Intercept	3.78
	(2.63)
Random portion	
Municipality	1.54
	(1.24)
Locality	0.00
	(0.00)
Dyad	10.41***
	(3.21)
Observations	963
Armed organization fixed effects	Yes
Year fixed effects	Yes
	First-stage
Fixed portion	
Indigenous	9.45
	(5.9)
Collective land	−0.43***
	(0.007)
Paramilitaries	0.002
	(0.04)
Strategic	−0.001
	(0.026)
Altitude	0.00
	(0.00)

(continued)

TABLE A2.6 (continued)

Cabecera	0.008
	(0.002)
Intercept	0.17
	(0.18)
Random portion	
Municipality	0.230
	(0.48)
Observations	963
Armed organization fixed effects	Yes
Year fixed effects	Yes

Note: Standard errors in parentheses. The standard errors for the second stage are estimated with the multilevel bootstrapping function of the lme4 package in R.
* p<0.05 ** p<0.01 *** p<0.001

ADDITIONAL EVIDENCE TO SUPPORT THE RELEVANCE OF THE INSTRUMENTAL VARIABLE

Chapter 5 used the potential influence of indigenous communities after the 1910s on the sampled communities as an instrument of high-quality institutions. In this section I provide additional evidence to support the relevance of the instrument. I describe how a Nasa community – the Nasa is one of the largest indigenous groups in Colombia – embarked in a process to recover their autonomy, cultivate their norms, and strengthen their institutions, and how that in turn enabled astonishing forms of risky collective action.[8] I rely on primary and secondary data, as well as on interviews conducted by my research team within the study of a sample of municipalities in 2006.

Located in the southwest of the country, Cauca is home to approximately half of Colombia's indigenous population. After building a strong, ethnic-based movement, the indigenous communities of the region consolidated a system of local governance widely supported by their members (Troyan 2008). The core of this movement was the Regional Indian Council of Cauca (CRIC), which was created in 1971 and represented the majority of Cauca's indigenous population, most of whom belong to the Nasa and Guambianos ethnic groups. The movement sought to recover and defend indigenous land, strengthen the *cabildos* (autonomous village councils),

---
[8] Part of this material was previously published in Arjona (2015).

ensure the implementation of indigenous laws, preserve indigenous culture, and train teachers in order to ensure education according to their culture and language (Sandoval 2008:42). The organization's impressive record of land recovery and formal political organization testify to its success: according to a renowned Nasa leader, "in the 1960s we had six *cabildos* and 200 hectares [of land]; today we have 122 *cabildos* and 570,000 hectares" (Verdad Abierta 2014).[9] The territory is divided into *resguardos* – major areas in which the indigenous communities have inalienable collective land ownership and the right to manage political and administrative affairs. In Cauca, the *cabildos*' laws are generally supported and valued as an essential part of the indigenous culture. Community members enthusiastically obey their *cabildo*'s decisions, even when they entail high risk, as will be shown later in the chapter.

Cauca has endured the presence of several armed actors over the years, especially the FARC. The indigenous movement has publicly rejected the presence of all state and non-state armed actors in their territory, as well as their attempts at social control and recruitment of indigenous peoples, and demanded respect for their culture and territories (Caviedes 2007:92). Despite being persecuted and victimized, these communities have sustained their resistance and mobilized against threats to their self-governance (Caviedes 2007; Rappaport 2007; Sandoval Forero 2008). Recently, they expelled FARC members as well as soldiers of the Colombian army from their territories, leading to tensions with both the government and insurgents (*El Tiempo* 2012).

The case of Toribío, a *resguardo* that is part of the CRIC, illustrates how legitimate and effective institutions developed by indigenous communities have allowed civilians to defy armed groups' rule and violence. According to our interviewees, the FARC arrived in Toribío in the early 1980s. In those early years, there was constant tension between the FARC and the community, but the *Cabildo* remained the undisputed authority among most residents. The FARC attempted to rule local life extensively, establishing rules over many spheres of life. Yet, the population disobeyed many of the group's rules. As an interviewee explained, "They [the FARC] imposed norms ... but civil society didn't really follow their rules. So, over time, the rules disappeared" (interview with local resident 2006).

Although the Nasa and the FARC share a long history of conflict, the tension between them reached its peak in the 2000s when Cauca became

---

[9] Sources differ regarding the number of hectares that the CRIC has recovered in their struggle. See for example (Hristov 2005:99; CRIC 2007:64).

highly strategic for the warring sides. In 2005, an analyst stated bluntly, "that who dominates the Colombian Massif [where Toribío is located] will determine the course of the war" (FIP 2005:28). As the FARC fought intensely to control the area, attacks against Toribío became more frequent. At the same time, the rebels intensified their efforts to subdue the population, trying to "impose their norms over those of the authorities of the *resguardo*" (Neiva 2009). Yet, the indigenous movement still did not give in. As a Nasa leader put it, "[the FARC] want to rule in our territory and we don't let them" (ibid.). Several events illustrate the kinds of risks that such resistance has entailed, and the strong collective action the community has maintained.

In 2004, Vitonás Noscué, the mayor of Toribío and a prominent indigenous leader, traveled to the department of Caquetá, in the south of the country. On his way back to Cauca, a FARC commander stopped him: "Why haven't you quit your post as mayor since we, the FARC, gave the order that all mayors quit?" Noscué replied: "Precisely for that reason. Because you do not give us orders. You are wrong because you were not the ones who elected us, it was the community and it is the community we obey." The commander decided to kidnap the mayor, who assured the guerrilla that the Indigenous Guard would soon rescue him (Neira 2005).

The Indigenous Guard is a nonviolent, civil defense organization created in 2001 by indigenous peoples in Cauca to protect their communities from armed actors. Community members of all kinds – men, women, teenagers, and elders – have volunteered to join the Guard. It is supervised by the *cabildo* and has about 6,000 members. It has alerted communities when armed actors were present, recovered bodies, and rescued kidnap victims (Ballvé 2006). After Noscué was kidnapped, about 400 members of the Guard scoured the mountains until they found the FARC and Noscué. Armed only with their ceremonial canes that symbolized the authority of the Guard, they surrounded the FARC and demanded the immediate release of Noscué. The FARC had no choice: killing 400 people would have been too politically costly, and it would have probably triggered a draconian response from the state.[10] They let Noscué go (Neira 2005).

---

[10] To illustrate, one of the largest attacks by the FARC killed 119 civilians in a rural area in the Chocó department in 2002. This event received massive attention by the media, political groups, NGOs, and international actors. The reputational effects of the attack were clearly large. The José María Córdoba bloc, the FARC unit responsible for the attack, made a public statement lamenting the event.

In 2009, the FARC's Sixth Front issued a death threat to three Nasa leaders in a pamphlet. The *cabildo* ordered the Indigenous Guard to make night rounds and alert everyone in the territory. A few months later, the FARC extended its warnings to all authorities of the *cabildo* as well as public servants in Toribío. The *cabildo* responded by calling for an extraordinary general assembly, which decided to prohibit the threatened individuals from quitting their posts and assigned each of them ten members of the Indigenous Guard as bodyguards (again only armed with their ceremonial canes). It also forbade parties and closed bars in order to reduce the likelihood of massacres. The *cabildo*'s governor summarizes their position bluntly: "they may kill one; they may kill two ... they may kill a hundred. But they won't kill us all" (Neiva 2009).

As of 2015, this community still carries on its struggle. During 2013, it publicly demanded all armed actors, including the national army, to abandon its territory. In July of 2013, after the army decided not to leave, at least 1,000 community members got together to physically remove the soldiers from their territory (León 2013). In 2014, the FARC killed Nasa leaders in Toribío. The delegation that was negotiating peace with the government in Cuba issued a public declaration offering apologies to the community (FARC 2014).

The astonishing levels of collective action of the community of Toribío, and its effect on resisting state and non-state armed actors, illustrates the relevance of the instrumental variable used in Chapter 5. In addition, it offers additional evidence to support the central contention of this book: that the quality of local institutions has radical effects on the ways in which civilian populations interact with armed actors.

Appendix 3
Supplementary Materials for Chapter 6

Table A3.1. presents strategic territory in documented cases of collective civilian resistance.

TABLE A3.1 *Sources on civilian resistance*[11]

Source	Name of community or organization	Strategic territory	Year when resistance started
Rueda (2003)	Association of Peasant Workers of Craré	Yes	1987
	Aguachica	Yes	1995
	San José de Apartadó and San Francisco de Asís	Yes	1996
	Pensilvania Alliance Alive Community	Yes	1997
Wabgou (2007)	Nasa indigenous community	Yes	1970s
Ramírez (2004a)	Peasant coca gatherers of Putumayo, Municipal Council of Rural Development, and ANUC putumayo	Yes	1996

(continued)

---

[11] This table includes sources published prior to 2010. There have been many other case studies and reports published since then. This exercise does not aim to be exhaustive. It is a plausibility test of the hypothesis according to which resistance tends to arise when negotiations fail between armed actors and communities in highly strategic territories.

TABLE A3.1 *(continued)*

Source	Name of community or organization	Strategic territory	Year when resistance started
Ramírez (2004b)	Coca gatherers (cocaleros) and Civic Movement for Integral Development of Putumayo	Yes	1996
Ramírez (2004b)	Putumayo	Yes	N. A.
Sección de Vida, Justicia y Paz (2002)	Several organizations including OREWA, Asociación Campesina Integral del Atrato (ACIA), Organización Campesina del Bajo Atrato (OCABA), and Asociación de Campesinos de Riosucio (ACAMURI), among others.	Yes	1997
Uribe (2004)	San José de Aparatadó	Yes	1996
Ferro & Uribe (2002)	Coca gatherers (cocaleros)	Yes	N. A.
Romero (2004)	SINTRAGRO and SINTRABANANO (unions)	Yes	1980s
Arenas (2004)	U'WA indigenous community	Yes	1993
CAVIDA (2002)	Afro-Colombian and Indigenous communities of the Cacarica region	Yes	N. A.
León (2004)	Caldono	Yes	N. A.
	Bolívar	Yes	N. A.
	Jambaló	Yes	N. A.
	Puracé	Yes	2001
Mitchell & Ramírez (2009)	Samaniego	Yes	1997
	Tarso	Yes	1997
	Sonsón	Yes	2001
Roldán (2009)	East Antioquia (Oriente Antioqueño)	Yes	2001
Esquivia & Gerlach (2009)	Montes de María	Yes	N. A.
Rojas (2008)	Afro-Pacific communities	N. A.	N. A.

Appendix 4
Supplemental Materials for Chapter 8

Chapter 8 uses the same dataset used in Chapter 5. However, in order to control for the factors that allow an armed group to successfully control a locality, the models are estimated only on observations on localities controlled by a single armed group. Since there is only one dyad in every locality–year, in Chapter 8 I estimate a three-level model (without the dyad as a level). The models for each level are the following:

$$Y_{tlm} = \gamma_{lm} + B_1 \chi_{tlm} + \zeta_1 Z_{t1} + \cdots + \zeta_{t-1} Z_{t-1} + e_{tlm} \quad (1)$$

$$\gamma_{lm} = \eta_m + B_2 \chi_{lm} + \delta_1 \Sigma_{g1} + \cdots + \delta_{g-1} \Sigma_{g-1} + \tau \Lambda + v_{lm} \quad (2)$$

$$\eta_m = B_0 + B_3 \chi_m + \gamma_m \quad (3)$$

The three-level model can be written in reduced form as follows:

$$\begin{aligned} Y_{tlm} =\ & B_0 + B_1 \chi_{tlm} + B_2 \chi_{lm} + B_3 \chi_m + \zeta_1 Z_{t1} + \cdots \\ & + \zeta_{t-1} Z_{t-1} + \delta_1 \Sigma_{g1} + \cdots + \delta_{g-1} \Sigma_{g-1} + \tau \Lambda \\ & + v_{lm} + \gamma_m + e_{tlm} \end{aligned} \quad (4)$$

Where the dependent variable Y (order or rebelocracy) in year t, locality l, within municipality m, is explained by a set of fixed coefficients B, time-varying and time-invariant explanatory variables at the level of the locality (χ_l), and the municipality (χ_m); $t-1$ year fixed effects (Z) and their corresponding coefficients (ζ); $g-1$ fixed effects for the armed organization (Σ) and their corresponding coefficients (δ); and a dummy indicating whether the group is a paramilitary organization, as opposed to a guerrilla one (Λ), together with its coefficient (τ). The random part of the model is given by a residual term for each level: one for the locality (v_{lm}), and one for the municipality (γ_m), together with the level-1 residual term for each observation (e_{tlm}).

There are only forty-eight observations with missing values. However, I estimated the models with ten datasets where missing values were imputed and the results are consistent.[12] The results are also robust to a linear time trend and to unit-specific time trends. For a discussion of model specification, see Chapter 5 and Appendix 2.

Table A4.1 presents the results of the linear multilevel models for recruitment.

TABLE A4.1 *Multilevel linear models for recruitment*

	Dependent variable: Recruitment			
	M1	M2	M3	M4
Fixed portion				
Rebelocracy	0.038***	0.038***		
	(0.002)	(0.002)		
Rebelocracy dev_mean			0.048***	0.039***
			(0.003)	(0.003)
Rebelocracy mean			0.023***	0.050***
			(0.004)	(0.004)
Paramilitaries	0.015	−0.109	0.190	0.145
	(0.109)	(0.106)	(0.113)	(0.095)
Resources		−0.0407*		−0.000377
		(0.0162)		(0.0139)
Resources mean				−0.154**
				(0.0590)
Paved		−0.0837**		0.0187
		(0.0291)		(0.0255)
Paved mean				−0.383**
				(0.0616)
State		−0.0408**		−0.0516***
		(0.0124)		(0.0108)
State mean				−0.174***
				(0.0213)
Ideology		−0.0728***		−0.0505
		(0.0208)		(0.0260)

(continued)

---

[12] I used the R package Amelia to perform the multiple imputation.

TABLE A4.1 (continued)

	Dependent variable: Recruitment			
	M1	M2	M3	M4
Ideology mean				−0.121***
				(0.0330)
Massacres		0.00361		−0.00214
		(0.0135)		(0.0111)
Massacres mean				0.00104
				(0.120)
Cabecera		0.0841		0.238
		(0.119)		(0.128)
Cabecera mean				−0.739***
				(0.0644)
Altitude		0.000		0.000
		(0.000)		(0.000)
Altitude mean				0.000
				(0.000)
(Intercept)	0.377**	0.542***	0.364**	1.064**
	(0.127)	(0.150)	(0.126)	(0.172)
Random portion (variance)				
Municipality	0.0326***	0.0465***	0.0380***	0.116***
	(0.026)	(0.031)	(0.027)	(0.058)
Locality	0.172***	0.168***	0.165***	0.183***
	(0.035)	(0.035)	(0.033)	(0.040)
Armed organization fixed-effects	Yes	Yes	Yes	Yes
Year fixed effects	Yes	Yes	Yes	Yes
Observations	1008	994	1008	994

Note: standard errors in parentheses.
*$p<0.05$
**$p<0.01$
***$p<0.001$

TABLE A4.2 *Linear multilevel models for recruitment (aggregate data at the dyad level)*

	(1)	(2)
Rebelocracy	0.067***	0.073***
	(6.01)	(6.70)
Paramilitaries	−0.174	−0.115
	(−1.96)	(−1.12)
Resources		−0.154
		(−1.12)
Paved		0.160
		(1.51)
State		−0.0575
		(−1.44)
Ideology		−0.0408
		(−0.48)
Massacre		0.0359
		(0.21)
Cabecera		0.0751
		(0.66)
Altitude		0.000
		(0.87)
Constant	0.034	−0.0414
	(0.54)	(−0.36)
Observations	109	106

Standard errors in parentheses.
Clustered standard errors at the municipality level
* $p<0.05$
** $p<0.01$
*** $p<0.001$

References

Abel, Richard L., 1974. "A Comparative Theory of Dispute Institutions in Society." *Law & Society Review*, 8(2), pp. 217–347.
Acemoglu, Daron, Robinson, James A., & Santos, Rafael J., 2013. "The Monopoly of Violence: Evidence from Colombia." *Journal of the European Economic Association*, 11(s1), pp. 5–44.
Acemoglu, Daron, Vindigni, Andrea, & Ticchi, Davide, 2010. "Persistence of Civil Wars." *Journal of the European Economic Association*, 8(2–3), pp. 664–676.
Acero, Luis Enrique, 2007. *Viota, Un Paraiso en los Andes Colombianos*. Bogotá: Corcas Editores.
Acker, Frank Van, 2004. "Uganda and the Lord's Resistance Army: The New Order No One Ordered." *African Affairs*, 103(412), pp. 335–357.
Ackerman, Robert M., 2002. "Disputing Together: Conflict Resolution and the Search for Community." *Ohio State Journal on Dispute Resolution*, 18, p. 27.
Adler, Paul S. & Kwon, Seok-Woo, 2009. "Social Capital: The Good, the Bad, and the Ugly." In Eric Lesser, ed. *Knowledge and social capital*. Woburn: Routledge.
Afshartous, David. "Determination of Sample Size for Multilevel Model Design." *Department of Statistics Papers, UCLA*.
Aguilera, Mario, 2001. "Justicia guerrillera y población civil 1964–1999." In B. de S. Santos & M. García Villegas, eds. *El Caleidoscopio de las Justicias en Colombia*. Bogotá: Siglo del Hombre Editores.
Aguilera, Mario, 2006. "ELN: Entre las armas y la política." In F. Gutiérrez Sanín, ed. *Nuestra Guerra Sin Nombre. Transformaciones del conflicto armado en Colombia*. Bogotá: Norma.
Aguilera, Mario, 2013. *Guerrilla y Población Civil. Trayectoria de las FARC 1949–2013*. Bogotá: Imprenta Nacional.
Ahmed, Azam, 2015. "Taliban Justice Gains Favor as Official Afghan Courts Fail." *New York Times*, 1 February 2015, p. A1.
Aitkin, Murray, Brian Francis and John Hinde and Ross Darnell, 2009. *Statistical modelling in R*. Oxford: Oxford University Press.

Albertus, Michael & Kaplan, Oliver, 2013. "Land Reform as a Counterinsurgency Policy Evidence from Colombia." *Journal of Conflict Resolution*, 57(2), pp. 198–231.

AnanthPur, Kripa, 2004. "Rivalry or Synergy?: Formal and Informal Local Governance in Rural India." *Development and Change*, 38(3) pp. 401–421.

Anderson, David, 2005. *Histories of the Hanged: The Dirty War in Kenya and the End of Empire*. New York: W.W. Norton.

Appleby, Joyce Oldham, Cheng, Eileen K., & Goodwin, Joanne L., 2001. *Encyclopedia of Women in American History*. Armonk, NY: Sharpe Reference.

Archila Neira, Mauricio, 1997. "El Frente Nacional: una historia de enemistad social." *Anuario Colombiano de Historia Social y de la Cultura*, 24, pp. 189–215.

Arenas, Luís Carlos, 2004. "La lucha contra la explotación petrolera en territorio U'wa: Estudio de caso de una lucha local que se globolizó." In Boaventura De Sousa Santos & Mauricio García Villegas, eds. *Emancipación social y violencia en Colombia*. Bogotá: Editorial Norma.

Arias, Enrique Desmond, 2006. *Drugs and Democracy in Rio de Janeiro: Trafficking, Social Networks, and Public Security*. Chapel Hill: University of North Carolina Press.

Arjona, Ana, 2008. "Armed Groups' Governance in Civil War: A Synthesis." Literature review commissioned by the Program on States and Security. Available at http://conflictfieldresearch.colgate.edu/wp-content/uploads/2015/05/Arjona.FINAL_.9.29.pdf [accessed January 5, 2016].

Arjona, Ana, 2009. "One National War, Multiple Local Orders: An Inquiry into the Unit of Analysis of War and Post-war Interventions." In P. Kalmanovitz & M. Bergsmo, eds. *Law in Peace Negotiations*. Oslo: Torkel Opsahl Academic EPublisher, pp. 199–242.

Arjona, Ana. 2014. "Wartime Institutions: A Research Agenda." *Journal of Conflict Resolution*, 58(8), pp. 1360–1389.

Arjona, Ana, 2015. "Civilian Resistance to Rebel Governance." In Ana Arjona, Zachariah Mampilly, & Nelson Kasfir, eds. *Rebel Governance in Civil War*. New York: Cambridge University Press.

Arjona, Ana, 2016a. "Civilians' Choices in Conflict Zones." Unpublished manuscript.

Arjona, Ana, 2016b. "Process-Driven Natural Experiments." Unpublished manuscript.

Arjona, Ana, 2016c. "State Capacity and the Prevention of Rebel and Criminal Governance: Beyond "Hearts and Minds." Under review.

Arjona, Ana, 2016d. "Institutions, Civilian Resistance and Wartime Social Order: A Process-Driven Natural Experiment in the Colombian Civil War." *Latin American Politics and Society*, 58(3), pp. 99–122.

Arjona, Ana, 2016e. "Recruitment in Civil War: An Institutionalist Approach". Under review.

Arjona, Ana & Kalyvas, Stathis, 2007. "Rebelling Against Rebellion: Comparing Insurgent and Counterinsurgent Recruitment." Presented at the Annual Meeting of the International Studies Association in Chicago.

Arjona, Ana & Kalyvas, Stathis, 2008. "Una Aproximación Micro al Conflicto Armado en Colombia: Resultados de una Encuesta a Desmovilizados de

Guerrillas y Grupos Paramilitares." In Freddy Cante, ed. *Argumentación, Negociación y Acuerdos*. Bogotá: Universidad del Rosario.

Arjona, Ana & Kalyvas, Stathis N., 2011. "Recruitment into Armed Groups in Colombia: A Survey of Demobilized Fighters." In Y. Guichaoua, ed. *Understanding Collective Political Violence*. London: Palgrave Macmillan, pp. 143–174.

Arjona, Ana, Kasfir, Nelson, & Mampilly, Zachariah, 2015. *Rebel Governance in Civil War*. New York: Cambridge University Press.

Austin, Peter, 2010. "Estimating multilevel logistic regression models when the number of clusters is low: a comparison of different statistical software procedures." *The international journal of biostatistics* (6) 1:1–18.

Autesserre, Séverine, 2009. "Hobbes and the Congo: Frames, Local Violence, and International Intervention." *International Organization*, 63(02), pp. 249–280.

Avila, Ariel, 2012. "De la Para-política a la Farc-política hay mucho trecho. Corporación Nuevo Arco Irirs." Available at www.arcoiris.com.co/2012/07/de-la-para-politica-a-la-farc-politica-hay-mucho-trecho/ [accessed on March 14, 2013].

Avila, Ariel, 2014. "Herederos de la parapolítica y personajes con vínculos con fuerzas ilegales con puesto en el Congreso." *Las 2 Orillas*. Available at www.las2orillas.co/herederos-de-la-parapolitica-y-con-vinculos-con-fuerzas-ilegales-tiene-puesto-en-el-congreso/ [accessed on January 20, 2015].

Baczko, Adam, 2013. "Judging in the Midst of Civil War." *Politix* 4.104: 25–46.

Balcells, Laia, 2010. "Rivalry and Revenge: Violence Against Civilians in Conventional Civil Wars." *International Studies Quarterly*, 54(2), pp. 291–313.

Balcells, Laia, 2017. *Rivalry and Revenge: The Politics of Violence in Civil War*. Forthcoming: Cambridge University Press.

Balcells, Laia & Justino, Patricia, 2014. "Bridging Micro and Macro Approaches on Civil Wars and Political Violence Issues, Challenges, and the Way Forward." *Journal of Conflict Resolution*, 58(8), pp. 1343–1349.

Ballvé, Teo, 2006. "Colombia's Women Warriors for Peace." *NACLA News*. Available at: https://nacla.org/news/colombias-women-warriors-peace.

Bangura, Yusuf, 2000. "Strategic Policy Failure and Governance in Sierra Leone." *The Journal of Modern African Studies*, 38(04), pp. 551–577.

Barnabas, B. & Zwi, A., 1997. "Health Policy Development in Wartime: Establishing the Baito Health System in Tigray, Ethiopia." *Health Policy Plan*, 12(1), pp. 38–49.

Barter, Shane, 2015. "The Rebel State in Society: Governance and Accommodation in Aceh, Indonesia." In A. Arjona, N. Kasfir, & Z. Mampilly, eds. *Rebel Governance in Civil War*. Cambridge University Press.

Barter, Shane Joshua, 2012. "Unarmed Forces: Civilian Strategy in Violent Conflicts." *Peace & Change*, 37(4), pp. 544–571.

Bateson, Regina. 2012. "Crime Victimization and Political Participation." *American Political Science Review*, 106(3): 570–587.

Beath, Andrew, Christia, Fotini, & Enikolopov, Ruben, 2013. "Winning Hearts and Minds Through Development: Evidence from a Field Experiment in Afghanistan." Presented at the American Political Science Association Annual Meeting.

Becker, Gary S., 1968. "Crime and Punishment: An Economic Approach." *The Journal of Political Economy*, 76, pp. 169–217.
Beckett, I.F.W., 2001. *Insurgencies and Counter-Insurgencies: Guerrillas and Their Opponents since 1750*. London: Routledge.
Bellows, John & Miguel, Edward, 2009. "War and Local Collective Action in Sierra Leone." *Journal of Public Economics*, 93(11–12), pp. 1144–1157.
Benavides Vanegas, Farid Samir, 2009. *La Movilización de Los Pueblos Indígenas Y La Lucha Por Sus Derechos En Colombia*. Barcelona: Institut Català Internacional per la Pau.
Bennett, Andrew & Checkel, Jeffrey T., 2014. "Process Tracing: From Philosophical Roots to Best Practices." In *Process Tracing: From Metaphor to Analytic Tool*. pp. 3–37.
Benson, Bruce L., 1989. "Enforcement of Private Property Rights in Primitive Societies: Law Without Government." *Journal of Libertarian Studies*, 9(1), pp. 1–26.
Bergen, Peter & Tiedemann, Katherine, 2012. *Talibanistan: Negotiating the Borders Between Terror, Politics, and Religion*. New York: Oxford University Press.
Berman, Eli, 2009. *Radical Religious and Violent: The New Economics of Terrorism*. Cambridge: MIT Press.
Berman, Eli & Laitin, David D., 2008. "Religion, Terrorism and Public Goods: Testing the Club Model." *Journal of Public Economics*, 92(10–11), pp. 1942–1967.
Bilz, Kenworthey, 2007. "The Puzzle of Delegated Revenge." *Boston University Law Review*, 87, pp. 1059–1112.
Blake, Damion. 2013. "Shadowing the State: Violent Control and the Social Power of Jamaican Garrison Dons." *Journal of Ethnographic and Qualitative Research*, 8, pp. 56–75.
Blattman, Chris & Annan, Jeannie, 2009. "From Violence to Voting: War and Political Participation in Uganda." *The American Political Science Review*, 103(2), pp. 231–247.
Blattman, Christopher & Miguel, Edward, 2010. "Civil War." *Journal of Economic Literature*, 48(1), pp. 3–57.
Bonilla, Laura, 2014. "Eln y el narcotráfico: una relación peligrosa." *El Espectador*, July 7.
Borrero, Camilo, 1989. "Acción Comunal y Política Estatal: ¿Un Matrimonio Indisoluble?" Centro de Investigación y Educación Popular, *Documentos ocasionales*, No. 57.
Bottia, Martha, 2003. "La Presencia y Expansión Municipal de las FARC: Es Avaricia y Contagio, Más que Ausencia Estatal." *Documento CEDE* 2003-03.
Boucoyannis, Deborah A., 2017. *From Roving To Stationary Judges: Power, Land, Justice, And The Origins Of Representative Institutions*. Forthcoming, Cambridge University Press.
Bowles, Samuel & Gintis, Herbert, 2002. "Social Capital and Community Governance*." *The Economic Journal*, 112(483), pp. F419–436.

Brady, Henry E., Collier, David and Seawright, Jason, 2010. "Refocusing the Discussion of Methodology." In Henry E. Brady & David Collier, eds. *Rethinking Social Inquiry: Diverse Tools, Shared Standards*. Lanham: Rowman & Littlefield Publishers, pp. 3–20.

Bryan, Mark L. & Stephen P. Jenkins, 2016. "Multilevel Modelling of Country Effects: A Cautionary Tale." *European Sociological Review*, 32(1), pp. 3–22.

Cabral, Amílcar, 1970. *National Liberation and Culture*. Syracuse: Syracuse University.

CAJAR, Colectivo de Abogados José Alvear Restrepo, 2008. "VIOTÁ 2003: ¿Meras coincidencias?.." Available at: www.colectivodeabogados.org/VIOTA-2003-MERAS-COINCIDENCIAS [accessed on May 27, 2010].

Caracol, 2011. "Guardia Indígena evitó el secuestro de dos médicos en el Cauca." Available at: www.caracol.com.co/nota.aspx?id=1441176 [accessed on September 10, 2012].

Caris, Charlie C. & Reynolds, Samuel, 2014. "ISIS Governance in Syria." *Middle East Security Report*, 22, pp. 1–41.

Cassar, Alessandra, Grosjean, Pauline, & Whitt, Sam, 2013. "Legacies of Violence: Trust and Market Development." *Journal of Economic Growth*, 18(3), pp. 285–318.

Castañeda, Dorly, 2014. *The European Approach to Peacebuilding: Civilian Tools for Peace in Colombia and Beyond*. New York: Palgrave Macmillan.

Caviedes, Mauricio (Editor), 2007. *Paz Y Resistencia: Experiencias Indígenas Desde La Autonomía*. Bogotá: Centro de Cooperacion Al Indigena Cecoin.

CAVIDA, 2002. *Somos tierra de esta tierra: Memoriade una resistencia civil*. Chocó

Central Intelligence Agency (CIA), 1966. "Banditry and Insurgency in Colombia." Unclassified CIA document. Available at www.cia.gov/library/readingroom/docs/DOC_0000598514.pdf [accessed on May 22, 2010].

Centro Nacional de Memoria Histórica (CNMH), 2009. *Recordar y narrar el conflicto. Herramientas para reconstruir memoria histórica*. Bogotá: Imprenta Nacional.

Centro Nacional de Memoria Histórica (CNMH), 2013. *¡Basta ya! Colombia: Memorias de guerra y dignidad*. Bogotá: Imprenta Nacional.

Chacón, Mario. 2004. "Dinámica Y Determinantes de La Violencia durante 'La Violencia' en Colombia." *CEDE* 16.

Chenoweth, Erica & Stephan, Maria J., 2011. *Why Civil Resistance Works: The Strategic Logic of Nonviolent Conflict*. New York: Columbia University Press.

CINEP, 2015. *Banco de Datos de Violencia Política*. Available at www.nocheyniebla.org/ [accessed on July 10, 2015].

Cliffe, Lionel, 1984. "Dramatic Shifts in the Military Balance in the Horn: The 1984 Eritrean Offensive." *Review of African Political Economy*, 30(30), pp. 93–97.

CNRR, Comisión Nacional de Reparación y Reconciliación, 2009a. "La Masacre De El Salado: Esa Guerra No Era Nuestra."

CNRR, Comisión Nacional de Reparación y Reconciliación, 2009b. "Trujillo, Una Tragedia que No Cesa. Primer Informe de Memoria Histórica de la ComisiónNacional de Reparación y Reconciliación".

CNRR, Comisión Nacional de Reparación y Reconciliación, 2011. *San Carlos: Memorias del Exodo en la Guerra*. Bogotá: Ediciones Semana.

Coase, Ronald, 1998. "The New Institutional Economics." *American Economic Review*, 140(1), pp. 72–74.

Cohen, Dara Kay, 2013. "Explaining Rape During Civil War: Cross-National Evidence (1980–2009)." *American Political Science Review*, 107(03), pp. 461–477.

Collier, Paul & Hoeffler, Anke, 2001. "Greed and Grievance in Civil War." *Oxford Economic Papers*, 56(4), pp. 563–595.

Comisión Colombiana de Juristas (CCJ), 2006. "Listado de víctimas de violencia sociopolítica en Colombia." Available at www.google.com/search?client=safari&rls=en&q=www.verdadabierta.com/.../asesinatos.../814-listado-ccj-3004-asesinados-por-+paramilitares&ie=UTF-8&oe=UTF-8 [accessed on September 13, 2010].

Connell, Dan, 2001. "Inside the EPLF: The Origins of the 'People's Party' & Its Role in the Liberation of Eritrea.' Revil Economy 28." *Review of African Political Economy*, 28(89), pp. 345–364.

Corporación Nuevo Arco Iris (CNAI), 2009. "¿El declive de la Seguridad Democrática?" *Revista Arcanos*, 13(15), pp. 4–94.

Crost, Benjamin, Felter, Joseph, & Johnston, Patrick, 2014. "Aid Under Fire: Development Projects and Civil Conflict †." *American Economic Review*, 104(6), pp. 1833–1856.

Cubides, Fernando, 1999. "Los Paramilitares y su Estrategia." In Deas and Llorente, eds. *Reconocer la guerra para construir la paz*. Bogotá: Cerec.

Cubides, Fernando, 2005. *Burocracias Armadas: el Problema de la Organización en el Entramado de las Violencias Colombianas*. Bogotá: Grupo Editorial Norma.

Darden, Keith, 2016. *Resisting Occupation in Eurasia*. Forthcoming, Cambridge: Cambridge University Press.

Dasgupta, Partha & Serageldin, Ismail, 2000. *Social Capital: Multifaceted Perspective*. Washington, DC: World Bank.

David Mason, T. et al., 2011. "When Civil Wars Recur: Conditions for Durable Peace after Civil Wars." *International Studies Perspectives*, 12(2), pp. 171–189.

Davies, James, 1962. "Towards a Theory of Revolution." *American Sociological Review*, 6, pp. 5–19.

Diaz-Cayeros, Alberto, 2011. "Indian Identity, Poverty and Colonial Development in Mexico." Presented at the Conference, *The Impact of Colonial and Post-Colonial Independence Institutions on Economic Development in Latin America*, Columbia University.

Dixit, Avinash K., 2007. *Lawlessness and Economics: Alternative Modes of Governance*. Princeton: Princeton University Press.

Doty, D. Harold & Glick, William H., 1994. "Typologies as a Unique form of Theory Building: Toward Improved Understanding and Modeling." *Academy of Management Review*, 19(2), pp. 230–251.

Downs, Alexander, 2008. *Targeting Civilians in War*. Ithaca, N.Y.: Cornell University Press.

Driscoll, Jesse, 2015. *Warlords and Coalition Politics in Post-Soviet States*. Cambridge University Press.

Dube, O. & Vargas, J.F., 2013. "Commodity Price Shocks and Civil Conflict: Evidence from Colombia." *The Review of Economic Studies*, 80(4), pp. 1384–1421.

Dubey, P.C., 2004. "Kangaroo Courts Hold Sway in Nepal Hinterland." *One World South Asia*, Available at: http://southasia.oneworld.net/article/view/90875/1/ [accessed February 19, 2007].
Dudley, Steven S., 2004. *Walking Ghosts: Murder and Guerrilla Politics in Colombia*. New York; London: Routledge.
Dunning, Thad, 2012. *Natural Experiments in the Social Sciences: A Design-Based Approach*. New York: Cambridge University Press.
Echandía, Camilo, 2008. "El fin de la invulnerabilidad de las FARC. El estado actual del conflicto armado en Colombia." *Nueva Sociedad*, No. 217, S.
Echandía, Camilo, 2013. "Narcotráfico: génesis de los paramilitares y herencia de bandas criminales." *Informes FIP*, 19, pp. 5–32.
Eck, Kristine. 2010. "Raising Rebels. Participation and Recruitment in Civil War." Phd Dissertation, Uppsala University.
El Espectador, 2015. "Los Escándalos del DAS." January 31.
El Tiempo, 1996. "Me Mataron Por Liberal." February 17.
El Tiempo, 1999. "Despeje: El Imperio de Las Farc." June 1.
El Tiempo. 2000. "El Miedo Ronda a Viotá." September 24.
El Tiempo, 2003a. "Avanzada Para en Viotá." June 23.
El Tiempo, 2003b. "Golpe a las Farc en Viotá." October 4.
El Tiempo, 2008, "Por Alianza Con 'Paras' en Masacre de Viotá, Destituyen al Capitán Édgar Arbeláez Sánchez." March 24.
El Tiempo, 2010. "El país no castigó a herederos de parapolíticos." March 15.
El Tiempo, 2012. "Indígenas Del Cauca Quieren Sacar a Farc Y a Ejército de Su Territorio." July 10.
El Tiempo, 2014. "Indígenas del Cauca, los más afectados del país por la violencia." November 7.
El Tiempo, 2015a. "Así quedó la lista de desaparecidos del Palacio de Justicia." October 21.
El Tiempo, 2015b. "Fiscalía pide juzgados especializados para casos de 'falsos positivos'." December 9.
Ellickson, R.C., 2009. *Order without Law: How Neighbors Settle Disputes*. Cambridge, MA: Harvard University Press.
Ellis, Stephen, 1998. "Liberia's Warlord Insurgency." In C. Clapham, ed. *African Guerrillas*. Oxford: James Currey Ltd.; Indiana University Press.
España, Irina & Sánchez, Fabio, 2010. "Industrialización regional, café y capital humano en la primera mitad del siglo XX en Colombia."
Espinosa, Nicolás, 2003. "Entre la justicia guerrillera y la justicia campesina. ¿Un nuevo modelo de justicia comunitaria?" *Revista Colombiana de Sociología*, 20, pp. 117–145.
Esquivia, Ricardo & Gerlach, Barabara, 2009. "The Local Community as a Creative Space for Transformation: The View of the Montes of María." In Virginia Marie Bouvier, ed. *Colombia: Building Peace in a Time of War*. Washington: U.S. Institute of Peace.
Evans, Alexander, 2009. "The Taliban as a Social Movement." In *Yale Afghanistan Forum*. New Haven: Yale University.
FARC & Bloque Martín Cabellero. 2014. "Lamentamos Lo Sucedido Con La Comunidad Nasa de Toribío." Available at https://resistencia-colombia.org/

index.php/dialogos-por-la-paz/comunicados/3797-lamentamos-sucesos-con-la-comunidad-nasa-de-toribio [accessed on January 12, 2015].

Fearon, James D. & Laitin, David D., 2003. "Ethnicity, Insurgency, and Civil War." *American Political Science Review*, 97(01), p. 75.

Felstiner, William L.F., 1974. "Influences of Social Organization on Dispute Processing." *Law and Society Review*, 9(1), pp. 63–94.

Ferro, Juan Guillermo & Uribe, Graciela, 2002. *El orden de la guerra: las FARC-EP, entre la organización y la política* 1. ed. Bogotá: CEJA, Centro Editorial Javeriano.

Ferro, Juan Guillermo & Uribe, Graciela, 2004. "Las marchas de los cocaleros del departamento de Caquetá, Colombia: Contradicciones políticas y obstáculos en la emancipación social." In Boaventura De Sousa Santos & Mauricio García Villegas, eds. *Emancipación social y violencia en Colombia*. Bogotá: Editorial Norma.

Finch, W. Holmes, Bolin, Jocelyn E., & Kelley, Ken, 2014. *Multilevel modeling using R*. Boca Raton: CRC Press.

Flora, Jan, Jeff Sharp, Cornelia Flora, and Bonnie Newlon. 1997. "Entrepreneurial Social Infrastructure and Locally Initiated Economic Development in the Non-Metropolitan USA." *Sociological Quarterly* 38: 623–645.

Fonseca Amador, Carlos. 1982. "Nicaragua: Zero Hour." In Tomas Borge et al., eds. *Sandinistas Speak*. New York: Pathfinder Press Book.

Förster, Till, 2015. "Dialogue Direct: Rebel Governance and Civil Order in Northern Côte d'Ivoire." In A. Arjona, N. Kasfir, & Z. Mampilly, eds. *Rebel Governance in Civil War*. Cambridge University Press.

Fumerton, Mario. 2001. "Rondas Campesinas in the Peruvian Civil War." *Bulletin of Latin American Research*, 20(4): 470–97.

Fundación Ideas para la Paz (FIP), 2005. "Las Elecciones del Macizo." *Siguiendo el conflicto: hechos y análisis de la semana*, 9, pp. 27–30.

Galeano, Myriam. 2006. *Resistencia Indígena en el Cauca*. Cauca: Consejo Regional Indígena del Cauca.

Galula, David, 1964. *Counterinsurgency Warfare; Theory and Practice*. New York: Praeger Security International.

Gambetta, Diego, 1993. *The Sicilian Mafia*. Cambridge, MA: Harvard University Press.

Gambetta, Diego, 1996. *The Sicilian Mafia: The Business of Private Protection*. Cambridge, MA: Harvard University Press.

García Villegas, Mauricio, 2008. *Jueces Sin Estado: La Justicia Colombiana en Zonas de Conflicto Armado*, Bogotá: Siglo del Hombre Editores.

García-Villegas, Mauricio & Espinosa, Jose Rafael, 2015. "The Geography of Justice: Assessing Local Justice in Colombia's Post-Conflict Phase." *Stability: International Journal of Security and Development*, 4(1), pp. 1–21.

Gates, S., 2002. "Recruitment and Allegiance: The Microfoundations of Rebellion." *Journal of Conflict Resolution*, 46(1), pp. 111–130.

Gberie, Lansana, 2005. *A Dirty War in West Africa: The RUF and the Destruction of Sierra Leone*. London: Hurst & Company.

Gelman, Andrew, 2007. "Struggles with survey weighting and regression modeling." *Statistical Science* 22(2): 153–164.

Gelman, Andrew & Jennifer Hill. 2006. *Data Analysis Using Regression and Multilevel/Hierarchical Models*. Cambridge: Cambridge University Press.

Gerring, John, 1999. "What Makes a Concept Good? A Criterial Framework for Understanding Concept Formation in the Social Sciences." *Polity*, 31, pp. 357–393.

Ghandour, Zeina B., 2010. *A Discourse on Domination in Mandate Palestine: Imperialism, Property and Insurgency*. New York: Routledge.

Gilligan, Michael J., Pasquale, Benjamin J., & Samii, Cyrus, 2014. "Civil War and Social Cohesion: Lab-in-the-Field Evidence from Nepal." *American Journal of Political Science*, 58(3), pp. 604–619.

Girling, J.L.S., 1969. *People's War: The Conditions and the Consequences in China and in South East Asia*. London: Allen & Unwin.

Gittitz, John S., 2013. *Administrando justicia al margen del Estado: las Rondas Campesinas de Cajamarca*. Lima: Instituto de Estudios Peruanos.

Giustozzi, Antonio. 2007. *Koran, Kalishnikov and Laptop: The Neo-Taliban Insurgency in Afghanistan*. New York: Columbia University Press.

Giustozzi, Antonio, 2014. "The Taliban's 'Military Courts'." *Small Wars & Insurgencies*, 25(2), pp. 284–296.

Giustozzi, Antonio, Franco, Claudio, & Baczko, Adam, 2013. *Shadow Justice: How the Taliban Run Their Judiciary*. Kabul: Integrity Watch Afghanistan.

Gómez, Augusto, 1991. *Indios, colonos y conflictos: una historia regional de los Llanos Orientales, 1870–1970*. Bogotá: Pontificia Universidad Javeriana.

González, Charity Coker, 2000. "Agitating for Their Rights: The Colombian Women's Movement, 1930–1957." *Pacific Historical Review*, 69(4), pp. 689–706.

González, Fernán, 1999. *Colombia, una Nación Fragmentada*. Bilbao: Bakeaz.

González, Fernán, Bolívar, Ingrid, & Vásquez, Teófilo, 2001. *Violencia Política en Colombia. De la nación fragmentada a la construcción del Estado*. Bogotá: CINEP.

González, Fernán E., 2003. *Violencia política en Colombia : de la nación fragmentada a la construcción del estado*. Bogotá, DC, Colombia: Centro de Investigación y Educación Popular (CINEP).

Gooty, Janaki & Yammarino, Francis J. 2010. "Dyads in Organizational Research: Conceptual Issues and Multilevel Analyses." *Organizational Research Methods*, 14(3), pp. 456–483.

Gould, Roger V., 1995. *Insurgent Identities: Class, Community, and Protest in Paris from 1848 to the Commune*. Chicago: University of Chicago Press.

Grosjean, Pauline, 2014. "Conflict and Social and Political Preferences: Evidence from World War II and Civil Conflict in 35 European Countries." *Comparative Economic Studies*, 56(3), pp. 424–451.

Groves, Robert M., 2004. *Survey Errors and Survey Costs*. Hoboken: John Wiley & Sons.

Guevara, Ernesto, Loveman, Brian, & Davies, Thomas M., 1997. *Guerrilla Warfare*, 3rd ed. Wilmington, DE: SR Books.

Gurr, Ted, 1970. *Why Men Rebel*. Princeton: Princeton University Press.

Gutiérrez Sanín, Francisco, 2003. "Heating Up and Cooling Down." *Paper presented at the workshop Obstacles to Robust Negotiated Settlements, Santa Fe Institute and Universidad Javeriana, Bogotá*.
Gutiérrez Sanín, Francisco, 2004. "Criminal Rebels? A Discussion of Civil War and Criminality from the Colombian Experience." *Politics & Society*, 32(2), pp. 257–285.
Gutiérrez Sanín, Francisco, 2008. "Telling the Difference: Guerrillas and Paramilitaries in the Colombian War." *Politics & Society*, 36(1), pp. 3–34.
Gutiérrez Sanín, Francisco & Barón, Mauricio, 2006. "Estado, Control territorial paramilitar y orden político en Colombia." In F. Gutiérrez Sanín, ed. *Nuestra guerra sin nombre. Transformaciones del conflicto en Colombia*. Bogotá: Norma, pp. 267–312.
Gutiérrez Sanín, Francisco & Giustozzi, Antonio, 2010. "Networks and Armies: Structuring Rebellion in Colombia and Afghanistan." *Studies in Conflict & Terrorism*, 33(9), pp. 836–853.
Gutiérrez Sanín, Francisco & Wood, Elisabeth Jean, 2014. "Ideology in Civil War Instrumental Adoption and Beyond." *Journal of Peace Research*, 51(2), pp. 213–226.
Gutiérrez Sanín, Francisco, Wills, María Emma, & Sánchez, Gonzalo, 2006. *Nuestra Guerra Sin Nombre: Transformaciones del Conflicto en Colombia*. Bogotá: Grupo Editorial Norma.
Guzmân, German, FALS, Orlando, & Umana, Eduardo, 1986. *La Violencia en Colombia*, 2 vols. Bogotá.
Habyarimana, James, Humphreys, Macartan, Posner, Daniel N., & Weinstein, Jeremy M., 2009. *Coethnicity: Diversity and the Dilemmas of Collective Action*. New York: Russell Sage Foundation.
Hancock, Landon E. & Mitchell, C.R., 2007. *Zones of Peace*. Bloomfield, CT: Kumarian Press. https://www.hrw.org/es/news/2005/06/14/colombia-proyecto-deja-intactas-las-estructuras-paramilitares [accessed on January 12, 2005].
Hartford, Kathleen, 1995. "Fits and Starts: The Communist Party in Rural Hebei, 1921–1936." In T. Saich, ed. *New Perspectives on the Chinese Revolution*. New York: Sharpe.
Haviland, Charles, 2006. "Parallel Justice, Maoist Style." *BBC News*, October 14, 2006.
Heilman, Jaymie, 2010. *Before the Shining Path: Politics in Rural Ayacucho, 1895–1980*. Stanford: Stanford University Press.
Helmke, Gretchen & Levitsky, Steven, 2004. "Informal Institutions and Comparative Politics: A Research Agenda." *Perspectives on Politics*, 2(04), pp. 725–740.
Helmke, Gretchen & Levitsky, Steven, 2006. *Informal Institutions and Democracy: Lessons from Latin America*. Baltimore: JHU Press.
Hendawi, Hamza & Abdul-Zahra, Qassim, 2015. "ISIS Is Making Up to $50 Million a Month from Oil Sales." *Business Insider*, available at www.businessinsider.com/isis-making-50-million-a-month-from-oil-sales-2015-10 [accessed on January 20, 2016].
Hernández Delgado, Esperanza, 2004. *Resistencia Civil Artesana de Paz: Experiencias Indígenas, Afro-Descendientes y Campesinas*. Bogotá: Pontificia Universidad Javeriana.

Heywood, Linda, 1989. "Unita and Ethinic Naitonalism in Angola." *The Journal of Modern African Affairs*, 27(1), pp. 47–66.

Hinton, William, 1966. *Fanshen; A Documentary of Revolution in a Chinese Village*. New York: Vintage Books.

Hobbes, Thomas, 2010. *Leviathan or the Matter, Forme, & Power of a Common-Wealth Ecclesiasticall and Civill*. I. Shapiro, ed. New Haven: Yale University Press.

Hobsbawm, E.J., 1971. *Primitive Rebels; Studies in Archaic Forms of Social Movement in the 19th and 20th Centuries*, 3rd ed. Manchester: Manchester University Press.

Hoover, Amelia, 2011. "Repertoires of Violence Against Noncombatants: The Role of Armed Group Institutions and Ideologies." PhD Dissertation, Political Science, Yale University.

Hox, Joop & van de Schoot, Rens, 2013. "Robust Methods for Multilevel Analysis." In Marc A. Scott, Jeffrey S. Simonoff, and Brian D. Marx, eds., *The SAGE Handbook of Multilevel Modeling*, p. 387.

Hristov, Jasmin, 2005. "Indigenous Struggles for Land and Culture in Cauca, Colombia." *The Journal of Peasant Studies*, 32(1), pp. 88–117.

Huang, Philip C.C., 2008. "Centralized Minimalism Semiformal Governance by Quasi Officials and Dispute Resolution in China." *Modern China*, 34(1), pp. 9–35.

Hultman, Lisa, 2007. "Battle Losses and Rebel Violence: Raising the Costs for Fighting." *Terrorism and Political Violence*, 19(2), pp. 205–222.

Human Rights Watch, 2000. "The Ties That Bind: Colombia and Military-Paramilitary Links." www.hrw.org/reports/2000/colombia/ [accessed on January 12, 2015].

Human Rights Watch (HRW), 2005. *Colombia – Proyecto deja intactas las estructuras paramilitares*.

Human Rights Watch, 2013. "El riesgo de volver a casa," www.hrw.org/es/report/2013/09/17/el-riesgo-de-volver-casa/violencia-y-amenazas-contra-desplazados-que-reclaman [accessed on January 12, 2015].

Human Rights Watch (HRW), 2015. "On Their Watch. Evidence of Senior Army Officers' Responsibility for False Positive Killings in Colombia." Available at www.hrw.org/report/2015/06/24/their-watch/evidence-senior-army-officers-responsibility-false-positive-killings [accessed on January 20, 2016].

Humphreys, Macartan & Weinstein, Jeremy, 2006. "Handling and Manhandling Civilians in Civil War." *American Journal of Political Science*, 52, pp. 429–447.

Humphreys, Macartan & Weinstein, Jeremy M., 2006. "Handling and Manhandling Civilians in Civil War." *American Political Science Review*, 100(03), pp. 429–447.

Isbell, Billie Jean, 1992. "Shinning Path and Peasant Responses in Rural Ayuacucho." In David S. Palmer ed. *The Shining Path in Perú*. New York: St. Martin's Press.

Jentzsch, Corinna, Kalyvas, Stathis N., & Schubiger, Livia Isabella, 2015. "Militias in Civil Wars." *Journal of Conflict Resolution*, 59(5), pp. 755–769.

Jiménez, Michael, 1988. "The Many Deaths of the Colombian Revolution: Region, Class and Agrarian Rebellion in Central Colombia." Presented at the Columbia University-New York University Conference on Andean History, New York City, December 9.

Johnson, D.H., 1998. "The Sudan People's Liberation Army and the Problem of Factionalism." In C. Clapham, ed. *African Guerrillas*. Oxford: James Currey, pp. 53–72.

Johnston, Patrick, 2004. "Timber Booms, State Busts: The Political Economy of Liberian Timber." *Review of African Political Economy*, 31, pp. 441–456.

Johnston, Patrick, 2008. "The Geography of Insurgent Organization and its Consequences for Civil Wars: Evidence from Liberia and Sierra Leone." *Security Studies*, 17(1), pp. 107–137.

Justino, Patricia, 2013. "Research and Policy Implications from a Micro-Level Perspective on the Dynamics of Conflict, Violence and Development." In P. Justino, T. Brück, & P. Verwimp, eds. *A Micro-level Perspective on the Dynamics of Conflict, Violence, and Development*. Oxford: Oxford University Press.

Kaldor, Mary, 1999. *New and Old Wars: Organised Violence in a Global Era*. Cambridge: Polity Press.

Kalyvas, Stathis N., 2006. *The Logic of Violence in Civil War*. Cambridge, New York: Cambridge University Press.

Kalyvas, Stathis N., 2015. "Rebel Governance during the Greek Civil War, 1942–1949." In A. Arjona, Z. Mampilly, & N. Kasfir, eds. *Rebel Governance in Civil War*. Cambridge University Press.

Kalyvas, Stathis N. & Balcells, Laia, 2010. "International System and Technologies of Rebellion: How the End of the Cold War Shaped Internal Conflict." *American Political Science Review*, 104(3), pp. 415–429.

Kalyvas, Stathis N. & Kocher, Matthew A., 2007. "How Free is 'Free Riding' in Civil Wars? Violence, Insurgency, and the Collective Action Problem." *World Politics*, 59(2), pp. 177–216.

Kamalendran, Chris, 2004. "The Inside Story of 'Eelam Courts'." *Sunday Times (Sri Lanka)*. Available at: www.sundaytimes.lk/021208/news/courts.html [accessed May 10, 2009].

Kaplan, Michael, 2015. "Amid Kunduz Takeover, Who Is Funding the Taliban? Iran, Drug Money Fuels Afghanistan Conflict." *International Business Times*. www.ibtimes.com/amid-kunduz-takeover-who-funding-taliban-iran-drug-money-fuels-afghanistan-conflict-2119267 [accessed on October 10, 2015].

Kaplan, Oliver, 2013a. "Nudging Armed Groups: How Civilians Transmit Norms of Protection." *Stability: International Journal of Security & Development*, 2(3), p. 62.

Kaplan, Oliver, 2013b. "Protecting Civilians in Civil War the Institution of the ATCC in Colombia." *Journal of Peace Research*, 50(3), pp. 351–367.

Kasfir, Nelson, 2002. "Dilemmas of Popular Support in Guerrilla War: The National Resistance Army in Uganda, 1981–86." Paper presented at LiCEPT. November, University of California, Los Angeles.

Kasfir, Nelson, 2004. "The Creation of Civil Administration By Guerrillas: The National Resistance Army and the Rwenzururu Kingdom Government in Uganda." Presented at the 2004 Annual Meeting of the American Political Science Association, Chicago, September 3.

Kasfir, Nelson, 2005. "Guerrillas and Civilian Participation: The National Resistance Army in Uganda, 1981–86." *The Journal of Modern African Studies*, 43(2), pp. 271–296.

Kattel, Mukunda, 2003. "Introduction to the 'People's War' and It's Implications." In Arjun Karki & David Seddon, eds. *The People's War in Nepal: Left Perspectives*. New Delhi: Adroit Publishers.

Kauffman, Arthur, 1999. *Filosofía del derecho*. Bogotá: Editorial Universidad Externado de Colombia.

Keen, David, 1998. "The Economic Functions of Violence in Civil Wars (special issue)." *The Adelphi Papers* 38(320), pp. 1–89.

Keister, Jennifer, 2009. "Social Contracts of Armed Groups: A Relational Contracting Approach to Rebel Governance." Paper presented at the conference Rebel Governance, New Haven, November.

Keister, Jennifer, 2011. "States Within States: How Rebels Rule." PhD Dissertation, Political Science, University of California, San Diego.

Kelsen, Hans, 2009. *General Theory of Law and State*. New Jersey: The Lawbook Exchange, Ltd.

Kerkvliet, Benedict J., 1977. *The Huk Rebellion: A Study of Peasant Revolt in the Philippines*. Berkeley: University of California Press.

Kinsella, Helen, 2011. *The Image Before the Weapon: A Critical History of the Distinction Between Combatant and Civilian*. Ithaca: Cornell University Press.

Knack, Stephen & Keefer, Philip, 1997. "Does Social Capital Have An Economic Payoff? A Cross-country Investigation." *The Quarterly Journal of Economics*, 112(4), pp. 1251–1288.

Kocher, Matthew, 2004. "Human Ecology and Civil War." PhD Dissertation, Political Science, University of Chicago.

Korf, Benedikt, 2004. "War, Livelihoods and Vulnerability in Sri Lanka." *Development and Change*, 35(2), pp. 275–295.

Kraja, Garentina, 2011. "Recruitment Practices of Europe's Last Guerilla: Ethnic Mobilization, Violence and Networks in the Recruitment Strategy of the Kosovo Liberation Army." Unpublished senior thesis, Yale University.

Kreft, Ita G.G. & Jan de Leeuw, 1998. *Introducing Multilevel Modeling*. Longon: Sage.

Kriiger, Jule et al., 2013. "1 2 It Doesn't Add Up." In Taylor B. Seybolt, Jay D. Aronson, & Baruch Fischhoff, eds. *Counting Civilian Casualties: An Introduction to Recording and Estimating Nonmilitary Deaths in Conflict*. Oxford University Press, p. 247.

La Serna, Miguel, 2012. *Corner of the Living: Ayacucho on the Eve of the Shining Path Insurgency*. University of North Carolina Press.

Lair, Eric, Massal, Julie, & Bonilla, Marcelo, 2000. "Acción colectiva e identidad entre los campesinos en un contexto de violencia: las rondas campesinas del norte del Perú y el movimiento armado Quintín Lame en Colombia." *Los movimientos sociales en las democracias andinas*, 132, p. 75.

LeGrand, Catherine, 1994. "Colonización y Violencia en Colombia: Perspectivas y Debate." En Machado (Compilador) ed. *El Agro y la Cuestión Agraria*. Bogotá: Tercer Mundo.

León, Juanita, 2004. *No somos machos, pero somos muchos: Cinco crónicas de resistencia civil en Colombia*. Bogotá: Editorial Norma.

León, Juanita. 2013. "Los Indígenas Del Cauca: El Dilema Más Difícil Para El Gobierno." *La Silla Vacía,* July 17. Available at http://lasillavacia.com/historia/los-indigenas-del-cauca-el-dilema-mas-dificil-para-el-gobierno-34734 [accessed January 12, 2015].

Levi, Margaret, 1989. *Of Rule and Revenue*. Berkeley: University of California Press.

Levinson, Charles, 2012. "Kidnapping, Spats on Docket of Syria Rebel Boss." *The Wallstreet Journal*, 17 August.

Lewis, Janet, 2010. *Ending Conflict Early: Incipient Stages of Insurgency and Counterinsurgency in Uganda*. Washington DC.

Lichbach, Mark, 1995. *The Rebel's Dilemma*. Ann Arbor: The University of Michigan Press.

Lockwood, David & Wrong, Dennis, 1994. "The Problem of Order: What Unites and Divides Society." *Contemporary Sociology*, 23(5), p. 757.

López, Claudia ed., 2010. *Y refundaron la patria. De como mafiosos y politicos reconfiguraron el Estado colombiano*. Bogotá: Random House Mondadori.

López, Claudia, 2016. *Adiós a las FARC. ¿Y ahora qué?* Barcelona: Random House Mondadori.

Lubkemann, Stephen C., 2008. *Culture in Chaos: An Anthropology of the Social Condition in War*. Chicago: The University of Chicago Press.

Lyall, Jason, 2014. "Process Tracing, Causal Inference, and Civil War." In Henry E. Brady & David Collier, eds. *Rethinking Social Inquiry: Diverse Tools, Shared Standards*. Lanham: Rowman & Littlefield Publishers, pp. 186–207.

Maas, Cora J.M., & Hox, Joop J., 2004. "Robustness Issues in Multilevel Regression Analysis." *Statistica Neerlandica*, 58 (2), pp. 127–137.

Maayeh, Suha & Sands, Phil, 2014. "Rebels' Court in Southern Syria an Alliance of Convenience Against Assad." *The National*. Available at: www.thenational.ae/world/middle-east/rebels-court-in-southern-syria-an-alliance-of-convenience-against-assad [accessed June 5, 2014].

Machado, Absalón, 1977. *El Café. De la Apacería al Capitalismo*. Bogotá: Punta de Lanza.

Machiavelli, Niccolò & Bondanella, Peter E., 1984. *The Prince*. Oxford [Oxfordshire]; New York: Oxford University Press.

Madariaga, Patricia, 2006. *Matan y matan y uno sigue ahí. Control paramilitar y vida cotidiana en un pueblo de Urabá*. Bogotá: Ediciones Uniandes.

Malaquias, Assis, 2001. "Diamonds Are a Guerrilla's Best Friend: The Impact of Illicit Wealth on Insurgency Strategy." *Third World Quarterly*, 22(3), pp. 311–325.

Mampilly, Zachariah, 2011. *Rebel Rulers: Insurgent Governance and Civilian Life During War*. Ithaca: Cornell University Press.

Manrique, Nelson, 1998. "The War for the Central Sierra." In S.J. Stern, ed. *Shining and Other Paths. War and Society in Peru, 1980–1995*. Durham: Duke University Press, pp. 193–223.
Mao, Zedong, 1978. *On Guerrilla Warfare*. New York: Anchor Press.
Marchal, Roland, 2007. "Warlordism and Terrorism: How to Obscure an Already Confusing Crisis? The Case of Somalia." *International Affairs*, 83(6), pp. 1091–1106.
McChrystal, Stanley A. & Hall, Michael T., 2009. *ISAF Commander's Counterinsurgency Guidance*. Kabul: International Security Assistance Force.
McClintock, Cynthia, 1998. *Revolutionary Movements in Latin America: El Salvador's FMLN & Peru's Shining Path*. Washington, DC: United States Institute of Peace Press.
McColl, Robert W., 1969. "The Insurgent State: Territorial Bases of Revolution." *Annals of the Association of American Geographers*, 59(4), pp. 613–631.
McDermott, Jeremy, 2014. "Las BACRIM y su posición en el hampa de Colombia." *Inside Crime*. April 11. http://es.insightcrime.org/investigaciones/las-bacrim-y-su-posicion-en-el-hampa-de-colombia [accessed January 23, 2014].
Medina Gallego, Carlos, 2009. "FARC–EP. Notas para una historia política 1958–2006." PhD Dissertation, Universidad Nacional de Colombia, Facultad de Derecho, Ciencias Políticas y Sociales.
Medina, Medófilo, 1980. *Historia del Partido Comunista Colombiano*. Bogotá: CEIS.
Merchán, Victor J., 1975. "Datos para la Historia Social y Económica y del Movimiento Agrario de Viotá y el Tequendama." *Estudios Marxistas: Revista colombiana de Ciencias Sociales*, 9(10), pp. 105–116.
Merchán, Víctor J., 1975. "La Autodefensa." *Estudios Marxistas: Revista colombiana de Ciencias Sociales*, N. 10.
Metelits, Claire, 2010. *Inside Insurgency: Violence, Civilians, and Revolutionary Group Behavior*. New York: New York University Press.
Milgram, Stanley & Yale U., 1963. "Behavioral Study of Obedience." *The Journal of Abnormal and Social Psychology*, 67(4), pp. 371–378.
Ministry of Interior of Colombia, 2012. "Plan Integral de Prevención y protección a violaciones de derechos humanos e infracciones al derecho internacional humanitario, Municipio de Viotá." Doc. AN-DH-P-01-F-01.
Mitchell, Christopher and Sara Ramírez, 2009. "Local Peace Communities in Colombia: An Initial Comparison of Three Cases". In Virginia Bouvier (Ed.). Colombia: Building Peace in a Time of War, pp. 245–270. Washington, D.C.: United States Institute of Peace.
Misión de Observación Electoral (MOE), 2010. "Informe de Observación Electoral de la Segunda Vuelta Presidencial." Comunicado de Prensa, June 20.
Molano, Alfredo, 1994. "Algunas Consideraciones sobre Colonización y Violencia." In Machado, ed. *El Agro y la Cuestión Agraria*. Bogotá: Tercer Mundo.
Molano, Alfredo, 2001. "La justicia guerrillera." *Boaventura de Sousa Santos y Mauricio García, Caleidoscopio de las justicias en Colombia*, Bogotá, CANH/CES/Uniandes/UN.

Moroni Bracamonte, José Angel & Spencer, David E., 1995. *Strategy and Tactics of the Salvadoran FMLN Guerrillas: Last Battle of the Cold War, Blueprint for Future Conflicts*. Westport, CT: Praeger.

Mouly, Cécile, Annette Idler, and Belén Garrido. 2015. "Zones of Peace in Colombia's Borderland." *International Journal of Peace Studies* 20(1): 51–63.

Mundlak, Yair, 1978. "On the Pooling of Time Series and Cross Section Data." *Econometrica: Journal of the Econometric Society*, 46(1), pp. 69–85.

Neira, Armando, 2005. "Corazón Valiente: Arquímedes Vitonás, el alcalde indígena de Toribío resiste, desarmado un prolongado ataque de las Farc contra su pueblo." *Semana*, April 24.

Neiva, José. 2009. "La Fuerza Del Ombligo." *El Malpensante*, available at http://www.elmalpensante.com/articulo/1462/la_fuerza_del_ombligo [accessed on January 12, 2015].

New York Times (NYT), 2010a. "Afghan Tribe, Vowing to Fight Taliban, to Get U.S. Aid in Return." January 27.

New York Times (NYT), 2010b. "As Marines Move in, Taliban Fight a Shadowy War." February 1.

New York Times (NYT), 2010c. "Taliban Exploit Openings in Neglected Province." July 29.

New York Times (NYT), 2015. "ISIS Women and Enforcers in Syria Recount Collaboration, Anguish and Escape." November 21.

Ngoga, Pascual, 1998. "Uganda: The National Resistance Army." Clapham, ed.

Nillesen, Eleonora & Verwimp, Philip, 2009. "Rebel Recruitment in a Coffee Exporting Economy." *Research Working Papers*.

Noche y Niebla, 2008a. "Falsos positivos por sectores sociales." No. 38, July.

Noche y Niebla, 2008b. "Terror e Inseguridad." No. 37. Ene.

Noche y Niebla, 2009. "Perfiles Totalitarios." No. 39. Ene.

Nordstrom, Carolyn, 1997. *A Differente Kind of War Story*. Philadelphia: University of Philadelphia Press.

North, Douglass C., 1990. *Institutions, Institutional Change and Economic Performance*. Cambridge, MA: Cambridge University Press.

North, Douglass C. & Weingast, Barry R., 1989. "Constitutions and Commitment: The Evolution of Institutional Governing Public Choice in Seventeenth-Century England." *The Journal of Economic History*, 49(4): 803–832.

O'Muircheartaigh, Colm & Pedlow, Steven, 2002. "Combining Samples vs. Cumulating Cases: A Comparison of Two Weighting Strategies in NLSY97." ASA Proceedings of the Joint Statistical Meetings. pp. 2557–2562. www.amstat.org/sections/srms/Proceedings/y2002/Files/JSM2002-001082.pdf [accessed February 10, 2013].

Offstein, N., 2003. "An Historical Review and Analysis of Colombian Guerrilla Movements." *Desarrollo y Sociedad*, 52(1), pp. 99–142.

Olson, Mancur, 1965. *The Logic of Collective Action; Public Goods and the Theory of Groups*. Cambridge, MA: Harvard University Press.

Olson, Mancur, 1993. "Dictatorship, Democracy, and Development." *The American Political Science Review*, 87(3), pp. 567–576.

Olson, Mancur, 2000. *Power and Prosperity : Outgrowing Communist and Capitalist Dictatorships*. New York: Basic Books.
Ostrom, Elinor, 1990. *Governing the Commons: The Evolution of Institutions for Collective Action*. Cambridge [England]; New York: Cambridge University Press.
Ostrom, Elinor, 1998. "A Behavioral Approach to the Rational Choice Theory of Collective Action." *American Political Science Review*, 92 (1), pp. 1–22.
Ostrom, Elinor & Ahn, T.K., 2003. *Foundations of Social Capital*. Cheltenham, UK; Northhampton, MA: Edward Elgar Pub.
Paige, Jeffery M., 1983. "Social Theory and Peasant Revolution in Vietnam and Guatemala." *Theory and Society*, 12(6), pp. 699–736.
Paige, Jeffery M., 1975. *Agrarian Revolution: Social Movements and Export Agriculture in the Underdeveloped World*. New York: Free Press.
Palacios, Marco, 2002. *El Café en Colombia 1850–1970. Una historia social, económica y política*, 3rd ed. Bogotá: Editorial Planeta.
Palacios, Marco, 2003. *Entre la legitimidad y la violencia: Colombia 1875–1994*. Bogotá: Editorial Norma.
Palacios, Marco & Safford, Frank, 2002. *Colombia: país fragmentado, sociedad dividida: su historia*. Bogotá: Editorial Norma.
Parkinson, Sarah Elizabeth, 2013. "Organizing Rebellion: Rethinking High-Risk Mobilization and Social Networks in War." *American Political Science Review*, 107(03), pp. 418–432.
Paul, B. & Demarest, W., 1998. *The Operation of a Death Squad in San Pedro la Laguna*. In R. Carmack, ed. *Harvest of Violence: the Maya Indians and the Guatemalan Crisis*. University of Oklahoma Press.
Pearlman, Wendy, 2013. "Emotions and the Microfoundations of the Arab Uprisings." *Perspectives on Politics*, 11(02), pp. 387–409.
Pécaut, Daniel, 1993. "Violencia y política en Colombia." In C.I. De Gregory, ed. *Democracia, etnicidad y violencia política en los países andinos*. Lima: IFEA-IEP.
Pécaut, Daniel, 1999. "From the Banality of Violence to Real Terror: The Case of Colombia." In Koonings & Kruijt, eds. *Societies of Fear*, pp. 141–167.
Pécaut, Daniel, 2001. *Guerra contra la sociedad* 1. ed. Bogotá, Colombiana: Editorial Planeta Colombiana.
Peña, Carina, 1997. "La guerrilla resiste muchas miradas." *Análisis Político*, No. 32.
Penhaul, Karl, 2001. "Guerrilla Justice / Colombian Civilians Sentenced in Rebel-Run Courts Are Put to Work Building Supply Roads in the Jungle." *Chronicle Foreign Service*, August 2.
Petersen, Roger Dale, 2001. *Resistance and Rebellion: Lessons from Eastern Europe*. Cambridge; New York: Cambridge University Press.
Petraeus, David H. et al., 2008. *The US Army/Marine Corps Counterinsurgency Field Manual*. Chicago: University of Chicago Press.
Picolli, Emmanuelle, 2009. "El pluralismo jurídico y político en Perú: el caso de las Rondas Campesinas de Cajamarca (Dossier)." *Íconos: revista de ciencias sociales*, 31, pp. 27–41.

Pizarro, Eduardo 2006. "Las FARC-EP,¿ repliegue estratégico, debilitamiento o punto de inflexión?." *Gutiérrez Sanín, Fernando; Sánchez, Gonzalo, Nuestra guerra sin nombre.* Bogotá: Norma, pp. 171–208.

Pizarro, Eduardo & Peñaranda, Ricardo, 1992. *Las FARC (1949–1966): de la autodefensa a la combinación de todas las formas de lucha* 1. ed., Bogotá, Colombia: UN Tercer Mundo Editores.

Pool, David, 2001. *From Guerrillas to Government: The Eritrean People's Liberation Front.* Oxford [England]: James Currey; Athens: Ohio University Press.

Popkin, Samuel L., 1979. *The Rational Peasant: The Political Economy of Rural Society in Vietnam.* Berkeley: University of California Press.

Potgieter, Jakkie, 2000. "Taking Aid from the Devil Himself: UNITA's Support Structures." In J. Cilliers & C. Dietrich, eds. *Angola's War Economy: The Role of Oil and Diamonds.* South Africa: Institute for Security Studies.

Prensa Rural, 2008. "Se devela la estrategia paramilitar del ejército en Viotá (Cundinamarca)." Available at: www.prensarural.org/spip/spip.php?article1326 [accessed September 10, 2010].

Putnam, Robert D., Leonardi, Robert, & Nanetti, Raffaella. 1993. *Making Democracy Work : Civic Traditions in Modern Italy.* Princeton, NJ: Princeton University Press.

Rabe-Hesketh, Sophia & Skrondal, Anders, 2008. *Multilevel and Longitudinal Modeling using Stata.* STATA press.

Radu, Michael & Arnold, Anthony, 1990. *The New Insurgencies: Anticommunist Guerrillas in the Third World.* New Brunswick, N.J.: Transaction Publishers.

Raeymaekers, T., Menkhaus, K., & Vlassenroot, K., 2008. "State and Non-state Regulation in African Protracted Crises: Governance Without Government?" *Afrika Focus*, 21(2), pp. 7–21.

Ramírez, María Clemencia, 2004a. "La política del reconocimiento y la ciudadanía en el Putumayo y la Baja Bota caucana: el caso del movimiento cocalero de 1996." In Boaventura De Sousa Santos & Mauricio García Villegas, eds. *Emancipación social y violencia en Colombia.* Bogotá: Editorial Norma, pp. 153–205.

Ramírez, María Clemencia, 2004b. "Estrategias de resistencia y organización campesina en un contexto de conflicto armado e ilegalidad: Construcción de cuidadanía en un marco de las políticas antidrogas y de desarrollo alternativo en el Putumayo." *Colombia a comienzos del nuevo milenio.* Cali: Universidad del Valle, Facultad de Ciencias Sociales y Económicas, Depto. de Ciencias Sociales.

Rappaport, Joanne, 2007. "Civil Society and the Indigenous Movement in Colombia: The Consejo Regional Indígena Del Cauca." *Social Analysis*, 51(2), 107–123.

Rasbash, Jon, & William J. Browne. "Non-hierarchical Multilevel Models." In Jon Rasbash and William J. Browne, eds. *Handbook of Multilevel Analysis.* New York: Springer, pp. 301–334.

Reno, William, 1998. *Warlord Politics and African States.* Boulder: Lynne Rienner Publishers.

Reno, William, 2011. *Warfare in independent Africa.* Cambridge University Press, 2011.

Reno, William, 2015. "Predatory Rebellions and Governance: The National Patriotic Front of Liberia, 1989–1992." In *Rebel Governance in Civil War.* Cambridge University Press.

Restrepo, Jorge & Spagat, Michael, 2005. "Colombia's Tipping Point?" *Survival*, 47(2), pp. 131–152.
Reyes, Alejandro, 1991. "Paramilitares en Colombia: Contexto, Aliados y Consecuencias." *IEPRI*, Ene.
Richani, Nazih, 2013. *Systems of Violence: The Political Economy of War and Peace in Colombia*. Suny Press.
Risse, Thomas, 2013. *Governance Without a State?: Policies and Politics in Areas of Limited Statehood*. Columbia University Press.
Robben, Antonius C.G.M., 2010. "Chaos, Mimesis and Dehumanisation in Iraq: American Counterinsurgency in the Global War on Terror." *Social Anthropology*, 18(2), pp. 138–154.
Roberts, Simon, 2013. *Order and Dispute: An Introduction to Legal Anthropology*. New Orleans: Quid Pro Books.
Roberts, Simon & Palmer, Michael, 2005. *Dispute Processes: ADR and the Primary Forms of Decision-making*. Cambridge, MA: Cambridge University Press.
Rohner, Dominic, Thoenig, Mathias, & Zilibotti, Fabrizio, 2013. "Seeds of Distrust: Conflict in Uganda." *Journal of Economic Growth*, 18(3), pp. 217–252.
Rojas, Catalina, 2009. "Women and peacebuilding in Colombia: Resistance to war, creativity for peace." In Virginia Marie Bouvier ed. *Colombia: Building Peace in a Time of War*. Washington: U.S. Institute of Peace.
Rojas, Erika, 2008. "Conflicto Armado y Comunidades Afro-pacíficas: La construcción de territorialidad e identidad en el municipio de de Olaya Herrera en medio del conflcito." Thesis, Political Science, Los Andes University. Bogotá.
Roldán. Mary J., 2009. "'Cambio de Armas': Negotiating Alternatives to Violence in the Oriente Antioqueño." In Virginia Marie Bouvier ed. *Colombia: Building Peace in a Time of War*. Washington: U.S. Institute of Peace.
Romanow, Zach, 2015. "Mapping the Syrian Crisis with the Carter Center." Carter Center. Available at: www.palantir.com/2014/06/mapping-the-syrian-crisis-with-the-carter-center/ [accessed February 5, 2016].
Romero, Mauricio, 2003. *Paramilitares y autodefensas, 1982–2003*, ed. Bogotá: Editorial Planeta.
Romero, Mauricio, 2004. "Los trabajadores banaeros del Urabá: de 'súbditos' a 'ciudadanos?" In Boaventura De Sousa Santos & Mauricio García Villegas, eds. *Emancipación social y violencia en Colombia*. Bogotá: Editorial Norma.
Romero, Mauricio & Valencia, León eds., 2007. *Parapolítica : la ruta de la expansión paramilitar y los acuerdos políticos* 2 ed. Bogotá, Colombia: Intermedio Editores.
Romero, Simon, 2009. "A Scandal Over Spying Intensifies in Colombia." *New York Times*, September 16.
Rubin, Barnett R., 2002. *The Fragmentation of Afghanistan: State Formation and Collapse in the International System*, 2nd ed. New Haven, CT: Yale University Press.
Rueda Mallarino, María, 2003. "Estrategias civiles en medio del conflicto: Los casos de las comunidades de Paz y de Pensilvania." Documentos CESO.
Ruiz Niño, Soledad, 1983. "Café, tecnología y sociedad municipal. Montengro, Villarica, Viotá." Research report, Political Science Department, Universidad de los Andes.

Sáfford, Frank & Palacios, Marco, 2002. *Colombia: Fragmented Land, Divided Society.*
Sambanis, Nicholas & Shayo, Moses, 2013. "Social Identification and Ethnic Conflict." *American Political Science Review*, 107(02), pp. 294–325.
Sanchez de la Sierra, Raul, 2015. *On the Origin of States: Stationary Bandits and Taxation in Eastern Congo.* Unpublished paper.
Sánchez, Fabio & Chacón, Mario, 2006. "Conflicto, estado y descentralización: del progreso social a la disputa armada por el control local 1974–2002." In IEPRI, ed. *Nuestra guerra sin nombre. Transformaciones del conflicto en Colombia.* Bogotá: Planeta.
Sánchez, Gonzalo, 1977. *Las ligas campesinas en Colombia.* Bogotá: Tiempo Presente.
Sandoval Forero, Eduardo Andrés, 2008. *La Guardia Indígena Nasa y el arte de la resistencia pacífica.* Medellín: Ediciones Colección Etnia, Fundación Hemera.
Schock, Kurt, 2005. *Unarmed Insurrections: People Power Movements in Nondemocracies.* Minneapolis: University of Minnesota Press.
Schubiger, Livia Isabella, 2015. *State Violence and Wartime Civilian Agency: Evidence from Peru.* Unpublished paper.
Scott, James, 1977. *The Moral Economy of the Peasant: Rebellion and Subsistence in Southeast Asia.* New Haven: Yale University Press.
Scott, James, 1979. "Revolution in the Revolution – Peasants and Commissars." *Theory and Society*, 7(1–2), pp. 97–134.
Sección de Vida, Justicia y Paz, 2002. *Situación de guerra y violencia en el departamento de Chocó. 1996-2002.* Bogotá: Conferencia Episcopal de Colombia.
Semana, 1999. "Un año después." November 11.
Semana. 2003. " '¿Meras Coincidencias?' " July 13.
Semana, 2013. "Las violentas cifras de las bacrim." April 15.
Semana, 2015. "La historia del coronel que se esfumó." January 31.
Shapiro, Ian, 2010. *Leviathan.* Yale University Press.
Shapiro, Martin, 1981. *Courts. A Political and Comparative Analysis.* Chicago: The University of Chicago Press.
Shewfelt, Steven, 2009. *Legacies of War: Social and Political Life after Wartime Trauma.* New Haven: Yale University.
Silver, Allan, 1965. "On Demand for Order in Civil Society: A Review of Some Themes in the History of Urban Crime, Police and Riot in England." Working Papers of the Center for Research on Social Organization, University of Michigan, No. 11, pp. 1–36.
Silver, Morris, 1974. "Political Revolution and Repression: An Economic Approach." *Public Choice*, 17(1), pp. 63–71.
Simmel, Georg, 1964. *Conflict; The Web of Group-affiliations.* New York: The Free Press.
Sinno, A.H., 2008. *Organizations at War in Afghanistan and Beyond.* Ithaca: Cornell University Press.
Skaperdas, Stergios, 2001. "The Political Economy of Organized Crime: Providing Protection When the State Does Not." *Economics of Governance*, 2(3), pp. 173–202.

Skarbek, David, 2011. "Governance and Prison Gangs." *American Political Science Review*, 105, pp. 702–716.

Skarpedas, S. & Syropoulos, C., 1995. "Gangs as Primitive States." In Gianluca Fiorentini & Sam Peltzman., eds. *The Economics of Organised Crime*. Cambridge, UK: Cambridge University Press.

Slater, Dan, 2010. *Ordering Power: Contentious Politics and Authoritarian Leviathans in Southeast Asia*. Cambridge: Cambridge University Press.

Sosnowski, Marika, 2015. "The Syrian Southern Front: Why it Offers Better Justice and Hope Than Northern Front." *Syria Comment*. Available at: www.joshualandis.com/blog/the-syrian-southern-front-why-it-offers-better-justice-and-hope-than-northern-front-by-marika-sosnowski/ [accessed August 15, 2015].

Staniland, Paul, 2014. *Networks of Rebellion: Explaining Insurgent Cohesion and Collapse*. Ithaca: Cornell University Press.

Starn, Orin, 1995. "To Revolt against the Revolution: War and Resistance in Peru's Andes." *Cultural Anthropology*, 10(4), pp. 547–580.

Steele, Abbey, 2016. "Unsettling: Displacement during Civil Wars." Unpublished manuscript. University of Amsterdam.

Stegmueller, Daniel, 2013. "How many countries for multilevel modeling? A comparison of frequentist and Bayesian approaches." *American Journal of Political Science*, 57(3), pp.748–761.

Stokke, Kristian, 2006. "Building the Tamil Eelam State: Emerging State Institutions and Forms of Governance in LTTE-controlled Areas in Sri Lanka." *Third World Quarterly*, 27, pp. 1021–1040.

Stoll, David, 1993 *Between Two Armies in the Ixil Towns of Guatemala*. New York: Columbia University Press.

Strachota, Krzysztof, 2015. "The Middle East in the Shadow of the Islamic State." *OSW Point of View*, 52, August, pp. 5–62.

Straus, Scott, 2008. *The Order of Genocide: Race, Power, and War in Rwanda*. Cornell University Press.

Sudman, Seymour & Bradburn, Norman M., 1982. *Asking Questions: A Practical Guide to Questionnaire Design*. San Francisco: Jossey Bass Publishers.

Suykens, Bert, 2015. "Comparing Rebel Rule Through Revolution and Naturalization: Ideologies of Governance in Naxalite and Naga India." In Ana Arjona, Nelson Kasfir, & Zachariah Mampilly, eds. *Rebel Governance in Civil War*. Cambridge: Cambridge University Press, p. 138.

Sweet, A.S., 1999. "Judicialization and the Construction of Governance." *Comparative Political Studies*, 32(2), pp. 147–84.

Taber, Robert, 1965. *The War of the Flea: A Study of Guerrilla Warfare Theory and Practise*. New York: L. Stuart.

Taussig, Michael T., 2003. *Law in a Lawless Land: Diary of a "limpieza" in Colombia*. Chicago: The University of Chicago Press.

Taw, Jennifer Morrison & Hoffman, Bruce, 1995. "The Urbanisation of Insurgency: The Potential Challenge to US Army Operations." *Small Wars & Insurgencies*, 6(1), pp. 68–87.

Taylor, Michael, 1988. "Rationality and Revolutionary Collective Action." In M. Taylor, ed. *Rationality and Revolution*. Cambridge [Cambridgeshire]; New

York Paris: Cambridge University Press; Editions de la Maison des Sciences de l'Homme.
Tejidos del Viento, 2014. "Tejiendo Memoria. Municipio Viotá." Report. Fundación Tejidos del Viento. http://soda.ustadistancia.edu.co/enlinea/paza tiempo/eje2/mod3/unidad3Tejidos_del_viento.pdf. [accessed on May 10, 2015]
Temple, Jonathan and Paul Johnson, 1998. "Social Capability and Economic Growth." *Quarterly Journal of Economics* 113: 965–990.
Theidon, Kimberly Susan, 2004. *Entre prójimos: el conflicto armado interno y la política de la reconciliación en el Perú*. Instituto de Estudios peruanos.
Third Congress of the International Communist, 2015. "Guidelines on the Organizational Structure of Communist Parties, on the Methods and Content of Their Work." Available at: www.marxists.org/history/interna tional/comintern/3rd-congress/organisation/guidelines.htm. [accessed on December 12, 2015].
Thompson, Loren B., 1989. *Low-intensity Conflict: The Pattern of Warfare in the Modern World*. Lexington, MA: Lexington Books.
Thompson, Robert Grainger Ker, 1983. *War in Peace: An Analysis of Warfare since 1945*. London: Orbis.
Tilly, Charles, 1978. *From Mobilization to Revolution*. Reading, MA: Addison-Wesley.
Tilly, Charles, 1985. "War Making and State Making as Organized Crime." In Peter Evans, Dietrich Rueschemeyer, & Theda Skocpol, eds. *Bringing the State Back In*. Cambridge: Cambridge University Press, pp. 169–191.
Torres, Maria Clara, 2004. "El surgimiento y apuntalamiento de grupos paramilitares." *Revista Controversia*, 183, pp. 50–80.
Tovar Pinzón, Hermes, 1997. *La estación del miedo o la desolación dispersa: el Caribe colombiano en el siglo XVI*. Bogotá: Editorial Planeta.
Trejo, Guillermo, 2009. "Religious Competition and Ethnic Mobilization in Latin America: Why the Catholic Church Promotes Indigenous Movements in Mexico." *American Political Science Review*, 103(3), pp. 323–342.
Trejo, Guillermo, 2012. *Popular Movements in Autocracies: Religion, Repression, and Indigenous Collective Action in Mexico*. Cambridge: Cambridge University Press.
Trinquier, Roger, 1964. *Modern Warfare; A French View of Counterinsurgency*. New York: Praeger.
Troyan, Brett. 2008. "Ethnic Citizenship in Colombia: The Experience of the Regional Indigenous Council of the Cauca in Southwestern Colombia from 1970 to 1990." *Latin American Research Review* 43(3), pp. 166–191.
Uribe de Hincapié, María Teresa, 2001. *Nación, Ciudadano y Soberano*. Medellín: Corporación Región.
Uribe de Hincapié, María Teresa, 2004. "Emancipación social en un contexto de guerra prolongada. El caso de la Comunidad de Paz de San José de Apartadó." In Boaventura De Sousa Santos & Mauricio García Villegas, eds. *Emancipación social y violencia en Colombia*. Bogotá: Editorial Norma.
Uribe de Hincapié, Maria Teresa, 2006. "Notas preliminares sobre resistencias de la sociedad civil en un contexto de guerras y transacciones." *Estudios PolÌticos*, 29, pp. 63–78.

Van Acker, Frank. 2004. "Uganda and the Lord's Resistance Army: The New Order No One Ordered." *African Affairs* 103(412): 335–357.

Van der Leeden, Rien, Karen Vrijburg, & Jan de Leeuw, 1996. "A review of two different approaches for the analysis of growth data using longitudinal mixed linear models: comparing hierarchical linear regression (ML3, HLM) and repeated measures designs with structured covariance matrices (BMDP5V)." *Computational statistics & data analysis*, 21 (5), pp. 583–605.

Varese, Federico, 2001. *The Russian Mafia: Private Protection in a New Market Economy*. Oxford: Oxford University Press.

Velandia, César Augusto, and José del Carmen Buitrago, 1989. *El Problema Indígena en el Sur del Tolima, 1950–1980*. Ibagué: Universidad del Tolima.

Vélez, Maria Alejandra, 1999. *FARC-ELN. Evolución y Expansión Territorial*. Bogotá.

Verdad Abierta, 2008. "Guillermo Torres' acepta masacre del Planchón." Available at www.verdadabierta.com/justicia-y-paz/versiones/527-autodefensas-campesinas-de-meta-y-vichada-carranceros/654-guillermo-torres-acepta-masacre-del-planchon [accessed on May 10, 2012].

Verdad Abierta, 2009a. "Así fue la guerra entre Martín Llanos y Miguel Arroyave." Available at www.verdadabierta.com/victimarios/2052-asi-fue-la-guerra-entre-martin-llanos-y-miguel-arroyave [accessed on June 15, 2012].

Verdad Abierta, 2009b. "Las Farc por dentro." Available at www.verdadabierta.com/procesos-de-paz/farc/2014-las-farc-por-dentro [accessed on December 12, 2013].

Verdad Abierta, 2010a. "Desmovilizado de las Auc hace nuevos señalamientos contra el coronel Mejía." Available at www.verdadabierta.com/la-historia/2514-desmovilizado-de-las-auc-hace-nuevos-senalamientos-contra-el-coronel-mejia [accessed on April 22, 2012].

Verdad Abierta, 2010b. "'El Diablo' de 'Martín Llanos' en Cundinamarca." Available at www.verdadabierta.com/las-victimas/4063-el-diablo-de-martin-llanos-en-cundinamarca [accessed on April 22, 2012].

Verdad Abierta, 2012. "Las sumas y restas de la justicia frente a la parapolítica." Available at www.verdadabierta.com/la-historia/4276-las-sumas-y-restas-de-la-justicia-frente-a-la-parapolitica [accessed on February 24, 2013].

Verdad Abierta, 2013. "De la curul a la cárcel." Available at www.verdadabierta.com/de-la-curul-a-la-carcel [accessed on February 24, 2013].

Verdad Abierta, 2014. "La Sangre Que Recuperó La Tierra de Los Nasa." Available at www.verdadabierta.com/lucha-por-la-tierra/5264-la-sangre-que-les-recupero-la-tierra-de-los-nasa [accessed on January 20, 2015].

Verdad Abierta, 2015. "El paramilitarismo en Colombia, ¿realmente se desmontó?." Available at www.verdadabierta.com/rearme/6121-el-paramilitarismo-en-colombia-realmente-se-desmonto [accessed on December 20, 2015].

Vidal Castaño, José, 2012. "Panorama del sindicalismo en Colombia." *Análisis*, 3, April, pp. 1–31.

Viterna, Jocelyn S., 2006. "Pulled, Pushed, and Persuaded: Explaining Women's Mobilization into the Salvadoran Guerrilla Army." *American Journal of Sociology*, 112(1), pp. 1–45.

Vlassenroot, Koen & Raeymaekers, Timothy, 2004a. *Conflict and Social Transformation in Eastern DR Congo*. Gent [Belgium]: Academia Press Scientific Publishers.

Vlassenroot, Koen & Raeymaekers, Timothy, 2004b. "The Politics of Rebellion and Intervention in Ituri: The Emergence of a New Political Complex?" *African Affairs*, 103(412), p. 28.

Volkov, Vadim, 2000. "The Political Economy of Protection Rackets in the Past and the Present." *Social Research*, 67(3), pp. 709–744.

Wabgou, Maguemati, 2007. "Pueblo Nasa. Identidades y Expresiones de resistencia Política. Serie de Investigaciones en Construcción." Universidad Nacional. Facultad de Derecho, Ciencias Políticas y Sociales. Instituto de Investigaciones Jurídico-Sociales Gerardo Molina (UNIJUS). No. 23. Universidad Nacional. Bogotá.

Weber, A. & Rone, J., 2003. "Abducted and Abused: Renewed Conflict in Northern Uganda." *Human Rights Watch*, Vol. 12.

Weber, Henri, 1981. *Nicaragua: The Sandinist Revolution*. London: NLB.

Weber, Max, 1968. *Economy and Society*. Berkeley: University of California Press.

Weinstein, Jeremy M., 2007. *Inside Rebellion: The Politics of Insurgent Violence*. Cambridge; New York: Cambridge University Press.

Weintraub, Michael, 2016. "Do All Good Things Go Together? Development Assistance and Violence in Insurgency." *Journal of Politics*, 78(4), DOI: 10.1086/686026.

Weldon, Thomas Dewar, 1953. *The Vocabulary of Politics*. Penguin Books.

Wickham-Crowley, Timothy P., 1987. "The Rise (and Sometimes Fall) of Guerrilla Governments in Latin America." *Sociological Forum*, 2(3), pp. 473–499.

Wickham-Crowley, Timothy P., 1991. *Guerrillas and Revolution in Latin America: A Comparative Study of Insurgents and Regimes since 1956*. Princeton, NJ: Princeton University Press.

Wickham-Crowley, Timothy P., 2015. "Transitions to and from Rebel Governance in Latin America, 1956–1990." In A. Arjona, Z. Mampilly, & N. Kasfir, eds. *Rebel Governance*. Cambridge University Press.

Williamson, Oliver E., 2002. "The Lens of Contract: Private Ordering." *The American Economic Review*, 92(2), pp. 438–443.

Wintrobe, Ronald, 1990. "The Tinpot and the Totalitarian: An Economic Theory of Dictatorship." *The American Political Science Review*, 84(3), pp. 849–872.

Wirpsa, Leslie, Rothschild, David, & Garzón, Catalina, 2009. "The Power of the Baston: Indigenous Resistance and Peacebuilding in Colombia." In Virginia Marie Bouvier, ed. *Colombia: Building Peace in a Time of War*. Washington: U.S.: Institute of Peace.

Wolf, Eric, 1969. *Peasant Wars of the Twentieth Century*. New York: Harper and Row.

Wolff, Michael Jerome 2015. "Building Criminal Authority: A Comparative Analysis of Drug Gangs in Rio de Janeiro and Recife." *Latin American Politics and Society*, 56(2), pp. 21–40.

Wood, Elisabeth, 2016. "Social Mobilization and Violence in Civil War and Their Social Legacies." In D. della Porta & M. Diani, eds. *The Oxford Handbook of Social Movements*. Oxford University Press.

Wood, Elisabeth Jean, 2003. *Insurgent Collective Action and Civil War in El Salvador*. New York: Cambridge University Press.
Wood, Elisabeth Jean, 2008. "The Social Processes of Civil War: The Wartime Transformation of Social Networks." *Annual Review of Political Science*, 11(1), pp. 539–561.
Wood, Elisabeth Jean, 2009. "Armed Groups and Sexual Violence: When Is Wartime Rape Rare?" *Politics and Society*, 37, pp. 131–161.
Wunsch, James S. & Ottemoeller, Dan, 2004. "Uganda: Multiple Levels of Local Governance." *Local Governance in Africa: The Challenges of Democratic Decentralization*, pp. 181–209.
Young, John, 1997b. *Peasant Revolution in Ethiopia*. New York: Cambridge University Press.
Young, Tom, 1997a. "A Victim of Modernity? Explaining the War in Mozambique." In Paul B. Rich & Richard Stubbs, eds. *The Counter-Insurgent State: Guerrilla Warfare and State Building in the Twentieth Century*. New York: St. Martin's Press.
Zahar, Mary-Joëll, 2001. "Proégés, Clients, Cannon Fodder: Civil-Militia Relations in Internal Conflicts." In Simon Chesterman, ed. *Civilians in War*. Boulder: Lynne Rienner Publishers.
Zambrano, Fabio, ed., 1998. *Colombia, País de Regiones*, Vol. II. Bogotá: CINEP.

Index

Note: Page numbers followed by letters *f*, *m*, *n*, and *t* refer to figures, maps, notes, and tables, respectively.

ACC. *see* Self-defense Forces of Casanare, Colombia
Aceh, Indonesia, 61
Afghanistan
   civilian agency in, 5
   rebel governance in, 34–35, 38
   see also Taliban
Africa
   aliocracies in, 32
   rebelocracies in, 33
   territorial control by rebel groups in, 44*n*
   see also specific countries
Afro-Colombian communities, 89
   land ownership in, 154
   negotiations with armed actors, 195–196
agrarian reform, in Viotá, Colombia, 17, 215, 219–223, 234
Ahrar al-Sham (Syria), 57
aliocracy, 3, 11, 28
   bargaining process and emergence of, 195, 197, 200
   benefits to armed groups, 12
   civilian cooperation under, 263
   civilian resistance under, lack of bargaining power in, 64–65
   collective resistance and emergence of, 196–201, 214
   in Colombia, 1, 2, 18, 194, 246–247
   determinants of, 3, 9, 18, 42*f*, 42*t*, 43, 62–63, 65, 82, 105

etymology of term, 3*n*
   examples of, 32
   institutional quality and, 144, 145*f*, 298
   paths to, 164–165, 193–201
   rebelocracy compared to, 12, 144*f*
   stages in construction of, 195–196
   state presence and, 145–146
   violence under, likelihood of, 30, 165
al-Nusra (Syria), 57
AMV. *see* Self-defense Peasant Forces of Meta and Vichada, Colombia
Angola, UNITA in, 33, 38, 45, 60
Apartadó, Antioquia (Colombia), 201, 206
April 19 Movement (M19), Colombia, 89, 91, 95*t*
Arbeláez, Édgar, 253
armed group(s)
   in Colombian civil war, 85, 89–90, 93, 94, 95*t*
   entry strategies of, 161, 173–179, 175*t*
   expansion during civil war, 178, 179, 267
   locally based, research needed on, 303
   preferences of, 44–45, 47
   presence of
      measuring, 308, 314
      types of, 24*f*
   and rebelocracy, preference for, 11, 18, 55–56, 82, 106, 214, 262
   security provided by, 7, 28, 181

387

armed group(s) (cont.)
    and social contracts, incentives for establishing, 9–10, 48–50
    stages in creation of social order by, 160–162, 161f
    and state, parasitic relations between, 253, 255, 301
    strategies toward communities, variation in, 5, 15, 17, 18, 24, 37–39, 81–82, 162–164, 163t
    taxation by, 7, 28, 182–183
    and territorial control, desire for, 7, 9, 44–45, 44n, 262
    territorial dispersal of, 43–44
    time horizon of, and wartime social order, 3, 9–10, 11, 42, 42f, 42t, 48–55, 82, 125, 298
    use of term, 24–25
    and wartime institutions, creation of, 7
    see also competition; discipline; recruitment; *specific groups*
army, Colombian, collusion with paramilitaries, 253, 255
Asia
    rebel governance in, 34, 38–39
    territorial control by rebel groups in, 44n
    see also specific countries
assumptions
    about civilian-combatant interaction, 5
    about civilian preferences, 47
    testing of, 4
    in theory of collective civilian resistance, 74–78
    in theory of wartime social order, 43–47, 106, 107t
    see also microfoundations
AUC (United Self-Defense Forces of Colombia), 91, 98
    collaboration with elites, 178
    collective work organized by, 190
    competition with ACC, 202–203
    indiscipline and disorder under, 207

BACRIM (emerging criminal bands), in Colombia, 93
Bananero Bloc (Colombia), 95t
Barco, Virgilio, 91
bargaining power, of civilians, 299
    under aliocracy, 64–65
    capacity for collective action and, 63–64, 194, 256

under disorder, 65
under rebelocracy, 63–64
Benavidez, Adelia, 250–252, 256
Betancourt, Belisario, 90
Bogota, Colombia
    Communist Party in, 220, 225, 247
    interviews conducted in, 207, 235, 283, 321–322, 323, 326t–328t
    and Viotá, 219, 220, 225, 235, 236, 245
Buenaventura, Valle del Cauca (Colombia), 200
Buitrageños (Colombia), 95t, 123n, 179n

cabildos (autonomous village councils), 351–352
Caimito, Sucre (Colombia), 194, 200
Calima Bloc (Colombia), 95t
Cano, Maria, 220
Caño Mochuelo, Arauca (Colombia), 196
Carranceros (Macetos), Colombia, 95t, 207
Casabianca, Tolima (Colombia), 184, 194
Castaño, Carlos, 98
Catatumbo Bloc (Colombia), 95t, 100
    former members of, in survey sample, 283f, 284, 322–323
Cauca, Colombia, indigenous movement in, 198–200, 208–209, 351–354
causal process observations (CPOs), 105, 109, 213
Centauros Bloc (Colombia), 95t, 202
China, People's Liberation Army (PLA) in
    political goals of, 59
    rebel governance by, 5, 38–39
civilian(s)
    preferences of, assumptions about, 47
    response to disorder, 203–204, 306
    survey of, 286–287, 286m
    see also communities
civilian agency, during war, 2, 4–6, 304, 306
    evidence for, 101, 261
    and social order, 41, 63, 187, 298–299
    see also bargaining power; resistance
civilian-combatant interaction
    armed competition and, 53, 203–204
    assumptions about, 5
    in Colombian civil war, reconstruction of, 4, 15, 170–171, 269, 316–324
    in daily life, 139, 141f, 144f, 186
    importance of understanding, 4, 8, 30–31, 40, 101
    intermediaries in, 191

Index   389

local context in, importance of, 308
negotiations in, 39–40, 195, 197, 200
and post-conflict outcomes, 4, 8, 31
and resistance, emergence of, 40
and social order, creation of, 161–162, 161f, 298
state presence and, 301
variation in, 5–6, 23–24, 204–205, 210–211
see also social contract
civilian cooperation
  under aliocracy, 263
  as dominant strategy, 67
  with FARC, in Viotá, 238–239, 244–246, 255–256
  judicial system and, 57–58
  obedience vs. spontaneous support, 46–47
  under rebelocracy, 11, 16, 18, 55–58, 106, 191–192, 262, 263, 304
  shift in, as survival strategy, 192
  social contract and, 48–50
  with Taliban, in Afghanistan, 6, 46
  and territorial control by armed group, 45–47
  use of term, 25
civilian resistance. *see* collective resistance; resistance
civil war(s)
  community role in shaping, 307
  Hobbes' description of, 47, 297, 312
  irregular, 4, 43, 297
  localist view of, 66
  quality of local institutions and likelihood of, 309
  social order in, 3, 9–13, 297
  see also Colombian civil war; social order, wartime
collective resistance
  absence of, and establishment of rebelocracy, 256–257
  and aliocracy, emergence of, 196–201, 214
  alternative explanations for, testing of, 257–260
  assumptions in theory of, 74–77
  and bargaining power of civilians, 63–64, 194, 256
  changes in community's capacity for, 75–76
  definition of, 63
  development during war, 302

expectations of, and armed groups' strategies toward communities, 11, 15, 42, 65, 82, 307
in highly strategic territories, 208–209, 210, 355t–356t
indigenous communities in Colombia and, 151–152, 196, 198–200, 208–209, 215, 351–354
institutional quality and, 3, 11–12, 18, 67, 68, 82, 144, 209–210, 246–247, 255–256, 260, 263
likelihood of, assessment by armed groups, 77–78, 83, 173, 250
to rebelocracy, 65–73, 196–197
role in evolution of civil war, 312
to Shining Path (Peru), 71–72, 304
studies of, 38–39
sustained nonviolent, effectiveness of, 260–261
violence against civilians and, 302, 305
violence used to test, 78, 83, 164, 170, 197–198, 305
in Zama, Viotá (Colombia), 249–252
Colombia
  agrarian reform in, 17, 215, 219–223, 234
  communities in, random sample of, 87, 102t, 112–114, 113m, 115f, 117, 118m, 313–315
  demobilization program in, 85, 91, 93, 282–284
  high-quality local institutions in, sources of, 150–151, 150f
  internal migration in, 151
  La Violencia in, 89, 96, 224–226
  rebel courts in, 34, 58, 61, 240–241
  topography and political fragmentation in, 88
  variation in local characteristics, 85
Colombian civil war, 88
  armed groups in, 85, 86, 89, 93, 94, 95t
  civilian-combatant interaction in, reconstruction of, 4, 15, 170–171, 269
  drug trade in, 45, 59, 86, 89, 93, 96, 99
  duration of, variation at subnational level, 85
  failed peace negotiations in, 90, 93
  origins of, 89, 96
  social order during, 14, 172, 172f
  societal costs of, 94

Colombian civil war (cont.)
    and study of wartime social order, 85
    see also guerrilla groups; paramilitary groups
Colombian Communist Party, 220n
    and FARC, 96, 236
    during *La Violencia*, 225
    in Viotá
        and agrarian reform, 220–221, 223, 224, 229–230
        decline of, 232, 235–236, 240
combatants
    demobilization program for, 85, 91, 93, 282–283
    former, survey sample of, 19, 282–285, 283f, 285m, 321–323
    guerrilla, characteristics of, 97
    paramilitary, characteristics of, 99
    see also civilian-combatant interaction
Communal Action Associations. *see* JACs
Communist Party of Colombia. *see* Colombian Communist Party
Communist Party of the Philippines (PKP), 52, 77
communities
    armed groups' strategies toward, variation in, 5, 15, 17, 18, 24, 37–39, 81–82, 162–164, 163t
    and civil war dynamics, 211, 307
    Colombian
        governance structure in, 116
        random sample of, 102, 102t, 112–114, 113m, 115f, 117, 118m, 313–315
        data collection on, 112–124, 313–329
        timelines in history of, 102, 119, 120f, 320
    use of term, 23–24
    in war zones, study of, 111–112, 124
    see also collective resistance; leaders; local institutions
competition, among armed groups
    and civilian bargaining power, 65
    and civilian-combatant interaction, 53, 203–204
    and disorder, 3, 10, 42, 42f, 42t, 51, 53–54, 126, 128f, 138, 157, 201, 202–205, 298
    effect on order, statistical model of, 133f, 134, 135f, 136–137, 137f
    measuring, 127
    and recruitment, 67n
    and short-term horizons, 10

state and, 79
and violence against civilians, 10, 44, 53, 54n, 65, 167–169, 202, 203, 204, 249, 305
cooperation. *see* civilian cooperation
Cordoba Bloc (Colombia), 95t
    former members of, in survey sample, 283f, 284, 322–323
counterinsurgency, civilian-combatant interaction and strategies for, 4, 8, 46
counterinsurgent irregular groups
    studies of, 34–35
    see also paramilitaries
courts, rebel, 56–58
    in Afghanistan, under Taliban, 34, 52, 57, 61
    benefits to armed groups, 61–62, 72–73
    in Colombia, 34, 58, 61, 240–241
    costs of running, 61–62
    in Indonesia, 61
    instrumental role of, 72–73
    Palestinian, 57, 61
    in Sri Lanka, under Tamils, 56–57
    in Syria, 57, 61, 62
Cuba, rebelocracy in, 34

data collection
    by armed groups. *see* intelligence gathering
    research. *see* empirical strategy; research design
dataset, on civilian-combatant interactions, 102t, 115, 122–124, 321
demobilization and reintegration program (DRP), in Colombia, 85, 91, 93, 282–284
democracy, capture of, 186–187, 242, 250–252, 307–308
Democratic Republic of Congo (DRC), rebel groups in, 38, 52, 59
discipline, of armed groups
    Colombian guerrillas, 98, 127, 205–206
    Colombian paramilitaries, 98, 127, 205–206
    and social contract, 51–52, 298
    see also indiscipline
disobedience, punishment for, under rebelocracy, 60–61, 191
disorder, in conflict zones, 3, 26–28, 26f
    civilian bargaining power during, 65
    civilian response to, 203–204, 306

Index   391

competition for territorial control and, 3,
    10, 42, 42f, 42t, 51, 53–54, 126,
    128f, 138, 157, 201, 202–205, 298
  examples of, 32
  indiscipline of armed group and, 3, 10,
    51, 55, 65, 126, 128f, 138, 157, 202,
    205–207
  measuring, 171
  natural resources and increased
    likelihood of, 131
  paths to, 161–162, 167–170, 201–209
  rebelocracy following, 204
  state presence and, 157
  strategic territories and, 12, 127
  time horizon of armed group and, 3, 10,
    42, 42f, 42t, 50–55, 82, 125, 298
  as transitory situation, 117
  in Viotá, Colombia, 248–249, 251
dispute institutions, 12, 68
  armed groups and creation of, 56–58,
    71–73, 183–184, 240–241
  and community's capacity for collective
    action, 71–72, 144
  importance of, 69–70
  in Nasa indigenous community, 351–353
  preexisting, and wartime social order,
    11–12, 68, 69–70, 81, 144, 299
  under rebelocracy, 71–73, 240–241
  role in transition to peace, 311–312
  in Viotá, Colombia, 225, 227
  see also courts
Domínguez, Rosa, 227
drug trade
  Colombian civil war and, 45, 59, 86, 89,
    93, 96, 99, 184–185
  Taliban and, 45

ecological fallacy problem, 87
economic activities, under rebelocracy, 59,
    184–185
  vs. aliocracy, 144f
  by guerrillas vs. paramilitaries, 138, 139f
  international image and, 60
  measures of, 331t
  quality of dispute institutions and, 69–70
  in Viotá, Colombia, 241
education, provision under rebelocracy, 62,
    189
elections, intervention by armed groups,
    186–187, 307–308
  FARC, 242, 250–252

    and violence, 315
ELN (Colombia), 91, 95t
  aliocracy under, 194
  Catholic Church and, 186
  discipline of, 98
  drug trade and, 89n, 98n
  emergence and expansion of, 89–90, 91,
    96
  former members of, in survey sample,
    283f, 284
  goals of, 96
  infiltration of politics by, 187
  organizational structure of, 97
  peace talks with, 90, 93
  regulatory practices of, 180
El Roble, Sucre (Colombia), 194
El Salvador, FMLN in, 38, 77
empirical strategy, 100
  data collection methods
    on civilians and combatants, 170–171,
      213, 282–287
    on communities, 112–124, 313–329
entry strategies, of armed groups, 161
  and rebelocracy, 173–179, 175t, 237
  see also intelligence gathering
environmental preservation, FARC and,
    184, 241
EPL. see Popular Liberation Army,
    Colombia
Eritrean People's Liberation Front, 33, 57
ERP. see People's Revolutionary Army,
    Colombia
Ethiopia, rebel governance in, 33, 57
Europe
  rebel governance in, 34, 49
  see also specific countries
extortion, armed groups and, 98, 99

failed state, concept of, 36
Farabundo Marti National Liberation Front
    (FMLN), El Salvador, 38, 77
FARC (Colombia)
  aliocracy under, 1, 2, 18, 194, 196, 214,
    246–247
  approach to communities in non-contested
    areas, 174, 175, 236–238
  civilian cooperation with, in Viotá,
    238–239, 244–246, 255–256
  civilian negotiations with, 197
  civilian resistance to, 194, 200
  collusion with politicians, 92

FARC (Colombia) (cont.)
    Communist Party and, 96, 236
    discipline in, 98
    dispute institutions under, 183, 240–241
    and drug trade, 45, 59, 98
    economic activities regulated by, 241
    emergence and expansion of, 89, 96, 267
    former members of, interviews with, 283f, 284, 324, 326t–327t
    goals of, 96
    ideological mobilization by, 177, 243–246
    and indigenous communities, 196, 198, 199–200, 208–209, 352–354
    indiscipline and disorder under, 206–207
    intelligence gathering by, 174
    intervention in politics, 187, 242–243, 250–252
    militiamen used by, 206, 248–249
    mobility regulation by, 182, 239
    natural resource protection under, 184, 241
    organizational structure of, 97
    peace negotiations with, 90, 91, 93
    and peasant communities, 203
    preference for rebelocracy, 214
    public goods provided by, 176, 178, 189–190
    rebelocracy under, 1, 2, 241–246
    recruitment by, in Viotá, 244–245
    social cleansing by, 176, 237, 238, 240
    social regulation by, 186, 239, 242, 244
    taxation by, 182–183, 248
    territorial expansion in 1990s, 91
    variation in strategies toward communities, 17–18, 353
    in Viotá, 1–2, 214, 234, 235–252, 254
Feminine Alliance (Colombia), 227
fieldwork. *see* empirical strategy
FMLN. *see* Farabundo Marti National Liberation Front
focus group, in Viotá, Colombia, 324
42nd Front (FARC, Colombia), 206, 235, 236, 240
43rd Front (FARC, Colombia), 196
Free Aceh Movement (Indonesia), 61
freedom of speech, regulation by armed groups, 185, 239
FSLN. *see* Sandinista National Liberation Front

GAM (Free Aceh Movement), Indonesia, 61
genocide, 45
Granada, Meta (Colombia), 180
Greece, rebel governance in, 34, 49
guerrilla groups, Colombian, 94, 95t
    characteristics of fighters, 97
    discipline of, 98, 127, 205–206
    dispute institutions and legitimacy of, 73
    and drug trade, 98
    emergence and expansion of, 89, 96
    entry strategies to build rebelocracy, 174–178, 175t
    ideological mobilization by, 175t, 176–177
    and indigenous communities, 196, 198, 199–200
    intervention in local elections, 187
    peace negotiations with, 90, 93
    public goods provided by, 139, 140f, 175t, 176, 178, 189–190
    rebelocracy and recruitment by, 292, 293f
    regulatory practices of, 139, 141f, 180
    social order under, 138, 172
    women in, 97, 207
    see also ELN; FARC
Guevara, Che, 36, 44

haciendas, in Viotá, Colombia, 217–219, 229
health services, under rebelocracy, 62, 189
Hilario (leader of Zama, Colombia), 230, 231, 243, 247
Hobbes, Thomas, 47, 297, 312
humanitarian relief
    civilian-combatant interaction and, 4
    local institutions and, 309–310

ideological mobilization, 164
    under aliocracy, 165
    as entry strategy for armed groups, 175t, 176–177
    FARC and, 177, 243–246
    under rebelocracy, 165, 166
ideology, of armed group
    and civilian resistance to rebelocracy, 65–66
    and recruitment, 274, 275f
    and social regulation of civilians, 186
    and wartime social order, 80, 301–302
India, Naga insurgencies in, 44n
indigenous communities, in Colombia, 89, 151
    and aliocracy, 195–196, 198–201

declaration of neutrality by, 201
influence of, measuring, 330–335
land ownership in, 154
negotiations with armed actors, 195
and quality of local institutions, 151–155, 153f
resistance to armed groups, 151–152, 196, 198–200, 208–209, 215, 340–354
indiscipline, of armed group
and disorder, 3, 10, 51, 53, 65, 126, 128f, 138, 157, 202, 205–207
effect on order, statistical model of, 133–134, 133f, 134f, 137, 137f
as free-riding problem, 51
measuring, 126–127, 333t
Indonesia, GAM (Free Aceh Movement) in, 61
infrastructure
under FARC, 243
under paramilitaries, 176n
under rebelocracy, 62, 189–190
institutional biographies, 15, 102t, 119–121, 120t, 320
vignettes surveys compared to, 121
institutions
definition of, 21–22, 22n
wartime, 2, 22
emergence of, 7
and post-conflict outcomes, 8–9
rebelocracy and, 11
and social order, 22
tendency to overlook role of, 6, 7–8
see also local institutions
instrumental variables approach, 100, 108, 111, 151
insurgent state, 43
intelligence gathering, by armed groups, 78, 161, 253
in construction of rebelocracy, 173–174
under rebelocracy, 191
and selective violence, 167
international image, rebelocracy and, 59–60
interviews
bias in, avoiding, 259
in-depth, 323–324
and local histories, building, 122, 323, 329t
long structured, 102
methodology used in, 316
participant selection, 315–316, 324t–328t
see also surveys

Iraq, civil war and disorder in, 32
irregular civil wars, 4, 43, 297
see also civil war(s)
ISIS (The Islamic State of Iraq and the Levant)
civilian cooperation with, 58
and interest in rebel governance, 304
services provided by, 62
Itagüí, Antioquia (Colombia), 178, 198

JACs (Communal Action Associations), Colombia
infiltration by armed groups, 174–175, 178, 179, 187–188, 238
in Viotá, 231, 233–234, 238, 239, 240–241, 246, 253–254

Kosovo, civil war in, 267

labor, armed groups and regulation of, 184–185, 190, 241
La Macarena, Meta (Colombia), 206
land reform. *see* agrarian reform
Latin America
rebel governance in, 33–34, 38, 62
territorial control by rebel groups in, 44n
see also specific countries
La Violencia (civil war), in Colombia, 89, 96
Viotá during, 224–226, 226n
leaders, community
armed actors and, 187–188, 198, 200
as determinants of collective resistance, 258
quality of dispute institutions and, 68
violence against, as measurement mechanism, 78, 83, 164, 198, 250
violence against, in construction of rebelocracy, 170, 179, 198
in Viotá (Colombia)
collaboration with FARC, 238–239
concentration of, 229–230, 233, 234–235
resistance to FARC, 1, 2, 247, 250–252
Leviathan (Hobbes), 47, 297
Liberal Party (Colombia), in Viotá, 224–225, 232–233, 238, 257
liberated zone, 43
Liberation Tamil Tigers of Tamil Eelam (LTTE), Sri Lanka, 32, 34, 44n, 56–57
Liberia
civil war and disorder in, 32
NPLF in, 39, 53

Liberia (cont.)
  rebel governance in, 39
Librea, Viotá (Colombia), 229
  Communist Party in, 229
  FARC penetration in, 238–239
  low institutional quality and cooperation with FARC in, 255–256
  rebelocracy under FARC in, 1, 2, 240, 256–257
  weakening of community organizing in, 232–233
Llanos, Martin, 179
local histories, constructing, 124, 323, 329t
local institutions
  biographies of, reconstruction of, 15, 102, 119–121, 120t, 320
  in indigenous communities, 151–155, 153f, 352
  infiltration by armed groups, 174–175, 178–179
  quality of, 67–68
    and armed groups' strategies to build order, 162–164, 163t
    and civil war, likelihood of, 309
    and collective resistance, 3, 11–12, 18, 67, 68–72, 82, 144, 209–210, 246–247, 255–256, 260, 263
    indigenous populations and, 151–155, 153f
    vs. leadership quality, as determinant of collective resistance, 258
    measuring, 121, 129, 330, 332t–334t
    and post-conflict outcomes, 310–312
    and recruitment, 263–264, 268, 278–281, 279f, 280f
    sources in Colombia, 150–151, 150f, 193
    in strategic territories, and social order, 127, 128f, 135f, 136, 145f, 146, 148–150, 149f, 299
    testing of hypothesis regarding, 17, 103
    and violence against civilians, 168, 306
    and wartime social order, 3, 9, 11–12, 15, 17–18, 68, 69–70, 81, 104, 144, 145f, 147–148, 147f, 148f, 155f, 157–158, 193, 260, 298–299
  role in civil war, further research needed on, 304, 312
  transformation during war, 266
  in Viotá (Colombia), 225–228
  community prosperity and weakening of, 230–233
  vs. state institutions, 231, 233
  strength in Zama, 233–235, 246–247
  see also dispute institutions; JACs
localist view of civil war, 66
long-term horizon of armed group, and social order, 3, 10, 41, 42f, 42t, 48–50, 82, 298
Lord's Resistance Army (LRA), 32, 37
Los Masetos (Colombian paramilitary group), 186–187
LTTE. see Liberation Tamil Tigers of Tamil Eelam

M19. see April 19 Movement, Colombia
macro-level changes, and short-term horizon of armed group, 54–55
Magangué, Bolivar (Colombia), 190, 207
Maoist rebels, in Nepal, 34, 57, 58
Mao Zedong
  on civilian cooperation, 46, 50
  on rebel governance, 36, 44
Martyrs of Guatica Front (Colombia), 95t
Medina, González, 253
Medio Atrato, Chocó (Colombia), 195
memory workshops, 102, 117–122, 117n, 316, 318–320
Merchán, Victor J., 217, 220, 224
  land gift to, 229, 234, 256
Metro Bloc (Colombia), 95t, 178
microfoundations
  definition of, 84
  testing of, 4, 16, 18–19, 100, 105, 107t
migration, in Colombia, 151
  of indigenous groups, and social order, 152–153
  to Viotá, 219–220
militias
  in civil wars, 86
  under FARC, 206, 248–249
  under rebelocracy, 191
  in slums of big cities, 29
mind mapping, 318–320, 319f
Mineros Bloc (Colombia), 95t
mobility, regulation by armed groups, 182, 239
Mojana Bloc (Colombia), 95t
Mozambique, Renamo in, 32

Index

Nasa indigenous groups (Colombia), 351
  local institutions of, 351–352
  resistance to FARC, 208–209, 352–354
National Liberation Army (Colombia). *see* ELN
National Patriotic Front of Liberia (NPLF), 39, 53
National Resistance Army (NRA), in Uganda, 33, 37
National Union for the Total Independence of Angola. *see* UNITA
natural resources
  exploitation by armed groups
    in Colombia, 89, 184–185
    and disorder, increased likelihood of, 131
    and need for civilian cooperation, 52
    and need for territorial control, 44–45
    prevalence of, 86
    and recruitment, 270–273, 274, 275*f*
    and social order in wartime, 14, 59, 128*f*, 129, 136, 136*f*
  protection by armed groups, in Colombia, 184, 241
negotiations
  between civilians and combatants, 39–40
  and aliocracy, emergence of, 195, 197, 200
  for peace
    in Colombian civil war, 90, 93
    disorder accompanying, 3, 54–55
Negro Antonio (FARC commander), 240, 241, 242, 243, 247, 250, 252
neo-paramilitaries, in Colombia, 93
Nepal
  Maoist rebels in, 34, 57, 58
  rebel courts in, 61
NGOs
  infiltration by armed groups, 178
  and institutional capacity of local communities, 76
Nicaragua, Sandinistas (FSLN) in, 77
Noscué, Vitonás, 208–209, 353
NPLF. *see* National Patriotic Front of Liberia
NRA. *see* National Resistance Army, Uganda
Nudo Paramillo, Córdoba (Colombia), 197

obedience, civilian, 46–47
  social contract and, 48–49
  see also disobedience
order, in conflict zones, 3, 21, 26–28
  civilian preference for, 50
  degree of, 27
  measuring, 171
  rebel preference for, 9
  social contract and, 26, 26*f*, 27
  see also social order, wartime

Pakistan, Federally Administered Tribal Areas (FATA) in, 24
Palestinian rebels, courts under, 57, 61
paramilitaries, 86
  competition with rebels, and disorder, 54
  rebelocracies established by, 34–35
paramilitary groups, Colombian, 86, 95*t*
  aliocracy under, 195
  armed competition with guerrillas, 204
  collaboration with local elites, 178, 179
  collusion with army, 253, 255
  collusion with politicians, 92
  competition among, 202–203
  discipline of, 98, 127, 205–206
  and drug trade, 96, 99
  emergence and expansion of, 90, 96, 267
  entry strategies to build rebelocracy, 174–178, 175*t*
  former members of, interviews with, 283*f*, 284, 326*t*–327*t*
  goals of, 96
  and indigenous communities, 198
  infiltration of local institutions, 174–175, 178, 179
  intervention in local elections, 186–187
  number of, 97
  organizational structure of, 98
  public goods provided by, 139, 140*f*, 175*t*, 189, 190
  rebelocracy and recruitment by, 292, 294*f*
  regulatory practices of, 139, 141*f*, 180
  relations with civilians, 204
  social cleansing by, 175*t*, 176
  social order under, 138, 172
  taxation by, 183, 254
  umbrella organization of (AUC), 91, 98
  violence by, 99, 168–169, 253–255
  in Viotá, 249, 252–255

Pasca, Cundinamarca (Colombia), 183, 194, 203, 207
Pastrana, Andrés, 91, 206
peace communities, 39, 54n
peaceful resistance, 6, 39, 260–261, 311
peace negotiations
  in Colombian civil war, 90, 93
  disorder accompanying, 3, 54–55
peasants, Colombian
  in agrarian movement, 17, 215, 219–221
  FARC and, 203
  growing apathy of, 232, 235, 238
  in haciendas, 217–219
  resistance to armed groups, 200
Peasant Self-defense Forces of Casanare, Colombia, 95t
Peasant Self-defense Forces of Córdoba and Urabá (ACCU), Colombia, 98
People's Liberation Army (PLA), China
  political goals of, 59
  rebel governance by, 5, 38–39
People's Revolutionary Army (ERP), Colombia, 95t, 194
Peru, Shining Path in, 34, 49, 59, 71–72, 304
Petraeus, David, 44
Philippines, communist rebels (PKP) in, 52, 77
PLA. see People's Liberation Army, China
political activities, armed groups and, 186–188
  under FARC, 242
  guerrillas vs. paramilitaries, 139, 140f
  measures of, 331t
  under rebelocracy, 59, 242
  under rebelocracy vs. aliocracy, 144f
politicians, collusion with armed groups, 59, 92
Popular Liberation Army (EPL), Colombia, 91, 95t
  emergence and expansion of, 89
  and unions, 177
post-conflict reconstruction
  civilian-combatant interaction and, 4, 8, 31
  disaggregated approach to, need for, 310
  local institutions and, 8–9, 310–312
predictability
  lack of, and disorder, 26–27
  social contract and, 26, 48
  state formation and, 7
  in war zones, 21–22
  see also order

private goods
  armed groups' strategic use of, 165, 167, 169, 174, 175, 175t, 178, 190, 237, 238, 243
  definition of, 163–164
  and FARC penetration in Viotá, 237, 238, 243
process-driven natural experiment, 17–18, 104, 109, 213
process tracing, use in research design, 104, 105, 152, 212–214
prostitution, regulation by armed groups, 180, 185
public goods, provision and regulation of
  armed groups strategies in, 175–176, 175t, 178, 189–190, 237, 238, 243
  and FARC penetration in Viotá, 237, 238, 243
  by guerrillas vs. paramilitaries, 139, 140f, 175t, 189–190
  measures of, 332t
  under rebelocracy vs. aliocracy, 144f
Puerto Gaitán, Meta (Colombia)
  elections in, manipulation of, 186–187
  paramilitary groups in, 179, 180, 195, 206, 207
  taxation in, 182
Puerto Parra, Santander (Colombia), 182, 183, 184, 191–192
Pumarejo, López, 223
punishment(s)
  of indisciplined combatants, in Colombia, 98, 99, 206
  monopolization of, and power, 56
  under rebelocracy, 60–61

rebel governance
  determinants of, 37–38
  literature on, 6, 32–40
  recent interest in, 35, 304
  variation in, 38–39
rebelocracy, 3, 10–11, 28
  aliocracy compared to, 12, 144f
  armed groups' preference for, 11, 18, 55–56, 82, 106, 214, 262
  armed groups' strategies leading to, 165–166, 173–179, 175t, 236–239
  and bargaining power of civilians, 63–64
  benefits to armed groups, 59, 191
  channels of rule under, 28–29

civilian cooperation under, 11, 16, 18,
    55–58, 106, 191–192, 262, 263, 304
civilian resistance to, quality of local
    institutions and, 3, 11–12, 18, 67,
    68–69, 196–197
civilian resistance under, 192
clandestine, 29
construction of, 173–179, 175*t*
costs of running, 60–62
determinants of, 3, 9, 82, 105, 138–150,
    139*f*–145*f*, 147*f*–149*f*
disorder followed by, 204
dispute institutions under, 71–73,
    240–241
domains of rule under, 28
etymology of term, 3*n*
examples of, 32–35
under guerrillas vs. paramilitaries,
    139–142, 142*f*
institutional quality and, 144, 145*f*,
    147–148, 147*f*, 148*f*, 155*f*, 298
and international image of armed groups,
    59–60
life under, 180–192, 239–246
measures of, 333*t*–334*t*, 335–340
past civilian resistance and, 156, 157*f*
prevalence of, 171, 172, 303–304
recruitment under, 19, 59, 106, 263–264,
    267–270, 272*f*, 273*f*, 276,
    277*f*–278*f*, 292, 293*f*, 294*f*, 295, 306
resources needed to sustain, 191
service provision under, 62
state presence and, 29, 181, 188
statistical models on, 127–150,
    147*f*–149*f*, 336–340
time horizon of armed group and, 3, 10,
    42, 42*f*, 42*t*
violence under, 30, 165, 166, 181, 305
in Viotá, Colombia, 1, 2, 239–246,
    256–257
recruitment, by armed groups
    alternative explanations for, testing,
        281–282
    coerced vs. voluntary, 264*n*
    comparison of joiners and nonjoiners,
        287–292, 289*f*–291*f*
    current theories of, 264–267
    in disputed territories, 67*n*
    FARC, in Viotá, 244–245
    by guerrillas vs. paramilitaries, 265*n*
    ideology and, 274, 275*f*
    individual agency and structural
        conditions for, 295–296
    natural resources and, 270–273, 274,
        275*f*
    after onset of war, 267, 295
    paths to, 268, 281
    quality of local institutions and, 263–264,
        268, 278–281, 279*f*, 280*f*
    under rebelocracy, 19, 59, 106, 263–264,
        267–270, 272*f*, 273*f*, 276,
        277*f*–278*f*, 292, 293*f*, 294*f*, 295, 306
    social order and, 19, 267–270, 290–292,
        291*f*, 295
    statistical models on, 274–281,
        276*f*–280*f*, 358*t*–359*t*
    territorial control and, 269, 270
    violence and, 274, 275*f*
Renamo (Mozambique), 32
research design, 14–19, 84
    advantages and limitations of, 106
    components of, 100, 101, 102*t*
    focus on Colombia, pros and cons of,
        85
    goals of, 100
    instrumental variables approach in, 100,
        108, 111, 151
    local histories in, 124, 323, 329*t*
    memory workshops in, 102, 117–122,
        316, 318–319
    multilevel models in, 111
    process-driven natural experiment in,
        17–18, 104, 109, 213–214
    process tracing in, 104, 105, 152,
        212–214
    significance of, 101
    surveys with local experts in, 122, 323
    vignettes surveys in, 102, 116–117, 121,
        317–318
resistance, civilian
    and aliocracy, 193–201
    civilian-combatant interaction and
        emergence of, 40
    definition of, 25, 63*n*
    disorder and, 306
    empirical literature on, 39–40
    external factors influencing, 83
    indigenous communities in Colombia
        and, 151–152, 196, 198–200,
        208–209, 215
    lagged, 156
    past, effect on rebelocracy, 156, 157*f*

resistance, civilian (cont.)
  peaceful/nonviolent, 6, 39, 260–261, 311
  prevalence of, 6, 39, 304
  under rebelocracy, 192
  rebelocracy and cost of, 58
  and social order in wartime, 11, 16
  theories of, 40
  types and effectiveness of, 63–64
  see also collective resistance
Revolutionary Armed Forces of Colombia. see FARC
Revolutionary Socialist Party (Colombia), 220
Revolutionary United Front (RUF), Sierra Leone, 39, 45, 53
Ricardo (Zama leader), 250
roads, construction and maintenance of
  under FARC, 243
  under rebelocracy, 62, 189–190
Rojas Pinilla, Gustavo, 225
RUF. see Revolutionary United Front
Rwanda, civil war in, 45
Rwenzururu Kingdom Government, in Uganda, 33

San Benito Abad, Sucre (Colombia), 187
San Bernardo, Toledo (Colombia), 187
Sandinista National Liberation Front (FSLN), Nicaragua, 77
Santos, Juan Manuel, 93
Santuario, Risaralda (Colombia), 178, 190, 191, 206
San Vicente del Caguán, Caquetá (Colombia), 206
security
  civilian preference for, 47
  and wartime social order, 7, 28, 181
Self-defense Forces of Casanare (ACC), Colombia, 202–203
  arrival in Viotá, 252–255
Self-defense Peasant Forces of Meta and Vichada (AMV), Colombia, 95t, 207
sexual conduct, regulation by armed groups, 180, 185
Shining Path (Peru)
  collective resistance to, 71–72, 304
  rebelocracy under, 34, 49, 59
short-term horizon of armed group
  conditions leading to, 10, 51–55, 82
  and disorder, emergence of, 3, 10, 41, 42f, 42t, 48, 50–55, 82, 125, 298

  strategies associated with, 167–170
Sierra Leone
  civil war and disorder in, 32
  rebel governance in, 39, 45
  RUF in, 39, 45, 53
social cleansing, in Colombian conflict zones, 49
  as entry strategy for armed groups, 175t, 176, 181, 237
  by FARC, in Viotá, 237, 238, 240
social contract, between civilians and combatants, 3, 171
  armed competition and breaches of, 54
  definition of, 26
  and order, 26, 26f, 27
  quality of preexisting local institutions and, 9
  rebel incentives to break, 54
  rebel incentives to establish, 9–10, 48–50, 52
  as solution to prisoner's dilemma, 49
  and violence, variation in armed groups' use of, 30
social order, wartime, 2
  civilian agency in shaping, 41, 63, 187, 298–299
  and civilian behavior, 306
  civilian-combatant interaction and emergence of, 161–162, 161f, 298
  Colombian civil war and study of, 85
  definition of, 22
  determinants of, 3, 11, 15–16, 41–42, 42f, 42t, 262
    testing of hypotheses regarding, 101, 124–138, 125f, 126f, 128f
  under guerrillas vs. paramilitaries, in Colombia, 138, 172
  ideology of armed group and, 80, 302–303
  importance of understanding, 30–31
  indigenous migration and, 152–153
  measures of, 116–117, 121–122, 171–172, 331t–334t
  multiple forms of, 162, 162f
  and post-conflict outcomes, 310
  quality of preexisting local institutions and, 3, 9, 11–12, 15, 17–18, 68, 69–70, 81, 104, 144, 145f, 147–148, 147f, 148f, 155f, 157–158, 193, 260, 298–299

and recruitment, 19, 267–270, 290–292, 291f, 295
stages in creation of, 19, 103, 160–162, 161f
state presence and, 78–80, 145–146, 147–148, 149f, 157, 300–301
statistical models of, 131–136, 133f–137f
in strategic territories with high-quality institutions, 127, 128f, 135f, 136, 145f, 146, 148–150, 149f
studies of, 22
theory of, 3, 9–13, 41–42
assumptions in, 43–47, 106, 107t
time horizon of armed group and, 3, 9–10, 11, 42, 42f, 42t, 48–55, 82, 125, 298
types of, 3, 10–13, 26–35, 26f, 41
in Colombia, 172, 172f
variation across space and time, 2, 3, 22–23, 35, 38–39, 87, 298
social regulation, by armed groups, 180, 185–186
FARC, in Viotá, 239, 242, 244
guerrillas vs. paramilitaries, 139, 141f, 180
measures of, 331t
under rebelocracy vs. aliocracy, 144f
Somalia, warlords in, 64
Spanish civil war, 168
spontaneous support, civilian, 46
ideology of armed group and, 80
need for, 47
social contract and, 49
Sri Lanka, Tamil Tigers (LTTE) in, 32, 34, 44n, 56–57
state
and armed actors, parasitic relations between, 253, 255, 301
and civilian-combatant interaction, 301
coexistence with rebelocracy, 29, 181, 188
failed, concept of, 36
insurgent, concept of, 43
presence of
measuring, 333t
and recruitment by armed groups, 273
rebelocracy and aliocracy compared to, 11
in Viotá, Colombia, 231, 233
and wartime social order, role in shaping, 12–13, 78–80, 145–146, 147–148, 149f, 157, 300–301

state building
dispute institutions and, 72–73
dynamics of civil war and, 31, 311–312
literature on, 7, 37
statistical analysis
limitations of, 16
of rebelocracy, 146–150, 147f–149f, 336–340
of recruitment, 274–281, 277f–283f, 358t–359t
use of, 100
strategic territories
collective resistance in, 208–209, 210, 355t–356t
high-quality institutions in, effect on social order, 127, 128f, 135f, 136, 145f, 146, 148–150, 149f, 299
violence toward civilians in, 170, 352
wartime social order in, 12, 74–75, 75t, 83, 128f, 130, 202
Sudan People's Liberation Army (SPLA), 57, 59–60
Sudan People's Liberation Movement (SPLM), 32, 59–60
surveys, 104
of civilians, 19, 286–287, 286m, 323
of ex-combatants, 19, 282–285, 283f, 285m, 321–323
with local experts, 122, 323
open- and close-ended questions in, 320–321, 331t–334t
with vignettes, 102, 116–117, 121, 317–318
Syrian civil war
and interest in rebel governance, 304
ISIS in, 58
rebel courts during, 57, 61, 62
recruitment in, 267

Taliban
civilian cooperation with, 6, 46, 49
and drug trade, 45
judicial system under, 34, 52, 57, 61, 61n, 73
social order under, spatial variation in, 24, 39
strategy in developing popular support, 57
strategy in fighting U.S. Army, 43
Tamil Tigers (Sri Lanka), 32, 34, 44n, 56–57, 61n

taxation, by armed groups
    FARC, 182–183, 248
    paramilitaries, 183, 254
    and wartime social order, 7, 28
Taylor, Charles, 53
Tellus, Viotá (Colombia), 229
    FARC influence on local institutions in, 240–241
    FARC penetration in, 237–238
    low institutional quality and cooperation with FARC in, 255–256
    rebelocracy under FARC in, 240, 256–257
    weakening of local institutions in, 232, 237
territorial control, by armed groups
    byproducts of, maximizing, 9, 45, 49, 58–60, 262
    civilian cooperation and, 45–47
    quest for, 7, 9, 44–45, 44n, 262
    rebelocracy and, 11, 18
    and recruitment, 269, 270
    see also competition
territories, strategic value of
    measuring, 129
    and wartime social order, 12, 74–75, 75t, 83, 128f, 130, 202
    see also strategic territories
Tierralta, Córdoba (Colombia), 181
    armed competition and violence in, 203, 204
    collective work in, 190
    indigenous communities in, 198
    interviews in, 323, 325t–326t
    labor control by paramilitaries in, 184
    taxation by paramilitaries in, 183
Tigray People's Liberation Front (TPLF), 33
time horizon of armed group, and wartime social order, 3, 9–10, 11, 42, 42f, 42t, 48–55, 82, 125, 298
timelines, community history, 102, 119, 120f, 320
Toledo, North Santander (Colombia), 207
Toribío, Cauca (Colombia), 208–209, 352–354
Torres, Guillermo, 180, 195, 207
Torrez Giraldo, Ignacio, 220

Uganda, rebel governance in, 33, 37
uncertainty
    competition among armed groups and, 202–203

disorder and, 3, 10, 27, 30, 32, 54, 55, 171
    dispute institutions and decrease in, 68
ungoverned spaces, use of concept, 36
unions, Colombian
    guerrilla groups and, 177
    in Viotá, 220, 221, 227, 234
UNITA (National Union for the Total Independence of Angola), 33
    and diamond extraction, 45
    international image of, concern about, 60
    variation in strategies toward civilians, 38
United Self-Defense Forces of Colombia. *see* AUC
Uribe, Alvaro, 92, 93

Vieira, Gilberto, 225
Vietcong, strategy in fighting U.S. Army, 43
vignettes surveys, 102, 116–117, 121, 317–318
    institutional biographies compared to, 121
Villanueva, Casanare (Colombia), paramilitary groups in, 179, 202
violence, armed groups' use of, 181
    under aliocracy, 30, 165
    and bargaining capacity during negotiations, 55
    and civilian cooperation under disorder, 65
    and collective resistance, 302, 305
    against community leaders, 170, 179, 198
    competition for territorial control and, 10, 44, 53, 54n, 65, 167–169, 202, 203, 204, 249, 305
    definition of, 163
    electoral campaigns and, 315
    high levels of, and community's capacity for collective action, 76
    in highly strategic territories, 170, 352
    ideology and, 80
    indiscriminate, 168, 306
    as measurement of collective action capacity, 67, 78, 164, 170, 197–198, 305
    paramilitary arrival and, 99, 168–169, 253–255
    as proxy for armed group presence, 308
    quality of local institutions and, 168, 306
    under rebelocracy, 30, 165, 166, 181, 305
    and recruitment, 274, 275f
    selective, 167–168, 306

Index

social order and variation in, 30
in strategic territories, 75
as tool for governing, 306
Viotá, Cundinamarca (Colombia), 212, 215, 216m
   agrarian reform in, 17, 215, 219–223, 234
   aliocracy under FARC in, 1, 2, 18, 246–247
   apathy in, 232, 235, 238
   civilian cooperation with FARC in, 238–239, 244–246, 255
   coffee crisis of 1990s in, 236, 239
   collective resistance to FARC in, 249–252, 256, 260–261
   communist ideology in, 214, 219–224, 228, 229–230, 231, 240
   disorder in, emergence of, 248–249, 251
   divergent development of villages in, 17, 212–214, 229–234, 257
   FARC in, 1–2, 214, 234, 235–252, 254
   hacienda period in, 217–219, 229
   interviews in, 323, 324t–328t
   JACs in, 231, 233–234, 238, 239, 240–241, 246, 253–254
   during *La Violencia*, 224–226, 226n
   leaders of, concentration in Zama, 229–230, 233, 234–235
   Liberal Party in, 224–225, 238, 257
   local institutions in, 225–228, 234–235
   militiamen in, 206, 248–249
   natural resource protection under FARC in, 184
   paramilitary arrival in, 249, 252–255
   prosperity and weakening of local institutions in, 230–233
   public services provided by FARC in, 189
   rebelocracy under FARC in, 1, 2, 235–246, 256–257
   recruitment by FARC in, 244–245
   self-defense groups in, 222, 224–225, 227
   state presence in, 231, 233
   taxation by armed groups in, 182–183, 248, 254
   violence in, 238n
   women's rights movement in, 227–228
   see also Librea; Tellus; Zama
voluntary support. *see* spontaneous support

war
   effects of, variation in, 8
   see also civil war(s); Colombian civil war
war zone, definition of, 23, 24f
Winners of Arauca (Colombia), 95t
women, Colombian
   FARC's appeal to, 244
   guerrillas, 97, 207
   interviewees, 316
   in local elections, 250–252
   participants in memory workshops, 119
women's rights movement, in Colombia, 227–228

youth
   FARC's appeal to, 244–245
   see also recruitment

Zama, Viotá (Colombia)
   aliocracy under FARC in, 1, 2, 246–247
   autonomy of, alternative explanations for, 257–260
   collective resistance to FARC in, 249–252, 256, 260–261
   concentration of local leadership in, 229–230, 233, 234–235
   paramilitary arrival in, 255
   strength of local institutions in, 233–235, 246–247

Other Books in the Series (*continued from page iii*)

Lisa Baldez, *Why Women Protest? Women's Movements in Chile*
Kate Baldwin, *The Paradox of Traditional Chiefs in Democratic Africa*
Stefano Bartolini, *The Political Mobilization of the European Left, 1860–1980: The Class Cleavage*
Robert Bates, *When Things Fell Apart: State Failure in Late-Century Africa*
Mark Beissinger, *Nationalist Mobilization and the Collapse of the Soviet State*
Pablo Beramendi, *The Political Geography of Inequality: Regions and Redistribution*
Nancy Bermeo, ed., *Unemployment in the New Europe*
Carles Boix, *Democracy and Redistribution*
Carles Boix, *Political Order and Inequality: Their Foundations and their Consequences for Human Welfare*
Carles Boix, *Political Parties, Growth, and Equality: Conservative and Social Democratic Economic Strategies in the World Economy*
Catherine Boone, *Merchant Capital and the Roots of State Power in Senegal, 1930-1F985*
Catherine Boone, *Political Topographies of the African State: Territorial Authority and Institutional Change*
Catherine Boone, *Property and Political Order in Africa: Land Rights and the Structure of Politics*
Michael Bratton and Nicolas van de Walle, *Democratic Experiments in Africa: Regime Transitions in Comparative Perspective*
Michael Bratton, Robert Mattes, and E. Gyimah-Boadi, *Public Opinion, Democracy, and Market Reform in Africa*
Valerie Bunce, *Leaving Socialism and Leaving the State: The End of Yugoslavia, the Soviet Union, and Czechoslovakia*
Daniele Caramani, *The Nationalization of Politics: The Formation of National Electorates and Party Systems in Europe*
John M. Carey, *Legislative Voting and Accountability*
Kanchan Chandra, *Why Ethnic Parties Succeed: Patronage and Ethnic Headcounts in India*
Eric C. C. Chang, Mark Andreas Kayser, Drew A. Linzer, and Ronald Rogowski, *Electoral Systems and the Balance of Consumer-Producer Power*
José Antonio Cheibub, *Presidentialism, Parliamentarism, and Democracy*
Ruth Berins Collier, *Paths toward Democracy: The Working Class and Elites in Western Europe and South America*
Daniel Corstange, *The Price of a Vote in the Middle East: Clientelism and Communal Politics in Lebanon and Yemen*
Pepper D. Culpepper, *Quiet Politics and Business Power: Corporate Control in Europe and Japan*

Sarah Zukerman Daly, *Organized Violence after Civil War: The Geography of Recruitment in Latin America*
Christian Davenport, *State Repression and the Domestic Democratic Peace*
Donatella della Porta, *Social Movements, Political Violence, and the State*
Alberto Diaz-Cayeros, *Federalism, Fiscal Authority, and Centralization in Latin America*
Alberto Diaz-Cayeros, Federico Estévez, Beatriz Magaloni, *The Political Logic of Poverty Relief*
Jesse Driscoll, *Warlords and Coalition Politics in Post-Soviet States*
Thad Dunning, *Crude Democracy: Natural Resource Wealth and Political Regimes*
Gerald Easter, *Reconstructing the State: Personal Networks and Elite Identity*
Margarita Estevez-Abe, *Welfare and Capitalism in Postwar Japan: Party, Bureaucracy, and Business*
Henry Farrell, *The Political Economy of Trust: Institutions, Interests, and Inter-Firm Cooperation in Italy and Germany*
Karen E. Ferree, *Framing the Race in South Africa: The Political Origins of Racial Census Elections*
M. Steven Fish, *Democracy Derailed in Russia: The Failure of Open Politics*
Robert F. Franzese, *Macroeconomic Policies of Developed Democracies*
Roberto Franzosi, *The Puzzle of Strikes: Class and State Strategies in Postwar Italy*
Timothy Frye, *Building States and Markets After Communism: The Perils of Polarized Democracy*
Geoffrey Garrett, *Partisan Politics in the Global Economy*
Scott Gehlbach, *Representation through Taxation: Revenue, Politics, and Development in Postcommunist States*
Edward L. Gibson, *Boundary Control: Subnational Authoritarianism in Federal Democracies*
Jane R. Gingrich, *Making Markets in the Welfare State: The Politics of Varying Market Reforms*
Miriam Golden, *Heroic Defeats: The Politics of Job Loss*
Jeff Goodwin, No *Other Way Out: States and Revolutionary Movements*
Merilee Serrill Grindle, *Changing the State*
Anna Grzymala-Busse, *Rebuilding Leviathan: Party Competition and State Exploitation in Post-Communist Democracies*
Anna Grzymala-Busse, *Redeeming the Communist Past: The Regeneration of Communist Parties in East Central Europe*
Frances Hagopian, *Traditional Politics and Regime Change in Brazil*
Mark Hallerberg, Rolf Ranier Strauch, Jürgen von Hagen, *Fiscal Governance in Europe*
Henry E. Hale, *The Foundations of Ethnic Politics: Separatism of States and Nations in Eurasia and the World*
Stephen E. Hanson, *Post-Imperial Democracies: Ideology and Party Formation in Third Republic France, Weimar Germany, and Post-Soviet Russia*
Michael Hechter, *Alien Rule*
Timothy Hellwig, *Globalization and Mass Politics: Retaining the Room to Maneuver*

Gretchen Helmke, *Courts Under Constraints: Judges, Generals, and Presidents in Argentina*
Yoshiko Herrera, *Imagined Economies: The Sources of Russian Regionalism*
J. Rogers Hollingsworth and Robert Boyer, eds., *Contemporary Capitalism: The Embeddedness of Institutions*
John D. Huber and Charles R. Shipan, *Deliberate Discretion? The Institutional Foundations of Bureaucratic Autonomy*
Ellen Immergut, *Health Politics: Interests and Institutions in Western Europe*
Torben Iversen, *Capitalism, Democracy, and Welfare*
Torben Iversen, *Contested Economic Institutions*
Torben Iversen, Jonas Pontussen, and David Soskice, eds., *Unions, Employers, and Central Banks: Macroeconomic Coordination and Institutional Change in Social Market Economics*
Thomas Janoski and Alexander M. Hicks, eds., *The Comparative Political Economy of the Welfare State*
Joseph Jupille, *Procedural Politics: Issues, Influence, and Institutional Choice in the European Union*
Stathis Kalyvas, *The Logic of Violence in Civil War*
Stephen B. Kaplan, *Globalization and Austerity Politics in Latin America*
David C. Kang, *Crony Capitalism: Corruption and Capitalism in South Korea and the Philippines*
Junko Kato, *Regressive Taxation and the Welfare State*
Orit Kedar, *Voting for Policy, Not Parties: How Voters Compensate for Power Sharing*
Robert O. Keohane and Helen B. Milner, eds., *Internationalization and Domestic Politics*
Herbert Kitschelt, *The Transformation of European Social Democracy*
Herbert Kitschelt, Kirk A. Hawkins, Juan Pablo Luna, Guillermo Rosas, and Elizabeth J. Zechmeister, *Latin American Party Systems*
Herbert Kitschelt, Peter Lange, Gary Marks, and John D. Stephens, eds., *Continuity and Change in Contemporary Capitalism*
Herbert Kitschelt, Zdenka Mansfeldova, Radek Markowski, and Gabor Toka, *Post-Communist Party Systems*
David Knoke, Franz Urban Pappi, Jeffrey Broadbent, and Yutaka Tsujinaka, eds., *Comparing Policy Networks*
Ken Kollman, *Perils of Centralization: Lessons from Church, State, and Corporation*
Allan Kornberg and Harold D. Clarke, *Citizens and Community: Political Support in a Representative Democracy*
Amie Kreppel, *The European Parliament and the Supranational Party System*
David D. Laitin, *Language Repertoires and State Construction in Africa*
Fabrice E. Lehoucq and Ivan Molina, *Stuffing the Ballot Box: Fraud, Electoral Reform, and Democratization in Costa Rica*
Mark Irving Lichbach and Alan S. Zuckerman, eds., *Comparative Politics: Rationality, Culture, and Structure,* 2nd edition
Evan Lieberman, *Race and Regionalism in the Politics of Taxation in Brazil and South Africa*

Richard M. Locke, *The Promise and Limits of Private Power: Promoting Labor Standards in a Global Economy*
Julia Lynch, *Age in the Welfare State: The Origins of Social Spending on Pensioner's Workers and Children*
Pauline Jones Luong, *Institutional Change and Political Continuity in Post-Soviet Central Asia*
Pauline Jones Luong and Erika Weinthal, *Oil is Not a Curse: Ownership Structure and Institutions in Soviet Successor States*
Doug McAdam, John McCarthy, and Mayer Zald, eds., *Comparative Perspectives on Social Movements*
Lauren M. MacLean, *Informal Institutions and Citizenship in Rural Africa: Risk and Reciprocity in Ghana and Côte d'Ivoire*
Beatriz Magaloni, *Voting for Autocracy: Hegemonic Party Survival and its Demise in Mexico*
James Mahoney, *Colonialism and Postcolonial Development: Spanish America in Comparative Perspective*
James Mahoney and Dietrich Rueschemeyer, eds., *Historical Analysis and the Social Sciences*
Scott Mainwaring and Matthew Soberg Shugart, eds., *Presidentialism and Democracy in Latin America*
Melanie Manion, *Information for Autocrats: Representation in Chinese Local Congresses*
Isabela Mares, *From Open Secrets to Secret Voting: Democratic Electoral Reforms and Voter Autonomy*
Isabela Mares, *The Politics of Social Risk: Business and Welfare State Development*
Isabela Mares, *Taxation, Wage Bargaining, and Unemployment*
Cathie Jo Martin and Duane Swank, *The Political Construction of Business Interests: Coordination, Growth, and Equality*
Anthony W. Marx, *Making Race, Making Nations: A Comparison of South Africa, the United States, and Brazil*
Bonnie M. Meguid, *Party Competition between Unequals: Strategies and Electoral Fortunes in Western Europe*
Joel S. Migdal, *State in Society: Studying How States and Societies Constitute One Another*
Joel S. Migdal, Atul Kohli, and Vivienne Shue, eds., *State Power and Social Forces: Domination and Transformation in the Third World*
Scott Morgenstern and Benito Nacif, eds., *Legislative Politics in Latin America*
Kevin M. Morrison, *Nontaxation and Representation: The Fiscal Foundations of Political Stability*
Layna Mosley, *Global Capital and National Governments*
Layna Mosley, *Labor Rights and Multinational Production*
Wolfgang C. Müller and Kaare Strøm, *Policy, Office, or Votes?*
Maria Victoria Murillo, *Political Competition, Partisanship, and Policy Making in Latin American Public Utilities*
Maria Victoria Murillo, *Labor Unions, Partisan Coalitions, and Market Reforms in Latin America*

Monika Nalepa, *Skeletons in the Closet: Transitional Justice in Post-Communist Europe*
Ton Notermans, *Money, Markets, and the State: Social Democratic Economic Policies since 1918*
Aníbal Pérez-Liñán, *Presidential Impeachment and the New Political Instability in Latin America*
Roger D. Petersen, *Understanding Ethnic Violence: Fear, Hatred, and Resentment in 20th Century Eastern Europe*
Roger D. Petersen, *Western Intervention in the Balkans: The Strategic Use of Emotion in Conflict*
Simona Piattoni, ed., *Clientelism, Interests, and Democratic Representation*
Paul Pierson, *Dismantling the Welfare State?: Reagan, Thatcher, and the Politics of Retrenchment*
Marino Regini, *Uncertain Boundaries: The Social and Political Construction of European Economies*
Kenneth M. Roberts, *Changing Course in Latin America: Party Systems in the Neoliberal Era*
Marc Howard Ross, *Cultural Contestation in Ethnic Conflict*
Roger Schoenman, *Networks and Institutions in Europe's Emerging Markets*
Ben Ross Schneider, *Hierarchical Capitalism in Latin America: Business, Labor, and the Challenges of Equitable Development*
Lyle Scruggs, *Sustaining Abundance: Environmental Performance in Industrial Democracies*
Jefferey M. Sellers, *Governing from Below: Urban Regions and the Global Economy*
Yossi Shain and Juan Linz, eds., *Interim Governments and Democratic Transitions*
Beverly Silver, *Forces of Labor: Workers' Movements and Globalization since 1870*
Theda Skocpol, *Social Revolutions in the Modern World*
Prerna Singh, *How Solidarity Works for Welfare: Subnationalism and Social Development in India*
Austin Smith et al, *Selected Works of Michael Wallerstein*
Regina Smyth, *Candidate Strategies and Electoral Competition in the Russian Federation: Democracy Without Foundation*
Richard Snyder, *Politics after Neoliberalism: Reregulation in Mexico*
David Stark and László Bruszt, *Postsocialist Pathways: Transforming Politics and Property in East Central Europe*
Sven Steinmo, *The Evolution of Modern States: Sweden, Japan, and the United States*
Sven Steinmo, Kathleen Thelen, and Frank Longstreth, eds., *Structuring Politics: Historical Institutionalism in Comparative Analysis*
Susan C. Stokes, *Mandates and Democracy: Neoliberalism by Surprise in Latin America*
Susan C. Stokes, ed., *Public Support for Market Reforms in New Democracies*
Susan C. Stokes, Thad Dunning, Marcelo Nazareno, and Valeria Brusco, *Brokers, Voters, and Clientelism: The Puzzle of Distributive Politics*

Milan W. Svolik, *The Politics of Authoritarian Rule*
Duane Swank, *Global Capital, Political Institutions, and Policy Change in Developed Welfare States*
Sidney Tarrow, *Power in Movement: Social Movements and Contentious Politics*
Sidney Tarrow, *Power in Movement: Social Movements and Contentious Politics, Revised and Updated Third Edition*
Tariq Thachil, *Elite Parties, Poor Voters: How Social Services Win Votes in India*
Kathleen Thelen, *How Institutions Evolve: The Political Economy of Skills in Germany, Britain, the United States, and Japan*
Kathleen Thelen, *Varieties of Liberalization and the New Politics of Social Solidarity*
Charles Tilly, *Trust and Rule*
Daniel Treisman, *The Architecture of Government: Rethinking Political Decentralization*
Guillermo Trejo, *Popular Movements in Autocracies: Religion, Repression, and Indigenous Collective Action in Mexico*
Rory Truex, *Making Autocracy Work: Representation and Responsiveness in Modern China*
Lily Lee Tsai, *Accountability without Democracy: How Solidary Groups Provide Public Goods in Rural China*
Joshua Tucker, *Regional Economic Voting: Russia, Poland, Hungary, Slovakia and the Czech Republic, 1990–1999*
Ashutosh Varshney, *Democracy, Development, and the Countryside*
Yuhua Wang, *Tying the Autocrat's Hand: The Rise of The Rule of Law in China*
Jeremy M. Weinstein, *Inside Rebellion: The Politics of Insurgent Violence*
Stephen I. Wilkinson, *Votes and Violence: Electoral Competition and Ethnic Riots in India*
Andreas Wimmer, *Waves of War: Nationalism, State Formation, and Ethnic Exclusion in the Modern World*
Jason Wittenberg, *Crucibles of Political Loyalty: Church Institutions and Electoral Continuity in Hungary*
Elisabeth J. Wood, *Forging Democracy from Below: Insurgent Transitions in South Africa and El Salvador*
Elisabeth J. Wood, *Insurgent Collective Action and Civil War in El Salvador*